CLASSICS IN VOTING BEHAVIOR

CLASSICS IN VOTING BEHAVIOR

Richard G. Niemi
University of Rochester

Herbert F. Weisberg
The Ohio State University

PRESS

A Division of Congressional Quarterly Inc.
Washington, D.C.

Copyright © 1993 Congressional Quarterly Inc.
1414 22nd Street, N.W., Washington, D.C. 20037

Printed in the United States of America

Second Printing

Cover design: Carol Crosby Black

Library of Congress Cataloging-in-Publication Data

Classics in voting behavior / [edited by] Richard G. Niemi, Herbert F. Weisberg.
     p.   cm.
    Includes bibliographical references and index.
    ISBN 0-87187-705-8 -- ISBN 0-87187-651-5 (paper)
 · 1. Elections--United States--History--20th century. 2. Voting-
-United States--History--20th century. 3. Party affiliation--United
States--History--20th century. I. Niemi, Richard G. II. Weisberg,
Herbert F.
JK1967.C4 · 1992
324.973--dc20   92-23085
                                                CIP

We dedicate this book to our wives,
Shirley Niemi and Judy Weisberg

CONTENTS

VI. HISTORICAL PERSPECTIVES

PREFACE

The inspiration for *Classics in Voting Behavior* came out of our work on another reader, *Controversies in Voting Behavior*. When we put together the second edition of *Controversies*, we chose all new articles to represent the best current work in the field, while recognizing that many readings from the first edition were still relevant. When we contemplated a third edition, the pressure to keep some of the earlier work was even greater. In some instances, the early work retained its original significance. For example, Burnham's and Rusk's work on nineteenth-century voting remains an important, and relatively unchanged, debate. In other instances, recent work was more easily understood if students were first introduced, even if briefly, to older, classic works that helped establish and define the field. For example, measurement questions about the party identification scale are most easily understood after one has seen Petrocik's display of "intransitivities."

CQ Press agreed that there was a role for reprinting and discussing the classic literature of the field, and *Classics in Voting Behavior* is the result. Thus, we now have two companion readers, either of which stands on its own, but which can be used together most effectively to provide a comprehensive overview of the modern era of voting behavior research.

As we gathered together the readings for *Classics*, our overriding principle was to select articles that have endured—either because their message remains fresh and valid today or because they provide the original insights into a modern, scientific understanding of public opinion and voting behavior. We began with the earlier *Controversies* editions and then expanded our scope to include pieces that had retained their prominence but, for one reason or another, had not been selected for those earlier editions. Consequently, *Classics* includes readings from the entire body of previous work. So we could include a much wider selection of pieces and because we recognized that in some instances the classic element could be conveyed using a small portion of a larger work, we have edited the readings. In some cases, we have selected very short sections. Even these few pages, however, enable students to grasp the flavor of the authors' ideas and evidence.

We hope our selections give students a sense of the early debates in the field, a feel for progress over the years in our understanding of voting, an awareness of the considerable continuity in voting behavior research, and, in some instances, an understanding of where the field now stands. Because even the large number of readings we have been able to include leaves out some important research, we have carried over from *Controversies* the idea of introductory essays that describe and summarize each of the controversies.

We would like to thank the many people who have helped us put this work together. Our first thanks go to the authors of the various articles included here. At Congressional Quarterly, we are especially grateful to David Tarr and Brenda Carter, who helped make the two-volume idea a reality. Shana Wagger was very helpful in keeping us on schedule while at the same dealing diplomatically and helpfully with our pleas for "just an extra few days." Jenny Philipson, Kerry Kern, and Laura Carter managed the day-to-day operations with skill and good humor. Our copy editor, Tracy Villano, worked hard to improve the writing. An anonymous reader helped us with a skillful, thorough assessment of the overall project as well as with detailed comments on our introductions.

We owe a special debt to BitNet, without which this volume could not have been completed on time. Our wives have been gracious, as usual, in understanding our pleas that we "have to work on the book." Finally, Weisberg would also like to acknowledge a sabbatical leave from The Ohio State University that gave him more time to work on this book and to thank the Department of Political Science at Rice University for providing a stimulating and hospitable environment for working on it.

R.G.N.
H.F.W.

INTRODUCTION

1. THE CLASSICS OF VOTING BEHAVIOR

The classics of voting behavior that we review here were written chiefly between 1950 and the early 1980s. These were the years that saw the beginning of the systematic study of individual voting behavior as well as the dominance of one paradigm and one source of survey data. By the end of the period, however, dissatisfaction with, and revisions to, the dominant paradigm and initial development of alternative and more varied data sources had occurred. That during this period we gained considerable knowledge about voting, as well as about public opinion and political participation more generally, cannot be doubted. What we learned, however, stirred controversies about all aspects of voting, and it is around these controversies that we organize the present volume. While the specifics of the controversies have changed over the years, the existence of alternative perspectives and conclusions has persisted. And the *topics* of controversy (for example, the nature of partisanship) have changed very little. Thus, the material we review and reprint is of considerable relevance to a contemporary understanding of voters and elections as well as crucial to an understanding of current research in voting behavior.

How to Study Voting

Methodology

Surveys are not the only way to understand voting. Indeed, the early study of voting amounted to journalistic or historical analysis of party positions, campaigns, and election results. Observers ascertained the meaning of an election by inspecting party platforms and listening to candidate speeches. It was assumed that voters were paying attention to what politicians were saying. Examination of election results over time yielded trends. And these presumably reflected corresponding changes in voter attitudes. The observers assumed that the intricacies of campaign organizations and events have some impact on individual voters and hence that the study of candidates' strategies, organizations, and personalities tells us something about ordinary voters.

These approaches continue to be used. Analysis of trends in election returns, for example, remains an important part of election-night reporting on television and of newspaper coverage the following morning. Reporters focus on the votes gained or lost by each party and sometimes on key districts that contain concentrations of important social groups. Unfortunately, such information can be misleading. For example, showing that the Republican vote in a particular district fell 10 percent from the previous election does not prove that 10 percent of the electorate switched from Republican to Democrat. Instead of attitude conversion, the change might reflect more complex patterns of population replacement (fewer Republicans among newly eligible voters or an increase of deaths among the Republican constituency) or voter mobilization (Democratic supporters turning out to vote at a higher rate in the more recent election, or Republican voters in the last election abstaining disproportionately in the more recent election). Additionally, a net change of 10 percent probably conceals much greater gross change, such as 30 percent of the Republican voters switching to the Democrats and 20 percent of the Democratic voters switching to the Republicans. Election returns, as well as platforms, speeches, and campaign activities, are not sufficient for studying electoral behavior.

The above illustrations do not mean that election returns, party positions, campaign information, and other such material are useless as sources of political information. Indeed, for earlier periods in our history, they may be the only available sources (see, for example, Chapters 29 and 30). And there are now statistical procedures for dealing with the "ecological fallacy" that bedevils attempts to use election returns to study individual behavior (see, for example, Goodman, 1959) and methods of content analysis that help us digest large volumes of written material. Still, the basic point remains: individual voting can best be understood by studying individuals.[1] As a result, surveys of the electorate have become a common means of understanding voting.

Of course, not all surveys provide reliable results. Indeed, one might wonder why one should accept any results based on surveys of perhaps 1,500 voters out of an electorate of millions. A complete explanation would require a lengthy statistical explanation (see, for example, Weisberg, Krosnick, and Bowen, 1989), but some brief points can be made, especially to underscore the point that reliable polls are not conducted haphazardly but according to scientific principles. Most important in conducting a survey is the way in which the sample is selected. Surveys that interview a few "typical" voters or that interview people at a single street corner should not be taken seriously, for there is no reason to believe that the people interviewed are typical of the electorate.[2] By contrast, the best scientific sampling procedures give everyone in the population an equal (or at least a known) probability of being part of the sample. Probability theory can then be used to estimate how close results for the sample are to those for the population of interest. For example, using conventional sampling techniques, a sample of about 1,500 people will give results that are generally (95 percent of the time) within 3 percent of the true result. Thus, a survey finding that 65 percent of the electorate supports a particular party can be interpreted as meaning that its level of support in the population as a whole is (almost certainly) between 62 and 68 percent.

There is inevitable error, of course, in attempting to describe a population with just a sample, but such error is generally tolerable. For example, it does not matter for most purposes if a party's support really is 62 percent or 68 percent. Moreover, the 3 percent error margin could be reduced, though that would generally not be cost effective, since cutting the error to, say, 1.5 percent would require the expense of 4,500 more interviews. Only when trying to predict a very close election might greater accuracy be necessary, and in such cases the pollsters prefer to admit that the election is "too close to call." Note, by the way, that the size of the sample is what matters for most purposes, not the size of the population. Thus, one would want about 1,500 interviews for a national sample or for a sample of the California electorate.

Aside from these sampling issues, the validity of a survey depends on the wording of the questions that are asked, and for this task mathematical principles are of less help. Different question wordings obtain different results, often only marginally different but occasionally very much so. At best, researchers "pretest" a question wording to make sure it is valid before using it in an actual survey. Sometimes, though, researchers gradually realize that a standard wording that has been used for years is not ideal and then change that wording, which can lead to problems in over-time comparisons (see Chapter 7). In any case, there is no perfect wording for survey questions, so dependence on wording is always important to acknowledge.

While potential problems with polls must be recognized, during the period covered in this volume surveys became the most important way to study voting.[3] Party positions, campaign organizations, and election returns are still studied intensively as well, but our main understanding of voting and elections is now through citizen interviews. This is reflected in the present volume, with most of the analyses reported here based on such surveys.

The Data Base

The articles in this book are based on special surveys rather than on commercial polls, such as the Gallup Poll. Why is this the case? The main reason involves what each is studying. The Gallup organization must forecast election results for their newspaper customers. Newspapers want to publish interesting stories, and predictions of election outcomes are certainly that. Gallup does very well in this prediction game. However, political scientists are typically studying the last election rather than the next. This is because they do not want to predict *who* will win a particular election so much as to understand *why* someone won. Some forms of prediction may eventually be possible (see Chapter 19), but political scientists want them to be firmly based on an explanation of past elections. Explaining election outcomes requires asking people many more questions than the commercial pollsters do. Voters cannot just be asked who they will vote for. They must be asked their feelings about each candidate, each party, each issue, how they obtained information on the election, how they voted in the past, and so on. This requires separate polls.[4]

Some academic political polls were reported in the 1920s, but the first important voting surveys were not conducted until the 1940s (see Table 1-1).

Table 1-1 Major Electoral Behavior Surveys and Major Reports on Them

Year	Study	Report
1940	Columbia University, Bureau of Applied Social Research, sample of Erie County, Ohio	P. Lazarsfeld, B. Berelson, and H. Gaudet, *The People's Choice,* Duell, Sloan & Pearce, 1944.
1944	National Opinion Research Center, national sample	
1948	Columbia University, Bureau of Applied Social Research, sample of Elmira, N.Y.	B. Berelson, P. Lazarsfeld, and W. McPhee, *Voting,* University of Chicago Press, 1954.
1948	University of Michigan SRC, national sample	A. Campbell and R. Kahn, *The People Elect a President,* SRC, University of Michigan, 1952.
1950	Columbia University, Bureau of Applied Social Research, four state samples	W. McPhee and W. Glaser, *Public Opinion and the Congressional Elections,* Free Press, 1962.
1952	University of Michigan SRC, national sample	A. Campbell, G. Gurin, and W. Miller, *The Voter Decides,* Row, Peterson, 1954. *See also* 1956 listing.
1954	University of Michigan SRC, pre-election national sample	A. Campbell and H. Cooper, *Group Differences in Attitudes and Votes,* SRC, University of Michigan, 1956.
1956	University of Michigan SRC, national sample	A. Campbell, P. Converse, W. Miller, and D. Stokes, *The American Voter,* Wiley, 1960.
1958	University of Michigan SRC, national sample, representation study	D. Stokes and W. Miller, "Party Government and the Saliency of Congress," POQ[a], Winter 1962. W. Miller and D. Stokes, "Constituency Influence in Congress," *APSR,*[b] March 1963. A. Campbell, "Surge and Decline," POQ, Fall 1960.
1960	University of Michigan SRC, national sample	P. Converse, A. Campbell, W. Miller, and D. Stokes, "Stability and Change in 1960: A Reinstating Election," *APSR,* June 1961. *See also* A. Campbell, P. Converse, W. Miller, and D. Stokes, *Elections and the Political Order,* Wiley, 1966.
1956-58-60	University of Michigan SRC, national sample, panel study	P. Converse, "The Nature of Belief Systems in Mass Publics," in D. Apter, *Ideology and Discontent,* Free Press, 1964.

Table 1-1 *(Continued)*

Year	Study	Report
1961	University of North Carolina, sample of South	D. Matthews and J. Prothro, *Negroes and the New Southern Politics*, Harcourt, 1966.
1962	University of Michigan SRC, national sample	
1964	University of Michigan SRC, national sample	P. Converse, A. Clausen, and W. Miller, "Electoral Myth and Reality: The 1964 Election," *APSR*, June 1965.
1966	University of Michigan SRC, national sample	
1967	NORC, University of Chicago, national sample	S. Verba and N. Nie, *Participation in America*, Harper & Row, 1972.
1968	University of Michigan SRC, national sample	P. Converse, W. Miller, J. Rusk, and A. Wolfe, "Continuity and Change in American Politics: Parties and Issues in the 1968 Election," *APSR*, December 1969.
1968	Opinion Research Corp., national sample	B. Page and R. Brody, "Policy Voting and the Electoral Process," *APSR*, September 1972.
1968	University of North Carolina, thirteen state samples	D. Kovenock, J. Prothro and Associates, *Explaining the Vote*, Institute for Research in Social Science, University of North Carolina, 1973.
1970	University of Michigan CPS, national sample	
1972	University of Michigan CPS, national sample	A. Miller, W. Miller, A. Raine, and T. Brown, "A Majority Party in Disarray," *APSR*, September 1976.
1972	Syracuse University, Onondaga County, N.Y.	T. Patterson and R. McClure, *The Unseeing Eye*, Putnam, 1976.
1974	University of Michigan CPS, national sample	
1976	University of Michigan CPS, national sample	A. Miller, "Partisanship Reinstated," *BJPS,*[c] April 1978.
1972-74-76	University of Michigan CPS, national sample, panel study	P. Converse and G. Markus, "Plus ça Change. . . : The New CPS Election Study Panel," *APSR*, March 1979.

Table 1-1 *(Continued)*

Year	Study	Report
1976	CBS/New York Times, national samples	
1976	Syracuse University, Erie County, Pennsylvania and Los Angeles	T. Patterson, *The Mass Media Election,* Praeger, 1980.
1978	University of Michigan NES, national sample	L. Maisel and J. Cooper, eds., *Congressional Elections,* Sage, 1981.
1978	CBS/New York Times, national and congressional candidate sample	G. Bishop and K. Frankovic, "Ideological Consensus and Constraint among Party Leaders and Followers in the 1978 Election," *Micropolitics,* No. 2, 1981.
1980	University of Michigan NES, national sample, panel study	W. Miller and J. M. Shanks, "Policy Directions and Presidential Leadership," *BJPS,* July 1982. G. Markus, "Political Attitudes During an Election Year: A Report on the 1980 Panel Study," *APSR,* September 1982.
1980	CBS/New York Times, national samples	
1982	University of Michigan NES, national sample	

Note: all the above studies involve postelection interviews. except for the 1954 preelection study, the 1961 study of the South, and the 1967 study of participation. Most also involve one or more preelection interviews.

[a] *Public Opinion Quarterly*
[b] *American Political Science Review*
[c] *British Journal of Political Science*

Continuous national political surveys began with the formation of the University of Michigan's well-known Institute for Social Research. The Survey Research Center (and more recently the Center for Political Studies) section of the institute has continued surveying up to the present day. The Michigan surveys are now administered by the National Election Studies under a continuing grant from the National Science Foundation, with researchers from universities across the country able to participate in preparing questions for the surveys and in analyzing the results. Special surveys have sometimes been conducted to study particular topics, but the Michigan surveys, with their hundreds of questions about the parties, the candidates, and the issues, have become the standard data base for the study of United States elections. Most of the studies reported in this book are based on these NES/CPS/SRC surveys.

There are several different patterns to the Michigan surveys used in this book. The usual pattern for presidential elections has been to interview the same people before and after the election. A desire to focus on electoral change, however, has led to some other study designs. An important variation is repeated pre-election interviews with the same person to analyze changes in vote intentions, as was done in the 1940 and 1948 Columbia studies and the 1980 NES study. Another important variant is interviewing the same people across election years so that voting change between elections can be examined, as was done in the 1956-58-60 and the 1972-74-76 Michigan "panel" studies. A final variation for presidential elections is weekly interviewing of different people throughout the election year, as was done in the 1984 NES "rolling thunder" (continuous monitoring) study.

A simpler study design has been used for congressional election years, with interviews conducted only after the election has taken place. The first Michigan study of a congressional election was a major study in 1958, which included interviews with the congressional candidates in those districts where they had interviewed voters. There were minor Michigan studies of the 1962, 1966, 1970, and 1974 congressional elections. By 1978 congressional scholars were doubting many of the findings from the 1958 study and were developing new theories of congressional voting. The 1978 survey became a major study of congressional voting, and resulted in a vast explosion of work on the topic, as shown in the section of this book on congressional elections. Similarly, specially designed studies in 1988, 1990, and 1992 have focused special attention on elections to the U.S. Senate.

The success of the University of Michigan scholars in conducting national election surveys led quickly to similar surveys in many other nations. Some of the early cross-national research represented attempts to replicate the Michigan surveys in other countries, but the concepts and questions developed in the American surveys often were found to be inapplicable in other settings (as discussed in Chapter 21). As a result, recent election studies have been typified by native researchers developing new questions and concepts based on their understanding of their countries. We have included mainly American studies in this book, though in our introductions we summarize many of the contributions of comparative studies to our overall understanding of voter behavior.[5]

How to Understand Voting

The Theory

There are countless ways to understand voting, but the period from 1950 to 1980 was dominated by a paradigm developed by the Michigan researchers. Two other potential paradigms were explored earlier by a Columbia research team. The 1940 Columbia study was based on a consumer preference model, in which each party was seen as presenting a product to the public, the campaign was seen as an advertising campaign during which the competing products were weighed by the public, and the voters were seen as recording their final choices when they stepped into the booth on election day. The problem with this model was that most people knew how they would vote even before the national conventions were held, particularly since President Franklin D. Roosevelt was running for a third term in office in 1940. People knew whether or not they were going to vote for him without listening attentively to the campaign. In the end, the Columbia researchers explained the 1940 election with a sociological model, relating voters' socioeconomic status (education, income, and class), religion, and place of residence (urban or rural) to their vote. These social group factors accounted for most of the observed differences in voting in their study of a single county, but it did not explain why those social group differences appeared; nor did it hold when applied by the Michigan scholars to their national sample in 1948. More complex consumer preference and sociological models might have been useful (and indeed have received attention in recent years), but the time had come for a sharp break with these early models.

The Michigan researchers analyzed the 1952 election using a social-psychological model. The major emphasis was on three attitudes: the person's attachment to a party, the person's orientation toward the issues, and the person's orientation toward the candidates. The emphasis on parties, candidates, and issues explicitly incorporated political variables into the voting model. A theory mapping how these three factors interrelate in their effects on the vote came in the landmark Michigan report on the presidential elections of the 1950s, *The American Voter*. A person's identification with a party became the core of the model. It in turn affected the person's attitude toward candidates and issues. The authors describe this in terms of a "funnel of causality." The phenomenon to be explained—voting—is at the tip of the funnel, but it is preceded by, and dependent on, a variety of factors. The funnel's axis is time. Events follow one another, converging in a series of causal chains and moving from the mouth of the funnel to its tip. Thus a multitude of causes narrows into the voting act. At the mouth of the funnel are sociological background characteristics (ethnicity, race, region, religion, and the like), social status characteristics (education, occupation, class), and parental characteristics (class, partisanship). All affect the person's choice of party identification, which is the next item in the funnel. Party identification in turn influences the person's evaluation of the candidates and the issues, which again takes us further into the funnel. The next part of the funnel features incidents from the campaign itself, as these events are reported by the media. Even closer to the tip are conversations the voter has with family and friends about the election. Finally comes the vote itself. While each of the prior factors affects the vote, the Michigan group concentrated on parties, candidates, and issues, rather than on the early social characteristics or the later communications network.

This remains the basic Michigan model (Beck, 1986), with a more explicit division today between what are designated long-term and short-term factors. Party identification is an important long-term factor affecting the vote. Issues and especially candidates are short-term factors specific to the election. This social-psychological model of the vote has affected virtually all later research, serving as the prime paradigm of the vote decision through most of the post-1950 period.

And it continues to affect research in other countries, even though it was eventually decided that a different model was more applicable for those settings.

One other model of voting became popular during the 1970s: the rational voter model. According to this model, voters decide whether or not to vote and which candidate to vote for on some rational basis, usually on the basis of which action gives them greater expected benefits. They vote only if they perceive greater gain from voting than the cost (mainly in time) of voting. In the usual formulation, they vote for the candidate closest to them on the issues. A major contribution of this approach is that it provides a more explicit and precise theoretical basis for voting decisions and for their analysis than do other approaches. If voters are rational in the sense indicated, then we can expect certain types of behavior in specific circumstances. In addition, the rational voter model lends itself more than others to predicting what effects changes in external conditions will have. The early work was more mathematical than empirical, but increasingly surveys became a mechanism for testing some of the conclusions of the rational voter model. If people with particular attitudes do not behave as predicted, then the assumptions of the theory might have to be revised. If their behavior is correctly predicted, then we can extend the theory further. Substantively, the major contribution of the rational voter approach has been to emphasize the role of issues, which were submerged in the early findings of the Michigan researchers.

The articles reprinted in this book reflect a variety of theories about voting. They are based largely on the social-psychological approach, sometimes modifying and adapting the Michigan model of the 1950s to accommodate later elections and new interpretations of voting. A few of the pieces, however, are strongly influenced by the rational voter perspective, most noticeably Fiorina's account of a rational voter theory of party identification (Chapter 24).

The Controversies

No sooner had the social-psychological model been proclaimed and the initial empirical findings on voting been reported than controversies erupted. As new studies were undertaken, the methods used became more varied and the statistics more sophisticated. The amount and quality of data increased as well. Controversies nevertheless remained.

One core controversy was mentioned above—the conflict between the social-psychological and the rational-choice models of voting. A second core controversy was between the Michigan model and the "revisionist school." The revisionists generally accepted the Michigan framework but objected to particular findings, such as the relative unimportance of issues in the Michigan results. By the early 1980s, many areas in the study of voting behavior witnessed debates between defenders of the Michigan results and the revisionists.

This book is organized around six major controversies evident during the first decades of voting behavior studies. Some of these controversies have been resolved, as when an early revisionist claim of major changes in voters' levels of ideological thinking was itself discovered to depend largely on changes in question wording. More often, the original positions are now seen as overly drawn: instead of debating whether people vote on the basis of party identification or issues, we now ask when each is important and which issues are paramount. Many of these early controversies continue: during the 1980s studies raised more serious questions about the stability of party identification than had been raised in the preceding era.

The various topics represented in the sections of this book are among the most important themes concerning voting and elections. We have selected some of the best available readings on these topics, though naturally we could not reprint all the top-quality research of prior years. Nevertheless, having worked through the material included here, the reader will have a substantial grasp of the basis of current controversies in the field.

NOTES

1. There may be exceptions to this statement, even for the present period. Kramer (1983), for example, makes a good argument that studying certain questions about economic voting might best be done with aggregate data. Experimental studies can also be useful, as in recent studies of the effects of television news (for example, Iyengar and Kinder, 1987).
2. Occasionally, however, small, in-depth surveys have also been useful even though not necessarily representative of the entire population. For example, the work of Lane (1962)—though based on a handful of respondents—was highly influential.
3. Interestingly enough, there was a resurgence in the use of other techniques to study voting during the 1980s (Niemi and Weisberg, 1992, chap. 1).
4. Commercial polls are now asking more questions of this kind (Niemi and Weisberg, 1992, chap. 1), but they still tend to be relatively short and therefore limited in scope.
5. A list of survey studies of voting around the world, and of articles and books based on them, is contained in de Guchteneire, LeDuc, and Niemi (1991).

FURTHER READINGS

The Role of Elections

Murray Edelman, *The Symbolic Uses of Politics* (Urbana: University of Illinois Press, 1964). Elections serve primarily a symbolic function.

Anthony King, "What Do Elections Decide?" in *Democracy at the Polls: A Comparative Study of Competitive Elections,* ed. David Butler, Howard R. Penniman, and Austin Ranney. (Washington: American Enterprise Institute, 1981). Review of the effects of elections on public policy formation.

Benjamin Ginsberg, *The Consequences of Consent: Elections, Citizen Control, and Popular Acquiescence* (Reading, Mass.: Addison-Wesley, 1982). The significance of elections for the establishment of popular influence and governmental authority.

Summary Statements of the Michigan SRC/CPS Theory of Voting

Angus Campbell, Philip E. Converse, Warren E. Miller, and Donald E. Stokes, *The American Voter* (New York: Wiley, 1960), chap. 2 (not in abridged version). Statement of the "funnel of causality" analogy.

Philip E. Converse, "Public Opinion and Voting Behavior," in *The Handbook of Political Science*, vol. 4, ed. Fred I. Greenstein and Nelson W. Polsby (Reading, Mass.: Addison-Wesley, 1975). Reactions to work that challenges *The American Voter* interpretations.

Herbert B. Asher, "Voting Behavior Research in the 1980s," in *Political Science: The State of the Discipline*, ed. Ada Finifter (Washington, D.C.: American Political Science Association, 1983).

Paul Allen Beck, "Choice, Context, and Consequence: Beaten and Unbeaten Paths toward a Science of Electoral Behavior," in *Political Science: The Science of Politics*, ed. Herbert F. Weisberg (New York: Agathon, 1986).

Books Reflecting a "Rational" Spatial Model Approach

Anthony Downs, *An Economic Theory of Democracy* (New York: Harper and Row, 1957). Formal statement of turnout and vote choice as rational behavior.

Morris P. Fiorina, *Retrospective Voting in American National Elections* (New Haven, Conn.: Yale University Press, 1981). Elections as referenda on past governmental performance.

James M. Enelow and Melvin J. Hinich, *An Introduction to the Spatial Theory of Voting* (Cambridge: Cambridge University Press, 1984). Mathematical treatment of elections over multidimensional issue spaces.

Books Studying Voting Across a Series of U.S. Elections

Norman H. Nie, Sidney Verba, and John P. Petrocik, *The Changing American Voter*, rev. ed. (Cambridge, Mass.: Harvard University Press, 1979). Revisionist look at the American voter.

Warren E. Miller and Santa M. Traugott. *American National Election Studies Data Sourcebook.* (Cambridge, Mass.: Harvard University Press, 1989). Compilation of responses and crosstabs to SRC/CPS political questions.

Paul R. Abramson, *Political Attitudes in America* (San Francisco: Freeman, 1983). Continuity and change from 1950s to 1980s in party loyalties, political efficacy, political trust, and other political variables.

Early English Language Books on Voting Behavior in Other Countries

Alan Arian, *The Choosing People: Voting Behavior in Israel* (Cleveland: Case Western Reserve University, 1973).

Don Aitkin, *Stability and Change in Australian Politics* (Canberra: Australian National University Press, 1977).

American Enterprise Institute series, *(Country) at the Polls*, various years.

Kendall Baker, Russell J. Dalton, and Kai Hildebrandt, *Germany Transformed*

(Cambridge, Mass.: Harvard University Press, 1981). Development of voter attitudes toward parties and politics in post-war Germany.

David Butler and Donald Stokes, *Political Change in Britain* (New York: St. Martin's Press, 1969, 1974). Approach and conclusions often parallel *The American Voter.*

Harold D. Clarke, Jane Jenson, Lawrence LeDuc, and Jon H. Pammett, *The Absent Mandate: The Politics of Discontent in Canada* (Toronto: Gage, 1984). Examines forces of change in Canadian politics in the 1970s and 1980s.

Max Kaase and Klaus von Beyme, eds. *Elections and Parties: Socio-Political Change and Participation in the West German Federal Election of 1976* (London: Sage, 1978).

Arend Lijphart, *The Politics of Accommodation: Pluralism and Democracy in the Netherlands* (Berkeley, Calif.: University of California Press, 1968).

Bo Särlvik and Ivor Crewe, *Decade of Dealignment* (Cambridge: Cambridge University Press, 1983). Declining role of parties in Britain in the 1970s.

Henry Valen and Daniel Katz, *Political Parties in Norway* (Oslo: Universitetsforlaget, 1964).

Kenneth D. Wald, *Crosses on the Ballot: Patterns of British Voter Alignment Since 1885* (Princeton, N.J.: Princeton University Press, 1983). Explores relationships between social divisions and the vote, especially for the period 1885-1910.

Books on Voting Behavior Across Several Different Countries

Seymour Lipset and Stein Rokkan, eds., *Party Systems and Voter Alignments* (New York: Free Press, 1967). Discussion of voting cleavages in several countries; set in a theoretical perspective.

Richard Rose, ed., *Electoral Behavior: A Comparative Handbook* (New York: Free Press, 1974).

Ian Budge, Ivor Crewe, and Dennis Farlie, eds., *Party Identification and Beyond* (London: Wiley, 1976). Questions utility of party identification in European countries.

Hans Daalder and Peter Mair, eds., *Western European Party Systems* (Beverly Hills, Calif.: Sage, 1983). Parties, turnout, and voting behavior in Europe.

Russell J. Dalton, Scott C. Flanagan, and Paul Allen Beck, eds., *Electoral Change in Advanced Industrial Societies: Realignment or Dealignment* (Princeton: Princeton University Press, 1984). Examines forces of change to political systems of Western democracies in the previous decade.

PART I: ELECTION TURNOUT

2. IS IT RATIONAL TO VOTE?

In theory, democracy rests on several principles. It assumes that citizens are interested in political affairs, discuss their government, and are motivated to participate in politics. It assumes that the citizens are well informed about government and decide how to vote on a rational basis. It assumes that voters have some meaningful choice between competing candidates. Perhaps the most basic of all aspects of democracy is the very act of voting. Without voting, democracy would not exist.

Clearly, these assumptions are not all correct. Some people do not vote or are actually prevented from voting. Lack of informed choice has often been a problem. And frequently people have not found the choice among candidates very meaningful. Yet all of these observations did little to affect democratic theory until quite recently. It was maintained that at least democracy *should* work this way, even if in reality it didn't always do so. In theory, democracy was still thought to rest on lofty principles.

Nonvoting Is Sensible and Acceptable

The proverbial monkey wrench was thrown into this thinking in the 1950s. One influential work was Anthony Downs's (1957) book, *An Economic Theory of Democracy*. Downs's approach differed from that conventionally used in political science. He emphasized a concept of political behavior based on a rational calculation of self-interest. This point of view is similar to that used in economic analysis, where the assumption is that individuals act so as to maximize their expected utility, which usually means minimizing dollar costs and maximizing dollar returns. Analyzing politics from a rational perspective, Downs argued, might provide a considerable degree of insight into some aspects of political behavior. It should be emphasized that Downs was not necessarily advocating rational calculations. And more important, if individuals in fact do act in this manner, it is not necessarily bad. Rather, just as the economic system works well (with some controls) when everyone maximizes his or her own utility, so the political system might work best when each individual acts primarily in his or her own interest. In any event, such a model—even if descriptively wrong in some respects—might aid our understanding of political behavior.

Using a rational decision-making approach, Downs reached conclusions that conflicted sharply with those of normative democratic theory. Downs's major conclusion on this topic is that it might indeed be irrational for people to vote, because the costs of voting outweigh the benefits derived from it. Moreover, many individuals who do vote do not find it in their self-interest to become well informed before voting. Once Downs pointed this out, the results seemed eminently sound. There are individual costs attached to voting—costs primarily in terms of time during which people could be doing other things. And the benefits from voting might be negligible. For example, if an individual sees almost no difference between the candidates in an election, it makes little difference which one wins. Moreover, since many individuals are voting, the chance that one person's vote will change the result is very small, though calculating the exact value is perhaps impossible. The costs of becoming informed are quite large, since paying attention to campaign issues takes much time, and it is often difficult to find out precisely what the candidates are saying anyway.

Though Downs's results may seem relatively straightforward, they ran directly counter to traditional democratic theory and opened up a new approach to the study of politics. But Downs's chief contributions with regard to voter turnout itself are the two conclusions noted above: both nonvoting and uninformed voting are often sensible from the perspective of particular individuals. Perhaps individuals *should* vote and *should be* informed, but we can no longer construct political theories that assume that everyone will be an informed voter.

Verba and Nie, in Chapter 3, provide another perspective on voting by reminding us that voting is only one of several forms of political activity. Different activities can be useful for different purposes, but voting is a "blunt" instrument.

Verba and Nie do not go so far as to say that voting is useless—in fact, they make a fairly strong case for voting—but they emphasize the rationality of other kinds of participation. Most important are what they call citizen-initiated contacts. These include contacts with government officials about particular problems faced by individuals and their families as well as contacts involving broader matters such as a school or a whole community. The key points are that the individual citizen chooses what the contact is about and that the nature of the problem and the solution are relatively specific. In contrast, in elections individuals don't choose what issues are involved, don't decide whom the choice is between, and often don't see that much of a choice actually exists. Given this difference, people are likely to find greater rewards in contacts they initiate than in voting.

Other types of activities (which Verba and Nie label "communal" and "campaign activity") lie between citizen-initiated contacts and voting in terms of direct, identifiable returns. These differences lead us to expect a variety of kinds of participation, with many individuals participating in one or two ways rather than in every way. That this is the case is shown by the summary of Verba and Nie's empirical study provided at the end of their chapter. But the important point from our perspective here is that Verba and Nie confirm what Downs's individualistic approach implied—that voting is typically one of the least useful ways of resolving private problems or of influencing specific governmental policies. At the same time, Verba and Nie's mention of communal participation begins to suggest that there may be collective and group-related aspects of participation that are omitted in Downs's individualistic approach, a perspective that has been examined in some later work (see Uhlaner, 1989).

The arguments provided by Downs and by Verba and Nie mean that nonvoting might be rational from each individual's point of view, though this does not necessarily suggest that this is the way citizens should behave. A natural question is, What implication does nonvoting have for the political system? Is a nation better off when large numbers of individuals fail to vote? Maybe it is rational for only half of the voting-age public to have voted in the 1988 United States presidential election, but is such low turnout desirable? Some authors have taken exactly that position. They suggest that low turnout is not only individually rational, but desirable as well. The best-known statement of this point of view was given by Berelson (1954), after one of the earliest empirical studies of voting. He points out the dangers of high interest (and, by implication, of high voting turnout):

> How could a mass democracy work if all the people were deeply involved in politics? Lack of interest by some people is not without its benefits. . . . Extreme interest goes with extreme partisanship and might culminate in rigid fanaticism that could destroy democratic processes if generalized throughout the community. Low affect toward the election—not caring much—underlies the resolution of many political problems. . . . Only the doctrinaire could deprecate the moderate indifference that facilitates compromise. (pp. 314-15)

Berelson's statement was actually part of a larger theory about the role of the mass public in a democracy. According to what became known as the "elitist" point of view, the responsibility for democracy's survival is in the hands of the political leadership. The individual citizen is not critical (in this view) so long as the elite acts responsibly. Berelson contrasted the normative theory of democracy with empirical findings and concluded that democratic theory was defective in emphasizing the citizen's role. Leadership characteristics are important. For nonleaders, he concluded that a range of behavior, including nonparticipation by many, is required.

Taken together, Downs and Verba and Nie provide an entirely new perspective on political participation and on voting in particular. Instead of arguing that every citizen should be an informed voter, the question now shifts to why anyone becomes informed and why anyone votes. Is voting actually useful in terms of some individuals' self-interest? And does voting actually make democracy work? Moreover, once we raise these questions, we should also ask whether voting should be encouraged. If nonvoting serves to facilitate compromise—or if most citizens' attitudes are irrelevant—perhaps citizens should be discouraged from voting rather than encouraged to vote.

Though we have not provided an exact chronology of studies, this stand was taken by several publications on voting and nonvoting. There also have been reactions to these views, and it is to these responses that we now turn. But the ideas that we have discussed so far cannot be wholly dismissed, and we shall return to them later.

Voting Is Rational and Essential

If Downs's analysis is carried to its logical conclusion, it suggests the possibility that no one will vote. The main components in Downs's analysis are C, the cost of voting; P, the probability that citizens will, by voting, affect the election outcome; and B, the extent to which an individual feels that one candidate will benefit him or her more than another ("the perceived candidate differential" or "differential benefit"). Gordon Tullock (1967, chap. 7) first formalized the notion that a person will vote if the expected gain (PB) exceeds the cost (C) of voting, where PB is the benefit from one's preferred candidate winning multiplied by the probability of affecting the election by one's single vote. But he argued that if each citizen has one vote, then the individual vote will have very little probability of affecting the total outcome. Thus, the probability (P) of affecting the outcome is very small, so PB will be very small, probably less than the cost for most individuals. It would seem as if it is irrational for most people to vote.

Riker and Ordeshook (1968) suggested that a different interpretation of the probability term P is required. What matters is the individual's perception of his or her chance of affecting the outcome of the election, and that in turn depends on how close the election is perceived to be. Individuals may consider the election close even if in some objective sense it is not. Riker and Ordeshook tested the notion that people are more likely to vote if the election is perceived to be close. Using data from the Survey Research Center 1952-1960 election studies, they found that perceived closeness does have an effect on turnout. In addition, they suggested that another term must be considered, which they labeled civic duty (D). One interpretation of the D term is analogous to a suggestion by Downs that individuals sometimes vote because they consider it in their long-term interest to help maintain democracy even if their short-run calculation suggests not voting. Thus, the complete formula is that the gains from voting are the expected benefit plus the sense of duty minus the costs: PB + D − C. A person would vote only if this quantity is greater than zero (that is, if the gains, including the sense of duty, outweigh the costs). In the original model without the duty term (D), voting is seen strictly as a means to obtain desired (short-term) ends, the benefits. Voting is instrumental to achieving those ends. By contrast, the model with the duty term treats voting as having value for its own sake. Voting is a way of expressing values rather than being solely instrumental.

The suggestion of adding a duty term is important, for in one sense it salvages voting for the rational individual. Citizens may conclude that their votes are unlikely to affect the outcome, that there is little advantage in one candidate over the other, and that the cost of voting is relatively high, and yet they may vote because it will help to preserve democracy for a later time when their votes may be more critical. But this formulation is not satisfactory to everyone. It seems to suggest that individuals almost never find it rational to vote in the short run, but vote only to preserve democracy. In other words, democracy is useful only for preserving itself. Moreover, if many individuals vote, then each individual can rationalize nonvoting. If it is in my self-interest not to vote in the short run, and if enough other individuals will vote so that democracy will be preserved, then there is no need for me to vote at all. But, of course, if everyone thought this way, then no one would vote. And yet people do.

One way out of this dilemma is to argue that P, the probability of affecting the election outcome, is irrelevant. Ferejohn and Fiorina (1974, p. 535) suggest that individuals may not ask themselves how likely they are to influence the outcome, but instead ask, "My God, what if I didn't vote and my preferred candidate lost by one vote? I'd feel like killing myself." If individuals decide on this basis, formally called a minimax regret rule, the relative sizes of the benefits (B) and the costs (C) are important. Clearly, the benefits are greater than the costs for some individuals, and for these people voting is rational. Thus, voting can be considered rational for some people, and democracy serves a purpose other than just to preserve itself.

Another possibility is that the probability (P) is actually quite large. This has been presumed in some game theoretic models of turnout, in which citizens' calculations of whether or not their votes will be pivotal depend on their estimation of everybody else's calculation as to whether their vote would be pivotal. For example, Palfrey and Rosenthal (1983, 1984) developed a model in which every voter has complete information about the preferences and costs for other voters and in which the P term approached 1 in equilibrium. This result may in fact apply for small electorates with substantial communication among possible participants. However, Palfrey and Rosenthal (1985) showed that in large electorates the inevitable uncertainty about the costs and preferences of other voters again yields a situation with a low subjective probability of affecting the election outcome and thus a low turnout rate.

Niemi (1976) suggested that the difficulty with the rational voter approach is that the cost of voting has been tremendously exaggerated. Particularly in presidential elections, the cost of voting is likely to be very small. Even the cost of becoming informed—at least informed enough to make a decision—is quite small. Moreover, there are costs attached to not voting, such as guilt feelings when others ask whether or not you have voted. Thus, even if the expected gain (PB) is quite small, this together with the costs of not voting may easily outweigh the relatively small cost of going to the polls. This point of view has the added advantage of emphasizing the variability of the cost term in different elections, a factor which has been largely ignored.

In a review of the literature on the rationality of turnout, Aldrich (1992) accepts Niemi's view of turnout as low cost but stresses that it is also a low benefit action. As a result, minor changes in the margin of either can affect turnout decisions, so get-out-the-vote drives can be effective in increasing turnout. Additionally, he argues that the duty term (D), should be seen more as a long-term investment in the political system, which makes the consumption model more compatible with rational-choice investment models. That is, voting once again becomes rational, though only because some of the elements in the vote decision have been reconceptualized.

The attention to the cost term in these works is well warranted. Even moderate voting costs in combination with a low expected gain *may* make voting irrational from the perspective of each individual. Or, to put it another way, small variations in cost may lead to sizable variations in the number of people who vote. While considerable progress has been made in reducing the legal barriers that have stood in the way of voting in presidential elections, the importance of this cost factor has still been all but ignored in the context of other elections. Factors such as registration by mail, more uniform voting dates throughout the nation, more polling places, longer hours for voting, and so on, should result in a considerable increase in turnout, particularly in elections that usually draw a small number of voters. The best estimate of the magnitude of this effect is by Rosenstone and Wolfinger (1978) (reprinted in the second edition of *Controversies in Voting Behavior*), whose analysis of 1972 Census Bureau surveys shows that the national turnout rate would have increased by 9 percent if all states had the same registration rules as the states with the most lenient registration procedures. Of course, state registration laws vary only slightly—for example, the presence or absence of Saturday or evening registration. European-type registration systems (where the government takes responsibility for maintaining an accurate list of eligible voters) would make an even greater difference in turnout. In a later study, Squire, Wolfinger, and Glass (1987) found that residential mobility was a major factor in not voting, presumably since many people do not change their voting registration after they move. They found that, in 1980, states with election-day registration had 18 percent higher turnout among people who had moved within the last six months than did movers in other states. They concluded that allowing movers to change their voting addresses at the same time as they change their mailing addresses would increase turnout by 9 percent; there might be a 2 percent Republican loss to Independents with such a change, but that is within the magnitude of sampling error.

Consideration of the cost term raised the second point made earlier: Should voting be encouraged or discouraged? Berelson's point of view suggested that it should be discouraged, or at least that low turnout has its advantages as well as its disadvantages. This elitist point of view was refuted by Walker (1966), who argued that low turnout, lack of interest, and apathy are not as benign as Berelson would have us believe. Drawing particularly on the experience of blacks in the United States, he argued that low turnout is not necessarily due to acceptance of the status quo but may instead indicate complete alienation from the political system. The resulting frustration can lead to unconventional forms of political participation, including violence. Moreover, Walker reminds us that for the classical democrat, political apathy is an object of intense concern because voting is supposed to do more than accept or reject the status quo. The very act of participation in the affairs of government is supposed to be an act of pride and self-respect for citizens. Acceptance of nonvoting would, from this point of view, totally corrode the very basis of democracy.[1]

Efforts have been made to determine empirically whether alienation is a prime cause of nonvoting. Converse with Niemi (1971) reported that all attitudinal factors for nonvoting were less frequent than legal (nonregistration) or personal (ill heath, flat tire, and so forth) reasons during the 1950s,[2] but this depends on the respondent's own explanation of not voting and does not explain why he or she was not motivated to register. The increased cynicism since the 1960s makes alienation a likely explanation of decreased turnout, and the popular press has already suggested as much.

Empirical tests, however, suggest that cynicism is not a powerful explanatory factor in presidential voting. Brody and Page (1973) considered the impact of two psychological factors on turnout in 1968—voter alienation, defined as liking none of the candidates, and voter indifference, defined as liking all of the candidates equally. The 1968 national election survey included a "thermometer question" in which respondents were asked to indicate how warm they felt toward several presidential contenders. A temperature of 50 was the neutral response, 100 indicated very warm feelings, 0 cold feelings. Brody and Page operationalized alienation in terms of the score a person gave to the presidential nominee he or she liked the most—a person whose favorite candidate had a score of 50 or less was termed alienated. A respondent who gave the three nominees the same score was termed indifferent. Alienation and indifference had definite effects on voting, but indifference accounted for a 17 percent drop in turnout, while alienation led to only a 10 percent drop in turnout. Moreover, only one-eighth of the sample was either alienated or indifferent by Brody and Page's measure, so neither effect had a large impact on turnout.

In a follow-up study, Weisberg and Grofman (1981) found a greater effect on turnout of satisfaction (rating both nominees above 50 on the thermometer) than of alienation in 1976; 29 percent of the respondents were satisfied with the candidates versus only 1 percent alienated. Further, they found that the lowest turnout rate was for neutrals (those who rated both candidates at 50), 13 percent below the concerned (those who rated one candidate above 50 and the other below 50). Altogether, they concluded that candidate-based abstention was limited in 1976. Instead, they suggested that habit is the best correlate of the turnout decision—habitual voters tend to keep voting while habitual nonvoters tend not to vote.

A Center for Political Studies report (Miller and Miller, 1976) on the 1972 election survey similarly analyzed the impact of two psychological factors on turnout. Political efficacy—the feeling that one can have an influence on government behavior—had a substantial impact with a 26 percent difference between high and low efficacy groups. By contrast, political trust had only a small impact, with cynics voting 9 percent less than those who trusted the government.

If these results are accepted, then current low turnout figures represent more than alienation and cynicism. On a more theoretical plane, they suggest that Walker's view of low turnout is empirically invalid at the present time and, by inference, is at least a questionable explanation of low turnout in the past. On the other hand, these analyses are far from definitive, and further studies of the impact of cynicism are to be expected.

Indeed, even the usual view that voting turnout in the United States is low has been questioned. At first blush the 50 percent turnout in presidential elections is embarrassingly below the 90 percent plus figures achieved in some European countries. However, Boyd (1981) implies that the voting rate in the United States is quite respectable. There are many more elections in this country than others. Whereas a parliamentary system such as England's might have only two elections (parliament and local) in a five-year interval, United States citizens might be called on to cast numerous votes in a four-year cycle of primary and general elections during presidential-election and midterm years, plus separate elections in odd-numbered years for state and/or local offices. Turnout might be low in the United States in any single election, but different voters are attracted to different elections. As a result, the proportion of the American public voting in any election during a four-year period might be close to the proportion in other countries. Voting is rational to the public, but different elections matter to different citizens.

Conclusion

Our view of voting has come almost full circle from where it began prior to the introduction of sample surveys and of rational political theory. What have we learned on the way? First, we have learned that nonvoting may mean several things—apathy, satisfaction with the status quo, cynicism—and should not be interpreted exclusively in terms of one of these causes. No doubt the importance of each of these factors varies, and it is an empirical question as to what impact each factor has in different times and places. To attribute nonvoting arbitrarily to one cause, and therefore to conclude that nonvoting is necessarily good or bad, is misleading. While we, like most Americans, lean toward the view that high rates of nonvoting are unsatisfactory, this view should not be accepted uncritically. Depending on the times, the circumstances, and the individuals, nonvoting can conceivably be an acceptable state of affairs.

Along with this viewpoint goes the finding that nonvoting may be individually rational, as Downs suggested. This view emphasizes the costs of voting and of participating generally. It suggests that, if we want to increase participation, we should reduce the costs of participation as much as possible. While in a sense this has always been known, the point takes on added significance when it is suggested that individuals may rationally decide that it is not in their self-interest to vote given the costs that are imposed. Consistent with this point of view would be an attempt to make voting virtually costless, which includes making registration automatic and thereby effortless. Though the location of voting booths may seem like a mundane problem, all of the factors that enter into the cost of voting, taken together, are a crucial factor in individual decisions about whether to vote. Manipulation of these costs is an important ingredient in the size of the turnout on our many election days.

Another conclusion that can be drawn from studies of turnout and voting involves a more accurate understanding of the role of voting in democratic government. As Verba and Nie indicate, other forms of political participation may be more rational than voting for many purposes. Yet they also point out that what voting lacks in the ability to convey information to leaders, it makes up for in the pressure put on the leadership. Voting cannot and should not be expected to decide particular policy alternatives, both because of the characteristics of individual voters that we shall observe later in the book, and because of the nature of the voting choice, as discussed by Verba and Nie. And yet in determining the general direction of government behavior, voting is a powerful means of control (Campbell, Converse, Miller, and Stokes, 1960, pp. 541-48). But the nature of that control can be known only through a better understanding of the individuals who make up the electorate—their political knowledge, their political attitudes, and the way in which they make political decisions. It is these factors that we consider in the remainder of this book.

A final point is that the readings in this section approach nonvoting as an individual decision, with remarkably little consideration of the organizational and group contexts of voting. Subsequent literature has turned more to these elements of the turnout decision.

Notes

1. An interesting middle ground in the debate between Berelson and Walker is provided by Converse (1964). From Converse's point of view, nonvoting itself may not be objectionable, but the sporadic participation of chronic nonvoters is. This point of view is most clearly expressed in an attempt to explain the mass support of the Nazi Party in Germany in the 1930s. Converse argues that chronic nonvoters who were uninformed and unsophisticated, but not necessarily pro-Nazi as such, were major contributors to the upsurge in Nazi voting. Thus the rise in Nazi voting was due not just to an increase in turnout, but to increased turnout among those who had previously been nonvoters out of apathy and ignorance. The soundness of this argument has been disputed by Shively (1972). Precise interpretation is difficult because conclusions must be based on an analysis of aggregate data.

2. Even as late as 1968, after passage of the Voting Rights Act of 1965 cut down on southern disfranchisement of blacks, 56 percent of nonvoting respondents (including southern blacks) cited legal reasons as the cause (CPS/SRC 1968 American National Election Study).

FURTHER READINGS

Empirical Studies of Nonvoting

Angus Campbell, Philip E. Converse, Warren E. Miller, and Donald E. Stokes, *The American Voter* (New York: Wiley, 1960), chap. 5, unabridged. One of the most complete early analyses of the correlates of turnout.

Philip E. Converse with Richard G. Niemi, "Non-Voting Among Young Adults in the United States," in *Political Parties and Political Behavior*, 2d ed., ed. William J. Crotty, Donald M. Freeman, and Douglas S. Gatlin (Boston:

Allyn & Bacon, 1971). Analysis of reasons given by respondents for not voting in the 1950s.

Herbert F. Weisberg and Bernard Grofman, "Candidate Evaluations and Turnout," *American Politics Quarterly* (1981) 9:197-220. Analysis of candidate-based correlates of nonvoting.

Raymond Wolfinger and Steven Rosenstone, *Who Votes?* (New Haven, Conn.: Yale University Press, 1980). Analysis of massive Census Bureau surveys on voting turnout.

Frances Fox Piven and Richard Cloward, *Why Americans Don't Vote* (New York: Pantheon, 1988). Popular analysis of the reasons for low voting rates.

Aggregate Analysis of Turnout

Stanley Kelley, Jr., Richard E. Ayres, and William G. Bowen, "Registration and Voting: Putting First Things First," *American Political Science Review* (1967) 61:359-79. Analysis of turnout figures in various cities in terms of differences in registration.

Jae-On Kim, John R. Petrocik, and Stephen N. Enokson, "Voter Turnout Among the American States: Systemic and Individual Components," *American Political Science Review* (1975) 69:107-23. Aggregate analysis of sociodemographic, electoral competitiveness, and legal correlates of turnout in 1960.

Empirical Analysis of Political Participation

Robert A. Dahl, *Who Governs?* (New Haven, Conn.: Yale University Press, 1961). Classical analysis of participation in local politics that provoked much reaction.

Norval D. Glenn and Michael Grimes, "Aging, Voting, and Political Interest," *American Sociological Review* (1968) 33:563-75. Voting remains steady into advanced maturity; political intere.: actually increases.

Lester W. Milbrath and M. L. Goel. *Political Participation*, 2d. ed. (Chicago: Rand McNally, 1977). Classification of participation types and summary of literature.

Sidney Verba and Norman H. Nie, *Participation in America* (New York: Harper and Row, 1972). Analysis of modes of participation, correlates of participation, and effects of participation in a national sample.

Margaret Conway, *Political Participation in the United States*, 2d ed. (Washington, D.C.: Congressional Quarterly Press, 1991). Textbook treatment of participation in American politics.

Comparative Analysis of Political Participation

Norman H. Nie, G. Bingham Powell, and Kenneth Prewitt, "Social Structure and Political Participation: Developmental Relationships," *American Political Science Review* (1969) 63:361-78, 808-32. Causal analysis of social experiences that explain growth of political participation in economically advanced nations.

Sidney Verba, Norman H. Nie, and Jae-On Kim, *Participation and Political*

Equality (Cambridge, Mass.: Cambridge University Press, 1978). Cross-national study of participation.

G. Bingham Powell, Jr., "American Voter Turnout in Comparative Perspective," *American Political Science Review* (1986) 80:17-43. Accounts for lower American turnout in terms of attitudes, party system, and registration laws.

Robert W. Jackman, "Political Institutions and Voter Turnout in the Industrial Democracies," *American Political Science Review* (1987) 81:405-23. Aggregate analysis of turnout differences between nations in 1960s and 1970s.

Russell Dalton, *Citizen Politics in Western Democracies* (Chatham, N.J.: Chatham House, 1988). Description of attitudes and coi.ventional and nonconventional participation in United States, Germany, France, and Great Britain.

Rationality of Voting

Anthony Downs, *An Economic Theory of Democracy* (New York: Harper and Row, 1957), chap. 14. Abstention from voting is rational, depending on the costs.

Gordon Tullock, *Toward a Mathematics of Politics* (Ann Arbor: University of Michigan Press, 1968), chap. 7. Emphasis on lack of expected gain from voting for the citizen.

William H. Riker and Peter C. Ordeshook, "A Theory of the Calculus of Voting," *American Political Science Review* (1968) 62:25-42. Importance of perceptions of how close the vote in an election will be.

John A. Ferejohn and Morris P. Fiorina, "The Paradox of Not Voting: A Decision Theoretic Analysis," *American Political Science Review* (1974) 68:525-36. Voting in order to not regret not voting.

Richard G. Niemi, "Costs of Voting and Nonvoting," *Public Choice* (1976) 27:115-19. Reconsideration of the costs of voting.

3. THE RATIONALITY OF POLITICAL ACTIVITY: A RECONSIDERATION

Sidney Verba and Norman H. Nie

The alternative modes of political activity, we have argued, represent different ways by which the citizen influences his government. This argument is supported by the findings reported in chapter 5 [of Verba and Nie] that different sets of orientations accompany the various types of activity. We can carry this argument a step further by considering more closely what it is that citizens expect to obtain—or can reasonably expect to obtain—from their participation; and how this differs from one mode to another. Participation is, to us, most importantly an instrumental activity through which citizens attempt to influence the government to act in ways the citizens prefer. But the alternative modes can produce different types of governmental response. In this chapter we look beyond our data to other studies to see how this is the case.

The problem relates to the current debate about the rationality of political activity.[1] It is not our purpose to enter the complexities of that debate, but some of the considerations involved highlight differences among our various modes of activity. And, in turn, the problem of rationality looks somewhat different when one has expanded one's notion of political activity beyond the electoral context. In particular, we can go beyond the question of whether it is rational to vote and whether citizens choose candidates rationally to the question of how the choice among alternative political activities relates to citizen needs and preferences.

The debate centers around the question: When citizens participate, do they do so rationally? For a citizen to do so, he must know what he wants in terms of a governmental response (for example, know what policy he wishes the government to pursue or know what benefit he wishes the government to provide), he must know what action is likely to increase the chances of the government providing what he wants, and he must act accordingly, taking into account the cost of that activity in relation to other uses of his time and effort. The citizen "inputs" some

Source: *Participation in America*, by Sidney Verba and Norman H. Nie, chap. 7. Copyright © 1972 by Sidney Verba and Norman H. Nie. Reprinted with permission of the authors.

Editor's Note: The data summarized in this chapter are based on a representative national sample of 2,549 respondents interviewed by the National Opinion Research Center in March 1967.

act of participation in the expectation that the government will "output" what he wants. If the former is appropriate to the latter—i.e., his participation increases the likelihood that the government will perform as he desires—the citizen is behaving rationally.

The clarity of the citizen's expectation is important. If one is really talking of governmental response to a citizen, the citizen's action must carry a message about his desires precise enough for the government to know how to respond to it. The citizen, in turn, must be able to tell, at least to some minimal degree, if the action of the government is responsive. To put it another way, an act of participation involves an hypothesis on the part of the participant that his act will lead to a desired response by the government. But for the act to be rationally instrumental, it must involve a *testable* hypothesis—i.e., the participant must be able to tell whether he has had any success. This suggests that the citizen's ability to act rationally in politics may depend on the nature of the political act, particularly on two of the dimensions we used to characterize political acts—the type of influence they exert (pressure or informational) and the scope of the outcome they can influence.

Most of the debate on the citizen as rational actor has dealt with him in his role as voter. And voters in general do not much measure up to the standards of rationality.

For one thing, the public has little information on which candidate takes which position during an election. In fact, they may know almost nothing about candidates. Miller and Stokes (1963) indicate that about half of their sample had heard or read nothing about either congressional candidate in their district and that only 25 percent had read anything at all about both candidates, still probably putting them a long way from having the information needed to make the kind of rational choice we have been discussing. And in an earlier study (see Lane and Sears, 1964, p. 61), it was found that less than half the public knew which party controlled the Congress—certainly a useful bit of information if one is to evaluate a candidate's potential performance.

In addition, it appears that few citizens know what they want. They do not have clear and consistent positions on the important issues of the day. Attitudes on public issues are lightly held, and answers to survey questions on specific issues facing the nation often appear to have a random quality (Converse, 1964). Nor do citizens have clear and consistent sets of issue positions. The absence of clear structure in citizen attitudes on the issues of elections is confirmed by Campbell et al. in their analysis in *The American Voter* of the "level of conceptualization" of voters (Campbell et al., 1960, chap. 10). Very few respondents (3.5 percent of voters) could be considered to have a political ideology of a clear sort (and even these people provide fairly vague notions of their political ideology if one reads the examples of answers). The kind of abstract conceptualization that could give structure to the electoral choice is almost completely missing. When citizens vote, they are more likely to be influenced by candidate images or by their traditional party affiliation than they are by the issue positions of the candidates or parties.

More recent attempts to find issue-voting (behavior consistent with our definition of rational participation) have found only a trace more of it than the authors of the classic analysis in *The American Voter* did. In some elections one finds more issue-voting than was found in 1956 by Campbell et al., in *The American Voter*, but still not much (Key, 1966; Converse, Miller, Rusk, and Wolfe, 1969). If respondents self-select the issues upon which to evaluate the parties, issue-partisanship (the perception of which party will more likely take the action you want on the issues most salient to you) predicts the vote better than when the issue is presented to the respondent by the researcher. But it still predicts the vote less well than does candidate image or party affiliation. And, as we shall argue, the procedure of allowing the respondent to choose the issue (RePass, 1971) is quite unrealistic.

Rationality and Contacting

But voting is only one mode of activity. These data on the relative lack of instrumental orientation toward the vote contrast sharply with our data on citizen-initiated contacts. Our respondents were asked about contacts that they initiated with government officials within and/or outside of the community. If they had initiated a contact, they were asked to identify the official and also to tell us the nature of the problem.

As one reads the answers to these questions one is struck by how relatively precise and instrumental the responses are. About one-third of all contacts, as we have noted, were on problems particularized to the individual or his family; the rest are more general in referent. As one could expect, the former type of contact involves requests for specific benefits and is clearly instrumental activity: the citizen knows what he wants and acts to obtain it. But even when the subject matter of the contact is a broader problem involving the entire community or the entire society, the problems tend to be fairly clear and specific. Citizens specify a problem area and a solution. And the choice of official to contact usually is quite appropriate: citizen-initiated contacts about school matters go to school officials or other relevant local officials, contacts about more general legislative matters go to state legislators or congressmen, contacts about the war in Vietnam go to one's senator, congressmen, or perhaps the President. This is not to argue a fantastically high level of sophistication about channels of influence among the citizenry. Rather, the data simply illustrate a circumstance in which citizens act politically with specific goals in mind and in ways that are quite appropriate for the achievement of these goals.

The main reason for this, we believe, is that in contacting, the citizen takes the initiative: he decides when to contact, whom to contact, and the subject matter of that contact. This is not to imply that the situation is totally unstructured for him and that he simply acts as he wants when the spirit moves him. He is constrained to act in certain ways by the channels available for contacting the government and he may be motivated to raise one particular problem or issue rather than another by governmental action or inaction in particular areas. But the agenda is set by the individual and quite freely chosen by him. Of the vast number of programs in which the government is engaged, he chooses one about which to complain; of the vast number of ways in which government activity impinges on his own life, he focuses on one for attention; of the vast number of things the government is not doing that might affect the individual, he brings up one for discussion. This choosing of the agenda by the individual is the main characteristic that differentiates citizen-initiated contacts from other modes of participation.

This choice guarantees that the issue of the participatory act is salient and important to the respondent. As many have pointed out, the personal "agendas" of citizens are fantastically varied. Each citizen has his own particular set of problems and concerns. These are usually close to his own life space, involving job, family, house. Or, if what concerns him is more general—war, high prices, the quality of schools, traffic problems, property taxes—there remains an almost infinite variety of personal sets of public issues.

A contact initiated by the citizen can be tailored to his specific set of problems. That this indeed seems to happen can be illustrated by one small piece of data. In addition to the questions on the subject matter of their contacts to officials, our respondents were asked to tell us the most important problems they faced in their personal and family lives and the most important problems that they saw facing the community. There were no constraints on the problems that could be mentioned, and the answers range widely. The answers to the question on the citizen's contact and the problems he perceived were coded into several hundred categories. Almost as many categories were necessary for coding the "contact" questions as for coding the "perceived problems" questions, despite the fact that many fewer respondents were answering contact questions. (About a third of our respondents had contacted an official, while almost everyone could name a personal or community problem.) What this indicates is that citizen-initiated contacting brings into the political system a set of concerns roughly as wide as the set of concerns that the citizenry faces.

Rationality and Voting

The situation facing the voter is sharply different. He does not choose the occasion to vote, nor does he choose the agenda; he doesn't choose the issues that divide the candidates, nor does he usually have much voice in choosing the candidates themselves. And given the fact that his own agenda is quite individual and may contain many and varied issues, it is unreasonable to expect that there will be a voting choice tailored to his own particular policy preferences at the moment. It is even more unreasonable to expect that the questions posed to him by interviewers about his views on the issues—issues he has not chosen— will elicit responses that will then clearly predict the vote.[2] His vote can only be a rather blunt instrument under these circumstances; it cannot have the sharpness and precision of the statements that accompany citizen-initiated contacts.

Given the lack of fit between the concerns of the individual and issues of the election, it is not surprising that issue-oriented voting is rare. Even if the citizen were motivated to vote on issues, the election usually offers an uncongenial setting. Given the multiplicity of issues in an election, there must be some way for the individual to simplify the choice situation into a meaningful dichotomy so that he can vote with a clear outcome in mind. This simplification of the choice situation can come about in one of two ways: the individual must have a clear and well-structured ideology and the parties must offer him a choice congruent with the ideology, or there must be some "overriding" issue in the election, and the parties must offer a clear alternative on that issue. An ideology allows a clear choice in a multi-issue situation, since such a belief system places individual issues into some overall structure. One then chooses a party in terms of its agreement with that ideology. But there is no need to spend time on this possibility, for there is little evidence that voters think in such ideological terms. Even if they did, the American parties would not offer them clear alternatives in those terms.

In the absence of an ideology that clearly sums up all issues and provides a general choice for the individual between the two political parties, the election can allow instrumental voting of a precise sort if there is an overriding issue. In this case, the individual believes that there is a single issue in the campaign compared with which other issues are minor and that one of the voting alternatives clearly is preferable to the others in relation to that issue. Under these circumstances, an individual can vote with the hope that his vote will increase the likelihood of a direct instrumental gratification—i.e., that his favorite party or candidate will win and carry out the policy he prefers in connection with the overriding issue.

But is this possible in the voting choice? It is certainly possible but unlikely. For one thing, such overriding issues do not often appear, and, second, the choice on the issue may not be clear. Actually, at the time we were conducting our study, there was an issue that seemed to be overriding—this was the issue of Vietnam. Our questionnaire contained a number of questions on it. In response to a completely open-ended question 66 percent of our sample said that the war in Vietnam was the most important problem facing the nation (74 percent if one takes into account the first and second most important problems), and many others simply referred to war. Ninety-one percent said that they worried about Vietnam.[3]

It would be hard to find a national issue upon which there was a greater focus of attention. But does this issue fit our criteria of an overriding one? Are individuals willing to vote on that issue alone and do they perceive a clear choice? In two additional surveys conducted closer to the 1968 election, respondents were asked how much importance they would give to a candidate's stand on Vietnam. In February 1968, 18 percent of a sample said that Vietnam would be more important than any other issue in making up their minds, and an additional 72 percent said that Vietnam would be important but that other issues would be important too. Only 4 percent said that the stand of the candidate on Vietnam would not be important. (Parallel data in June 1968, are 12 percent, 83 percent, and 6 percent respectively.)[4] At least for the group that says it will be the most important issue for them, the war in Vietnam fulfilled the first criterion for an overriding issue. But they are still a small part of our sample.

And what of the second criterion: that the individual is offered a choice on the issues by the political parties? Whether the parties did offer a choice on the issue is a question that can be answered in many ways. Let us look at the question from the point of view of the voter: Did *he* see a choice? A few survey results are relevant. In our survey in 1967 (in which 65 percent said that Vietnam was the most important issue facing the country), 66 percent agreed with the statement that it would make no difference which party was in power as far as Vietnam was concerned. (Eleven percent disagreed slightly with that statement, and 11 percent disagreed strongly.)

More telling, perhaps, is the public's perception of the position of the candidates on the issue. In a study of the 1968 election (by Brody, Page, Laulicht, and Verba), respondents were asked to place various candidates on a seven-position "hawk-dove" scale based on where they thought the candidate stood on the Vietnam issue. Most citizens saw little or not difference between the candidates. The average perception of the position of the candidates placed Nixon at 4.4 on the scale, Humphrey at 4.1 (i.e., on the average, Humphrey was seen as a touch more dovish that Nixon, but only a touch). In contrast, citizens placed George Wallace at 6.5. Looked at another way, over half (57 percent) of the citizens who assigned a place to both major party candidates placed them in the same position or within one scale point of each other (Brody and Page, 1972).

The data strongly suggest that the candidates were not perceived by the public as offering widely divergent alternatives on the subject of Vietnam. In addition, there is evidence that as the election campaign progressed, the issue became less and less important, perhaps because the two candidates most similar on Vietnam were chosen (Brody, Page, Verba, and Laulicht, 1969). And an intensive analysis (by Brody and Page, 1972) of the public speeches of the two candidates shows a combination of convergence and vagueness—both of which make issue-voting difficult. The specific case of Vietnam does not demonstrate that an overriding issue might not emerge in some election. But the relatively stringent criteria that would have to be met before one could say that the individual was voting with a specific policy outcome in mind suggest that the situation will be rare. And, of course, we are familiar with the general tendency of election campaigns to blur political issues.[5]

This is not to argue that voting on the basis of ideology or clear issue perception is impossible. Quite the contrary. In our view, the reason why such voting is rare lies within the nature of the collective decision made during an election, not in the incompetence or "irrationality" of the voter. Given a candidate who makes a strong ideological appeal—that is, takes a strong and consistent position on a large number of issues—one might find more voters responding in those terms. Or given a candidate who taps some deeply felt and widely shared issue, one might find more voters voting instrumentally with a fairly precise goal in mind. Thus, Field and Anderson (1969), in their comparison of the 1964 election with the data reported on the 1956 election in *The American Voter*, find that there is more reference to ideological terms in the 1964 Johnson-Goldwater race. References to explicit ideology rise from 9 percent in 1956 (they use a somewhat different definition of this than do the authors of *The American Voter*) to 16 percent in the 1960 [election] to 24 percent in the 1964 election. The rise in frequency of ideological references in 1960 suggests that the base year of 1956 in

The American Voter may have been a year of abnormally low levels of political controversy. But even the level of ideological reference found in 1964—and we are really dealing here with such general political terms as *liberal* and *conservative*—is hardly impressive given the type of political appeal made by Goldwater. Nevertheless, the difference between 1964 and 1956 does suggest that the nature of the choice situation—as exemplified by the two presidential candidates—structures the type of response available.

More relevant to our argument is the 1968 election, in which the Survey Research Center found, among those who voted for George Wallace, clear goal orientation consistent with the appeal that Wallace had been making (Converse et al., 1969). In contrast to the appeal of Goldwater in 1964, in which there was some response in general ideological terms, Wallace's appeal was in terms of a specific set of overriding issues (race, crime, the urban crisis) of great salience to a group of voters and on which the candidate was taking a strong and clear position. As the Survey Research Center analysts correctly point out, this example indicates that issue-oriented voting is possible, given the right set of issues that are deeply felt and salient to a group, as were the race and urban issues in 1968. But the fact that this type of instrumental voting appears in relation to a third-party candidate and for only a small segment of the population indicates that this is not yet the mainstream orientation of the American public to the voting choice.

The difficulty in using the vote to satisfy the specific desires of citizens can be seen quite clearly if we compare the responses reported in *The American Voter* where respondents favored a party or candidate because of some expectation of a specific beneficial outcome with the responses we received on the subject matter of citizen contacts.

Two differences seem to stand out. In relation to contacts, the individual seems to be looking forward: He is asking for some future benefit from the government. In relation to the vote, he is likely to be looking backward, even when he is focused on a specific instrumental goal. Thus *The American Voter* authors refer to the frequent appearance among "nature of the times" respondents of comments about promises that have not been kept. And the one woman quoted who mentions a specific particularized reason for favoring one party over another (Campbell et al., 1960, p. 244) refers to "the good wages my husband makes." V. O. Key, Jr. (1966, p. 61), who makes the strongest argument for the rationality of the voter (in our terms, for his ability to make choices with a specific political outcome in mind) makes that argument in terms of the ability of the voter to make rational evaluations of past performance rather than clear demands for future performance.

The second reason why expectations of specific gratification in response to one's vote differ from such expectations in response to citizen-intitiated contacts is that, in some sense, such expectations are appropriate in the latter case and inappropriate in the former. The individual who contacts the government with a salient and specific outcome in mind engages in more reasonable behavior than does the individual who sees the election as related to the particular specific problem that is most salient to him at the time. (Though, as the Wallace campaign reminds us, candidates—probably third-party candidates—can sometimes tap such issues.)

This may explain why the type of answers we quote as to the subject matter of citizen-initiated contacts—answers we consider to indicate some precise understanding of political needs—are the type that, when they appeared in answer to the question of what one likes about the parties or candidates in *The American Voter*, were coded in one of the lowest categories in terms of conceptualization; the "nature of our times" category. The point is that the individual can select the agenda of a contact, and he does so in the context of the specific problems that are troubling him at the time. However, in relation to the vote, one of two things may happen: on the one hand, he may respond to the agenda as offered to him in the election, but he will do so in vague terms (as when he gives general or group-oriented answers to open-ended questions) or in inconsistent and changeable terms (as when he answers questions on specific issues) because the agenda presented to him is not of his choosing and does not reflect the problems he faces most immediately. On the other hand, if he does respond to the election in terms of his own salient and specific problem, his response is inappropriate because the election rarely revolves around that problem at all or, if it does, it will certainly not revolve around that problem alone. Or one can look at this from the point of view of our distinction between pressure and information as means of influencing the government. The voting situation is an uncongenial one for conveying specific citizen preferences because there is no way to cram that information into the vote, whereas one can express precise information when one contacts a leader.

In the light of these considerations, it is no wonder that issue orientations have no larger role in the voting choice. Nor is it any wonder that those who attempt to develop a calculus from which one can infer that it is reasonable for a citizen to bother to vote—given the small impact he can have on the election—have had to turn to variables such as the gratification one receives from fulfilling a civic duty (Riker and Ordeshook, 1968). This preserves the rationality of the vote—if it makes you feel good, it's rational to do it—but it hardly makes voting an instrumental act aimed at obtaining some beneficial governmental action. And mere habit may play a role in voting turnout. As our data in chapter 5 [of Verba and Nie] indicated, voting specialists are characterized by habitual attachment to a political party and relatively little emotional concern with the issues. As we shall show later, the likelihood of voting can be partially explained simply by the length of time one has been an eligible voter, a fact consistent with an habitual basis of voting. Last, one of the prime characteristics of voting—the ease of the act and the lack of initiative required—makes it likelier that citizens will vote even if they see no specific gain from the outcome.

The difference between citizen-initiated contacts and voting supports our contention that contact mechanisms and electoral mechanisms represent different systems for relating citizens to the government. Both elections and citizen-initiated contacts represent simplifying mechanisms whereby individual preferences are converted into social choice, i.e., mechanisms whereby the vast multiplicity of demands and needs that citizens have can be communicated to the government and allocations of societal resources can be made relevant to these needs and demands. But the voting and contact mechanisms work in different ways. In the election, we are dealing with social choice for the entire society. The preferences of citizens are simplified by being channeled into a limited number of choices: a choice among a few parties, or between those parties and abstention. Under such circumstances, the individual is unlikely to find a voting choice that allows him to make an instrumental decision relevant to the specific set of salient problems that face him at the time of the election—problems that our data (and the data of others) tell us are likely to be highly particularized, involving the health of the individual, his economic situation, and the condition of his neighborhood, as well as more public issues (see Cantril, 1965). It is unlikely that a candidate will stand for the specific set of goals the individual has or even that the set of problems that concern him most will become the subject of the election.

The problem is not specific to the American two-party system. The fact that electoral choice in the United States is often reduced to that between two political parties intensifies both the simplification of the choice and its incongruence with the specific set of problems facing the individual. If there were more parties offering more specific programs, the individual could tailor his voting choice somewhat more to his own specific salient needs and problems. (And it is not accidental that the best example of issue-oriented voting—Wallace in 1968— involves a third-party candidate.) But that does not solve the problem of social choice. The more parties, the more an individual may find one party that comes close to his particular set of preferences. But the choice means less in terms of influencing governmental policy, because the party elected will be a minority party and will have to form some coalition with other parties to enter a government.[6] It is not the number of parties, but the making of a social choice for the whole society that leads to the distance between the vote and the particular salient preferences of the individual.

Citizen-initiated contacts represent an alternative way of simplifying social choice. This is done by decomposing the choice to the individual level. These contacts often deal with particularized problems; in many cases the response to a contact would have major impact on the individual without affecting the overall allocation of societal benefits in more than marginal ways. But the sum total of all such contacts and the myriad responses to them do represent a mechanism for social allocation without the clear necessity of general social choice. By decomposing social choice to a vast number of specific interactions with the government, the structure of citizen-initiated contacts may represent an important means of achieving instrumental goals from the government, goals that are close to the most salient problems felt by the individual.

The contrast between the vote and citizen-initiated contacts leads to further comment on the American public. Research on political beliefs has led to the conclusions that the American public rarely approaches political matters with a clear and well-defined perception of the issues, that the public is ill-informed, its political beliefs lightly held and quickly changeable, its view of political matters vague and distant, and that politics and political controversy lack salience, i.e., the individual is more likely to be concerned with his own narrow day-to-day problems than with the issues that excite the few politically involved and sophisticated citizens. This view of the American public has usually been derived from studies of political matters in which, to use our phraseology, the agenda has been set for the individual by others. (Sometimes the agenda is set by the researcher who comes to the respondent with fixed alternative questions about political matters the researcher considers important.) This view also derives from studies of electoral choice, in which individuals are not found to have a clear issue-oriented view of the meaning of the election. It derives from studies of attitudes on foreign policy, in which the individual is found to know and care little about the foreign-policy choices of the government; and it derives from studies of the consistency and stability of attitudes on major public issues when the individual is asked to take sides on some such issue. For this realm of politics, the view of the public is accurate and relevant (Converse, 1964; Campbell et al., 1960; McClosky, 1964; Almond, 1950).

Our only objection is to a tendency to consider such a position representative of the sum of the citizens' relations with the government. Our data on the content of citizen-initiated contacts show a citizenry involved with the government in ways that are highly salient to them, on issues that they define, and through channels that seem appropriate. What we are suggesting is that on matters of the politics of everyday life, citizens know what they want.[7]

Furthermore, we ought to make clear that in contrasting voting and citizen-initiated contacts, we do not intend to praise the latter as a means of participation and criticize the former. Quite the contrary. A system based on individual contacts would allow adequate citizen control over the government only if access to those contacts were equally available for all and, more important, if there were no significant "macro" policy issues that had to be decided. As some data to be presented later will show, the former condition does not hold. Access to contacting is not as widespread as access to the vote. And the latter condition does not hold either. Social policy has to be made. Particularized contacts can be effective for the individual contactor but they are inadequate as a guide to more general social policy.

The point is that if one wants to maximize popular control over governmental activities that affect the lives of citizens, both types of mechanisms—the contacting and the electoral—are needed. Because governmental policies are almost always quite general, their application to a specific individual in a specific situation involves particular adjustments or decisions made by low-level government officials. Insofar as this is the case, the ability of the citizen to make himself heard on such a matter—by contacting the officials—represents an important aspect of citizen control. Though such contacts may be important in filling the policy gaps and in adjusting policy to the individual, effective citizen control over governmental policy would be limited indeed if citizens related to their government only as isolated individuals concerned with their narrow parochial problems. The larger political questions would remain outside popular control. Therefore, though electoral mechanisms remain crude, they are the most effective for these purposes.

Thus, despite much of what we have said, the vote remains probably a most effective means for citizen control over leaders. Even if the individual voter has little power over the election outcome, the set of all voters is powerful indeed. But the comparison of voting with citizen-initiated contacting helps us comprehend why it remains such an inadequate mechanism for citizen control, an inadequacy that may lie less in the incapacities of the citizenry than in the nature of the electoral mechanism itself.

Indeed, as we shall demonstrate in Chapter 19 [of Verba and Nie], voting *in combination with other acts* is a most potent political force. Other acts have, as we suggested, more information-carrying capacity. On the other hand, votes are most powerful in applying pressure on leaders. When the two coexist—pressure plus information—participation is, as we shall see, most effective. Even if the vote can carry little information, voting can make governmental leaders more sensitive to other more informative messages coming from citizens.

The Rationality of Communal and Campaign Activity

For the purposes of illustrating the differences in the ways the modes of activity relate the citizen to his government, the contrast between voting and citizen-initiated contacts is the most important and illuminating. We can fill out the picture by looking briefly at communal and campaign activity.

Much of what has been said about contacting can also be said about communal activity. Indeed, one of the component acts of the communal mode of participation involves contacting officials on a social issue. In these cases, the citizen acts, as we have suggested, with fairly specific goals and with fairly good selectivity in terms of the officials chosen for contact. The other component of communal participation involves activity in cooperation with others—informal cooperation with friends, neighbors, fellow-workers or other citizens of similar interest—or activity through formally organized groups. Such activity is particularly widespread in America. Over a century ago, Tocqueville commented on the distinctive amount of such activity in the United States. And recent data on participation in a variety of nations (Almond and Verba, 1963, chap. 7; Verba, Nie, and Kim, 1971, p. 36) suggest that participation through cooperation with others is the mode of activity for which the rate in the United States far exceeds rates found elsewhere.

Insofar as citizens are cooperating with others in attempting to influence governmental policy, one would not expect that the average citizen can set the agenda as freely as he can when he is contacting on his own, for he has to consider the views of the others with whom he cooperates. Nevertheless, such group-oriented activity should resemble contacting more than it does activity in the electoral process in terms of its ability to satisfy the most direct instrumental needs of the citizen. Citizens tend to become involved in groups that deal with problems salient to them. The problems are not as particular as the problems brought by those who contact on personal and family matters; they may indeed be general social problems of the community. But the citizen will choose to become involved in relation to problems that touch him. Parents become active in school groups; sportsmen in groups concerned with recreational facilities. The cooperation may involve informal relations among like-minded citizens, but the very term *like-minded* makes clear that the participants will be those for whom the problem is salient. Or the cooperation may involve activity through formal organizations, but citizens tend to join organizations that relate to things they consider important.

In this sense, communal activity (and, in particular, those activities carried on in cooperation with others) may combine some of the advantages of contacting with those of voting. Communal activity engaged in concert with one's fellows can deal with fairly specific problems that are high on the agenda of citizens—problems that affect some specific group to which they belong or problems that affect the community as a whole. In this sense they have the specificity and information-carrying capacity of contacting. On the other hand, the fact that citizens are joining together to act politically increases the potential influence that they can have, especially when the issue involved is broader than those associated with particularized contacting.[8] Whether these activities are those of formally organized interest groups or of informal groupings of citizens coming together for a specific purpose, they form an important part of the participatory system in the United States.

Last, we can consider campaign activity. The campaign activist is, in some sense, in the same position as the voter. He may have somewhat more control over the agenda of the election—he may be active in nominations and in issue selection—but it is unlikely that the average campaign activist has much voice in these matters either. But because campaign participation requires more time, effort, and initiative than voting, it is hard to see it as motivated solely by habit or sense of civic obligation.

How then does the campaign activist get instrumental benefits? Is it rational for him to be active? Several answers are possible. In the first place, campaign activists do differ from ordinary voters in having clearer issue orientations. As our data in chapter 5 [of Verba and Nie] made clear, campaign activists score higher on the scale of issue extremity than any other type of political actor, except the complete activists.[9] In addition to their stronger and more consistent issue positions, they tend to have a better developed ideological view of the differences between the parties than do ordinary citizens (Marvick and Nixon, 1961). Thus, in terms of their own orientations to politics, campaign activists may be better equipped than the average citizen to vote "instrumentally." They are more likely to have clear and consistent policy views and to see policy differences between the parties. Yet, these activists may also be blocked from successfully pursuing instrumental goals within the electoral process by the same thing that blocks voters: They do not control the agenda of the election and therefore that agenda is unlikely to match their own.

What happens under such circumstances? There are no national data on this subject, but Eldersveld's data on party workers in Detroit are most revealing in the light of our discussion of elections and instrumental gratification. He finds that for lower-echelon party workers (which is what most of our campaign activists are), one must distinguish between the motivations for initial involvement in partisan activity and the motives for remaining active.

... while grass roots workers may have been recruited under the guise of the "voluntaristic-idealistic-impersonal task-oriented" concept of party work, ... these precinct leaders in large numbers change motivational direction during their careers. Many become disillusioned; the majority articulated personal demands, needs, and satisfactions to be derived from party activity. In reality this means that the majority of precinct leaders changed their motivational relationship to the party.... They either became disillusioned, or they conceptualized their relationship in terms of social friendship satisfactions (66 percent of the Democrats, 49 percent of the Republicans), a desire to be "in the know" and gain prestige in the neighborhood (4 percent of the Democrats, 6 percent of the Republicans), or they saw other personalized satisfaction such as the enjoyment of the "fun and excitement" of a campaign (6 percent of the Democrats, 4 percent of the Republicans).[10]

In short, then, party activists may join parties because of some instrumental goal, a belief that they can influence governmental policy in some desired direction. However, over time, these goals become less important and side benefits become more important. On the lower levels, these side benefits tend to be social in nature (one enjoys party work, meets others, etc.), while on the upper level they are both social and material (one makes business connections, etc.). This finding is consistent with our findings on the high issue orientation of partisan activists and with our view of the electoral process as a relatively uncongenial setting for participation oriented toward dealing with issues one considers important. It may be that the ineffectiveness of the electoral mechanism for satisfying specific policy goals means that activists either adopt alternative goals that do not depend on governmental responsiveness, or drop out. We will return to this subject in chapter 12 [of Verba and Nie], where we will present contrasting data on the two parties.

The Participation Input: A Summary

In Part I [of Verba and Nie] we have attempted to analyze and describe the participation input: How much participation is there, of what kind, and from what people? In this chapter we have attempted to demonstrate that the alternative modes of participation do in fact differ in the kinds of benefits that citizens can reasonably expect from them. For some modes of participation, means-ends calculations are more difficult than for others, but when one looks across the range of alternative activities open to the citizen one may find a greater degree of instrumental and rational activity than is sometimes assumed. And where one finds rather ill-developed means-ends calculations—as in relation to voting—the source may lie in the nature of the electoral system itself at least as much as it lies in the incapacity of the average voter.

It may be useful now to tie together what we have found about the participation input. Table 3-1 summarizes a good deal of what we have found. In column A we list the six types of participants that we have found to fit the patterns of activity of American citizens, and we give the proportion of the population that falls into each of these types. In column B we characterize their respective patterns of activity, and in column C we indicate how these activities fit our theoretical dimensions of participation. In column D we give the main characteristics of each group in terms of political orientations, a pattern of orientations that, we believe, confirms the meaningfulness of the distinctions we make among the types of political actors. In column E we indicate the social composition of the various activist groups. In short, one can tell from Table 3-1 how many people are active in America, the ways in which they are active (and in particular, the all-important question of the types of outcome their activity can influence), and their social characteristics.

The participation input summarized in Table 3-1 suggests a quite variegated pattern of participation in the United States, not a mere division of the population into several different activity levels. This is not simply to say that there are many different kinds of activities open to citizens. Rather the data reported in Part I [of Verba and Nie] support a stronger conclusion: that there are several different systems of participation in the United States.

There are several justifications for this stronger conclusion. In the first place, we have found that the various political acts in which citizens can engage form meaningful patterns and constitute particular modes of activity. Second, we have found that there are groups of citizens who "specialize" in one mode of activity or another. It is true that there are some citizens who engage in all modes of activity and some who do nothing, but substantial numbers of citizens limit their activity fairly closely to one mode or another. Third, we found that the alternative types of activists have distinct patterns of orientation to politics that are consistent with our analysis of the implications for the various ways citizens can participate. And, last and probably most important, we have shown that the alternative patterns of activity relate the citizen to his government in different ways: They can influence different kinds of governmental decisions, and they allow the participant to exercise more or less influence over the result of his participatory attempt.

What Are the Alternative Systems of Participation?

First, there is the system of particularized contacting, a channel of participation that permits citizens to seek a variety of decomposable benefits from the government—benefits that aid only them. Through this system of participation, the individual citizen may seek some government service or may seek to stop some government activity that is impinging on his life. This system of participation does not touch on the great issues of policy, and perhaps for that reason little attention has been paid to it. But the government affects our lives in so many small ways that this would appear to be a critical channel, and if it were closed to some groups, they would be severely deprived. Indeed, life would be much more difficult even in the most democratic society if there were no means available to obtain minor adjustments and dispensations from general government policy, especially when that policy is made on such a grand scale and at places so distant from the lives it affects.

Particularized contacting is an activity carried on by all sorts of citizens—by some who are active in other ways, by some who are not. This reflects the fact

Table 3-1 The Participation Input: A Summary

A Type of Participant	B Pattern of Activity	C Theoretical Dimensions Activity Pattern	D Leading Orientations	E Main Social Characteristics
The inactives (22%)	No activity		Totally uninvolved, no interest, skill, sense of competence, or concern with conflict.	Lower socioeconomic levels and blacks are overrepresented, as are older and younger citizens (but not middle-aged ones) and women.
The voting specialists (21%)	They vote regularly, but do nothing else.	Broad collective outcomes, counterparticipants, and low initiative.	Strong partisan identity but otherwise relatively uninvolved and with low skills and competence.	Lower socioeconomic levels are overrepresented. Older citizens are overrepresented, as are those in big cities. Underrepresented in rural areas.
The parochial participants (4%)	They contact officials on particularized problems and are otherwise inactive.	Particularized outcomes, no conflict, and high initiative.	Some political skill (information) but otherwise no political involvement.	Lower socioeconomic groups are overrepresented, but blacks are underrepresented. Catholic rather than Protestant. Big cities rather than small towns.

The communalists (20%)	They contact officials on broad social issues and engage in cooperative activity. Vote fairly regularly, but avoid election campaigns.	Collective outcomes (but may be narrower than those of elections), high initiative, and relatively no conflict.	High sense of community contribution, involvement in politics, skill and competence. Nonpartisan and avoid conflict.	Upper socioeconomic levels very overrepresented, blacks underrepresented. Protestant rather than Catholic. Overrepresented in rural areas and small towns; underrepresented in big cities.
The campaigners (15%)	Heavily active in campaigns and vote regularly.	Broad collective outcomes, moderate to high initiative, and relatively conflictual.	Politically involved, relatively skilled and competent, partisan and involved in conflict, but little sense of community contribution.	Overrepresentation of upper-status groups. Blacks and particularly Catholics overrepresented. Big-city and suburbs rather than small towns and rural areas.
The complete activists (11%)	Active in all ways.	All characteristics of all acts.	Involved in politics in all ways, highly skilled and competent.	Heavy overrepresentation of upper-status groups. Old and young underrepresented.
Unclassified (7%)				

that such activity deals with myriad specific problems affecting all sorts of people. Those citizens who limit their activity to particularized contacting are a special type. We have labeled them *parochial participants,* for though they have the skill and initiative to engage in fairly difficult activity, they show no involvement in political life in the broader sense.

Next we have uncovered the communalist system of participation, whereby citizens alone or, more often with others, attempt to deal with the more general problems of their communities or of particular groups. The problems are not so narrow as those dealt with via particularized contacting, but they are nevertheless problems that are specifically pertinent to the individuals or groups active in this way. The activity also seems to be relatively nonconflictual, either because the goal is some general benefit to the community or because it is some benefit to the specific group of activists but is not seen by others as affecting them negatively. Much of this activity seems to consist of mobilizing community resources or one's fellow citizens to deal directly with community problems or to induce the government to do so.

The communalists' attitudes fit their activity: They have a high sense of contribution to the community and a general involvement in politics, but they seem to avoid conflict. As we have suggested, activity of this sort is found more frequently in the United States than in a variety of other countries—a fifth of the U.S. citizenry concentrate on this form of participation. However, data presented in chapter 13 [of Verba and Nie] suggest that such activity flourishes under conditions that may be disappearing in America. If so, the system of political participation in the United States will lose an important and distinctive component.

The third and fourth modes of participation with which we have dealt involve the electoral system. One way citizens take part is via an active role in the campaign process. Our data show that almost a third of the citizenry participate in some way in this process, and that over 15 percent concentrate on this form of political involvement. When we add this 15 percent to the even larger number of communalists, we see two vigorous, yet separate, systems whereby private citizens can and do attempt to influence the direction of our political life. But campaign activity differs from communal activity because the issues of the former are less specific to the participants and because they involve more conflict.

The last mode of activity is voting. We find a substantial proportion of citizens (21 percent) who limit their activity to this—but it is not nearly so large a group as other studies have suggested. And although we have found the vote to be a rather limited mode of engagement, there would appear to be few other available mechanisms whereby the preferences of all citizens can simultaneously be taken into account, giving them some control over the selection of leadership. Furthermore, some data to be presented in chapter 19 [of Verba and Nie] will indicate that although voting may have minimal effectiveness as a channel for communicating the specific needs and desires of a particular participant, when aggregated across all citizens and especially when combined with other activities conveying more information, it remains a most powerful system for insuring the responsiveness of elites.

Each of the modes of participation is distinctive and each, therefore, forms an important component of the overall system of participation in the United States. It is a rich and complex system. But it is also a system for which all the components are not equally accessible to all citizens.

Notes

1. There is a wide literature on this subject. Some of the most important works are Campbell et al. (1960, chap. 10), Converse (1964), McClosky (1964), Key (1966), Shapiro (1969), and Riker and Ordeshook (1968).
2. RePass (1971) shows that one can better predict the vote if one uses attitude position on the issue that the respondent chooses as most salient to him. But, though this removes some artificiality in political science research on voting by giving freer rein to the problems the respondent himself considers important, it adds a new artificiality. Our contention is that it is unrealistic for the individual to be allowed to choose the agenda of the election, for indeed the issues are not posed by him but by the parties and the candidates.
3. The data on Vietnam are from a series of studies of attitudes on that issue conducted by Richard A. Brody, Jerome Laulicht, Benjamin I. Page, and Sidney Verba. For some reports on these data see Brody, Page, Verba, and Laulicht (1969), Brody and Page (1972), and Rosenberg, Verba, and Converse, 1970).
4. See Brody, Page, Verba, and Laulicht (1969).
5. That individuals do not approach the vote with a clear perception of alternatives ought not to be taken to imply that citizens are somehow failing in their obligations to have such clear perceptions. The obvious point is that they receive precious little help from the parties or candidates for this. See Kelley (1960). As he puts it:

    > Contemporary campaign discussion is often of such a character that it is unlikely to help voters much in their efforts to arrive at a wise choice of public officials. It may, in fact, have quite the reverse effect. Campaign propagandists obscure the real differences between candidates and parties by distortion, by evasiveness, and by talking generalities (p. 80).

    > Anyone who examines the course of discussion in campaigns can hardly fail to conclude that it is often as well designed to subvert as to facilitate rational voting behavior. What candidates say frequently lacks relevance to any decision voters face, exposes differences in the views of candidates imperfectly, and is filled with evasions, ambiguities and distortions. (p. 51)

    On this general subject, see also Downs (1957).
6. The classic political science debate over forms of electoral system, particularly the choice between proportional representation and single-member district systems, is relevant here. See also Downs (1957).
7. This is consistent with the finding that individuals manifest issue positions with more consistency on local issues and on specific issues than on general political issues. Luttbeg finds that the mass-elite distinction in terms of consistency of attitudes found on national issues does not apply to more local ones. See Luttbeg (1968).
8. The vast literature on pressure groups in America is relevant here. Stein Rokkan makes one of the best and most explicit cases for the importance of group activity as a

means of filling in the gaps left by electoral competition. See his chapter on Norway in Dahl (1966).

9. See [Verba and Nie,] chap. 5, Figure 5-2. See also McClosky, Hoffmann, and O'Hara (1960).

10. See Eldersveld (1964, pp. 290-92). A study of the incentives for the maintenance of activism among precinct party officials in North Carolina and Massachusetts found a similar stress on personal satisfactions. See Bowman, Ippolito, and Donaldson (1969). Marvick and Nixon (1969) find a greater stress on concern for public issues as a reason for party activism among their sample in Los Angeles, but their question may be such as to engender "official justifications." However, they also find a heavy stress on social gains from party activity. On this subject, see also Salisbury (1965-66).

PART II: IDEOLOGY

4. DO VOTERS THINK IDEOLOGICALLY?

Major voting studies in the 1950s and early 1960s led to the conclusion that mass electorates were very unsophisticated. While political commentary among elites and in the press is traditionally carried out using concepts such as liberalism and conservatism, studies beginning with *The American Voter* showed that most voters were blissfully ignorant of these notions, interpreting politics in terms of narrower concepts of group interests instead and often without benefit of any issue-based content whatsoever. But just as the role of issues in voting decisions grew in the 1960s and 1970s (see Chapter 9) so the level of ideological thinking was thought to have grown. Moreover, the studies documenting the absence of ideological thought were mostly American, and there was some suggestion that European mass electorates routinely understood the concepts of left and right as applied to politics. Finally, new methodological approaches suggested to some that the assumption of minimal understanding was misleading even for the 1950s. Thus, a considerable amount of writing in the 1970s and early 1980s was devoted to the question of just how widespread ideological thinking is.

An Unsophisticated Electorate

Most discussions of ideological thinking in the electorate can be traced back to one of two works—*The American Voter* and Converse's (1964) "belief systems" paper. In *The American Voter* (Campbell et al., 1960, chap. 10), the authors categorized individuals into one of four "levels of conceptualization" according to how they discussed politics when asked what they liked and disliked about the two parties and their presidential candidates. Only the top group—a mere 2½ percent of the electorate—was considered to have shown clear evidence of ideological thinking. Another 9 percent showed some form of ideological thought. The remainder of the sample responded to parties and candidates in terms of group benefits (42 percent), the "goodness" or "badness" of the times (24 percent), or, incredibly, without any real issue content (22½ percent).

Converse's work was even more devastating. First, he found that opinions on policy items often failed to be related to one another. One might have thought that voters with a liberal opinion on one issue would tend to have a liberal opinion on other issues—even if they were not able to describe their views in ideological terms. Yet attitudes were not constrained in this way. Second, Converse found that some respondents failed to express any attitude at all on policy items that were thought to be among the most important at the time. Third, in a portion of his article reprinted here as Chapter 5, Converse shows that among those who gave a response, the way in which they responded over time suggested that they might be responding randomly. In the most extreme instances, as many as 70 percent of the respondents either confessed themselves ignorant or gave responses that suggested that their answers might be changing at random over the years. "Nonattitudes" and a lack of ideological constraint were thus added to the characterization of the American voter.[1]

In the next decade or so, the thesis of an unsophisticated electorate underwent intense criticism. In addition, even writings that lent support to that view often contained qualifications to earlier, unbridled statements about the electorate's abilities. Thus, it is easy to be blinded to the fact that research continuing into the 1980s contained numerous indications of very restricted ideological thinking and very limited understanding of ideological concepts and terminology.

A follow-up to Converse's original study, the Converse and Markus article reprinted here as Chapter 8, has this dual character. The study reports the results of a panel survey in which respondents were interviewed several times over the period 1972-1976. The study replicated the earlier survey from which Converse had concluded that nonattitudes and lack of constraint were primary features of the electorate.

In their report of the new panel, Converse and Markus emphasize the very high stability of party identification, several new issues on which stability is surprisingly high (suggesting that real attitudes were present), and the intermediate-level stability of candidate evaluations. Yet they make it clear that opinions on many issues were no more stable in the 1970s than in the 1950s. The initial results may have been exaggerated—as when some interpreted the most extreme results as showing that the vast majority of the electorate was expressing nonattitudes generally—and the new panel reveals some variability in stability rates that was not previously apparent. But to the extent that the earlier study showed an absence of strong, meaningful opinions on issues, the newer results for these issues support the very same conclusion. Indeed, Converse and Markus refer to the new panel data as "very nearly a carbon copy" of the earlier results. This is rather surprising in light of other changes in the 1960s, above all the apparent increases in constraint over the same period. As Converse and Markus point out, even if the increased constraint is artifactual, owing to changes in question wording, one might well expect greater attitude stability on the same basis.[2]

Other writings at that time contain similar dual results. Levitin and Miller (1979), for example, note that "well over half" the electorate can express some ideological sentiment and that ideological labels have "political significance" for a wide class of voters. Yet they also write of "considerable slippage" in the connection between ideological thinking and electoral decisions. In the end they conclude that perhaps 15-20 percent of the electorate has coherent ideological views, and they write that "our demonstration of the extent to which ideological sentiments do not translate directly into policy preferences is entirely congruent with the research of Converse, Klingemann, Stimson and others who have documented the lack of ideological thinking in mass electorates in the United States and Europe" (pp. 769-70).

Klingemann's work is often cited to document increased ideological thinking in the United States and relatively greater understanding of ideological terms in Europe (see below), but the thrust of his major effort is entirely congruent with the quotation above. Klingemann studied the level of ideological sophistication in five European countries surveyed in the 1970s. The results, of course, varied in detail across countries and also demonstrated that voters are not easily packaged into pure categories of ideologues and nonideologues. Nevertheless, summarizing his chief measure of ideology, Klingemann concluded that "the thesis that there is an extraordinarily thin layer of respondents with high ideological competence is thus supported on a cross-national scale" (1979a, p. 245). In fact, from a third (Germany) to two-thirds (Great Britain) of the sample in each country was classified as showing no ideological conceptualization. In a similar vein, Norpoth (1979) observed that voters often relied on party alignments in government rather than on ideology for voting cues.

Also largely supporting the notion of an unsophisticated electorate are papers by Conover and Feldman (1981) and by Howell (1983). As in other work at that time, Conover and Feldman took it for granted that many voters express feelings about liberals and conservatives and willingly place themselves on a dimension anchored by these terms. What they questioned was the meaning of these labels for the general electorate. Very often, they argued, ideological labels are "largely symbolic in content and non-dimensional in structure" (p. 369). Individuals respond to ideological terminology, but "causality runs primarily from evaluations of ideological labels to self-identification" (p. 372) rather than the other way around. Howell (1983, p. 2) added that "ideological identification is not only largely symbolic, but for many is also affected by the very short term events surrounding a particular campaign." Self-identifications changed frequently in 1980 and in a way that suggested that they were responding to candidate evaluations.[3]

Finally, in the late 1970s and early 1980s there was an important series of methodological articles related to the specific question of attitudinal constraint in the general public. Nie and Andersen (1974) showed an apparently substantial increase in constraint in the 1960s and 1970s compared to the 1950s. Several researchers, however, independently noted that changes in the format of survey questions in 1964 and 1968 might account for these observed increases. Particularly persuasive was the "split sample" study of Sullivan, Piereson, and Marcus, in which the changes observed from the 1950s to the 1960s were replicated at one time point by using both the old one-sided question format and the new balanced format. A portion of their article—a classic example of the combination of experimental design with survey research—along with relevant material from the Nie and

Andersen work, are reprinted here as Chapters 6 and 7. While Sullivan et al. are extremely persuasive and suggest strongly that there was no real increase in constraint, we reprint Nie and Anderson as well because it was widely cited and because other developments in the 1960s (see Chapter 23) indicated that change, or at least potential change, remained an important issue. What is most important for our purposes, however, is that the end result of this line of inquiry was the conclusion that there was no major increase in constraint after 1964.[4]

On another methodological front, Smith (1980) criticized the "levels of conceptualization" measure as both unreliable and invalid.[5] Significantly, Smith concluded that if the "levels" are indeed "false measures of ideological sophistication," then the changes observed in these measures were also misleading. This along with other results implied "that there was a change in the sophistication of the language in which people talked about politics, but no change in the sophistication of the underlying evaluative processes" (p. 695). Collectively, these and other critiques (for example, Margolis, 1977; Hurley and Hill, 1980) raised serious questions about whether or not voters in the issue-laden and polarized 1960s and 1970s were in any sense more sophisticated than those in the issueless and nonideological 1950s.

A (Reasonably) Ideological Electorate

In contrast to the work just reviewed, many writings in the 1970s and early 1980s emphasized that voters are reasonably sophisticated—not budding analysts to be sure, but far from the truly unsophisticated cretins portrayed earlier. Three themes were emphasized: increased ideological awareness, greater awareness in Europe than in the United States, and more recognition of the importance of ideological terms for the electorate. Each of these will be summarized briefly. In addition, a number of important criticisms have been made of the way in which the early studies measured ideology; these will also be reviewed.

Changes in the electorate are apparent in numerous writings, but they are most forcefully stated in *The Changing American Voter*. Using identical measures from 1952 on, the authors found that the proportion in the electorate who could reasonably be called ideologues (or near-ideologues) was relatively low in the 1950s—reaching its nadir in 1956—but rose substantially during the 1960s. (The level dropped a bit in the 1970s but remained above the 1950s level.[6]) They also elaborated on Nie and Andersen's (1974) apparent finding of substantial increases in the degree to which attitudes were constrained; to a greater extent than before, those who took liberal positions on one issue also took liberal positions on other issues. In both cases—the rise in levels of conceptualization and in constraint—the increase occurred at all levels of education. Thus, the changes could not be attributed to the very considerable increase in education levels in those decades.

As we noted earlier, these analyses have come under serious attack owing to measurement questions. Yet they could not be dismissed too quickly since the apparent increases in ideological thinking were not isolated developments. The dramatic decline in party loyalties and party-based voting and the equally eye-catching increase in issue voting (see Chapters 9 and 23) suggest at a minimum that voters in the 1960s and 1970s were paying more attention to the substantive content of political arguments. At an elite level, candidates such as Barry Goldwater, George Wallace, and George McGovern were describing themselves in ideological terms, creating an atmosphere that made greater understanding by the electorate at least plausible. While these concomitant changes by no means proved that voters were becoming more ideologically oriented, they caution us against too quickly rejecting the direct evidence as methodological artifacts. Moreover, even if the studies were correct in showing that improved survey questions were responsible for the increase in ideological constraint, the appropriate interpretation may be that there was more constraint in the 1950s than was initially realized.

While *The Changing American Voter* contains the most forceful statement of an increasingly ideological electorate, independent analyses also support this trend. For example, codings of the levels of conceptualization that conform closely to the original version yield the same increase in the 1960s and 1970s compared to the 1950s (Hagner and Pierce, 1982, p. 788; Miller and Miller, 1976, p. 844).[7] The change is most apparent in the top category, as shown in Table 4-1 (although Converse, 1975a, countered that the proportion of the population in the top two categories combined has remained amazingly stable, as if half the population is permanently consigned to completely nonideological responses). More significantly, perhaps, similar changes apparently occurred in Europe. The direct evidence is very limited, but Klingemann (1979a, pp. 226, 233) found a slight upward trend in Germany between 1969 and 1974 and a probable difference (hampered by different questions and codings) in Great Britain between 1963 and 1974.

In a different way, the Converse and Markus article reprinted here also supports, if not increased ideological thinking, at least the foundation for such thinking. Recall that the original panel results (Converse, 1964, and Chapter 5) were widely interpreted as showing that many individuals had "nonattitudes," suggesting that voters hardly thought about issues at all, to say nothing of putting them together in some larger framework. The report of the 1972-1976 panel, while showing similar, low over-time correlations on issues repeated from the 1950s, also found some issues on which over-time stability was quite high. Ideological thinking does not automatically follow, but a basis for it at least existed. Significantly, the issues with the highest stability were moral and racial in nature, the very issues that are arguably the heart of the new ideology (see Chapter 8).

At about the same time that researchers were discovering these over-time differences, others were finding evidence of ideological thinking in Europe. Much of the evidence concerned awareness of the terms left/right to describe political conflict. Such an awareness was evidently widespread. Inglehart and Klingemann (1976), for example, reported that in nine European countries, self-placement on a left/right scale was greater than identification with any of the political parties, often as high as 85-90 percent. Similar results were reported by Barnes (1971), Klingemann (1979b, p. 279), and Holmberg (1981, p. 196).[8] While the meaning

Table 4-1   Distribution of the Levels of Conceptualization, 1956-1980

Levels of Conceptualization	1956	1960	1964	1968	1972	1976	1980
Ideologues	12%	19%	27%	26%	22%	21%	21%
Group Benefit	42	31	27	24	27	26	31
Nature of the Times	24	26	20	29	34	30	30
No Issue Content	22	23	26	21	17	24	19
Total	100%	99%	100%	100%	100%	101%	101%
N	(1740)	(1741)	(1431)	(1319)	(1372)	(2870)	(1612)

Source: Knight (1990, p. 72)

attached to the terms was often vague, many of the respondents were able to place multiple parties on such a scale with a high degree of accuracy (for example, in Holmberg, 1981, p. 201; Sani, 1974). Another analysis showed consistently higher continuity coefficients in Sweden than in the United States (Niemi and Westholm, 1984), including very high stability on left/right self-placement. The authors pointed out that the results may reflect "stability by proxy," owing to the strong positions taken by the political parties, and may indicate no greater understanding of political arguments. Nonetheless, at a minimum, they indicate recognition and repetition, if not understanding, of ideological terms along with a lower level of nonattitudes. At the extreme, some authors interpreted findings such as these as indicating that European politics is primarily motivated by ideology, and that ideology plays the role in Europe that party identification does in the United States (Percheron and Jennings, 1981; van der Eijk and Niemöller, 1983).

Still a third emphasis in recent work has been on the extent to which ideological terms are related to political behavior. In a sense, this emphasis has its origin in Lane's (1962) early work on personal ideologies. In contrast to Converse's analysis of ideology in relatively short interviews with thousands of respondents, Lane employed in-depth interviews with small numbers of respondents (typically a dozen). Lane's working-class respondents were quite articulate in their discussions of politics, although they did not necessarily put the political world together in the same way that academic political scientists might expect. Instead of using what we might consider the conventional liberal or conservative ideologies, they frequently had their own "personal ideologies." Lane's work showed that ideological thinking was more widespread than mass surveys suggest, but the potential impact on politics is limited when different citizens have their own personal ideologies rather than sharing a more general common ideology.

Lane's focus on what constitutes ideological thinking led to some controversy over how to interpret *The American Voter*'s findings on levels of conceptualization. For example, are "group benefits" comments nonideological? Or might they be the way in which the working class phrases ideological concerns? After all, saying that one party is better than another for workers or the poor very much expresses the class conflict notion that is fundamental to socialist ideology. Even the usual emphasis on party identification in voting might not be incompatible with an emphasis on ideology. Voters may learn early that one party represents their ideological interests and may subsequently use party identification as a short-cut for ideology.

This emphasis on how ideological terms are related to political behavior is most forcibly stated in work by Levitin and Miller (1979). While they make it clear, as noted above, that understanding of ideological terms is often minimal, they nonetheless conclude (p. 769) that "ideological location is an important factor in shaping voters' choices on election day." Or again (p. 751), "[liberal and conservative] labels have political significance for [Americans'] political attitudes and election day decisions." Implicit in their formulation is that the importance of ideology goes well beyond the small, sophisticated group of voters commonly referred to as ideologues.

Less explicit about the relationship between ideology and individual voters, but highly influential nonetheless, were macro-level interpretations of contemporary electoral change. The much heralded "new politics," for example, was often discussed in ideological terms (Dalton, 1988). And since interpretations of day-to-day events are in terms of elite attitudes and behavior, it is easy to forget the lessons of other work, which indicate that elite interpretations may not filter very far down into the general electorate (see note 3). Thus, for example, it is tempting to interpret gains by the environmental "Green" party in Germany in 1983 as ideologically based, but in reality those voters might be no more informed about the Greens' policies than were many who voted against Lyndon Johnson in the 1968 primaries.[9] Thus, both academic and popular interpretations of recent events reinforced the assumption of increased ideological thinking.

Finally, in contrast to the articles cited earlier, some methodological critiques supported the notion of a reasonably sophisticated electorate. Starting with Achen's (1975) analysis, the main bone of contention was over the meaning of the low correlations observed (as in the Converse and Markus chapter) for attitudes expressed at two or more points in time. The low level of continuity could signify large amounts of real attitude change. However, the low level of continuity in individual attitudes during the panel studies of the 1950s and 1970s was not accompanied by the sharp shifts in aggregate positions that would be expected if real change were occurring. So everyone seemed to agree that real attitude change was quite limited. The remaining possibilities were that respondents vacillate because of nonattitudes (Converse's argument, which was discussed at the beginning of this chapter) or that the survey questions are unreliable (so that poor or ambiguous wording causes random fluctuations).

If one is willing to make certain assumptions about the behavior of the measurement errors that occur when one asks survey questions, it is fairly straightforward to "correct" the over-time correlations for the limited reliability of the questions (as Converse and Markus do for party identification). Studies doing so (Achen, 1975; Erikson, 1979; Judd and Milburn, 1980) found that respondents were highly stable in their attitudes despite the variations in their manifest responses. To the degree that these criticisms of the original over-time analysis are correct, the electorate has a strong foundation for an ideological outlook on politics. However, the appropriateness of the assumptions about the measurement errors can be challenged. Thus, in their chapter, Converse and Markus defend their interpretation over Achen's, arguing that the problem lies with the nature of the citizenry rather than with the survey questions.

Conclusion

In concluding their chapter on the levels of conceptualization, Nie, Verba, and Petrocik (1976, p. 122) wrote that "our conclusion must be a middle of the road one: there has been a substantial change in the way the public conceptualizes politics, yet there is evidence for inertia as well." A similar conclusion applies more broadly to the question of whether or not voters think ideologically. On the one hand, empirical research has forever ruined our picture of mass electorates as comprised of idealized good citizens. Along with that fictional person's high levels of political interest, knowledge, and participation, we must discard an all-encompassing ideological view of politics and a clear understanding of political coinage such as liberal/conservative and left/right. Too many results—those cited in the first part of this chapter and others—have found voters like Butler and Stokes's "army" respondent whose understanding and use of ideological thinking are minimal at best.[10] Too many attempts have been made to lower the standards required to declare voters ideological—only to find that many voters still could not qualify.

At the same time, we need not paint a picture of the electorate as unqualifiedly and forever ignorant of ideological perspectives, as perhaps was the impression when *The American Voter* declared that at best 2½ percent of the electorate truly deserved to be called ideologues. The evidence of a reasonably sophisticated electorate, such as the apparent growth in understanding of ideological terms and examples in the United States and abroad of high over-time stability, are too widespread to be dismissed lightly. Similarly, better understanding of our methodology—simply recognizing that there is some unreliability in the survey questions—adds to the understanding that voters are not devoid of somewhat larger, overarching perspectives on the political scene.

Thus our conclusion, like that of *The Changing American Voter,* must be a middle-of-the-road one: voters both here and abroad are neither super-sophisticated nor abysmally ignorant. Individuals form a continuum, with a small group at the very top in knowledge and sophistication, but only a small group as well who are totally uninformed. The only surprise is that it has taken us so long to realize that this truism applies to ideological thinking and all aspects of political knowledge just as it applies to most other subjects.

On the way to this conclusion, we also learned that ideological thinking varies over time and space. The level of ideological thinking depends in part on the party system, the candidates, and even the specific appeals made in a given year. It is impossible to conclude that some fixed percentage of the electorate is ideological, whatever the definition we use. But it is possible to conclude that ideological thinking ebbs and flows and that it will always play a role, but probably never an exclusive one, in electoral politics.

NOTES

1. There was also some supportive evidence from Great Britain (Butler and Stokes, 1969) and France (Converse and Dupeux, 1962). Evidence of another sort was found in a classic article by Prothro and Grigg (1960). Upward of 95 percent of their respondents professed agreement with such principles as "the minority should be free to criticize majority decisions," yet far fewer agreed with specific statements that seemed to be logical expressions of these principles.
2. The apparent increases in constraint and the finding that it was owing to changes in question wording are reviewed below. The latter findings were just becoming available when Converse and Markus published their work.
3. Yet another relevant study is that by Bishop and Frankovic (1981), which replicated Converse's (1964) comparison of an elite sample (congressional candidates) with a cross-section survey of voters. Bishop and Frankovic's data from 1978 and Converse's data from 1958 both showed considerably greater attitudinal constraint among the elite than among the general population sample.
4. An equally valid point, which has often been overlooked, is that the Sullivan et al. findings suggest that constraint was higher in the 1950s than had been estimated by Converse (1964).
5. Though developed in *The American Voter*, the specific versions studied by Smith were from Field and Anderson (1969) and Nie, Verba, and Petrocik (1979).
6. Nie, Verba, and Petrocik (1979). See also the corrections in Nie, Verba, and Petrocik, 1981.
7. Miller and Miller did their own coding for 1972 and used the Klingemann and Wright coding for 1968 (first reported in Converse, 1975a). There is a 5 percent discrepancy between Hagner and Pierce's and Miller and Miller's estimate for 1972, about 1 percent of which is probably accounted for by the latter's exclusion of unclassified respondents. For still another measure, see Field and Anderson (1969). These various analyses are not entirely independent, of course, since they rely largely on the same data and often on very similar techniques.
8. It turns out that Americans are also surprisingly familiar with the terms left/right and the more familiar liberal/conservative. However, strict comparisons with European data are hampered by small but important methodological differences (Klingemann, 1979a, pp. 229-30).
9. It was discovered at the time of the New Hampshire primary that ". . . more often than not, McCarthy voters were upset that Johnson had failed to scourge Vietnam a good deal more vigorously with American military might, which is to say they took a position diametrically opposed to that of their chosen candidate" (Converse et al., 1969, p. 1095).
10. His explanation of "left" and "right": "when I was in the Army you had to put your right foot forward, but in fighting you lead with your left. So I always think that the Tories are the right party for me and that the Labour party are fighters" (Butler and Stokes, 1969, p. 209).

FURTHER READINGS

The Nature of Ideological Thinking

James W. Prothro and Charles M. Grigg, "Fundamental Principles of Democracy: Bases of Agreement and Disagreement," *Journal of Politics* (1960) 22:276-94. Public acceptance of democratic ideology does not extend to the specifics of democracy.

Angus Campbell, Philip E. Converse, Warren E. Miller, and Donald E. Stokes, *The American Voter* (New York: Wiley, 1960), chap. 10, unabridged; chap. 9, abridged. Analysis of "level of conceptualization"of politics by the electorate.

Philip E. Converse, "The Nature of Belief Systems in Mass Publics," in *Ideology and Discontent*, ed. David E. Apter (New York: Free Press, 1964). Full statement of results about ideology.

Herbert McClosky and John Zaller. *The American Ethos: Public Attitudes toward Capitalism and Democracy*. (Cambridge, Mass.: Harvard University Press, 1984). Discrepancies between elites' and the general public's views of democratic principles and practices.

Pamela Johnston Conover and Stanley Feldman. "The Origins and Meaning of Liberal/Conservative Self-Identification," *American Journal of Political Science* (1981) 25:617-45. Ideological identifications have largely symbolic meanings.

The Ideological Level of the Electorate

Norman H. Nie, Sidney Verba, and John R. Petrocik, *The Changing American Voter* (Cambridge, Mass.: Harvard University Press, 1976), chaps. 7-9. Increased ideological thinking in the 1970s.

Christopher H. Achen, "Mass Political Attitudes and the Survey Response," *American Political Science Review* (1975) 69:1218-231. Emphasis on low question reliability causing apparent lack of ideology.

James A. Stimson, "Belief Systems: Constraint, Complexity, and the 1972 Election," *American Journal of Political Science* (1975) 19:393-417. Politics is viewed unidimensionally by the most able half of the electorate.

Teresa E. Levitin and Warren E. Miller. "Ideological Interpretations of Presidential Elections," *American Political Science Review* (1979) 73:751-71. Ideological labels, even when misunderstood, have political significance for the political attitudes and voting decisions of Americans.

Comparative Studies of Ideology

David Butler and Donald E. Stokes, *Political Change in Britain* (New York: St. Martins, 1969), chap. 9. Finds that voter reactions to parties are not satisfied by a single left/right continuum.

Ronald Inglehart and Hans D. Klingemann, "Party Identification, Ideological Preference, and the Left/Right Dimension Among Western Mass Publics," in *Party Identification and Beyond*, ed. Ian Budge, Ivor Crewe, and Dennis

Farlie (London: Wiley, 1976). Use of left/right terminology greater in Europe than in United States.

Ronald Inglehart and Hans D. Klingemann, "Ideology and Values," in *Political Action*, Samuel H. Barnes et al. (Beverly Hills, Calif.: Sage, 1979). "Postmaterialist" ideas, their distribution, and their relationship to political participation in five countries.

Annick Percheron and M. Kent Jennings, "Political Continuities in French Families: A New Perspective on an Old Controversy," *Comparative Political Studies* (1981) 13:421-36. Argues that the French electorate interprets politics with the left/right dimension more than with party identification.

Richard G. Niemi and Anders Westholm, "Issues, Parties, and Attitudinal Stability: A Comparative Study of Sweden and the United States," *Electoral Studies* (1984) 3:65-83. Greater attitudinal stability in Sweden than in the United States.

5. THE STABILITY OF BELIEF ELEMENTS OVER TIME

Philip E. Converse

... All of our data up to this point have used correlations calculated on aggregates as evidence of greater or lesser constraint among elements in belief systems. While we believe these correlations to be informative indicators, they do depend for their form upon cumulations among individuals and therefore can never be seen as commenting incisively upon the belief structures of individuals.

It might then be argued that we are mistaken in saying that constraint among comparable "distant" belief elements declines generally as we move from the more to the less politically sophisticated. Instead, the configuration of political beliefs held by individuals simply becomes increasingly idiosyncratic as we move to less sophisticated people. While an equally broad range of belief elements might function as an interdependent whole for an unsophisticated person, we would find little aggregative patterning of belief combinations in populations of unsophisticated people, for they would be out of the stream of cultural information about "what goes with what" and would therefore put belief elements together in a great variety of ways.

For the types of belief that interest us here, this conclusion in itself would be significant. We believe however, that we have evidence that permits us to reject it rather categorically, in favor of our original formulation. A fair test of this counterhypothesis would seem to lie in the measurement of the same belief elements for the same individuals over time. For if we are indeed involved here in idiosyncratic patterns of belief, each meaningful to the individual in his own way, then we could expect that individual responses to the same set of items to different points in time should show some fundamental stability. They do not.

A longitudinal study of the American electorate over a four-year period has permitted us to ask the same questions of the same people a number of times, usually separated by close to two-year intervals. Analysis of the stability of responses to ... "basic" policy questions ... yields remarkable results. Faced with

Source: "The Nature of Belief Systems in Mass Publics," in David Apter, ed., *Ideology and Discontent.* Copyright © 1964 by The Free Press of Glencoe, a Division of The Macmillan Company. Reprinted with permission of David Apter.

the typical item of this kind, only about thirteen people out of twenty manage to locate themselves even on the same *side* of the controversy in successive interrogations, when ten out of twenty could have done so by chance alone.

While we have no comparable longitudinal data for an elite sample, the degree of fit between answers to our issue items and congressional roll calls is strong enough to suggest that time correlations for individual congressmen in roll-call choice on comparable bills would provide a fair estimate of the stability of an elite population in beliefs of this sort. It is probably no exaggeration to deduce that, in sharp contrast to a mass sample, eighteen out of twenty congressmen would be likely to take the same positions on the same attitude items after a two-year interval. In short, then, we feel very confident that elite-mass differences in levels of constraint among beliefs are mirrored in elite-mass differences in the temporal stability of belief elements for individuals.

We observed much earlier that the centrality of a specific belief in a larger belief system and the relative stability of that belief over time should be highly related. From our other propositions about the role of groups as central objects in the belief systems of the mass public, we can therefore arrive at two further predictions. The first is simply that pure affect toward visible population groupings should be highly stable over time, even in a mass public, much more so in fact than beliefs on policy matters that more or less explicitly bear on the fortunes of these groupings. Second, policy items that do bear more rather than less explicitly upon their fortunes should show less stability than affect towards the group *qua* group but more than those items for which contextual information is required.

Figure 5-1 gives strong confirmation of these hypotheses.[1] First, the only question applied longitudinally that touches on pure affect toward a visible population grouping is the one about party loyalties or identifications. As the figure indicates, the stability of these group feelings for individuals over time (measured by the correlation between individual positions in two successive readings) registers in a completely different range from that characterizing even the most stable of the issue items employed.[2] This contrast is particularly ironic, for in theory of course the party usually has little rationale for its existence save as an instrument to further particular policy preferences of the sort that show less stability in Figure 5-1. The policy is the end, and the party is the means, and ends are conceived to be more stable and central in belief systems than means. The reversal for the mass public is of course a rather dramatic special case of one of our primary generalizations: The party and the affect toward it are more central within the political belief systems of the mass public than are the policy ends that the parties are designed to pursue.

Figure 5-1 also shows that, within the set of issues, the items that stand out as most stable are those that have obvious bearing on the welfare of a population grouping—the Negroes—although the item concerning federal job guarantees is very nearly as stable. In general, we may say that stability declines as the referents of the attitude items become increasingly remote, from jobs, which are significant objects to all, and Negroes, who are attitude objects for most, to items involving ways and means of handling foreign policy.

Figure 5-1   Temporal Stability of Different Brief Elements for
Individuals, 1958-60

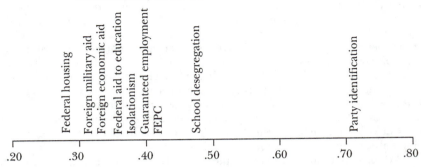

Note: The measure of stability is rank-order correlation (tau-beta) between individuals'
positions in 1958 and in 1960 on the same items.

Although most of the less stable items involve foreign policy, the greatest instability is shown for a domestic issue concerning the relative role of government and private enterprise in areas like those of housing and utilities. Interestingly enough, this issue would probably be chosen by sophisticated judges as the classically "ideological" item in the set, and indeed table VII [in Converse] shows that the counterpart for this question in the elite sample is central to the primary organizing dimension visible in the matrix. Since the item refers to visible population groupings—"government" and "private business"—we might ask why it is not geared into more stable affect toward these groups. We do believe that measures of affect toward something like "private business" (or better, perhaps, "big business") as an object would show reasonable stability for a mass public, although probably less than those for more clearly bounded and visible groups like Negroes and Catholics. The question, however, is not worded in a way that makes clear which party—government or private business—will profit from which arrangement. Lacking such cues, the citizen innocent of "ideology" is likely to make rather capricious constructions, since the issue is probably one that he has never thought about before and will never think about again except when being interviewed.

In short, all these longitudinal data offer eloquent proof that signs of low constraint among belief elements in the mass public are not products of well knit but highly idiosyncratic belief systems, for these beliefs are extremely labile for individuals over time. Great instability in itself is *prima facie* evidence that the belief has extremely low centrality for the believer. Furthermore, it is apparent that any instability characterizing one belief sets an upper limit on the degree or orderly constraint that could be expected to emerge in static measurement between this unstable belief and another, even a perfectly stable one. While an aggregate might thus show high stability despite low constraint, the fact of low stability virtually ensures that constraint must also be low. This kind of relationship between stability and constraint means that an understanding of what underlies high instability is at the same time an understanding of what underlies low constraint.

The fact that we have asked these questions at more then two points in time provides a good deal of leverage in analyzing the processes of change that generate aggregate instability and helps us to illuminate the character of this instability.[3] For example, in Figure 5-2 we discover, in comparing our indicators of the degree of instability associated with any particular belief as they register between t_2 and t_3 with the same figures for t_1 and t_2, that estimates are essentially the same. This result is an important one, for it assures us that within a medium time range (four years), differences among issues in degree of response stability are highly reliable.

Far more fascinating, however, is another property that emerges. Quite generally, we can predict t_3 issue positions of individuals fully as well from a knowledge of the t_1 positions alone as we can from a knowledge of their t_2 positions alone. In other words, the turnover correlations between different time points for these issues tend to fit the scheme shown in Figure 5-2.

It can be shown that there is no single meaningful process of change shared by all respondents that would generate this configuration of data.[4] In fact, even if we assume that there is a relatively limited number of change processes present in the population, we find that only two such models could generate these observations. The first of these models posits that some of the respondents managed in a deliberate way to locate themselves from one measurement to another on the opposite side of an issue from the one they had selected at the preceding measurement. It would have to be assumed that a person who chose a leftish alternative on a certain issue in the first measure would be motivated to remember to seek out the rightish alternative two years later, the leftish again two years after that, and so on. Naturally, an assumption that this behavior characterizes one member of the population is sufficiently nonsensical for us to reject it out of hand.

Once this possibility is set aside, however, there is only one other model involving a mixture of two types of process of change that fits the observed data. This model is somewhat surprising but not totally implausible. It posits a very sharp dichotomy within the population according to processes of change that are polar opposites. There is first a "hard core" of opinion on a given issue, which is well crystallized and perfectly stable over time. For the remainder of the population, response sequences over time are statistically random. The model does not specify what proportions of the population fall into these two categories: This matter is empirically independent, and it is clear that the size of the turnover correlations between any two points in time is a simple function of these relative proportions.

In view of our earlier remarks, this "black and white" model is credible in its assumption that a mass public contains significant proportions of people who, for lack of information about a particular dimension of controversy, offer meaningless opinions that vary randomly in direction during repeated trials over time. We may be uncomfortable, however, at using a model that suggests such a rigid and polar division of the population, leaving no room for the "gray" area of meaningful change of opinion or "conversion." In this respect, while the

Figure 5-2   Pattern of Turnover Correlations Between Different
Time Points

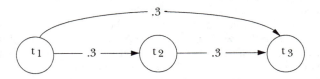

randomness posited by the model is a discouraging property substantively, it is an empowering property mathematically, for aggregate randomness has certain predictable consequences. For example, if the model were to fit the data, we would know that some people who are responding to the items as though flipping a coin could, by chance alone, supply the same responses at three trials in a row and would therefore have response paths indistinguishable from those of perfectly stable respondents but for entirely different reasons. While we could not enter the stable group and "tag" such random people, we would at least have an excellent estimate of the number of them that lingers after three trials to pollute the set of genuinely stable respondents. Most important, however, is the fact that the very character of the model makes it possible to test quite rigorously the goodness of fit of the data to the model.

For our initial test, we singled out the issue that seemed on *a priori* grounds most likely to fit the model. It was the most "ideological" item in the battery yet the one that had shown the highest degree of temporal instability: the question about the respective roles of private enterprise and government in areas like housing and electrical power. It is important to understand in detail the grounds on which this item was chosen. The model requires that some people have unswerving beliefs on the subject and that other people have no beliefs at all. It also requires that there be no middle ground, no set of people whose beliefs on the subject are in the process of evolution. For these requirements, the "government *vs.* private enterprise issue," more than any of the others, seemed "sheltered" from meaningful change. This isolation was true in two senses. First, it involved a very basic area of political controversy, and people understanding the stakes involved in a more ideological way would not be readily dissuaded from their respective positions. Secondly, while events like the crisis at Little Rock and exposés of waste in foreign aid were occurring in this period to touch off meaningful evolutions of opinion, little was occurring that might intuitively be expected to shake true beliefs on one side or the other. At the same time, of course, the relationships to be judged in the item were sufficiently remote and abstract from the experience of most people to make many meaningless responses likely.

The fit between the data collected at three time points on this issue and our black and white model was virtually perfect.[5] This result lends remarkable assurance that our understanding of the "change" processes affecting the issue responses was accurate: The only change that occurred was random change. We naturally went on to apply this test of fit to the other issues, for which the black and white model had seemed less credible. And indeed, these other items showed a somewhat poorer fit with the model. None strays a great distance, but it is unlikely that any would survive significant tests of goodness of fit.[6] What, then, can we say about the character of beliefs touched by these other items?

Strictly speaking, as soon as we encounter data that depart in any significant measure from the black and white model, we lose all mathematical anchors, in the sense that, unless we insert a variety of restrictive assumptions, the number of models (even simple ones) that could logically account for the data becomes very large indeed. Despite this loss of power, the existence of one issue that does fit the black and white model perfectly provides at least an intuitive argument that those that depart from it in modest degrees do not require a totally different class of model. In other words, we come to suppose that these other items depart from the model only because of the presence of a "third force" of people, who are undergoing meaningful conversion from one genuine opinion at t_1 to an opposing but equally genuine opinion at t_2. This "third force" is small, and the dominant phenomenon remains the two segments of the population, within one of which opinions are random and within the other of which opinions have perfect stability. Nevertheless, the presence of any third force suffices to disrupt the fit between the data and the black and white model, and the degree of departure is a function of the size of the third force.

It should be reiterated that this view cannot be subjected to any unequivocal mathematical test but rather depends for its reasonableness upon the excellence of the fit shown by one issue and the approaches to fit shown by the others. It seems likely that responses to other issues of a similar type are generated in similar fashion. And while it is true that competing attitude models could be applied to describe most of these data, their assumptions simply lose all plausible ring when confronted with the results from the private-enterprise issue.[7]

Or, in another vein, the discouragingly large turnover of opinion on these issues in the total mass public might be taken as evidence that the questions were poorly written and thus extremely unreliable—that the main lesson is that they should be rewritten. Yet the issues posed are those posed by political controversy, and citizens' difficulties in responding to them in meaningful fashion seem to proffer important insights into their understanding of the same political debates in real life. More crucial still, what does it mean to say that an instrument is perfectly reliable *vis-à-vis* one class of people and totally unreliable *vis-à-vis* another, which is the proper description of the black and white model? The property of reliability is certainly not inherent *solely* in the instrument of measurement, contrary to what is commonly supposed.

As another check on the question of reliability, we decided to examine the temporal stability of belief elements of this sort among very limited sets of people whose broader interviews gave us independent reasons to believe they had particular interest in narrower belief areas (like the Negro question). We took advantage once again of interviews with a good deal of open-ended material, sifting through this voluntary commentary to find people who had shown "self-starting" concern about particular controversies. Then we went back to the relevant structured issue questions to examine the stability of these belief elements for these people over time. The turnover correlations for these limited subpopulations did increase substantially, beginning to approach the levels of stability shown for party identification (see Figure 5-1). Once again, the evidence seemed clear that extreme instability is associated with absence of information, or at least of interest, and that item reliability is adequate for people with pre-existing concern about any given matter.

The substantive conclusion imposed by these technical maneuvers is simply that large portions of an electorate do not have meaningful beliefs, even on issues that have formed the basis for intense political controversy among elites for substantial periods of time. If this conclusion seems self-evident, it is worth reflecting on the constancy with which it is ignored and on the fact that virtually none of the common modes of dealing empirically with public beliefs attempts to take it into account. Instead, it is assumed that a location must be found for all members of a population on all dimensions of controversy that are measured. Our data argue that, where any single dimension is concerned, very substantial portions of the public simply do not belong on the dimension at all. They should be set aside as not forming any part of that particular issue public. And since it is only among "members" of any given issue public that the political effects of a controversy are felt (where such "effects" include activated public opinion expressed in the writing of letters to the editor, the changing of votes, and the like), we come a step closer to reality when we recognize the fragmentation of the mass public into a plethora of narrower issue publics.

NOTES

1. The items portrayed in Figure 5-1 are [described in Converse's article].
2. We regret that we did not get measures of pure affect for other groupings in the population, for all population members. A copious literature on intergroup attitudes in social psychology contains, however, much presumptive evidence of extreme stability in these attitudes over time.
3. Unfortunately we lack the longitudinal data for elites that would permit the following analysis to be comparative. Let us keep in mind, however, that the relatively high constraint among belief elements already demonstrated for elites is almost certain proof of high stability of these elements over time as well. The phenomenon we are analyzing is thus a mass not an elite phenomenon.
4. More technically, such a configuration is mathematically incompatible with the assumption based on simple Markov chain theory that a single matrix of transition probabilities can account for the change process. For the benefit of the nontechnical reader, we use the phrase "change process" in the singular to denote a single specified matrix of transition probabilities.
5. The logic of the test is rather simple. If the model pertains, then any respondents who change sides of an issue between t_1 and t_2 are from the random part of the population, while those who do not change sides are a mixture in known proportions of perfectly stable people and random people who happened to have chosen the same side twice by chance. If we divide the population into these two parts on the basis of their t_1 and t_2

patterns and if the model is appropriate to the situation, then the turnover correlations between t_2 and t_3 for each of the two divisions of the population are determinate. The purely random group should show a correlation of .00 between t_2 and t_3; the adulterated stable group should show a correlation that falls short of unity as a direct function of the known proportions of random people still in the group. For our critical test, the original total-population turnover correlation (1956-1958) was .24. With the population properly subdivided as suggested by the model, this over-all correlation could be expected to fork into two correlations between t_2 and t_3 of .00 and .47, *if the model was applicable.* The empirical values turned out to be .004 and .49.

6. For instance, in terms parallel to the expectations of the final sentence of footnote 5, the correlations may fork into a pair that are .07 and .35, rather than .00 and .47.

7. For example, a random path of responses would be laid down over time by a set of people for whom the content of the item was very meaningful, yet put each individual in such a quandary that his pro-con response potential balanced exactly at .50-.50. In such cases, it could be assumed that slight rewording of the item, making it "harder" or "easier" in a Guttman sense, would shift the response potentials away from this .50-.50 balance and would thus begin to produce correlations between individual responses over time. This view cannot be challenged in any decisive way for issues generating responses that depart from our black and white model, since, in these cases, a distribution of the population continuously across the total range of response probabilities is entirely compatible with the data. It is even possible to describe the empirical situation surrounding the private-enterprise item in these terms. The problem is that such a description seems patently absurd, for it implies that the question was somehow constructed so that the content drew highly unequivocal responses from one class of people but left all the rest in perfect and exquisite conflict. Intermediate classes—people with probabilities of responding to the content positively at a level of .6, .7, .8 or .9—are simply not necessary to account for the data. Such a description lacks verisimilitude. Our assumption is rather that, had the private-enterprise item been rendered "harder" or "easier" in a Guttman sense, the respondents we call "random" would have *continued* to respond randomly, at least across a zone of items so broad as to bracket any plausible political alternatives. In other words, the problem is not one of specific wording that puts the respondent in particularly delicate conflict; it is rather that the whole area from which this item is drawn is so remote to the respondent that he has not been stimulated to any real opinion formation within it.

6. MASS BELIEF SYSTEMS REVISITED: POLITICAL CHANGE AND ATTITUDE STRUCTURE

Norman H. Nie with Kristi Andersen

... One of the newer "common wisdoms" derived from survey techniques has to do with the absence of ideology in the American public. Ideology has many meanings, but one of its components is usually a high degree of consistency among political attitudes—attitudes on a wide range of issues falling into clear liberal and conservative tendencies And this component has been found to be particularly lacking in the American mass public.

... In this paper we propose to examine the structure of mass attitudes over the past 16 years. We will show that there have been major increases in the levels of attitude consistency within the mass public. ...

The Data

The analysis is based on data gathered by the Survey Research Center at the University of Michigan in conjunction with its national election studies. Between 1952 and 1972, the Survey Research Center (SRC) has interviewed a representative sample of some 1,500 to 2,700 adult Americans in each of the presidential elections and in several of the off-year congressional elections. The respondents in each of these surveys were asked questions about their attitudes on a wide variety of political issues. Many of these opinion questions appear in only one or two of the surveys, but a set of questions covering five basic issue-areas is available for each of the presidential election years from 1956 through 1972 and for the 1958 congressional election. Similar questions were asked of a national sample in a survey which was administered by the National Opinion Research Center (NORC) in the spring of 1971.

The five issue-areas for which we have comparable data over the entire time period are: [social welfare, welfare measures specific for blacks, and size of government, racial integration in the schools, and the Cold War].... The questions to be used in the analysis are, with minor variations in wording and coding, identical at all points in time.... Coding categories were reordered

Source: *Journal of Politics* (1974) 36: 540-87. Reprinted with permission of the publisher.

wherever necessary to range from conservative to liberal. . . . Answers to questions which originally permitted more than three codes were collapsed so that responses to all questions conformed to a unified trichotomous format of: (1) conservative; (2) centrist; (3) liberal. (Gamma is used as our basic measure of association.) Refusals, those with no opinions, and those giving "don't know" responses were always excluded from the analysis. . . .

Summarizing the Growth of Ideological Consistency

The timing as well as the scope and magnitude of the growth of attitude consistency can be seen most clearly in the summary measures presented in Figure 6-1. Plotted through time in this figure are three measures of attitude consistency. The solid line presents the overall index of constraint—a simple average of the ten correlations [for each year]. The line composed of dashes is the index of domestic attitude consistency and is computed by the average for each year of the correlations among the four domestic issue-areas. The dotted line is the average correlation of the four domestic issues with attitudes on the cold war.

The difference between the two periods—1956 to 1960 and after 1964—is quite striking. In the earlier period the overall index hovers around .15, but in 1964 and each year thereafter it is at about .40. The overall index of constraint has therefore increased by over two and one-half times. The index of domestic attitude constraint shows the same basic patterns. Through 1960, the index is slightly below .25, but in 1964 it climbs to about .50 and stays there in all subsequent years.

The pattern with regard to the index of the relationship between attitudes on domestic issues and positions on the cold war indicates an equally dramatic and similarly timed increase in ideological constraint. In 1956, just a few years after the end of the Korean War, the average relationship between liberal/conservative attitude on the domestic issues and the desirability of a tough stand on the international Communist threat (including attitudes on the desirability of sending American soldiers abroad to fight communism) was almost zero. In 1964 and thereafter, on the other hand, the correlation between domestic attitudes and keeping American soldiers abroad (in Vietnam specifically in 1968, '71, and '72) and otherwise taking a tough or conciliatory stand on the cold war rose to around .25. In other words, in contrast to the situation in the mid-fifties and early sixties, foreign policy attitudes, at least as measured by position on the cold war, have increasingly become part of the public's general stance on the issues.

To summarize our findings thus far: the existing description of low levels of attitude consistency in the mass public and the absence of an over-arching liberal/conservative ideology indicated by this lack of consistency no longer appears accurate. From 1964 onward, attitudes in the mass public on the issues of social welfare, welfare measures specific for blacks, racial integration in the schools, and positions on the cold war are substantially intercorrelated. That it, those who are liberal in one of these issue-areas tend to take liberal positions on the others, and the same is true for those at the conservative end of the attitude continuum. . . .

Figure 6-1   Changes in Attitude Consistency, 1956-72

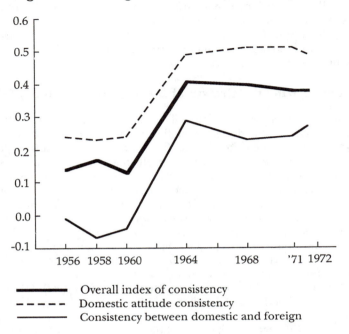

———————   Overall index of consistency
‐ ‐ ‐ ‐ ‐   Domestic attitude consistency
———————   Consistency between domestic and foreign

Changing Levels of Education in the Mass Public: A Possible Explanation

What has been responsible for the changes in the structure of mass beliefs in so short a period of time? . . . The first place to look for the source of the growth of attitude consistency is an increase within the mass public in the "ideological capacities" stressed by the theory. . . .

[However,] with regard to both overall and domestic attitude consistency, the fact is that the sharp increases in levels of attitude constraint which occurred between 1960 and 1964 took place among both the highly educated and those with little formal education. The implication of [this] finding . . . is that the growth of attitude consistency within the mass public is clearly not the result of increases in the population's "ideological capacities" brought about by gains in educational attainment. . . .

The Changing Salience of Politics: An Explanation

. . . as was the case with the hypothesis involving education, we need to examine the levels of attitude consistency over time among the interested and uninterested. . . . We can see that the growth of interest does not alone account for the rise of liberal/conservative ideology because consistency has gone up among the interested and uninterested alike, just as it has gone up among both the educated and less educated. However, while increased educational attainment appeared to play almost no role in the growth of attitude consistency, increases in political interest (or the salience of politics) . . . have played a very significant role. Between 1960 and 1968, it was among the growing group of citizens interested in politics that one found the largest increase in attitude consistency. . . . By 1968 and 1972, however, the interest-based explanation seems to fall apart. . . . [Nevertheless, the salience of politics is still relevant; detailed analysis shows that] in 1972 it is this group [those who are politically disenchanted] alone which has caused the level of ideological constraint to remain high despite a decline in positive political interest.

Summary

. . . the important point is that the pattern of attitudes found among Americans in the 1950's was a transient phenomenon and not an inevitable characteristic of mass politics. Of course, the pattern that emerged in the 1960's may be transient as well, but that does not change our argument about the lack of inevitability of the earlier pattern. Indeed, our data suggest that not only specific political attitudes but the *structure* of mass attitudes may be affected by politics in the real world. The average citizen may not be as apolitical as has been thought. . . .

7. IDEOLOGICAL CONSTRAINT IN THE MASS PUBLIC: A METHODOLOGICAL CRITIQUE AND SOME NEW FINDINGS

John L. Sullivan, James E. Piereson, and George E. Marcus

Much of the research conducted during the 1950s on public attitudes and opinions concluded that citizens at large did not think about politics in a conceptual way, were unable to organize their political attitudes along ideological lines, and exhibited great instability in their opinions on political issues (Campbell, Converse, Miller, and Stokes, 1960, chap. 9; Converse, 1964). Some writers went so far as to conclude on the basis of this research that coherent political attitudes simply do not exist in the mass public (Converse, 1970). However, many recent studies of American public opinion and electoral behavior have stressed the degree to which citizens have become more sophisticated and ideological in their assessments of issues, parties, and candidates. There is evidence, for example, that the use of ideological concepts in the mass public significantly increased in the aftermath of the 1964 campaign (Pierce, 1970; Field and Anderson, 1969). Moreover, it further appears that there are now higher levels of constraint in the mass public than there were in the 1950s and, hence, more stable political attitudes (Nie and Andersen, 1974; Nie, Verba, and Petrocik, 1976, chap. 7).

Taken as a group, these studies point to the decade of the 1960s, and particularly to the presidential campaign of 1964, as an important transitional period during which the relatively issueless politics of the Eisenhower-Kennedy period gave way to the heated conflicts over civil rights, Vietnam, crime, and government corruption that dominated national politics between 1964 and 1974. As the parties began to offer candidates who took distinct positions on these issues, they provided important ideological cues to voters and, in so doing, raised the stakes of politics in general. As these studies apparently prove, then, the dynamics of this period created a more coherent and ideologically consistent set of attitudes in the American public.

The argument is, of course, a plausible one, given the political events that occurred between 1956 and 1974. However, there are good reasons to question

Source: *American Journal of Political Science* (1978) 22:233-49. Reprinted with permission of University of Texas Press. © 1978 by the University of Texas Press.

the thesis and to suspect that these claims about changes in the structure of public attitudes have been exaggerated. This paper raises several questions about the validity of previous studies (Nie and Andersen, 1974; Nie et al., 1976, Chapter 7) which suggest that levels of constraint in the mass public greatly increased between 1956 and 1974. Our argument is that levels of constraint probably did not change substantially during this period, but that reported changes were largely due to subtle changes in the survey instruments used to measure the concept. We will not be able to demonstrate this directly, because new measures cannot now be taken. The argument does rest, however, upon evidence that is as strong as we can possibly obtain at this late date.

Changing Levels of Constraint?

The major recent work on changing levels of constraint has been done by Nie and his associates (1974, 1976). Using SRC national election surveys taken between 1956 and 1972, along with two NORC surveys taken in the early 1970s, they claim to "demonstrate . . . that there has been a major increase in the level of attitude consistency within the mass public" (1976, p. 123).

[Their] results seem to point to some significant change in the structure of public attitudes beginning in 1964. However, there were important changes in question wordings beginning with the 1964 survey which suspiciously coincide with the changes in correlations across issue areas. Before 1964, the items were one-sided statements which were followed by queries as to whether respondents had opinions on the statements; if they did, they were asked to agree or disagree. . . . Beginning in 1964, respondents were presented with two-sided statements, followed by queries as to whether they had been interested enough in the issue to favor one side over the other. If the answer was yes, they were asked to indicate which side they favored; a middle category was used for those who did not favor either side.[1] Of the two formats, the latter is clearly the more valid, since it presents both sides of the issue on equal terms. The questions used prior to 1964, on the other hand, are worded in a way that promotes "agree" responses, regardless of ideology, since the alternatives are not made evident to respondents. In this sense, the items used since 1964 are more reliable measures of the left-right dimension than those used prior to 1964.

Not only were the question formats changed, but the meanings of the items were also altered in some cases. For example, the aid to education question was substantially altered beginning with the 1964 survey. Prior to 1964, the statement assumes that cities and towns need assistance in providing education; in addition, it refers only to building schools, a particularly difficult problem in the 1950s. It is, indeed, difficult to disagree with this statement, since it says if local units need help in building schools, the federal government should lend assistance. Even a solid majority of strong Republicans agreed with this statement (68 percent in 1956) though presumably many of them would have preferred the cities and towns to handle the problem *if* they could. The question posed in 1964 was more general, and referred to providing education, not merely to building schools. It also more clearly focused the liberal-conservative difference over local versus national authority. The same is true of the item used to measure the black welfare dimension. Prior to 1964 it simply stated that the government should prevent discrimination in jobs and housing, while the newer version specified the government in Washington, again more clearly relating the issue to the liberal-conservative dimension. In short, the questions used after 1964 tended to be more general, more clearly related to the liberal-conservative dimension as we understand it, and thus more likely to produce higher inter-item correlations than those used prior to 1964. The suspicion arises, therefore, that the changing levels of constraint reported by Nie and associates are merely artifacts of changed measurement instruments.

The question of whether the pattern of correlations was due to real changes in public attitudes or to changed measurement instruments (or both) cannot be definitively settled at this late date. New measures will not settle it, since the political context is irrevocably changed. Nor can we simply analyze the reliability of the original items, since the same basic unit of information is used to measure both the degree of item or test reliability and the level of constraint. One could consider all of the questions as measures of the liberal-conservative dimension and compute a reliability coefficient of them, but this would be a function of the inter-item correlations, which is precisely the same information used to measure the level of constraint. Given this under-identification, additional information must be obtained.

Our strategy was to select two independent random samples of adult respondents and to administer to each sample one of the two versions of the questions used to measure constraint between 1956 and 1972. Thus, one sample was given the questions used prior to 1964 and the other sample was given those used in 1964 and thereafter. If the item-item correlations are higher in the sample presented with the new questions, we can reasonably infer that differences in measurement instruments most probably accounted for the apparent increase in constraint found in the post-1960 surveys. If the correlations are not systematically different, on the other hand, we can conclude that real changes probably produced the correlations, or at least that the patterns were not due to changed question formats.

Though convincing, such evidence would not be categorical. It could be possible that some complex interaction of electoral history and question wording could explain findings consistent with our formulation. Therefore, even if the new question wording generates higher levels of constraint today, it would not rule out the possibility that in the 1950s the old questions provided a valid basis for measuring the left-right dimension, while today it does not. Readers should thus be aware of the limits of our analysis, which apply with equal force, however, to that of Nie and associates.

The Twin-Cities Samples

In order to test the hypothesis that the changing patterns of correlation were due to changes in question formats, we conducted two independent surveys in Minneapolis and St. Paul, Minnesota, during the Spring and Summer of 1976.

One sample of respondents was asked the newer set of questions (post-1964) while the other was asked the older set (pre-1964). Two independent random samples of size 300 were selected from the Twin Cities city directories, which include a listing of all adults in Minneapolis and St. Paul. Interviews were completed with 200 persons using the old items and with 198 persons using the new items, a response rate of about 66 percent.

In order to make comparisons between samples, the samples should more or less reflect the demographic characteristics of the larger community, and they should be similar to one another in these respects. The demographic characteristics of the Twin Cities population, as well as those of our two samples, show that the samples are quite similar and that both are representative of the larger population. Given two such random samples, then, any systematic differences in the correlations between samples can be fairly attributed to the different question formats. We do not mean to say, of course, that the exact correlations generated from these samples can be freely generalized to the country at large. We are, in fact, less interested in the sizes of the correlations than in the *differences* in the correlations between the samples.

Findings and Analysis

The results from our split-half sample of the Twin Cities area are reported in Table 7-1. These are the gammas for each issue pair using the pre- and post-1964 question formats. As the figures show, the differences in the correlations between our two samples are quite similar in size to the differences found in the SRC data before and after 1964. For example, referring to the SRC data, the mean for the first pair of issues (welfare/black welfare) under the old question wording is .31 while under the newer question wording the mean is .47. In our survey, the gamma for this issue pair under the old wording is .28 while under the new wording it is .43. In the original SRC data, then, the increase was .16, while between our control samples the increase was .15 (see Table 7-2). On the second pair (welfare/integration), the increase in the SRC data was .23 (from .13 to .36) while between our control samples the increase was .19 (from .11 to .30).

Table 7-1   Correlations (Gammas) for Old and New Questions: Twin Cities Samples, 1976

	Old Question Wording	New Question Wording
Welfare/Black Welfare	.28	.43
Welfare/Integration	.11	.30
Welfare/Size of Government	.09	.14
Black Welfare/Integration	.35	.58
Black Welfare/Size of Government	.09	.06
Integration/Size of Government	.20	.26

Table 7-2   Differences in Item-Item Correlations in National Surveys (Pre- and Post-1964) and Twin Cities Samples

	National Surveys (New Question Wording Mean Minus Old Question Wording Mean)	Twin Cities Samples (Old Question Wording Minus New Question Wording)[b]
Welfare/Black Welfare	.16	.15
Welfare/Integration	.23	.19
Welfare/Size of Government[a]	−.10	.05
Black Welfare/Integration	.23	.23
Black Welfare/Size of Government[a]	.08	−.03
Integration/Size of Government[a]	−.07	.06

[a] The size of government issue changed after 1968, making comparisons difficult between data sets collected at different times. We have therefore used the 1972 correlations for this issue as the basis for comparison with the pre-1964 means in the national surveys.

[b] These figures are based upon the correlations in Table 7-1.

The only exceptions to this pattern are those pairs which include the size of government issue, and this result is consistent with that reported by Nie and associates. This pattern thus supports their view that the size of government issue has become orthogonal to the left-right dimension, even when measured with the newer question formats.

The changes in the correlations in both data sets are summarized in Table 7-2. Here we compare the changes in the average correlations before and after 1964 in the SRC data with the differences in our own samples. The differences for the item pairs over time in the SRC national surveys are closely matched by the differences found in the Twin Cities surveys taken at one point in time. This is especially true of the three pairs that do not contain the size of government question. Given the changes in the meaning of this particular issue over time, comparisons based upon it are bound to be risky. Even so, the differences in the two data sets among pairs containing the size of government issue are comparable, though the calculations for the SRC data are based upon a "correction" for the change in meaning of the issue after 1968 (see the footnote to Table 7-2).

The pattern of these results suggests that the level of constraint in the mass public has not increased greatly over the past two decades, as others have argued, but rather that it merely *appears* to have increased because of the ways in which it has been measured. Changes in measurement instruments rather than real changes in the structure of public attitudes are probably the real cause of the pattern of correlations reported by Nie and associates. Our own view is that the questions used in the national surveys before 1964 did not adequately capture the liberal-conservative dimension, and therefore it is not surprising that studies using these items should have found lower levels of constraint in this period than in the later period during which more reliable measures were used. The fact that levels of constraint differed so substantially and so consistently between our two control samples strongly suggests that the differences over time reported by others are spurious.

. . . [In] addition, it is important to note that the differences between the "interested" and "not interested" groups in the national surveys are not particularly large (the former increases by .29, the latter by .19), and it is doubtful that they are large enough to sustain the "interest" explanation put forth by Nie and associates. This explanation, of course, rests upon the claim that the increases were much more substantial among the interested than among the disinterested group. Since these differences are not large, and since they are comparable to those found in our control samples, we are not inclined to reject our hypothesis that they were caused by changes in question formats. Readers, meanwhile, may judge for themselves.

A Note on Response-Set Bias in the Pre-1964 Questions

One obvious problem with the pre-1964 questions is that they are burdened with a serious response-set bias. As noted earlier, these questions are posed in such a way that it is difficult to disagree with them. One's immediate impulse is to agree, regardless of the supposed ideological content of the questions. The items used in 1964 and after, however, do not introduce this bias since they pose both sides of an issue and then allow respondents to choose between them. The latter is a much more valid and reliable procedure, both for measuring attitudes as well as levels of constraint.

We can get a preliminary idea of how this may have influenced the results reported by Nie and associates by looking at some figures from the SRC surveys of 1956 and 1964 and from the Twin Cities survey. The figures in Table 7-3 report the proportions of respondents in these samples giving the "liberal" response to the various questions listed along the margins. It is apparent that the pre-1964 questions did tend to promote "agree" responses. The first four issues listed include the three social welfare items (job guarantee, aid to education, and medical assistance) and the black welfare item. For all of these, the liberal response is to "agree." There was overwhelming agreement with these statements on the 1956 survey, ranging from 61 percent agreeing with the statement on medical care to 74 percent agreeing with the aid to education statement. As the table shows, we found very similar results using these items in 1976 in our own survey. When the questions are turned around, however, so that a liberal response requires one to disagree with the statement, the proportion of these responses declines substantially. This probably explains, in part, why the proportions of liberal responses to the school integration and size of government items are so low, though one could argue that these differences coincidentally reflect public sentiments. There are, in addition, vast differences in the proportions of liberal responses given to these questions in 1956 and 1964. The items used in 1964, on balance, produce more consistent marginals and they tend to produce fewer liberal responses, particularly on those first four welfare items.

Table 7-3   Response Bias in Pre- and Post-1964 Questions: Percent "Liberal" Responses to Old and New Question Formats (1956 and 1964 National Surveys and 1976 Twin Cities Survey)

	Pre-1964 Questions			Post-1964 Questions		
		Percent Liberal			Percent Liberal	
Issue	*Liberal Response*	*1956 SRC*	*Twin Cities*	*Liberal Response*	*1964 SRC*	*Twin Cities*
Job Guarantee	Agree	63	68	Support Fed. Guarantee	36	43
Aid to Education	Agree	74	70	Support Fed. Aid	38	39
Medical Care	Agree	61	73	Support Fed. Help	59	71
Black Welfare	Agree	79	69	Support Fed. Role	45	53
School Integration	Disagree	44	26	Support Fed. Role	48	40
Size of Government	Disagree	32	33	Gov't Not Too Strong	52	37

Among these items, the only ones producing comparable results across the years are the medical assistance questions. Otherwise, the differences are large, both in the national surveys and in the Twin Cities surveys.

Moreover, it will be observed that these differences in support for social welfare policies between 1956 and 1964 do not make any sense when one considers the actual politics of the period. If these figures are to be believed, support for welfare policies declined substantially between 1956 and 1964, a dubious proposition. If there ever was a high tide of support for welfare legislation in the United States in the postwar period, it probably occurred in 1964 or shortly thereafter; and if there was a low tide, it must have occurred sometime in the 1950s. In this case, the survey results defy our usual understanding of the period. The only way to make sense out of these results, in our view, is to attribute them to changed question formats.

It is impossible to determine exactly what impact this response bias had upon the item-item correlations, because it is confounded with other biases arising from question wording. In addition, we do not know what the correlations would have been in the absence of such biases.

Our own guarded judgment is that response bias existed in the earlier surveys, but that its impact is very difficult to assess. Suffice it to say, others who would attempt longitudinal studies with the national election surveys should bear this difficulty in mind. But, given our earlier presentation, this particular bias does not appear as the serious question wording bias in measuring changing levels of constraint before and after 1964.

Concluding Comments

The burden of this presentation has been to suggest that constraint in the mass public probably did not increase very much between 1956 and 1972; rather, reported changes were due to modifications in the survey items used to measure constraint. Though the evidence presented is not entirely conclusive, we believe it is strong enough to make it difficult to maintain that the structure of public attitudes has changed substantially since the 1950s.[2]

This conclusion raises some questions about recent revisionist research in the areas of public opinion and electoral behavior. It has become commonplace to observe that the findings reported by Campbell et al. in *The American Voter* (1960) were too heavily influenced by the consensus politics of the 1950s, and that the conflicts of the 1960s brought about important changes in the American electorate. Thus, the earlier findings were time-bound, and conflicts with these findings based upon more recent data can be chalked up as political change. The results reported above suggest that we may be overestimating the degree of real change that took place during the 1960s. Instead, the discipline of political science may have improved its techniques of measuring public attitudes during this period. This "learning," in turn, may have produced different but more reliable findings as time passed, and these changes were then projected onto the public instead of being perceived as changes internal to the discipline. This should not be pushed too far, lest we imply that electoral researchers have merely been talking to themselves. But it does raise fundamental questions about the entire enterprise.

NOTES

1. We cite as an example the questions on economic welfare. The 1956 wording: "The government in Washington ought to see to it that everybody who wants to work can find a job. Now would you have an opinion on this or not?" (If Yes): "Do you think the government *should* do this?" (Agree strongly; agree, but not very strongly; not sure; disagree, but not very strongly; disagree strongly.) The 1964 wording: "In general, some people feel that the government in Washington should see to it that every person has a job and a good standard of living. Others think the government should just let each person get ahead on his own. Have you been interested enough in this to favor one side over the other?" (If Yes): "Do you think that the government should see to it that every person has a job and a good standard of living *or* should it let each person get ahead on his own?" [eds.]
2. Brunk (1978) has performed an experiment similar to ours, using college students as respondents. His results are identical to ours.

8. PLUS ÇA CHANGE...
THE NEW CPS ELECTION STUDY PANEL

Philip E. Converse and Gregory B. Markus

   ...Analysts of the sequence of national election studies generated with National Science Foundation help by the Center for Political Studies at the University of Michigan have been frustrated for some time at the lack of long-term panel linkages—the reinterviewing of the same respondents—in successive replications of the basic study design. The 1976 presidential election marked the completion of the first large-scale panel segment, stretching back to 1972, since the original four-year panel was completed in 1960....

   Of course the study of electoral change has scarcely withered away in the interim for lack of full longitudinal studies.... Hence it will be helpful background if we review, with a brevity verging on oversimplification, some of the chief findings from the original panel, as well as revisions provoked by subsequent independent samples on into the early 1970s.

The Original 1956-60 Panel and Later Findings

   ...The major analyses of the panel-specific data from the 1956-58-60 reinterview sample were never reported in a self-contained monograph. However, some of the more surprising empirical facts to emerge from those analyses played an influential role in the senior author's essay, "The Nature of Belief Systems in Mass Publics" (Converse, 1964). Stripped to its essentials, one brute fact which could only have arisen from long-term longitudinal data was the discovery that *at the individual level,* the stability of party identifications in the 1956-60 period vastly outstripped the stability of individual positions on even the most stable of the major political issues of the period.

   Such stability of party identification had been suspected for some time on the basis of the noteworthy inertia of marginal distributions for the variable in independent cross-section samples throughout the 1950s. In fact, that suspicion had been central in some of the major theses of *The American Voter* (1960). However, inertia of marginals, or minimal net change, is not at all incompatible

   Source: *American Political Science Review* (1979) 73: 32-49. Reprinted with permission of the publisher.

with the possibility of high rates of *gross* change, or rapid individual-level "turnover." Indeed, while time series data on distributions of mass opinions on major political issues were somewhat more truncated because of the flux of salient issues from one election to the next, where repeated cross-section measurement did exist for political issues, the marginals were often as inert in the 1950s as those for party identification.

Therefore it was particularly striking to discover that beneath the net stability of party identification lay a very marked degree of gross, or individual-level stability; whereas the inertia or net stability of opinion distribution on major political issues concealed an equally surprising degree of individual-level turnover which appeared to be almost a Brownian motion. Let us be careful not to overstate the case. Party identification was *not perfectly* stable for individuals over the 1956-58-60 panel observations, in the sense that all individuals located themselves in the same one of seven possible categories in each ensuing measurement. Substantial numbers changed to an adjacent location on the continuum, and a very few appeared to move long distances (5-7 "slots") across the continuum. Similarly, it was not true that the individual-level data on issue positions showed no stability whatever. For one thing, there was significant variation from issue to issue, in patterns that seemed decodable; and in any event, even the issues with the greatest individual-level turnover showed some significant degree of continuity, as indexed by the correlation of each issue with itself over time departing reliably above zero.

Nonetheless, the contrasts in stability between party and issue positions remained absolutely stark, and we would find it hard to be impressed with any theory of the dynamics of these political attitudes which failed to encompass such contrasts. One implication seemed to be that party loyalties had a considerable primacy in the attitude systems involved. In the 1950s, at least, issue positions were but weakly aligned with partisanship, in the minds of the voters, in any event. Perceived linkages between parties and issues were, by and large, vague and contradictory as well. We opined at the time (Campbell, et al., pp. 179-83) that a major cause of the confusion might be that "actual" party differentiation on the major issues was at low ebb in the mid-fifties, a guess that later proved to have some merit. However, in the modest degree that partisanship and issue positions did co-vary, the contrasts in stability from the panel data suggested that it was likely that these issue preferences were more often brought into line with prior partisanship than the reverse. Once again, there is no need to exaggerate the case: surely issue positions could affect partisanship for occasional individuals at any time, and at some occasional junctures might do so for larger fractions of the population. But it seemed well-nigh impossible to square the panel contrasts in party and issue stability with a model in which the preponderant causal flow was, in any intermediate term, from issue position to partisanship, at least in the late 1950s.

Cross-Section Sample Findings from the 1960s

Although no full-blown panels of the national electorate were followed in the 1960s, there was ample sign of major trends in these matters by the middle years of the decade. While change was rapid on many fronts, some of the most impressive evidence involved the party-issue nexus.

Burnham (1968) noted that after a lengthy period in which the aggregate distribution of party identification had remained nearly constant, the first signal change began in the middle 1960s with a rising proportion of the electorate refusing to report identification with either party and insisting on being classed as independents, thereby swelling the neutral middle of the party identification continuum. This apparent erosion in feelings of party loyalty among American voters, caught at an incipient stage by the first Burnham accounts, has since proceeded majestically in the same direction for close to a decade, and certainly must rank by now as change of massive magnitude. . . .

Where issue positions of the public are concerned, Nie (with Andersen, 1974) has advanced some provocative analyses suggesting that soon after 1960, voter policy preferences began to take on a much firmer "muscle tone" than was characteristic of data from the 1950s. This change is largely indexed by a marked increase in the cross-sectional correlations among issue positions in the 1960s, as opposed to their feeble level of the preceding decade. The reality of the issue trends charted by Nie has been subject to somewhat more controversy than attends the brute empirical facts of erosion in party loyalties, since some (Bishop et al., 1978; Sullivan et al., 1978) have suggested that the changes may be more an artifact of shifts in question format in the Michigan series than true secular change. However this matter may be resolved, the Nie thesis has strong face validity at least, since increased public attention to policy cleavages is almost another way of describing the onset of political turbulence of the type characterizing American politics for the past dozen years.

Moreover, the Nie thesis receives supplementary support from changes observed in linkages between partisanship, issue positions, and voting decisions. For example, Pomper (1972) pointed out that voter perceptions of party differences on policy issues showed more clarity by 1964 than had been true in the first panel period of the late 1950s. The citizen was more likely to see differences between the parties on policy matters, and the alignment between partisanship and issue preferences had heightened as well. In the most exhaustive recapitulation of these trends, Nie, Verba and Petrocik (1976) have shown that the election-by-election correlations between party identification and the vote, as compared with issue-vote correlations, changed after the early 1960s: the apparent weight of partisanship in the voting decision had undergone significant decline, while the weight of policy preferences showed a marked advance.

Again the magnitude of these trends, as well as their durability into the 1970s, remains subject to scholarly dispute (see, for example, Margolis [1977] on Pomper). Similarly, the longer-range import of the differences before and after the early 1960s is subject to basic disagreement. Some see these changes as secular and permanent or even accelerating into the future. Others see one or the other political period as the American norm, interrupted by an era of aberration. Still others see the two periods as local minima and maxima, with a putative normal lying somewhere between.

Nevertheless, some of the component changes are beyond dispute as empirical facts, and taken as a *gestalt*, they have a great deal of intuitive appeal.

The parts fit together admirably, and correspond nicely with impressions most of us who lived through both periods would have harbored in any event.

It is against this backdrop that the advent of the new 1972-74-76 panel version of the Michigan election series is particularly welcome. . . . One precious class of information—the continuity or individual-level stability of the key variables—cannot be squeezed from the independent-replication design. In fact, it cannot even be deduced from other attendant slice-of-time facts with much reliability, as we shall shortly see. And given the intervening work on electoral change, some of the first-cut expectations as to how the new panel data might look are extremely straightforward. Apparently party is down, and issues are up. The main question to be asked of the new panel data would merely seem to be "by how much?"

We shall reveal the general answer rapidly, for its explication can easily occupy us for the rest of this article. Where party and issues are concerned, and *with respect to those facets of change which a panel design is uniquely equipped to illuminate,* our first-cut explorations show that *the 1972-76 panel data are very nearly a carbon copy of those from the 1956-60 panel!* That is, the individual stability of party identification, relative to that for policy preferences, is just about as great for the latter period as for the former.

We shall spend most of the rest of this chapter trying to clarify just what those initial results do and do not mean. . . .

The Case of Party Identification

. . . There is no need to do a panel study to monitor change in either the mean or the variance of a distribution. Successive independent cross-section samples can perform this task equally well. The information a panel study uniquely supplies involves the continuity in positioning of the same individuals over time. One index of such continuity is the proportion of the panel on or near the main diagonal of the cross-tabulation of the same variable between waves. While such expressions are commonly used, they are weak summarizations not only because of the arbitrary nature of the category width that constitutes the "stable" diagonal, but also because the resulting proportions are strongly influenced by the number of categories into which the variable is partitioned, so that comparisons across variables of different category "length" become nonsensical. An obvious improvement is to deal with a summary expression of correlation or regression.

. . . While it is technically quite possible that individual-level continuity correlations for party identification have remained at their high levels of the late 1950s despite the shrinking variance of the distribution [i.e., the well known increase in the proportion of independents], it would not intuitively seem very likely. After all, the descriptors commonly applied to the surge in independence talk of the "erosion" of these identifications, and the "destabilization of partisanship." While such terms are entirely proper, they would certainly seem to imply a major unraveling of individual-level continuities in party preference, even in the stability of relative locations. Moreover, at a less intuitive and more technical level, if error variances remain constant while true variances of a variable decline, then the magnitude of correlations involving the variable will be attenuated.[1] Thus the natural shrinkage of observed variance of party identification might be expected on these grounds alone to dilute the continuity correlations correspondingly.

Some years back we suggested that this might not turn out empirically to be the case with party identification (Converse, 1975a), since the only scrap of a national panel conducted during the 1960s—a couple hundred stray cases reinterviewed between 1964 and 1966—showed continuity correlations which were virtually identical to those estimated from the 1956-60 panel, despite the fact that this panel lapped over into the period in which the variance of identification reports had begun to shrink palpably. Therefore we are not entirely surprised to discover that the continuity correlations calculated for party identification from the new 1972-76 panel are just about as high as they were in 1956-60. In absolute terms they are a hair smaller, but the difference is too slight for statistical significance. Probably the drop is in some degree real, as one would expect from the truncation of variance in the later period. However, the stunning fact is that the decline is simply vestigial: if one could say from the 1956-60 panel that individual-level continuity correlations for party identification with a two-year time lapse ran in the low .80s, one can make exactly the same statement for the 1972-76 panel.

For reasons that should be apparent, the magnitudes of continuity coefficients are specific to the size of the time interval elapsing between measurements. In processes of progressive (that is, not cyclical) change, they can be expected to decline as the interval becomes more extended. Indeed, this property emerges clearly in the party identification data. The four-year correlations are less than those calculated for a two-year interval; and the latter are smaller than correlations formed for measurements separated by only a few weeks in time, as is the case when the party identification item is applied to the same sample in both the pre-election and post-election questionnaires. Therefore continuity correlations in general only have meaning as they are tagged with some specific time interval. If we stick with the two-year correlations in order to encompass comfortably the data from the two-wave, 1964-66 mini-panel, then we find the following best estimates for two-year continuity correlations:[2]

$$
\begin{array}{ll}
\text{The 1956-60 period} & = .835 \\
\text{The 1964-66 mini-panel} & = .836 \\
\text{The 1972-76 period} & = .813
\end{array}
$$

There are several ways of processing these raw continuity coefficients into more refined components. One of the easiest partitions, dependent on having at least three waves of measurement, is to break the raw coefficients into (1) a reliability component, reflecting the complement of the proportion of error variance; and (2) a "true" stability coefficient, reflecting the degree to which the measurement at two points in time would be correlated if there were not intrusion of unreliability. Such procedures have been described by Heise (1969), and refined a further step by Wiley and Wiley (1970). These manipulations rest, as always, on a series of assumptions about the character of the data and the attendant error structures. One of the less pleasing sets of assumptions—that the measurement reliability (Heise) or the absolute error variances (Wiley and Wiley) are constant from wave to wave in a given panel sequence—can be relaxed in the case of the 1956-60 panel, where instead of three waves of measurement of party identification we can profit from five.[3] While it is regrettable that party identification was measured only three times in the new panel (1972 pre-, 1974, and 1976 pre-), there is sufficiently striking consistency between the two panels to enable us to use the additional information afforded by the first panel to reassure ourselves concerning various assumptions which must be made for the later batch of panel data. Also, of course, we can proceed no further with the mere two waves offered by the 1964-66 mini-panel, although the data presented above also give some assurance that we are dealing with process parameters which have a considerable stability in the intermediate term.

There are other assumptions embedded in calculations of the Heise or Wiley and Wiley type that are not entirely well met by the data. Thus, for example, there is reason to believe that both the measurement reliability and the true stability of the party identification item is less than nicely homogeneous over the population. In later, more complicated assays of these data, we shall take such characteristics into fuller account. Nonetheless, as first-cut approximations, it is worth seeing what can provisionally be estimated concerning the relative proportions of change due to unreliability, as opposed to "true change," in these longitudinal measurements.

Where they can be compared most fully (as in the five-wave panel), calculations of the Heise and Wiley and Wiley type give virtually identical estimates with these data. Both calculations agreed that the main source of the slight decline in overall continuity between the two large panels is a slight increase in unreliability, exactly as one would expect if the main change in the data were a shrinkage in the time variance.[4] In both calculations, the decline in reliability is roughly from (a central tendency of about) .88 in the first panel to about .84 in the second.[5] Once this slight decline in reliability is set aside, as it is when we calculate the true stability coefficients, we find comparisons of the following sort as our best estimates for the two-year interval:

	1956-58-60	1972-74-76
Two-year stability (Heise style)	.951	.972
Two-year stability (Wiley style)	.958	.972

The homogeneity of these estimates, both between calculation methods and more especially across two periods in which the nature of party identification has seemed so different, when other facets of change in the variable are considered, is very striking. There are a variety of ways of expressing the implications of these findings. We shall postpone some of the broader theoretical implications for our conclusions. For now, we might briefly consider what the above data imply for the long-term "staying power" of party identifications at the individual level.

If we merely knew that the raw two-year continuity correlation for party identification was about .82 (as a period-free average), then we might be tempted to conclude that over a period of 16 (2^4) years, we could only expect a continuity of .45 (or $.82^4$), a value which would not be entirely impressive. However, if we trust the above estimates as to the proportion of observed change which is mere unreliability of measurement, then we would expect the 16-year *observed* (i.e., error-attenuated) stability coefficient to look something like .73 (or .86 [$.96^4$], where the .86 is the period-free reliability estimate) instead of .45. This is a vastly different picture of the long-term individual-level stability of the variable, especially as it is appropriate to square these two values, yielding a contrast in shared temporal covariance of .53 instead of .26. And we feel considerably less cavalier about cycling hypothetically over longer periods of time in this way, once we have at least some shred of assurance, which the above data give, that the true stability of the party identification measures is remarkably close to stationary across two political periods in which, in other senses, it has been subject to major change.

However, even this assumption is subject to challenge. After all, the decline in reported strength of partisanship has proceeded secularly from 1965 to 1975. While our panel observations in 1964-66 and 1972-76 bracket the beginning and end of this fascinating period, they leave uncovered a crucial segment of time from 1966 to 1972. Perhaps it was in this six-year interval that continuity correlations on party identification might have registered a distinct sag.

Here again we can import a crucial datum which suggests that the stationarity of these continuity correlations has been complete over the past two decades. In 1973 Jennings and Niemi (1977) reinterviewed the parents of their 1965 graduating high school students, who had originally been interviewed in 1965. In principle this is a 1965-73 panel, covering exactly the years that we are missing in our national samples. The difficulty is that these parents cannot be seen as a proper sample of the adult electorate, even though they may be a perfectly honest national sample of a more restricted population.

What the Jennings-Niemi respondents have in common is having been parents of high school seniors in 1965. This means that they are a very homogeneous age cohort, relative to the electorate as a whole. The group lacks newer and younger voters completely and, given their association with children not dropping out of high school, they should show higher than normal social status. Now it can be calculated that if such respondents were really representative of the full electorate, and if our panel continuity coefficients were truly stationary in the long run, then over an eight-year span these respondents should show a continuity correlation for party identification of .76. However, the age and class bias of the Jennings-Niemi respondents would lead one to expect a slightly higher figure. It turns out that the observed figure for the party identifications of the Jennings-Niemi parents over the 1965-1973 interval is .79. This value is either right on target or, if anything, a shade high: certainly an hypothesis which maintains that continuity sagged between our panel points of 1966 and 1972 finds no comfort whatever in these data. All of the available evidence, then, suggests that there has been no change in the individual-level continuity of party identification over the past 20 years, despite an incontestable change in the likelihood of reported partisanship.

The Continuity of Policy Preferences in the '50s and the '70s

A comparative examination of the individual-level stability of preferences on political issues poses somewhat different analysis problems, chiefly because while the two major parties have long been constants of the political scene, the objects of issue orientation are in perpetual evolution. The issue positions which seemed central to political controversy in the early 1970s were somewhat different from those central in the late 1950s. Moreover, the election studies have been for some time measuring issue positions in a different format than was used in the late 1950s, and there are reasons to expect that these pure methods changes should affect some of the process parameters which interest us (Bishop et al. and Sullivan et al., 1978).

Hence strict comparisons of issue continuities are impossible. Nevertheless, there are some matches between issue items from the panel studies of the two periods which are tighter than others, so that some rough comparisons are possible. Moreover, the continuity correlations for issue positions in the original panel fell within a range which was vastly different from the values for party identification, and therefore it is of interest to see how even the newer issues are behaving in these terms in the more recent panel. We shall begin with a few of the closer matches and then summarize the general trends over all of the new panel issues as a set.

One issue item in the later panel was worded identically to the original 1956-58-60 study. This is a foreign policy question, in agree-disagree form, intended to tap isolationism:

> "This country would be better off if we just stayed home and did not concern ourselves with problems in other parts of the world."

Despite the identical wording of questions, there were minor variations in format. Most notably, the item responses were handled dichotomously in the new panel, whereas they had been spread out into four main points ("strong agree" to "strong disagree") in all waves of the original panel. Also in the last two waves of the first panel, a "filter" was added to assess whether respondents felt they had an opinion on the matter. Both of these format differences would seem likely, by conventional wisdom at least, to dull the correlations surrounding the more recent application of the isolationism item, other things being equal.

Unfortunately, this foreign policy item was asked only in 1972 and 1976 in the second panel, so we can only make direct comparisons with the four-year (1956-60) continuity correlation from the first panel. Since the same limitation applies to the only other plausible foreign policy item match, we shall take that item in the same breath, even though item wording is much less parallel. Both panels had an item on foreign aid, although with the following variation in wordings:

> (1956-60) "The United States should give economic help to the poorer countries of the world even if those countries can't pay for it."

> (1972-76) "The United States should give help to foreign countries even if they don't stand for the same things we do."

The same differences in response categories pertain for these foreign aid items as for the isolationism item.

The four-year continuity correlations for these foreign policy items are as follows:

	1956-60		1972-76	
	r	(N)	r	(N)
U.S. Stay Home	.347	(1086)	.309	(1113)
Foreign Aid	.292	(1009)	.264	(1039)

The similarities between the two panels are quite impressive. And if there is any merit in our a priori expectation that format differences would tend to attenuate the more recent panel results by some small amount, it would be hard to argue that these continuity estimates are any less stationary than those for party identification, although of course they fall at a totally different level of correlation.

In the original panel, foreign policy preferences tended to be among those issue items of lesser individual-level stability. We shall see that the case is exactly the same in the new panel. Domestic issues in the old panel fell into two substantive domains: social welfare policy and civil rights policy. Both domains are represented with three-wave issue items in the new panel, although the item format is always different, and the wording shows greater or lesser variation.

The nearest thing to a match among the social welfare items involves questions about government guarantees of employment. The old agree-disagree item has been changed to a forced-choice format, with two contrasting substantive alternatives. Moreover, in this case—in contrast to the foreign policy items—response alternatives for the new panel are *more* numerous than for the old, with a 7-point rating scale being used to replace the four-category agree-disagree form. Thus, by the same reasoning as used before, we might expect slightly higher correlations with the new panel than with the old. Despite such differences in form, the intent of the two items is surely identical:

> (1956-60) " 'The government in Washington ought to see to it that everybody who wants to work can find a job.' Now would you have an opinion on this or not? (IF YES) Do you think the government should do this?"

> (1972-76) "Some people feel that the government in Washington should see to it that every person has a job and a good standard of living. Suppose that these people are at one end of this scale—at point number 1. Others think the government should just let each person get ahead on his own. Suppose these people are at the other end at point number 7. And, of course, some other people have opinions somewhere in between. Where would you place yourself on this scale, or haven't you thought much about this?"

For these items, asked in all three major waves of both panels, the average two-year continuity correlation in each study is:

	1956-60	1972-76
Government Job Guarantee	.457	.493

Again, we may well be struck by the similarity in values between the two periods, especially by comparison with the much more stable party identification items, or the visibly less stable foreign policy questions. Or if we want to pay attention to the small differences in absolute values between the two estimates, the value for the new panel is in fact slightly higher, as format changes would have led us to believe.

In civil rights, an item on school desegregation occurs in both panels, although it is another instance in which the question was only asked twice (1972 and 1976) in the second panel. The latter item is a forced-choice version of the earlier form, with those respondents claiming no opinion being filtered off in both instances.

> (1956-60) "The government in Washington should stay out of the question whether white and colored children go to the same school."

> (1972-76) "Do you think the government in Washington should see to it that white and black children go to the same schools, or stay out of this area as it is not its business."

In general we would expect the forced-choice version to produce slightly more discriminating measurement and hence higher correlations; yet the item in the second panel was only scored as a dichotomy, instead of the four-point agree-disagree scale used originally. Therefore there are no very clear expectations as to pure methods differences in the continuity correlations. The actual four-year correlations are, however, very similar:

	1956-60		1972-76	
	r	(*N*)	r	(*N*)
School Desegregation	.397	(1059)	.410	(714)

By this time it will not be surprising if the reader is beginning to find the parallels between all of these panel results, despite a decade and a half of intervening political change, as eerie as these parallels have seemed to us.

We have by now exhausted all of the issues for which very close matches in wording and intent, if not in format or in letter, are available.[6] While the similarities in individual-level stability for these well-matched items are striking, we should not conclude that the issue materials from the new panel more generally look just like those from the earlier data set. This is true chiefly because there are new issues present in the 1972-76 panel which are not inheritances from the past; and these items sometimes have a different cast in continuity terms.

A good example is provided by the civil rights issue concerning school busing to promote racial integration. This issue was not even in the air at the time of the earlier panel, so that its absence from those interviews was not at all a matter of editorial oversight, but rather a token of a truly different environment of policy debate. The issue is also of particular interest because casual observation would suggest that this issue, probably more than any other in the civil rights area or, for that matter, the total arena of policy debate, has had an inflammatory or polarizing quality that has bitten deep into even relatively inattentive segments of the public. In other words, if as we have earlier suggested, it is true that the general levels of these continuity correlations reflect the degree to which items tap into more or less thoroughly crystallized attitude structures (where the limiting case of no crystallization whatever is the "non-attitude"), we would expect rather substantial continuity correlations for the busing items. This expectation is sustained. The best estimate of the two-year continuity correlation is .575, a value still falling very well below the corresponding value for party identification, but nonetheless significantly higher than that registered for any issue items in the whole 1956-60 panel.

There are at least two other issues new to the 1972-76 panel which show even higher continuity values. These items are not only new: together they seem to stand for a coherent *class* of issue which was not even of much salience in the 1950s. One is a 7-point scale where the extremes involve the legalization of marijuana at one end, and the setting of higher penalties for its use at the other. The other is an item on abortion, in which the respondent is asked to choose between four levels of lenience in availability, essentially bounded by "under no circumstances" at one end and "at any need" on the other. Neither of these items was asked in the middle wave in 1974, so that only estimates of the four-year continuity correlations are available. As we have pointed out, coefficients over this time lapse tend to run lower than their two-year counterparts. Thus, for example, if the school busing issue runs about .574 for a two-year lapse, it stands at .535 for a four-year lapse. The only two issues which exceed it are marijuana and abortion, with *four*-year coefficients of .640 and .617, respectively.

These are high values, and they seem clearly associated with a class of moral issues of the kind brought to salience by the counterculture confrontations of the preceding decade. Indeed, the only other specific issue item with a four-year continuity correlation over .50, in addition to marijuana, abortion and busing, is an item on whether women should have an equal role with men in business and government, or should keep their place in the home (.519). Again, this is an item which pits the cutting edge of new mores against an array of traditional values.

For those who have worked in other political cultures, it is not entirely surprising that such moral issues should have a deeper resonance among those not normally attentive to much political controversy than is true for policy debates of most other kinds. Perhaps these uncommon magnitudes represent something other than a sharper crystallization of attitudes across a larger fraction of the electorate than is true of other issues, but for the time being such would seem to be the most plausible diagnosis.

There is one other item, not referring to a specific policy issue or for that matter any "new" issue at all, but relevant to a large range of issues, which also shows a four-year continuity correlation over .50, although the high value occurs under a special configuration of circumstances important to make clear. This item is the ideological item involving self-placement on a 7-point liberal-conservative scale, with a four-year continuity correlation of .564. The special circumstances arise because the correlation is being figured on a much more limited fraction of the population than is true of any of the other specific issues. This high attrition occurs because such a continuity correlation can only be computed for those respondents who choose some content response at both years involved in the correlation. On items like the abortion question, almost all respondents choose a content alternative, so that the continuity correlation refers to a quasi-totality of the electorate. On the liberal-conservative item, however, over one-third of the population must be set aside at the outset as missing data, either because they say they do not know their position or because they accept a "no-opinion" filter.

It may seem surprising that only as few as 35 percent or so fail to give content locations on two successive administrations of this ideological scale, and hence do not figure in the continuity correlations, when for many years items asking people what the labels "liberal" and "conservative" mean have shown some 40 percent or so who do not know. The implication is either that some people who would not profess to know what political difference is intended are nonetheless choosing a location on the continuum, or that the 40 percent value has changed, although it had not changed even after we were deep into the turmoil of the 1960s. Unfortunately, the item tapping the meaning of the terms was never asked in any of the five waves of the new panel. However, work in Western Europe has made it clear that people who locate themselves on an analogous left-right scale despite confession that they do not understand what the terms mean politically, tend in large numbers to place themselves at the exact midpoint of the continuum offered (e.g., Converse and Pierce, 1970). This is an easy solution when one is unsure of the significance of the extremities. And indeed, the midpoint of the United States scale is very well populated also. In fact, in the turnover cross-tabulations of the liberal-conservative scale, the cell which marks the exact center on both administrations tends to be two to three times as populous as any other cell in the matrix.

Hence the special circumstances which appear to sustain the high liberal-conservative continuity correlations seem to be that better than one-third of the population is removed at the outset; and among the remaining two-thirds, substantial numbers express their uncertainty by persistently locating themselves at dead center, thereby not adding to the continuity correlation, but not detracting much from it either. It is likely that for those with truly crystallized positions on the liberal-conservative continuum, the individual-level stability of position is very high, even as high or higher than party identification. But this fraction of the population is likely to be quite limited.

In our discussion we have introduced a number of issues or meta-issues which were not present in the original panel, but are new entrants in the 1972-76 period. All of these items discussed show higher levels of continuity than the most stable issues in the original panel. This might lead to a conclusion that levels of continuity in issue positions are up quite notably, if not because of heightened continuity from issues that can be specifically matched across the panels, at least because issues newly arisen in the real world are of a kind that tap more sharply crystallized opinion.

One can defend a very modest version of this argument if one limits attention to the two or three moral issues. However, a number of other "new issues" in the panel have not been discussed, and these generally show levels of continuity that are utterly redolent of issues in the 1956-60 period. Thus, for example, two items which have overtones of the "law and order" themes of the past decade—one dealing with repercussions of urban unrest, another dealing with protection of the rights of accused persons as opposed to stopping crime at all costs—show two-year continuity coefficients of about .36 and .45 respectively, values which are very middling relative to the range "normal" for domestic issues late in the 1950s. An item addressed to the possibility of a more or less progressive taxation rate shows a four-year value of about .31, and the figure is only .28 for an item asking whether the federal government has become too powerful. The latter figures are *lower* than any parallel figures to be found for domestic issues in the original panel.

To summarize, then, we have found that where specific issues can be directly matched, continuity values seem amazingly stationary across the two panels. One type of issue not salient in political debate in the late 1950s—moral or counterculture issues—do show signally higher continuity values than any other specific issues in either panel. Once beyond these moral issues, however, even new issues do not in general show any higher levels of continuity than the old.

A great deal of work of a more probing sort can be done with these issue materials. For example, more intensive investigations of the apparent substantial error structures in these responses are possible, particularly as some few of the new panel issues have been applied on four waves instead of merely three. Such empirical wedges are important to arrive at a proper diagnosis as to what these error structures really mean. Achen (1975) has concluded that the low levels of continuity marking issue responses occur simply because the items are unreliable, probably because of poor wording. It was the amazingly low "test-retest" reliability of the 1956-58-60 panel issues that touched off our earlier investigations as to why this degree of unreliability occurred, and led to our conclusion that the low apparent reliabilities were not simply a function of the items themselves in a shoddy-wording sense, but rather were a joint function of the substance of the items and the variable degree of attitude crystallization which more and less attentive respondents brought to the particular substance (Converse, 1964, 1970).

We still feel our interpretation is preferable to Achen's revision. Among other things, Achen's explanation does not give as much help in understanding why high political elites show higher continuity coefficients and hence apparently higher reliabilities than does the mass public, even when asked to respond to the very same simplistic issue items, although this difference is the most direct corollary of our original interpretation. Nor does the Achen interpretation prepare us to expect that the same team of question-writers who manage to word questions quite effectively regarding personal morals cannot find comparably effective wording when asking about foreign policy debates. Again, we need only imagine that disagreements about personal morals grip more people more vitally than do debates over foreign affairs in order to fold the new findings nicely into our original interpretive structure.

The important point is that the new panel data base offers a challenging field for investigating some of these differences more thoroughly.[7] For the moment, however, it seems fair to conclude that the individual-level relative stability of issue positions in the American public has changed only slightly between the two panels, and that no significant change whatever can be discerned where the same issue substance can be matched across the two eras.

Evaluations of Political Figures

Of the original Survey Research Center triad of parties, candidates and issues, all empirical work of a panel type has focused to date on parties and issues, for the simple reason that the 1956-60 period bridged two presidential elections with no continuity of candidates. The same lack of continuity marks the 1972-76 interval. However, the new panel does include multiple evaluations, on a thermometer scale, of the most prominent partisan political figures in the land, even if not running for president. It is naturally of interest to ask how stable these personality evaluations are, by comparison with the high stability of party identification and the relatively low stability of personal positions on political issues. Therefore we shall close our review of some of the first panel findings with a brief consideration of these raw continuity results.

Ratings of Hubert Humphrey, Ted Kennedy, Scoop Jackson, Richard Nixon and George Wallace were drawn in 1972, 1974 and 1976. In addition, a rating of George McGovern was applied in 1972 and 1976. Over all instances, the 100-point thermometer scale was explained and then names were offered *seriatim* as stimulus words for evaluation. The continuity correlations available for these political figures are summarized in Table 8-1. A number of provisional observations about this array are fairly obvious.

One is that the levels of continuity correlations across six of the most prominent political figures of the era covered by the new panel show a very wide range of variation. While it is not perfectly certain in what currency such comparisons should be made, we find it reasonable to square the above correlational values and speak in terms of the proportions of temporal covariance involved in the various evaluations. In this currency, evaluations of Kennedy appear some 2½ to 4 times more stable than evaluations of Jackson. Given such variation, it is tempting to try to explain its sources. One hypothesis might be that the stimulus words "Henry 'Scoop' Jackson" are more poorly worded as question items than the stimulus words "Edward 'Ted' Kennedy," and that hence the Jackson item is simply less reliable. A plausible rival hypothesis, and one that we considerably prefer, is that more American voters bring more meaning to the Kennedy name than to the Jackson name, have more crystallized attitudes toward it as a stimulus, and hence respond more stably to it. The apparent reliability is not, by this construction, a function of the measuring instrument taken in a vacuum, but rather a product of the interaction between content and the variable degree of meaning this content has for various citizens.

However, a second observation helps to keep us from considering these continuity correlations too woodenly as though they were test-retest reliability coefficients. Although it may not dazzle the unaided eye, the pattern of continuity coefficients for evaluations of Richard Nixon are quite unique relative to all other contents of the new panel discussed to date. We know from the panel marginals

Table 8-1   Continuity Correlations in the 1972-76 Panel: Six Major
Political Figures

	Continuity Correlations	
	Average, 2-Yr. Ests.	4-Yr. Ests.
Edward "Ted" Kennedy	.722	.671
George Wallace	.683	.609
Hubert Humphrey	.592	.531
Richard Nixon	.585	.461
George McGovern	—	.554
Henry "Scoop" Jackson	.445	.343

Source: 1972-74-76 panel study of the national electorate carried out by the Center for Political Studies, University of Michigan.

(as if we needed them!) that true change in evaluation of Richard Nixon between 1972 and 1974 or 1976 was of massive proportions. In 1971, according to the Gallup Poll, the American people considered Richard Nixon the most admirable person in the entire world. His thermometer ratings in the 1972 wave of the panel confirm this level of adoration, since he received a mean rating of 65-66 in that year, relative to a rating of 52 or 53 for popular figures like Kennedy or Humphrey. By 1974 he had tumbled into the high 30s, and by 1976 to 31.

Thus there is a major injection of real change in the Nixon case, although as we have seen, it may or may not have been a type of change that affects the stability of relative individual positions. That is, it remains possible that people who were wildly enthusiastic about Nixon in 1972 merely were reduced to lukewarm feelings about him by 1976; and those just mildly warm were reduced to cool feelings, etc., such that there was little leap-frogging of individual positions. What is peculiar about the Nixon pattern, however, is that a good deal of true change (in the latter sense) was touched off by the Watergate drama. If we make the relevant Heise calculations for the Nixon case, we find that quite uniquely relative to all other panel materials, true change competes on nearly equal terms with unreliability in explaining why the raw continuity coefficients are as low as they are.

A final observation concerning Table 8-1 returns us to the main themes of this essay. We introduced the panel data on personages by way of asking where "candidates"—broadly construed—fit in the hierarchy of continuities defined up to now by parties and issues, given prior panel material. If we are correct in our interpretation of the reasons why Kennedy evaluations are so much more stable than those for Jackson, then it should be clear that we could generate variations in these continuity coefficients for political leaders almost at will, by playing with the known prominence of such figures. In the limiting case, we could probably generate a continuity coefficient approaching zero with a stimulus like "Senator

Zablocki," although it is reasonable to imagine that a persistent "ethnic vote" might keep such coefficients from actually touching zero.

Nevertheless, while it would be a chimera to imagine that some restricted range of continuity coefficients could reliably encompass any political figures whatever (by comparison with parties or issues), it is reasonable to limit our attention to the few truly prominent (in a mass-public sense) political personages in the land, just as the authors of the voting surveys try to restrict their issue measurements to the most salient policy cleavages of any particular period. And if we make such a limitation, then the data in Table 8-1, coupled with those cited earlier for parties and issues, might strongly suggest that in the hierarchy of continuity that these panel data help to establish, evaluations of major political leaders might properly be wedged in between parties as the most stable objects of orientation in terms of relative voter positioning, and issue positions as the least. Thus major political personages in any given epoch may serve as important cynosures of attention for the electorate, and as significant cues for other more substantive forms of political evaluation.

Summary and Implications

Figure 8-1 provides a handy graphic summary of the continuity correlation information that we have reviewed. In a nutshell, this summary says that apart from the emergence of some political cleavages having to do with traditional moral values in the later period, there has been scarcely any change in the comparative continuity of party and issue positioning between the two eras, despite manifold reasons to expect not only change, but change of major proportions. The individual-level continuity of party attachments continues to dwarf that for issue positioning in the 1972-76 period, as it did in 1956-60. And affection and dislike for the most prominent political leaders of the epoch seem to show levels of continuity which—again absent the moral issues—clearly lie between parties and issues.

... An implication which is of great theoretical importance flows from the hierarchy of continuities across parties, leaders and issues suggested in Figure 8-1, and is relevant for controversies over the prevalence of issue voting. It is not hard to imagine that attitudes which show higher individual-level stability have causal primacy relative to less stable attitudes. If this simple surmise is meaningful, then it would seem that where political evaluations are concerned, a party $\gg$ leader $\gg$ issue flow may be dominant, even across periods as disparate as those before and after 1960.

It must be kept in mind that the new panel data are merely suggestive in this regard, rather than definitive. Even the gross discrepancies in continuity between partisanship and issue positioning cannot guarantee that party identification is nearly always causally primary when party feelings are discovered to be aligned with issue preferences. Among other things, we must remember that there are only two major parties, whereas the number of political issues which may exercise one or another voter is legion. Thus it would always be possible, if indeed a bit strained, to imagine that the typical voter might be viscerally gripped by one issue

Figure 8-1 Continuities in Public Response to Parties, Leaders, and Issues

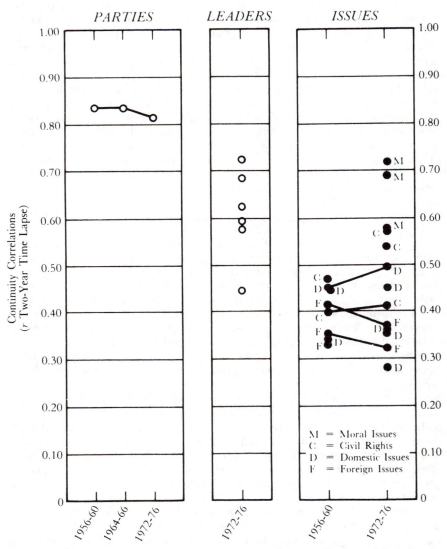

Note: Where items can be plausibly matched between panel segments, the respective data points are linked by a trend line. The whole figure is expressed in the currency of *two*-year continuity correlations. Where only four-year correlations are available, plausible two-year interpolations have been made to permit inclusion of a maximal number of observations.

Source: Panel studies of the national electorate carried out by the Center for Political Studies, University of Michigan.

out of some 30 in the active universe in some period, with very uncrystallized attitudes on the other 29. If party positions on such crucial but idiosyncratic issues remained constant over long periods of time, these policy preferences might totally dictate party identifications, at the very same time that measurement over a dozen or so of the 30 potential issues might show very high aggregate instabilitiy, since only one voter in 30 would, on the average, be gripped by each.

While such a model remains conceivable, it is obviously not the most plausible reading of current data. The huge discrepancies in individual-level continuities between party loyalties on one hand and issue positions on the other, particularly in view of what now seems to be their long-term constancy, argues for an overwhelming primacy of the party term when party-issue congruence does occur. However, further causal modeling work with the new panel, profiting from some of the kinds of estimates presented in this report, can mold more incisive conclusions from what must remain only suggestive ones at this point.

The additional fact, also made clear by the new panel data, that reactions to political leaders display levels of continuity intermediary between partisanship and policy preferences, raises a number of further interesting possibilities. Such a data configuration may, for example, suggest a significant margin for policy leadership available to major political figures, whereby admirers are quite susceptible to influence leading them to adopt policy positions more congruent with those espoused by their heroes. Or again, the greater continuity in evaluation of leaders as compared with issue positions may simply reflect the fact that party attachments anchor *both* leader assessments and issue positions, but do so more effectively in the case of leaders because the common voter can maintain much more firm and unequivocal cognitive links between parties and their most prominent leaders than between parties and positions on various issues.

This is obviously not the place to begin sorting out such possibilities. However, the first-cut results from the new CPS panel are striking indeed. They already rule out some constructions which might be placed upon the electoral history of the past decade, and begin to draw into focus a number of new research questions which, with more refined "milling" of the panel data, we may well be able to answer effectively.

NOTES

1. Note, however, that this expectation is contingent on an error variance which is gaining in size relative to the true variance. In the more general case, the continuity correlation is in theory independent of the variances of the component distributions.
2. All correlations are calculated on the basis of party identification as a seven-point, integer-scored scale. Here as at some other points in this article, precise numbers of cases are difficult to provide, since the estimates are more often than not "synthetic," resting on multiple bases. Thus, for example, the value of .835 is based on an averaging of four different estimates available in the 1956-60 panel for the correlation after about

a two-year interval. While all of these values are very similar in appearance, each is based on a rather different number of cases.

3. In addition to the full-blown fourth wave present on ICPSR tapes due to a full-sample application of the party identification item in the post-election as well as the pre-election study for 1960, a stray set of 165 cases were re-asked the party identification question in the 1956 post-election study as well. Estimates from this mini-sample are of course less stable than their counterparts in the four other waves. However, where comparisons are possible, they are so gracefully consistent with what can be learned from the pre- and post-1960 waves that we do not have much hesitation in using them to yield the additional degrees of freedom provided by a fifth wave. Naturally, in all relevant calculations, we take account of the fact that the points of observation are very unequally spaced in real time.

4. Actually, our detailed calculations show not only no shrinkage in the error variance, but if anything a slight absolute increase. Thus the decrease in reliability (or the proportion of true variance to total variance) has a double source.

5. Throughout this chapter we are providing mere "bottom-line" estimates that conceal more detailed consideration of angularities in the data. One such angularity being momentarily ignored in this statement, although dealt with in our calculations, is the presence of some systematic progression of the unreliability term across waves of the same panel.

6. There is one other pairing, also in civil rights, where a somewhat rougher match might be made. In the first panel, a question inspired by the FEPC legislation of the time asked about the appropriateness of the government attempting to ensure that Negroes get "fair treatment in jobs and housing." In the second panel, respondents were asked whether the government should make "every possible effort to improve the social and economic position of blacks and other minority groups." These are divergent questions, both in substance and in group of reference, although there is some obvious kinship between them. The first item was in four-point agree-disagree form; the second was in forced-choice, seven-point scale form. The average two-year continuity correlations in the first instance was .468; in the second, a somewhat higher .535.

7. We postpone consideration of the detailed partitioning of the issue items into reliability and stability components, since a proper treatment requires taking account of differing response variances in different population segments. However, it may be of interest to note that a simple partitioning of these issue items, ignoring the complications, suggests that the unreliability component of responses greatly outruns a true change component, just as was true for the original panel.

PART III: VOTE DETERMINANTS

9. WHAT DETERMINES THE VOTE?

A continuing question in voting behavior is what determines the vote. Are people's votes primarily issue-determined, with voters choosing between candidates on the basis of the great issues of the day—or, for that matter, the minor issues of the moment? Or are votes primarily based on reactions to political candidates? Is voting really party-based, with voters choosing on grounds of habitual affiliation with a particular party? Or is voting based on age-old social cleavages, such as class, religion, and ethnic divisions?

Much research has been devoted to sorting out the relative importance of these different causes of the vote. The early research typically found that party and candidate factors were the more important, with issues rarely playing much of a role. This conclusion was highly controversial, in part because voting on the basis of issues was deemed more "rational" by some observers than voting on the basis of candidate characteristics, partisan appeals, or group divisions—and these observers believed that political men and women were rational actors. It was eventually concluded, however, that issues are in fact important, but this opened the door to an interesting intellectual puzzle: could researchers sort out the relative contributions of parties, candidates, and issues? And since there are many issues, can researchers determine the contribution of each one, or at least of each type of issue? In this chapter we deal with two of these controversies: are issues important, and can we sort out the relative importance of different causes of the vote?

Absence of Issue Voting

The original view was that voting must be based on issues, since parties and candidates spend so much time during election campaigns discussing and debating issues. The early empirical voting studies, however, found that the public had a very limited knowledge of the issues, leading to the conclusion that other determinants must be more important.

The Columbia University studies of 1940 and 1948, for example, found that voters often decided how to vote before the campaign, and thus before issues were even raised. They found that voters often perceived the issue positions of candidates incorrectly, and thus concluded that issues could not be important. Similarly, *The American Voter* reported that on 16 different issues in 1956 only 18 to 36 percent of the electorate satisfied what the authors considered three prerequisites for issue voting: being familiar enough with the issues to have an opinion, knowing what the government is doing on the issue, and believing the parties differ on the issue. Converse's (1964) conclusion that some issues were marked by "nonattitudes," with respondents answering questions virtually randomly simply to satisfy the overinsistent interviewer, further emphasized the relative unimportance of issues in voting.

If voting was not issue-based, then social groups, party, and/or candidate factors must predominate. The Columbia research stressed the social group factors, as was discussed in the introduction to this book. Even today, many reports on elections give considerable attention to how different groups vote. But most students of American voting behavior agree that it is necessary to delve deeper into the voter's political attitudes in understanding the vote, rather than just to observe the person's demographics.

The American Voter was the first to emphasize the importance of party identification in the vote decision. Most Americans generally consider themselves either Republican or Democrat and vote accordingly in most elections. Not only is long-term partisanship a direct cause of the vote, but it also affects the way people view the candidates and the issues, which are short-term influences on the vote. In addition, the first causal modeling effort (Goldberg, 1966), discussed later, supported the view that partisanship was more significant than candidate evaluations or attitudes on issues.[1]

Some observers might view party voting as less rational than issue voting, but that need not be the case. If people initially choose to identify with a party because they generally agree with it on the issues, then they can use their party identification as a short cut in deciding how to vote at later elections without taking time to research all the issues. As we will see in later sections of this book, issues can also still be important in changing a person's partisanship. A person may change from one party to another if the latter provides better alternatives on the issues over the course of several elections. Thus issues retain some importance in this theory.

The Michigan studies have also emphasized the importance of candidates in voting decisions. After all, if issues are not important, and if partisanship and social group factors are stable, then the dramatic changes in the vote from one election to the next must be the result of the changing cast of candidates. This conclusion was first reached by Stokes (1966) in a statistical decomposition of voting results that was later updated through 1980 by Miller and Wattenberg (1981). The Michigan surveys included a set of questions asking people what they liked and disliked about both major parties and presidential nominees. The responses were categorized in terms of six components of the vote: attitudes toward the Republican candidate, the Democratic candidate, domestic issues, foreign issues, parties as managers of government, and group-related issues. Statistical analysis of these responses showed that the group factor was strongly pro-Democratic throughout this period. The domestic issue component favored the Democrats through 1964, but the Republicans gained the advantage in the Nixon campaigns and in 1980. Party performance and foreign issues helped the Republicans (except in Barry Goldwater's 1964 campaign), though the impact of party performance was negligible after 1964 (and foreign policy had minimal impact in 1976). The most significant variation, however, was in the candidate factor, which varied from very strongly pro-Republican in 1956, when Dwight Eisenhower was reelected in a landslide, to very strongly Democratic in 1964, when Lyndon Johnson gained his landslide victory. The candidate factor clearly provided the dynamism of electoral politics. According to this analysis, the Republicans have been able to win the White House so frequently since the 1950s, despite the Democratic lead in party identification, largely because they generally have managed to nominate better-appreciated candidates.

Is the importance of the candidate factor necessarily an indication that voters are not capable of dealing with political issues—or of voter "irrationality," as it was phrased in the 1960s? Not really. If the candidate factor simply reflected whether or not the voter liked the candidate's smile, then the candidate emphasis would represent nonsubstantive voting. However, it is fully reasonable to vote on the basis of *some* candidate characteristics—for example, whether a candidate is seen as competent to carry out his or her issue promises. And studies indicate that reactions to candidates are generally of this type. For example, Popkin, Gorman, Phillips, and Smith's (1976) analysis of George McGovern's 1972 defeat showed that his loss was due more to concerns about his competence than to his position on the issues. As a result, it is important to disentangle the separate dimensions underlying the candidate factor. Markus's (1982) analysis of new candidate trait questions, included in the 1980 election study, showed that candidate competence and candidate integrity are separate, independent dimensions of reactions to presidential candidates. Voting on the basis of the competence or integrity of the candidate is certainly rational, even though it is not issue voting.

The major theme of voting studies in the mid-1960s was thus the irrelevance of issues. A careful rereading of these studies makes clear that the authors realized that issues *could be* more important at other points in history, that issues can be important in ways other than directly influencing the vote, and that over the long term a person's party identification can change in response to the issues. However, the usual impression of the early literature is that voters in any single election followed the irrational appeals of party and candidates rather than rationally considering the issues. In short, voters were fools.

The Prevalence of Issue Voting

But are voters fools in any one election? The importance of issues has been emphasized most by those observers who want to view the voter as a rational political actor and who view issue voting as more rational than voting on the basis of party or candidate considerations. As pointed out in the preceding pages, it is often entirely rational to employ party and candidate considerations in deciding how to cast a vote, though the more general conclusion is that issue voting best demonstrates the seriousness of the citizen when choosing how to cast his or her vote. The first chapter of this book gives an outline of the rational voter approach, particularly Downs's (1957) work. Briefly, rational voters would be expected to calculate how much they differ from each candidate on the issues and then vote for the candidate to whom they are closest. This approach is incorporated in the Page and Jones and the Markus and Converse chapters in this section, though with differences between the researchers on how important such issue calculations turn out to be.

The first empirical work to argue that voters are calculating observers was a posthumous book by V. O. Key, Jr. (1966), *The Responsible Electorate.* Key argued that vote change between elections was the result of voter satisfaction or dissatisfaction with the performance of the administration. As an example, three-fifths of the 1956 Eisenhower voters who became dissatisfied with Eisenhower's performance as president voted for John F. Kennedy in 1960. According to Key, this showed that "voters are not fools"—they can vote on the basis of issues, and particularly on the basis of their satisfaction (or dissatisfaction) with the administration. While Key's emphasis on issues led to important reexamination of this subject by political scientists, his own evidence had limitations. It relied on respondents' recall of how they voted in the preceding election, a recall that is not always accurate. In addition, Key's research did not handle a problem known as "projection"—people may decide how to vote on grounds unrelated to administration performance, but then report satisfaction or dissatisfaction with the incumbent administration so as to be consistent with that planned vote. This problem is most apparent when Key's data (1966, p. 46) showed that voters who were dissatisfied with the Roosevelt farm policy were most likely to switch their votes in 1940, though few historians would regard that election as a major referendum on agriculture.

Key's book also introduced an important concept into the issue literature. He reminded us that issues would be important only when the parties (or candidates) differed on them. He called this the "echo chamber effect," where the electorate can just echo back whatever alternatives they are provided. If the candidates do not really differ on the issues, then they will be unimportant, as was the case in the election of 1956. On the other hand, when candidates present stark issue contrasts, as in the 1964 and 1972 elections, then the electorate does indeed respond. From Key's perspective, then, the lack of issue voting is not a fault of the electorate; it is a fault of a party system that does not provide the electorate with real issue choices.[2]

Key's emphasis on the importance of issue clarity was further amplified by subsequent examination of the role of "candidate ambiguity" in campaigns, as in the selection from Page and Brody (Chapter 11). Page and Brody accept Key's point that issues can be important in an election only when there are issue differences in the campaign. They look at the controversy over the Vietnam War— a likely candidate for the major issue of the 1968 presidential campaign. In fact, the Michigan election surveys found it to be unimportant. In an analysis of campaign speeches, Page and Brody show that candidates Richard Nixon and Hubert Humphrey both gave ambiguous messages regarding their positions on the war. In the portion of their work reprinted here, their analysis of mass surveys shows that this ambiguity led to perceptions of minor differences between the two candidates. In this vacuum of objective information, subjective processes predominated. They show that partisans who were anti-war tended to think that their party's nominee was dovish, while those who favored a militaristic solution tended to think their party's nominee agreed with them. Issues are not important when the candidates are purposely ambiguous. By the 1972 election there were unambiguous candidate differences on Vietnam; correspondingly, analysis (Abramson, Aldrich, and Rohde, 1983, chap. 6) shows the war played a more important role in voting that year.

In sharp contrast to the lack of clear distinction between Nixon and Humphrey on the Vietnam War issue, Converse, Miller, Rusk, and Wolfe (1969) showed that the George Wallace third-party candidacy in 1968 was an issue candidacy. Wallace was the governor who had resisted federal efforts to desegregate Alabama schools. His anti-establishment issue stances were effectively communicated to the public, as evidenced by higher correlations between thermometer ratings and issue positions on civil rights, law and order, and Vietnam for Wallace than for Nixon or Humphrey. (Converse, Miller, Rusk, and Wolfe also showed that the anti-Vietnam war candidacy of Eugene McCarthy in the early primaries actually received considerable support from Democrats who wanted a more militaristic solution to the war than that of incumbent president Lyndon Johnson. McCarthy's primary votes were interpreted as anti-war, but apparently voters were voting against the incumbent without necessarily supporting the issue positions of his challenger.)

Whereas Key used Gallup data for his evidence on issue voting and Brody and Page used specially commissioned surveys, RePass (1971) made use of the Michigan data in his reconsideration of issue importance. RePass pointed out that the Michigan findings of low issue voting were based on questions that did not really concern issues. When respondents were asked what they liked and disliked about the parties and candidates, their attention was being directed away from issues. Consequently, the low level of issue responses should not be a surprise. Even when the voters were asked about issues, they were all asked about the same issues, and ones decided on in advance by the questionnaire writers rather than by the voters themselves. According to Converse's (1964) discussion of "issue publics," one would expect that different citizens would be most concerned about different issues—Americans of eastern European descent would be concerned about foreign policy with respect to that region of the world, and so on. Yet the evidence against issue voting was largely based on the assumption that the same issues should concern everyone. RePass instead made use of a question asking people to name the "most important problems" facing the government in Washington. He found that people listed problems, perceived party differences on those problems, and recognized party positions on those issues fairly accurately. He found that issues were about as important as party in 1964, but in the absence of proper questions he could not tell whether this would have been true in the elections studied in *The American Voter*. This shows that not even the 1964 election provided Johnson an issue mandate on any single issue.

In contrast to RePass's methodological focus, which might alter the interpretation of the 1950s, Pomper's (1972) was more substantive and was directed to change over time. Pomper's analysis of the 1956-1968 surveys showed that issues became more important after 1960. Beginning in 1964 there were large differences in the proportions of Democrats and Republicans who took liberal positions on issues, more people perceived differences between the parties on the issues, and more people perceived the Democrats as more liberal on those issues. Pomper explained this change as the result of greater differences between the parties in the 1960s than in the 1950s, an explanation in keeping with Key's echo chamber argument.

This evidence was somewhat controversial. Margolis (1977) showed that large numbers of respondents were not asked the questions that Pomper was analyzing because they were not at all familiar with the issues involved. Nevertheless, a large volume of work—epitomized by *The Changing American Voter* (Nie, Verba, and Petrocik, 1976)—supported the proposition that the public became more issue-oriented in the 1960s. Times had changed. The politically quiescent 1950s was followed by a turbulent decade marked by the Civil Rights revolution, urban riots, and a land war in Vietnam and its accompanying protest. The issues still would not matter if the candidates took ambiguous stands, as in 1968, but in general the importance of issues seemed to have increased.

There were several major restatements of the importance of issues in voting in the late 1970s and early 1980s. The first was by Carmines and Stimson in their paper excerpted in this section (Chapter 12). It makes an interesting distinction between "hard" and "easy" issues. Hard issues (like the pace of withdrawal from Vietnam in the 1972 election) are more difficult for voters to comprehend than are easy ones, so hard issues will be important only for voters with high levels of political information, while easy issues will be important for voters with high levels of information as well as for those with low information levels. Carmines and Stimson argue that there is a large amount of issue voting when easy issues are involved in an election. They use the racial issue as an example of an easy issue, arguing that it had a major impact on some recent elections even though it was not raised explicitly. Finally, they claim that realignments are more likely to occur around easy issues. In their more recent work (Carmines and Stimson, 1989) they suggest that a realignment occurred in the 1960s and 1970s around the racial issue.

A second major recent statement of the importance of issues is Fiorina's (1981b) analysis of "retrospective voting." Fiorina distinguishes between prospective voting, in which citizens vote for the candidate or party making the best promises for the future, and retrospective voting, in which citizens vote on the basis of past party performance. With an argument reminiscent of Downs's, Fiorina claims that it is rational for citizens to vote against a party when it has not performed well in office, using such retrospective assessments to make inferences about prospective performances by that party. Indeed, it may be more rational to vote retrospectively than to cast a prospective vote on the basis of campaign promises that the candidate may not keep.

Fiorina models the vote as a function of retrospective evaluations and future expectations,[3] with past partisanship (in the previous election) controlled. His results emphasize the importance of the retrospective terms, both directly and working through future evaluations. For example, Fiorina finds evaluations of Gerald Ford's presidential performance, feelings about the Nixon pardon, future expectations about inflation and unemployment, relative trust of Carter and Ford, and a judgment about which has the most appropriate presidential personality to have significant effects on the vote in 1976 once 1974 partisanship is controlled, where future economic expectations are based on retrospective evaluations of the government's economic performance and evaluations of Ford's presidential performance are "mediated" retrospective evaluations. Miller and Wattenberg (1981) offered a retrospective interpretation of the 1980 election, arguing that Reagan won more out of citizen dissatisfaction with Carter's performance (retrospective voting) than out of a preference for Reagan's conservative policy promises (prospective voting).

A third major restatement of the role of issues has to do with the importance of economic issues. This work itself has generated a considerable amount of controversy (see Niemi and Weisberg, 1992), which we shall not review here. In any case, whether stated in terms of easy issues, retrospective voting, or economic determinants, there is much greater emphasis on the role of issues in voting today than there was a few decades ago. Indeed, we think that the role of issues is one controversy that has been largely settled. Few political scientists would now characterize the electorate as always issueless or as chronically unequipped to deal with issues (whether due to intelligence or interest). Particular campaigns may be more or less issue-oriented, and some candidates and some voters stress issues more than others. But there is no doubt that issues often play an important role in elections, especially in salient campaigns, such as for the presidency. Having arrived at this conclusion, however, does not settle all disagreements about issue voting, as we shall see in the next section.

The Relative Importance of Parties, Candidates, and Issues

Rather than just debate whether or not issues are important in influencing individual voting decisions, some researchers have tried to disentangle the relative influences of party, candidate, and issue factors. A causal model of the vote decision that attempted to do just this was first offered by Goldberg (1966) for the 1956 election. Partisanship was portrayed as affecting issue positions, candidate evaluations, and the vote; issue positions were seen as affecting both candidate evaluations and the vote; and candidate evaluations affected the vote. Goldberg found the candidate factor to be much more important than issues. Partisanship, however, was the most important causal factor, both directly and indirectly through its effects on the way people viewed the candidates and the issues.[4] Hartwig, Jenkins, and Temchin (1980) extended Goldberg's analysis to all of the elections between 1956 and 1976. The importance of issues increased over time, while partisanship correspondingly declined in importance, though neither changed as sharply as Schulman and

Pomper (1975) reported when they looked at only three of these elections. This work heartened those who were looking for issue effects on voting, while providing added evidence to those who were arguing that the American party system was dealigning (see also the discussion of the declining relationship of party to vote in this period in the reading by Nie in Chapter 23). Still, summing direct and indirect effects, the issue factor was always the least important of the three, and party always first.

This early causal model of the vote soon proved more simplistic than our evolving theoretical understanding of voting. For one thing, its emphasis on determining the relative importance of party, candidate, and issue factors ignores the fact that they do not operate separately. It is difficult to disentangle their separate effects, and their combined effects may be of greater interest. For example, dissatisfaction with an incumbent's handling of a problem could be both a candidate and an issue factor at once, as could concern with the competence of a challenger to handle a particular issue. Thus, concern with McGovern's "foolish" proposals in 1972 (such as his proposal to give every person in the United States one thousand dollars) or concern with Carter's competence (his inability to get the hostages out of Iran) were simultaneously candidate and issue factors, and any attempt to allocate them to just one category is artificial.

Furthermore, the early causal model of the vote was simplistic in treating causation as unidirectional. It did not explore the effects of voting on partisanship (which will be examined more carefully in a later section of this book) or the effects of candidate orientation on issue views. Brody and Page, in the excerpt in Chapter 10, show that the relationship between issue position and voting could actually be the result of two psychological processes—projection and persuasion— instead of actual policy voting. True policy voting occurs when voters first decide their own issue stands and then choose to vote for the candidate nearest them on the issues. Projection occurs when voters just assume their preferred candidate agrees with them on the issues, whereas persuasion occurs when voters modify their own issue positions to conform to those of the candidate they support. As Brody and Page show, the confounding effects of projection and persuasion must be removed to determine the true magnitude of issue voting. Beyond that, projection and persuasion effects are interesting to study in their own right, since they represent the combined effects of candidate and issue factors working together, a sort of interactive effect that was missed in the early causal models. Because Goldberg's causal model assumed only unidirectional causation with issue position affecting candidate evaluation but not vice versa, he was unable to test for projection and persuasion effects.

To test for reciprocal causation requires moving beyond the "recursive" (one-way) causal models to more complicated "nonrecursive" (two-way) models. Moving beyond one-way causation models is complicated in that regular regression analysis ("ordinary least squares") cannot be employed. Instead, a special "simultaneous equation" procedure is required, adding predictors which would affect one of the variables caught in the reciprocal causation but not the other (such as finding demographic variables that theoretically will affect partisanship but not issue position or candidate evaluation directly). These are termed "exogenous" variables in that they are outside the model. They affect variables inside the model but are not themselves affected.

Jackson (1975b) provided the first such model of the vote decision in 1964, with party identification both affecting and being affected by candidate evaluations. He found that partisanship is affected by evaluations of the candidates on the issues, so that treating partisanship as a wholly exogenous variable, as done in earlier causal models, was incorrect. Even his model, however, did not allow for the impact of candidate evaluations on issue positions.

The readings in this section by Page and Jones and by Markus and Converse are state-of-the-art causal models of the vote decision. The Page and Jones chapter (13) analyzes 1972 and 1976 data. Their model permits a full range of reciprocal relations between party, candidate, and issue terms, while recognizing the further direct impact of the candidate's personal characteristics on the candidate evaluation. As noted, the only way to determine the relative importance of the reciprocal paths is to include some exogenous variables in the model. For example, Equation 2 in Page and Jones's reading assumes that the respondent's relative closeness to the two candidates is affected by the respondent's race, age, sex, education, and income. These demographic variables, however, are assumed not to affect directly the respondent's relative evaluations of the candidates or current partisanship. They treat the vote as a function of only relative candidate evaluation, feeling that any increase in explanation that partisanship would provide is just a reflection of the imperfections of the candidate rating data that underlie the relative candidate evaluation calculation. Comparative candidate evaluations are found to affect comparative policy evaluations, showing that projection, persuasion, and other rationalization mechanisms do affect the issue term in voting models. The issue factor was found to be most important in 1976, with personal qualities of the candidates a close second, and partisanship third. By contrast, in the "clear choice" election of 1972, the issue factor predominated so much so that the other variables provide little further explanation.

The Markus and Converse chapter (14) employs the more powerful 1972-1974-1976 panel study to examine the determinants of voting in 1976. By using panel data, Markus and Converse can incorporate reciprocal causal effects through lagging variables. For example, they can assume that issue stands at one point in time affect issue stands at a later time. They are also able to model both projection and persuasion effects, seeing how respondents' issue stands at an earlier time are affected by their candidate evaluations. They find projection effects to be low but significant, persuasion effects on three of their five issues, and projection a fifth stronger than persuasion. Candidate evaluations are found to depend on perceived candidate personalities, partisanship (which also has a substantial indirect effect through perceived candidate personalities), and issues. Vote is portrayed as basically dependent on candidate evaluation, with partisanship having a direct impact only when respondents are fairly neutral between the candidates.

The Markus and Converse methodology is more complicated than that of most previous studies because it includes lagged variables and interaction terms in many of its equations. This may make their study more appropriate than previous studies, but it also makes its results harder to interpret. Fortunately, Markus and Converse generally include extra tables to help interpret the results. For example, Table 14-1 in their chapter can be used to understand their findings on the determinants of 1976 party identification. According to their Equation 6, partisanship in 1976 is affected by the respondent's partisanship in 1972 as well as by whether and how the respondent voted in 1972. The table shows that 1976 partisanship is predicted to be most Democratic (as indicated by the most negative value in the table) for those strong Democrats in 1972 who voted for McGovern in that year.[5] Strong Democrats who did not vote in 1972 were somewhat less Democratic in their 1976 identification, while strong Democrats who voted for Nixon in 1972 were even less Democratic in their 1976 identification. All in all, looking down the columns of Table 14-1, whether and how people voted in 1972 affected their 1976 partisanship by less than a point (on the seven-point partisanship scale). By contrast, looking across the rows of that table, a person's 1976 partisanship is determined more by his or her 1972 partisanship, with more than a three point difference between 1972 strong Democrats and strong Republicans in 1976 partisanship, regardless of how they voted in 1972.

The differences in results of these two chapters for the 1976 election reflect the difficulties inherent in such modeling. A large number of decisions must be made as to which variables affect which others and how to operationalize the variables with questions from the surveys. The exact specification and operationalization decisions have a great effect on the results of simultaneous equation modeling. The Page and Jones piece is particularly sensitive to the choice of exogenous variables. For example, shouldn't race be affecting partisanship in their model as well as policy preferences, since blacks are much more Democratic in their partisanship than are whites? The Markus and Converse piece is similarly sensitive to its modeling assumptions. For example, if short-term effects on party identification are to be *tested*, shouldn't short-term effects on partisanship be included explicitly in their model as well as long-term effects? Also, the models incorporate partisanship in very different ways and operationalize the issue factor differently. Finally, the results differ in that Page and Jones treat candidate evaluation as equivalent to the vote, while Markus and Converse are interested in the increment that partisanship adds when the person is approximately indifferent between the candidates.

What is equally important, though, is to emphasize the similarities between these two efforts. They agree that a simultaneous equation approach is necessary. They both recognize the existence of projection and persuasion effects, though only Markus and Converse are able to provide separate estimates of each. They both represent much more complex attempts to incorporate party, candidate, and issue factors into a model of voting than did the previous models, though Markus and Converse find candidate characteristics to have the largest direct effect on candidate evaluations in 1976 while Page and Jones find issues of greater importance.

In a later study, Markus (1982) used panel data for 1980 to develop a dynamic model of the vote decision in that year. Projection effects are again evident, while persuasion effects are not. Evaluations of both Jimmy Carter and Ronald Reagan were strongly affected by their perceived competence. Candidate integrity also was important as regards evaluations of Reagan, whereas dissatisfaction with Carter's performance strongly detracted from ratings of Carter. Issues in the sense of policy distances also worked against Carter to a small degree, but dissatisfaction with Carter's performance (which Markus treats as an issue factor) was the dominant influence.

It is important to note that these statistical decompositions of the vote themselves became controversial in the 1980s as political psychologists applied modern social psychological ideas to the voting decision. For example, a number of authors reexamined how voters react to political candidates (Abelson, Kinder, Peters, and Fiske, 1982; Lodge, McGraw, and Stroh, 1989; Marcus, 1988), while Rahn, Aldrich, Borgida, and Sullivan (1990) constructed a model of the vote from a cognitive perspective.

Conclusion

As noted, one controversy about issue voting has been resolved. Issues are often important, and voters are capable of deciding on the basis of them. However, in the mid-1970s one would also have guessed that a clear judgment on the relative importance (both within and across elections) of the determinants of voting would be obtained as soon as better data and more powerful analysis techniques were employed. Now that has been done, but without achieving any consensus as to the relative importance of the different voting determinants. Indeed, what we have learned is that it is a false question to ask how party candidates and issue factors act independently.

As is now apparent, the use of more complicated models and better data do not necessarily provide definitive conclusions. Instead, these models prove very dependent on their exact assumptions, whether these are the simultaneous equations models of Page and Jones and Markus and Converse, or the economic models. A different set of assumptions would yield different results. Similarly, a different set of operational indicators could yield different results. The models are always going to be vulnerable to these matters of assumption and operationalization, and so consensus now seems beyond reach.

At the same time, there is growing agreement on some considerations beyond the fact that issues can be important. Researchers who construct individual-level models now accept that rationalization processes affect the measurement of policy voting, and they agree that projection is more common than persuasion. Voters are more likely to assume the candidate they like agrees with their issue positions than to accept the issue positions of the candidate they like. The results also show that effects are reciprocal, so that simple one-way causation models no longer suffice.

There remains more disagreement, however, on the importance of partisanship. Some models find major partisanship effects (and the dynamic models are most likely to do so), other models find minor partisanship effects, and some models omit the partisan term completely. Also, the original emphasis on determining the relative importance of party, candidate, and issue factors may have been misplaced. As we have seen, they do not necessarily operate separately (as in the case of projection and persuasion effects), and they can be difficult to disentangle. Beyond this, the more complex causal models of the vote are more interesting in terms of development of a theory of voting than are simplistic attempts to separate party, candidate, and issue factors. Thus, we are left with indeterminacy, but at the same time we have available some very useful attempts to construct general models of voting.

Finally, we note the fact that research on voting in other nations differs in several respects from the type of analysis discussed here. For one thing, the candidate factor is typically given much less attention, especially for countries in which the public votes for members of parliament rather than directly for a president or prime minister. This difference makes concern over reciprocal causation between issue position and candidate evaluation less serious. At the same time, there is more interest in other countries in the impact of social characteristics on the vote. The party system in many of these countries is based on social distinctions, which Lipset and Rokkan (1967a) argue reflect the cleavages of earlier days—among them center-periphery (including linguistic conflicts), and state-church, land-industry, and owner-worker cleavages. Often researchers feel that partisanship need not be considered per se, since it is simply a reflection of these social cleavages. The relevance of party identification will be taken up further in Chapter 21.

NOTES

1. Causal modeling is a statistical procedure for determining the relative importance of independent variables in explaining a dependent variable; this procedure is particularly useful when complicated causal linkages are hypothesized (such as a recursive system in which one variable causes two others, and all three of these variables cause the ultimate dependent variable).
2. Downs's (1957) spatial model of party competition shows that, under specified assumptions, the optimal issue positions of the parties converge to the median voter's position, so rational behavior by the parties can lead to their not offering real choices to the electorate. Ambiguity is useful for politicians, in that more voters can then think those politicians agree with them on the issues (see especially Page, 1978).
3. Fiorina differentiates between two types of retrospective evaluations. Simple retrospective evaluations (SRE) include the person's satisfaction with such things as personal financial situation, foreign policy, civil rights, and so on. By contrast, mediated retrospective evaluations (MRE) are summary judgments that are influenced by the respondent's prior dispositions and information sources. MREs include evaluation of presidential performance and government economic performance. They are affected by the SREs and by prior partisanship. Fiorina also makes allowance for future expectations (FE), such as which party the voter expects to handle economic problems better in the next four years, which presumably are based on retrospective evaluations and partisanship.
4. Also, Goldberg concluded his paper with a detailed discussion of how to test the relative importance of these factors correctly if appropriate data were available, a discussion

which proved to be very close to what Markus and Converse (chap. 14) did when such data became available.

5. The value of this entry can be calculated from the results the authors present for Equation 6. Remember that they scored partisanship -3 (strong Democrat) to $+3$ (strong Republican), voting 0 (abstainers) and 1 (voters), and Democratic and Republican voters 0 (No) and 1 (Yes). Then for a strong Democrat who voted for McGovern, ID $1976 = -.37 - .20(1) + .49(0) + (.63 + .10(1))$ $(-3) = -.37 - .20 + (.73) (-3) = -2.76$.

FURTHER READINGS

The Role of Issues

V. O. Key, Jr., *The Responsible Electorate* (Cambridge, Mass.: Harvard University Press, 1966). Began the reconsideration of issues.

David E. RePass, "Issue Salience and Party Choice," *American Political Science Review* (1971) 65:389-400. Issue importance depends on how questions are asked.

John H. Kessel, "The Issues in Issue Importance," *American Political Science Review* (1972) 66:459-65. Alternative interpretations of findings showing increased issue importance.

Gerald M. Pomper, "From Confusion to Clarity: Issues and American Voters, 1956-1968," *American Political Science Review* (1972) 66:415-28. Voters increasingly perceive consistency between parties and issue positions.

Michael Margolis, "From Confusion to Confusion: Issues and the American Voter (1956-1972)," *American Political Science Review* (1977) 71:31-43. Challenges interpretations of a more issue-oriented electorate.

Benjamin I. Page, *Choices and Echoes in Presidential Elections* (Chicago: University of Chicago Press, 1978). Emphasizes role of ambiguity of candidate positions in elections.

Bo Särlvik and Ivor Crewe, *Decade of Dealignment* (Cambridge, England: Cambridge University Press, 1983). Decomposition of importance of specific issues in change in voting results from 1974 to 1979 British elections.

Edward R. Tufte, *Political Control of the Economy* (Princeton, N.J.: Princeton University Press, 1978). Voting on the basis of economics, with the argument that the government manipulates the economy to improve its chances for reelection.

D. Roderick Kiewiet, *Macroeconomics and Micropolitics: The Electoral Effects of Economic Issues* (Chicago: University of Chicago Press, 1983). Personal and especially national economic experiences influence voting behavior.

The Role of Candidates

Donald E. Stokes, "Some Dynamic Elements of Contests for the Presidency," *American Political Science Review* (1966) 60:19-28. Candidates provide the main reason for voting change between elections.

Herbert F. Weisberg and Jerrold G. Rusk, "Dimensions of Candidate Evaluation," *American Political Science Review* (1970) 64:1167-85. First empirical analysis of candidate competition space.

Statistical Models of the Vote Decision

Morris P. Fiorina, *Retrospective Voting in American National Elections* (New Haven, Conn.: Yale University Press, 1981). Development of the ideas of retrospective voting and party identification as a running tally of partisan evaluations.

Analysis of Vote Determinants in Other Countries

Kendall L. Baker, Russell J. Dalton, and Kai Hildebrandt, *Germany Transformed* (Cambridge, Mass.: Harvard University Press, 1981). Causal analysis of vote determinants in Germany in 1960s and 1970s.

Vote Prediction

Stanley Kelley, Jr., and Thad W. Mirer, "The Simple Act of Voting," *American Political Science Review* (1974) 68:572-91. Develops simple predictor of the vote and compares it with other predictors.

Spatial Modeling of Political Competition

Anthony Downs, *An Economic Theory of Democracy* (New York: Harper and Row, 1957), especially chap. 8. This was the first work on spatial modeling.

Donald E. Stokes, "Spatial Models of Party Competition," *American Political Science Review* (1963) 57:368-77. Leading critique of Downs's analysis.

Otto A. Davis, Melvin J. Hinich, and Peter C. Ordeshook, "An Expository Development of a Mathematical Model of the Electoral Process," *American Political Science Review* (1970) 64:426-48. Nonmathematical statement of early multidimensional spatial model.

William H. Riker and Peter C. Ordeshook, *An Introduction to Positive Political Theory* (Englewood Cliffs, N.J.: Prentice-Hall, 1973), chaps. 11, 12. Summary of work on spatial modeling.

10. THE ASSESSMENT OF POLICY VOTING

Richard A. Brody and Benjamin I. Page

The voter has the option of voting or of abstaining; if he votes, he chooses among candidates. By "policy voting" we mean the extent to which these behaviors are caused by the voter acting in accord with his policy preferences. The question with which we are here concerned is: How do we know whether and to what extent "policy voting" has taken place in a given election? The process of obtaining this knowledge is what we mean by the "assessment of policy voting.". . .

A Question of What Causes What

If it is true . . . that voters vote for the candidates proximal to them on the issues, then the processes relevant to the perception of that proximity become pertinent in assessing the extent of policy voting. These processes are pertinent because we may wish to exclude from our definition of policy voting some behaviors which they describe.

Consider the elements of the model depicted in Figure 10-1: If we relax the assumption of recursivity [one-way causation] and permit the voter's evaluations of the candidates (or his vote) to cause his perceptions of their stands or his own policy position or both, we can distinguish three "proximity" processes. . . .

The first process, "Policy Oriented Evaluation," is depicted in Figure 10-1. It describes the cases in which the prior held policy position of the voter and his perceptions of the candidates' positions (which are presumably independent of each other) *cause* his evaluation. Thus, in the slice of time considered by this model or covered in a cross-sectional survey, the voter's position and perception are invariant, and evaluations vary in accord with the issue proximities.

Suppose we change the invariant elements of this model: If perceptions and evaluations were invariant and the respondent's own position yielded to or formed around the position he believed was held by the candidate he favored (or intended

Source: *American Political Science Review* (1972) 66:450-58. Reprinted with permission of the publisher.

Figure 10-1 Necessary and Sufficient Conditions for Policy Voting

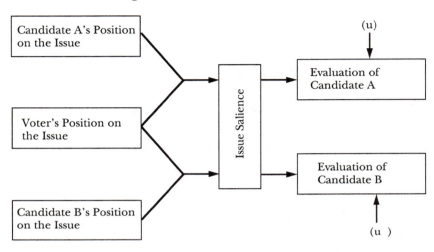

to vote for), we would say that the voter had been "persuaded" by the candidate. "Persuasion" may be a perfectly legitimate political process, but in the slice of time being considered here, it is an effect of, not a cause of, candidate evaluation. In these terms, we cannot say that the voter who is persuaded is evaluating or voting on the basis of policy.

The third process stems from allowing the perceived position of the candidate to vary with the voter's own position and his evaluation of the candidate. Under this model, a voter could see a candidate as close to himself on an issue because he otherwise felt positive about the candidate, and he could see other candidates as distant from him on the issue(s) because he felt negative about them for other reasons. In other words, a voter would "project" his own (or a nearby) stand into candidates he favored. We are reluctant to call those who project "policy voters."

Both persuasion and projection have been found to operate in the American electorate. Berelson, Lazarsfeld, and McPhee (1954, pp. 220-22) found these processes operating on policy stands as clear as President Truman's position on Taft-Hartley repeal; we found them operating on the less clear Vietnam policy positions of candidates Nixon and Humphrey in 1968 (Page and Brady, 1972).

The presence of these two "alternate" processes in the electoral system makes it inappropriate to declare policy-oriented evaluation *the* cause of the correspondence between issue proximity and voting behavior. We need some means for examining the potential for "persuasion" and for "projection" and of estimating them as separate processes. . . .

11. POLICY VOTING AND THE ELECTORAL PROCESS: THE VIETNAM WAR ISSUE

Benjamin I. Page and Richard A. Brody

Most theories which hold that the preferences of the public affect policy making are predicated on the assumption that elections link opinions with policies. Electoral links, in turn, are thought to depend upon the ability of citizens to take account of their policy preferences when deciding how to vote. For that reason "issue voting" has been a focus of research by scholars concerned with empirical democratic theory. . . .

The Study

The 1968 presidential election, coming at the height of the war in Vietnam, offered an opportunity to examine these questions. . . .

Beginning in February 1968, we commissioned a series of nationwide opinion surveys, designed primarily to discover how Vietnam entered into public perceptions and evaluations of presidential candidates, and into the final voting decision.[1] In addition, the Survey Research Center of the University of Michigan, carrying out its usual election study for the Inter-University Consortium for Political Research, agreed to include some of our key items in its questionnaire. The November 1968 findings reported in this paper come from our analysis of the SRC data; findings concerning previous months are drawn from the ORC/IEP surveys.

In each survey, respondents were asked to indicate what Vietnam policy they preferred, on a seven-point rating scale. The scale was introduced by a prologue in which it was stated that opinions about Vietnam differed; some people favored all necessary measures to achieve a complete military victory; others favored immediate American withdrawal from Vietnam; and others, of course, had opinions somewhere in between. The interviewer then displayed a printed card with the numbers 1 through 7 arrayed at equal intervals along a line. Point number 1 was labeled "immediate withdrawal," and point number 7 "complete

Source: *American Political Science Review* (1972) 66:979-95. Reprinted with permission of the publisher.

military victory." Other points were designated only by numbers. Respondents were then asked where on this scale they would place themselves, or whether they had no opinion. . . .

We examined the relationship between votes for Richard Nixon and Hubert Humphrey in 1968, and Vietnam policy preferences, as measured on our seven-point scale and by a similar three-alternative item. It is apparent that Vietnam policy preferences did not have a great effect on voting for the major party candidates in 1968. . . . We are left, however, with the question of why such a potent issue had so little effect on voting. . . .

The average American perceived Nixon and Humphrey as standing very close together on the escalation/de-escalation dimension. With seven distinct points to choose from, in fact, the average perceptions of Nixon's and Humphrey's positions on the Vietnam scale were only one-third of one point apart. . . .

In order to explain the widespread failure to perceive a difference between the candidates, it is not necessary—at least in this case—to postulate that people were unable to perceive clearly. The candidates' campaign speeches reveal that there was, in fact, rather little difference between Nixon's and Humphrey's stated positions on Vietnam policy. . . .

Candidate Ambiguity and Policy Voting

The similarity between Humphrey's and Nixon's Vietnam positions can account for an absence of Vietnam voting among more than half of the voters—those who didn't see much difference between the two. But what of the large minority of voters who did perceive a difference of two or more points on the seven-point scale? Did they vote their Vietnam preferences? If so, why didn't they bring about a strong relationship between opinion and vote in the population as a whole?

Part of the answer is apparent when we look at the full distribution of perceptions. Those who saw a big difference between the candidates' positions were quite unable to agree which candidate was more of a hawk, and which more of a dove. To be sure, the majority considered Nixon more hawklike, but over one-third thought that Humphrey was more of a hawk than Nixon.

Among those who thought Humphrey more hawklike than Nixon, the tendency [of hawks to vote for Nixon, doves for Humphrey] was reversed: hawks voted strongly for Humphrey, and doves for Nixon. These people of course counterbalanced some of the doves who voted for Humphrey and hawks who voted for Nixon. Their effect was to decrease the relationship. It does not follow, however, that Americans voted their Vietnam preferences to a greater extent than indicated. On the contrary, most people's perceptions were too confused to play a part in voting decisions.

Those who saw a big difference between Humphrey and Nixon—a difference in either direction—were generally perceiving each candidate as standing wherever they wanted him to stand. They projected their own opinions onto their favored candidate. Among Republicans, who mostly favored Nixon, extreme hawks thought that Nixon was an extreme hawk; extreme doves thought

Table 11-1   Projection of Nixon's Vietnam Position by Republicans Who Saw a Substantial Difference Between Nixon and Humphrey

Perception of Nixon's Stand	*Policy Preference on Vietnam*					
	Immediate Withdrawal				*Complete Military Victory*	
Immediate Withdrawal	20% (4)	0 (0)	0 (0)	0 (0)	0 (0)	3 (4)
	55 (11)	42 (10)	19 (5)	4 (1)	14 (3)	25 (30)
	20 (4)	25 (6)	54 (14)	7 (2)	9 (2)	23 (28)
	0 (0)	33 (8)	23 (6)	89 (25)	55 (12)	43 (51)
Complete Military Victory	5 (1)	0 (0)	4 (1)	0 (0)	23 (5)	6 (7)
	17 (20)	20 (24)	22 (26)	23 (28)	18 (22)	100 (120)

Note: Tau b = .50. Correlation ratio (eta) = .376. This table is based on Republicans who voted and who perceived a difference of more than one point on the Vietnam scale between Nixon's position and Humphrey's. Scores of "2" and "3" and of "5" and "6" on the seven-point scale have been combined.

he was an extreme dove; and those in the middle thought that Nixon stood in the middle! The relationship between opinion and perception was quite strong. (See Table 11-1.) Similarly, among Democrats, extreme hawks tended to think Humphrey was an extreme hawk; extreme doves thought Humphrey an extreme dove; and those in the middle thought he stood in the middle.[2] (See Table 11-2.) Moreover, Republicans tended to perceive Humphrey as taking a position quite different from their own opinion.[3]

Many of those who saw a big difference between Nixon and Humphrey, in other words, were responding to their own wishes. Their perceptions were the result of intended vote, not the cause. These people were not engaged in policy voting.

This finding does not, on its face, cast great credit upon the American voter: it seems to support the view that voters are ignorant and incapable of rational political decisions. Again, however, it is not necessary to rely entirely upon an

Table 11-2 Projection of Humphrey's Vietnam Position by Democrats Who Saw a Substantial Difference Between Nixon and Humphrey

	Policy Preference on Vietnam					
Perception of Humphrey's Stand	*Immediate Withdrawal*				*Complete Military Victory*	
Immediate Withdrawal	28% (11)	17 (4)	2 (1)	4 (1)	2 (1)	9 (18)
	23 (9)	46 (11)	20 (12)	36 (10)	12 (5)	24 (47)
	21 (8)	21 (5)	53 (32)	18 (5)	17 (7)	30 (57)
	18 (7)	13 (3)	18 (11)	36 (10)	19 (8)	20 (39)
Complete Military Victory	10 (4)	4 (1)	7 (4)	7 (2)	50 (21)	17 (32)
	20 (39)	12 (24)	31 (60)	15 (28)	22 (42)	100 (193)

Note: Tau b = .33. Correlation ratio (eta) = .211. This table is based on Democrats who voted and who perceived a difference of more than one point on the Vietnam scale between Nixon's position and Humphrey's. For clarity in presentation, scores of "2" and "3" and scores of "5" and "6" have been combined. This collapsing does not materially affect the form or strength of the relationship.

explanation based on voters' deficiencies. Further examination of the candidates' behavior shows that Nixon and Humphrey both made it quite easy to misperceive their Vietnam positions, and quite hard to vote on the basis of the slight differences which actually existed. Both candidates were very vague and ambiguous. . . .

Again we must push the inquiry one step further, and ask why Nixon and Humphrey were both so ambiguous. The case of Vietnam is consistent with theories which suggest that ambiguity may be the rule in candidates' rhetoric. Vagueness defuses issues. If a candidate is vague, he fails to gain new support which might come from those who would agree with his position, if he took one; but he also avoids alienating the many who would not agree with his position, whatever it was. In many cases, or even all cases, ambiguity might profit a candidate more than any single specific position could.[4]

Still, evidence from the study of a single issue does not permit generalizations about the electoral process. The question of candidates' ambiguity, like that of convergent issue positions, must be answered in the context of a cross-section of issues. If it is the case that candidates are always ambiguous, that would constitute a way in which candidates' behavior and the electoral process itself regularly inhibited issue voting. . . .

NOTES

1. The surveys were conducted in February, June, August, and November 1968 by the Opinion Research Corporation (Princeton, New Jersey) for the IEP project. In addition to the present authors, the project includes Jerome Laulicht and Sidney Verba.
2. The greater strength of the relationship for Nixon may in part reflect his greater ambiguity on Vietnam, which made projection easier; but it also results from the fact that Republicans tended to like Nixon more than Democrats liked Humphrey. Republicans therefore felt a greater need to make their perceptions of Nixon's position congruent with their own opinions.
3. Negative projection of the opposing candidate's position was more marked among Republicans than Democrats. Only 5 percent of these Republicans saw Humphrey standing at exactly the same point as themselves, compared to the 14 percent which would have been expected on the basis of the marginals. The overall negative relationship was significant at better then $p = .001$, by a chi-square test. The corresponding relationship for Democrats' perceptions of Nixon was not significant at the $p = .10$ level, however. The reason for this difference appears to be that Republicans felt negative toward Humphrey, but Democrats were merely neutral about Nixon and had less reason to project his position away.

   All these tables are based only on voters who saw a large difference between the candidates. Projection was also widespread among other groups, such as nonvoters, but it was much less common among voters who saw little difference between Nixon and Humphrey.
4. Similar reasoning is given in Downs (1957, pp. 135-37). Candidate ambiguity is predicted under special circumstances in Shepsle (1972).

12. THE TWO FACES OF ISSUE VOTING

Edward G. Carmines and James A. Stimson

... Our understanding of issue voting is not likely to be clear, precise, or comprehensive until we know much more about the core "issue" in issue voting, the decision calculus used by voters to link their policy concerns to voting choices. As a first step toward that comprehensive understanding, we need to question whether "issue voting" is a single phenomenon. Our argument is that it is not, that there are two theoretically different and empirically identifiable types.

Issue voting of the first type involves conscious calculation of policy benefits for alternative electoral choices. This "hard-issue" voting has its intellectual roots in the Downsian tradition (Downs, 1957). It presumes that issue voting is the final result of a sophisticated decision calculus; that it represents a reasoned and thoughtful attempt by voters to use policy preferences to guide their electoral decision. Citizens, after examining the policy positions represented by candidates in a given election, vote for that candidate who is closest to them in some (probably multiple) issue space (Davis et al., 1970; Brody and Page, 1972; Frohlich et al., 1978). Hard-issue voting should be best exemplified, at least in degree, among those who have the conceptual skills to do it well.

The second type of issue voting (which we shall denote "easy") occurs when a particular issue becomes so ingrained over a long period that it structures voters' "gut responses" to candidates and political parties. Because gut responses require no conceptual sophistication, they should be distributed reasonably evenly in the voting population. It can be argued of course that this second type of issue voting is merely a simplified version of the first. But we shall argue that the distinction between them is fundamental, that they involve different decision processes, different prerequisite conditions, different voters, and different interpretations. . . .

Source: *American Political Science Review* (1980) 74:78-91. Reprinted with permission of the publisher.

The Attributes of Easy Issues

Most of what is written about "issues" is descriptive of what we have called "hard" issues. We focus here, in counterpoint, on the attributes of the easy issue.

If we ask the question, "What makes an issue easy?" we would be asking what makes possible a gut response elicited equally from well-informed and ill-informed, from interested and uninterested, from active and apathetic voters. Three such requisites are these:

1. The easy issue would be symbolic rather than technical.
2. It would more likely deal with policy ends than means.
3. It would be an issue long on the political agenda.

Each of the requisites has a simple rationale. Symbolic conflicts are readily communicated to mass publics. Technical issues are not. As prescriptions for public problems, technical policies require knowledge of important factual assumptions to be appreciated. Symbolic issues may be presented *and understood* simplistically.

Easy issues must almost inevitably concern the ends of public policy rather than the means. In part, this is simply the first requisite restated; the means of public policy are usually more technical than symbolic. In part, it is because preferences about policy ends can arise from the common prejudices of the mass culture. Normative premises are not by definition informed; neither do they need to be articulated.

The easy issue, finally, is likely to be an unresolved conflict long in the public eye. Even if the first requisites were met, a new issue would not be likely to find its way to the "gut" of those paying least attention to politics. Simplicity alone is not enough, but with time and simplicity an issue can permeate the electorate.

A last, more speculative, attribute of the easy issue is not a requisite, but a consequence. The availability of the easy issue for electoral choice we take to be a system-determined attribute. Simply put, sometimes easy issues are offered to the electorate and sometimes they are not. Whether a given easy issue was employed by a given voter in an election depends more crucially upon whether the choice was offered than upon the ability of the voter to make such a choice (Prewitt and Nie, 1971). Hard issues we posit to be always available; the degree to which they are employed is voter-dependent. More interested, more informed, and more involved citizens are more likely to discriminate by hard issues than their less interested, less informed, and less involved counterparts.

This last attribute could form an important link in the solution of the unresolved problem of explaining over time variation in issue voting. But it must remain only an informed speculation here. We turn now to two real-world issues that exemplify the easy/hard distinction.

Desegregation and Vietnam: Easy and Hard

Racial desegregation is a protypically easy issue—in fact, the issue that led us to think about the consequences of easy-issue voting. Although the policy conflicts involved in desegregation can be detailed in great complexity, we think it reasonable to assume that the typical voter sees in it a simple issue. Some support for that assumption can be found in our operational indicator of desegregation attitudes (a factor score derived from a variety of racial materials), which is most clearly defined by items which ask simply for respondent preferences for more or less segregation in American society. Desegregation is symbolic (Sears et al., 1979); there are virtually no technical or pragmatic issues in it. And it has been around a very long time now. The least-informed segments of both black and white communities respond meaningfully to the question of desegregation; it is that easy.

It is an issue, finally, on which parties and candidates have staked out relatively unambiguous positions—most notably in the 1964 presidential election. The clarity of positions on desegregation during that electoral contest can be seen in a simple statistic: the Survey Research Center did not discover a single black Goldwater supporter in its nationwide election survey (cited in Greenstein, 1970, p. 26). The 1964 presidential election, we believe, had a powerful and lasting effect on racial desegregation—perceptions that led to a slow but permanent reshaping of underlying party loyalties (Stimson and Carmines, 1977).

The Vietnam War was quite a different issue. The issue was badly muddled in 1968 when the country was deeply divided about the war (Verba and Brody, 1970) but Nixon and Humphrey took similar positions (Page and Brody, 1972). War and peace are simple enough ends, but the candidates did not offer that choice. Instead, the electorate was presented with alternative plans (one of them "secret") to end the war (Page, 1978). The issue had been changed but not particularly clarified by 1972 (Steeper and Teeter, 1976), when one candidate promised to end the war by immediate withdrawal and the other claimed already to have resolved it by his harder-line approach. While antiwar activists may have seen a wide gulf separating the candidates' positions, we believe most voters saw the issue in far more narrow terms, focusing mainly on the speed and conditions of withdrawal. The confusion was heightened, finally, by the fact that Democratic presidents had initiated and vigorously prosecuted the war while the Republican incumbent had sharply reduced the number of U.S. troops in Vietnam. With strong sentiment for ending the war running in the electorate, moreover, the alternative candidate scenarios increasingly focused debate on the return of prisoners of war, American postwar prestige, and the like. The relative efficacy of the not terribly different strategies was the issue.

The pace of withdrawal from Vietnam (the "choice" offered in the 1972 presidential election) was clearly a hard issue by our criteria. The issue, as presented, was pragmatic, not symbolic. It dealt with the best means of ending the war, but with nearly universal agreement on the ultimate end. And it was an issue of relatively brief duration, lasting at most the length of American involvement in the war, but probably a good deal less than that, since the nature of the issue changed as the war evolved.

Our classification of desegregation and Vietnam into theoretical categories rests, in the end, on empirical knowledge. Racial desegregation could be complex and Vietnam simple if the issues had evolved that way in the political system *and if voters saw them that way.* All issues have intrinsically simple and complex facets; which particular facets predominate at a given time is an empirical question. We have no doubt that desegregation was (and is) seen as a simple issue. For evidence that Vietnam was not at all simple in 1972, see Steeper and Teeter (1976). . . .

Political Inferences and the Easy-Issue Voter

Political analysts observe issue voting and infer sophistication. That inference is clearly problematic in view of our finding that there is a second type of issue voting that is not sophisticated at all. Indeed, as we have seen, easy-issue voting is found most frequently in the least-sophisticated portion of the electorate. Thus it is clear that issue voting, as it has been traditionally conceptualized and measured, overestimates the amount of sophisticated policy calculation going on in the electorate. This is the most direct implication of our findings. But the question of "how much" issue voting is only part of a larger theoretical quandary that begins with the questions "who?" "where?" and "when?" and ends with "what does it all mean?"

We have seen that some traditionally postulated correlates of issue voting are uncorrelated with easy-issue voting.* When the easy-issue voters are included as issue voters, these relationships are weaker than they would be if only hard-issue voters were counted. This suggests that these indicators predict not issue voting per se, but sophisticated calculation (i.e., hard-issue voting). Other theoretically critical correlates of issue voting would be expected to behave the same way.

Some of the meaning of issue voting can be found from studying *where* it occurs. A regional analysis of several recent elections would, for example, point to the South as the homeland of issue voting, an anomaly for current conceptions. The South, with its prevailing low educational levels and politics of one-party factionalism, is hardly the place to search for unusual sophistication in voting behavior. And indeed the South is not unusually sophisticated, because while it contains disproportionate numbers of issue voters, it has disproportionately few hard-issue voters. The difference, of course, lies in the large number of voters—at both ends of the spectrum—who respond only to our easy issue, race.

These findings also shed some light on the debate over whether the lack of issue voting observed in some times and places derives from inherent limitations of the citizen/voter or from inadequacies of choice offered by the political system. It may well be that the two conflicting theories each account for a different kind of issue voting. Sophisticated calculation requires both cognitive ability and attention to political life, neither of which is likely to vary much from year to year. We would expect a gently upward trend in sophisticated calculation over time from the upward trend in mean education level of the electorate. Easy-issue voting, on the other hand, requires neither cognitive ability nor attention to politics, and is

---

* Editors' note: The correlations between easy-issue voting and measures of sophistication were −.04, −.01, and .01 (all statistically insignificant) for education, information, and activism, respectively. For hard-issue voting, the correlations were .09, .21, and .15 (all statistically significant).

free to vary with the availability of easy issues. When easy issues are present, as seems certainly to have been the case for the New Deal era and to a lesser extent, the post-1960 period, increases in issue voting are observed. When easy issues are absent, as in the 1950s, issue voting is considerably more modest because it is concentrated among hard issues.

This suggests that easy-issue voting may occur in waves or surges, as a response to the relatively rare occasions when parties engage in the hazardous behavior of staking out opposing positions on a deeply felt issue. The surge of easy-issue voting is not an encouraging phenomenon for those who would hinge the viability of democracy on the ability of citizens to choose rationally between alternative issue positions of parties and candidates. The surge in issue voting seems likely to occur on a large scale only when choices are simplistic. In light of this account, one should not be surprised that the authors of *The American Voter* (Campbell et al., 1960) did not discover high levels of issue voting for the 1952 and 1956 presidential elections. By that time the easy issues associated with the New Deal had declined in salience but had not yet been replaced by the emerging issue of race. Nor are we surprised by the higher levels of issue voting that researchers have discovered in the post-1960 presidential elections. But the lion's share of this increase, we believe, is owing to the easy issue of race, not to hard issues. Increased issue voting therefore says little about the political sophistication of the American electorate.

Isolating the easy issue and the unsophisticated easy-issue voter is useful, finally, as a bridge between historical accounts of electoral realignment and the modern voting studies. The historical accounts specify a prominent role for the lowest common denominator of the mass electorate in the issue-based overthrow of old party systems. But association of issue voting with voter sophistication in the voting studies would predict that the unsophisticated would be the last to adjust their electoral behavior to an issue cleavage cutting across the party system. The emergence of the easy issue is a plausible resolution of this apparent dilemma. The crystallizing factor that precipitates realignments must, we believe, revolve around easy—not hard—issues. For only easy issues are salient enough over a long enough period to encourage parties to provide relatively clear and simple choices. And these are the only kinds of choices that provide parties the opportunity to change their minority or majority status, to become beneficiaries (or victims) of the unfolding realignment process. Hard issues, on the other hand, are too complicated and too subtle to provide a basis for a *major* reshuffling of party supporters. While their effects on the party system may be dramatic in the short term—as Vietnam was in 1972—their long-term impact is likely to be inconsequential. . . .

13. RECIPROCAL EFFECTS OF POLICY PREFERENCES, PARTY LOYALTIES, AND THE VOTE

Benjamin I. Page and Calvin C. Jones

Students of political behavior have long been interested in the extent of "policy voting," that is, the degree to which citizens take account of the public policy stands of candidates when they cast their votes. They have sought to discover the importance of policy orientations in voting, and how they compare with such factors as long-term partisan loyalties and perceptions of the character and personal qualities of the candidates. Answers to such questions are thought to bear not only upon the workings of individual psychology, but also upon theories of democratic politics (in terms of the rationality and cognitive capacities of the citizenry) and upon various theories of the decision process in voting.

Unfortunately, more than 30 years of research have left many issues unresolved. Varying conceptions of the central variables and differing methods of measurement and analysis have led to widely divergent conclusions, even on such apparently straightforward matters as whether policy positions, party loyalties or candidates' personal characteristics were more important in a given election, or whether or not policy concerns increased in importance in the 1960s and 1970s in comparison with the 1950s.[1] It is our purpose to further this research with some new empirical evidence. In doing so we must also complicate matters, suggesting that virtually all past voting studies have erred by ignoring the possibility of reciprocal causal effects among the central variables of the electoral process.

Among the few exceptions is the work of Jackson (1975b), whose non-recursive voting model of the 1964 election specified causal interdependence between partisan affiliations of voters and their evaluations of the public policy stands of the parties and candidates. Although we argue below that Jackson's model omits certain crucial reciprocal linkages, it was the first instance of a system of structural equations to consider the roles of partisanship and policy orientations as dependent, as well as independent variables, and represented a major step forward in electoral research. More recent papers by Achen (1976) and Markus (1976) also allow for some reciprocal causal links.

Source: *American Political Science Review* (1979) 73:1071-90. Reprinted with permission of the publisher.

Within the last several years survey data have become available which allow researchers to design and test sophisticated electoral process models. Yet, while a great many scholars have seized upon these data to improve their operationalizations of central electoral variables, few seem to have recognized all of the implications of the newer constructs (e.g., the "proximity" measures of candidate policy evaluations) for the task of specifying the equation, or system of equations in their statistical models. We will present below a full non-recursive voting model. For data we have turned to the 1972 and 1976 presidential election surveys conducted by the Center for Political Studies (CPS) at the University of Michigan. These are the first election studies to include the measures we believe necessary for constructing an adequate model of the electoral process.

One-Way Causation: Recursive Models of Voting

Most published voting studies to date, from the simplest to the most complicated, have been based upon some form of recursive model of the voting decision. Causation in these models is assumed to operate in one direction only, typically from policy preferences and/or party affiliation and/or candidate evaluations to the vote.[2] We intend to specify and estimate a non-recursive model, in which causation may be reciprocal, simultaneously operating in both directions among several pairs of variables. For comparative purposes, however, we first consider some typical recursive models and their results. We begin with a simple bivariate model which postulates that citizens' policy preferences uniquely determine their voting choice.

We conceptualize the voting choice somewhat differently from usual. Most past researchers have focused on a dichotomous dependent variable—the respondent's prospective or retrospective report of his or her vote for one of the major party candidates. We prefer to analyze the respondent's net comparative evaluation of the opposing candidates, as measured by the arithmetic difference between the scores given to each of the candidates on the CPS "feeling thermometer" scales.[3] The candidate thermometer scores can be argued to represent rather well what utility prospective voters think they would gain or lose from the election of a given candidate. The difference between thermometer scores for Democratic and Republican candidates, then, represents the net gain (or loss) in utility which the citizen would expect to receive as a result of the election of the Republican rather than the Democratic candidate. In this sense, it closely resembles Downs' concept of the "expected party differential" (1957).

Past empirical work has shown that such comparative evaluations of candidates, whether measured by the difference in thermometer scale scores or by a net count of positive and negative open-ended comments about the parties and candidates, are excellent predictors of voting decisions (Brody and Page, 1973; Kelley and Mirer, 1974). In both 1972 and 1976, according to our own analysis, over 95 percent of the voters who scored one candidate higher than the other on the thermometer scale reported voting for that candidate. Ordinary least squares regression of the binary vote measure upon a trichotomization of the net comparative evaluation measure resulted in standardized regression coefficients or betas of .81 for 1976 and .87 in 1972, with corresponding gammas of .95 in both years.

It can be argued that party loyalties have some direct effects upon the vote in breaking ties when citizens evaluate the opposing candidates equally. We would contend, however, that here partisanship is as likely to be a dependent variable, if anything, and that the apparent additions to explanatory power by party and other variables may merely reflect the imperfection of thermometer scores as measures of the overall utility expected from the election of candidates.

Comparative evaluations, in other words, are so closely related to the vote that they can be substituted for the binary measure in our analysis. Such a substitution has the advantage of providing a continuous variable which can be related to other continuous variables without need for transformations such as logit or probit—which in fact would conflict with our theoretical specification of an expected utility decision rule—in order to capture more accurately the underlying mathematical function associated with the vote for a particular candidate. It also has the advantage (important for our non-recursive models below) of clearly conceptualizing the attitude immediately proximal to the voting act as one which can conceivably affect, as well as being affected by, other attitudinal variables. Put most simply, we believe that the voting intention is not only a dependent variable, but may be an independent variable as well.

We will now consider several alternative measures of issue orientations, in each case—for the sake of simplicity—dealing with a summary measure of many policy preferences rather than trying to estimate separate effects for different policies. The first, which we will call the "Policy Preference Index," is a weighted linear composite of respondents' scores on a series of closed-ended policy items: the CPS self-rating scales. It resembles the policy index used by Nie, Verba and Petrocik (1976).

A second approach to measuring policy orientations makes use of a simple net count of pro-Republican minus pro-Democratic policy-related comments offered in response to the CPS open-ended questions concerning likes and dislikes for the major parties and candidates. It is similar to the policy variables used by Stokes (1966). This measure (which we have labeled "Net Policy Comments") allows respondents to define their own policy concerns, rather than imposing the same scales of policy alternatives upon everyone: it counts policy orientations as meaningful only when they are salient enough to be mentioned spontaneously by a respondent.[4]

We need a third measure of policy orientation in order to take account of the theoretical literature on spatial modeling which has grown out of the work of Hotelling (1929), Downs (1957), Davis, Hinich and Ordeshook (1970), and others. This literature specifies precisely how policy voting could occur in terms of an individual's decision calculus. It argues that voters take into account their perceptions of the policy proposals of the candidates as well as their own preferences, and that they vote for the candidate whose policy stands are perceived to be closer to their own preferences. Depending upon where the candidates actually stand and where the voters perceive them to be, there might or might not, according to these theories, be a linear relationship between voters' policy preferences and their intended vote. There should, however, always be a direct relationship between comparative policy distances and evaluation of the candidates.

Accordingly, we computed an indicator of "Comparative Policy Distances" between candidates and voters. There are various ways to construct policy distance measures; ours uses the CPS closed-ended, self-rating policy preference scales together with the associated perceptions of candidates' stands to construct a single, relative distance between the respondent and both candidates. That is, absolute distance measures were computed between the voter's preferred position and the perceived positions of the Republican and Democratic candidates on each policy scale. For each voter, distance from the Republican was then subtracted from his or her distance from the Democrat, and the resulting signed, algebraic scores were weighted and summed over all policy scales. The result tells which candidate a voter feels closer to, and by how much.[5]

Ordinary least squares estimates (standardized) of the effect of issues upon the vote, using each of these three policy measures and the simple bivariate model, [were obtained]. Plainly it makes a difference how policy orientations are measured. The first two estimates, based on simple policy preferences (.36) and open-ended policy comments (.41), are similar and of moderate size. The latter is slightly larger, suggesting that policy comments may indeed more accurately reflect issues of real concern to voters. But more striking is the fact that the third estimate, using policy distances, is considerably larger (.63) than the other two. On the face of it, this seems to support the argument that spatial models do a superior job of specifying the form and process of the voting decision. However, there is an alternative explanation which we will deal with later: namely, that distance or proximity estimates of policy voting may be artificially inflated when the possibility of reciprocal causation is ignored.

In order to round out the bivariate approach to explaining the vote, we [obtained] separate estimates of the effects of two non-policy variables, subjective party attachments and evaluations of the candidates' personal and leadership qualities. Subjective partisanship is measured by the usual CPS seven-point classification of "party identification" based on whether, generally speaking, respondents consider themselves Democrats, Republicans, Independents or whatever. In magnitude, the effect of partisanship (.57) ranks between the estimates for "Policy Preferences" and "Policy Comments," on the one hand, and "Comparative Policy Distances," on the other. This result highlights a problem faced by scholars interested in the relative importance of partisanship and policy concerns in the voting process. Obviously, a great deal depends upon how one defines and measures policy orientations at the outset.

We measured reactions to candidates' personalities by counting the net number of pro-Republican minus pro-Democratic comments in response to the CPS open-ended questions, including only those comments focusing on personal or leadership qualities and quite devoid of policy or partisan content. The standardized estimate of the effect of candidates' personal qualities on evaluations (.63) is bigger than that for subjective partisanship, policy preferences or policy comments, and equal in size to the bivariate coefficient for our comparative policy distance measure.

The most obvious objection to all these estimates is that they take account of only one independent variable at a time. If policy orientations, partisan commitment and evaluations of candidate character each have some independent influence on the voting decision, and if these variables are even moderately collinear, then the bivariate estimates will be biased. Under the usual circumstances (i.e., positive correlations among the regressors), the bias would be upward, so that bivariate methods are quite likely to overestimate the extent of policy voting—or, for that matter, the extent of party or candidate voting (Johnston, 1972). Some of the work of Boyd (1972), Pomper (1975), Aldrich (1975), Miller et al. (1976) and others is subject to this criticism. Particularly vulnerable is the issue-by-issue "normal vote" technique, since issues may be collinear with each other as well as with other variables.

Of course, most analysts are aware of this problem and incorporate two or more independent variables in their voting models. It is common, for example, to include one or another measure of policy orientations together with partisan loyalties. . . .

Two-Way Causation:
Non-recursive Models of the Vote

. . . Undeniably, much of the confusion in debates over policy voting stems from the use of different policy measures, different specifications of equations, and different estimation techniques. Researchers simply talk past one another, treating findings as if they were inconsistent when they are not. In principle this problem is easily solved; it is merely necessary to be precise about what is being claimed, rather than talking in global terms.

A more fundamental problem with such analyses, however—a problem confounding most of the existing literature on voting behavior—is an incorrect assumption of one-way causation. The error of this assumption is most obvious in models employing policy proximity or distance measures. Clearly, citizens may tend to vote for the candidate to whom they feel closest on matters of public policy. Yet it seems to us quite possible—in fact likely—that citizens whose initial vote intentions may be formulated on non-policy grounds, can and do convince themselves that the candidates they prefer stand closer to them on the important policy issues. Just such a pattern is suggested by social-psychologists' studies of "projection" or "selective perception"; it also follows theoretically from the rational calculus of citizens operating with less than perfect information. Lacking other evidence, voters might reasonably infer that a candidate who agrees with them on most matters also would agree with them on any new policy matter that comes up. Thus perceived policy distances may be consequences as well as causes of intended votes. There is some empirical evidence, in Berelson et al., *Voting* (1954) and elsewhere, that overall evaluations of candidates do in fact affect perceptions of candidates' policy stands.

By this logic, two-way causation . . . might well bias upward the estimates of policy voting in any recursive model using proximity measures of this kind, even those which "control" for partisanship and other independent variables (Shapiro, 1969; RePass, 1971; Aldrich, 1975; Miller et al., 1976).

It must be recognized, however, that much the same problem can occur in voting models which employ policy measures that do not explicitly include perceptions of candidates' stands. For example, recall that policy comments are drawn from responses to the CPS questions concerning party and candidate likes and dislikes. Implicit in each response is a judgment—that is, a perception—about where the parties or candidates stand on policies salient to the voter. Despite the open-ended, voluntary character of these responses, they could still be based upon rationalized and/or incorrect perceptions of the candidate or party positions. In other words, policy comments, too, may be consequences as well as causes of overall candidate evaluations, which again could lead to inflated estimates of the extent of policy voting (Stokes, 1966; Campbell, Converse, Miller and Stokes, 1960; Pomper, 1975; Kagay and Caldeira, 1975).

Moreover, we see no reason to assume that voters' policy preferences themselves are unaffected by general candidate evaluations. When an attractive candidate takes a strong stand on a matter of public policy, might he or she not persuade some supporters—especially those for whom the issue is of comparatively low salience—to bring their opinions into agreement? Or, less grandly, might not some of a candidate's supporters, in lieu of genuine opinions, give facile responses to policy questions corresponding to what they think their preferred candidate stands for? Because candidates are often ambiguous, it can be argued that such persuasion effects are likely to be less important than the effects of projection or selective perception, but we see no reason to exclude altogether the possibility that persuasion occurs.

In short, we are suggesting that all analyses which postulate policy variables to be recursive, uni-directional influences on candidate evaluations or vote choices may be overestimating the extent of policy voting. All the previously cited voting studies (except those by Jackson, Achen, and Markus), and many others not cited, are offenders in this respect. Even the pioneering causal model of Goldberg (1966) is entirely recursive and subject to this criticism, as is the recent work of Nie, Verba and Petrocik (1976).

At the same time, we maintain that the many researchers who do not use policy proximity measures or some other means for taking explicit account of perceived candidate positions are likely to *under*estimate the degree of relationship between policy orientations and intended votes. There is no a priori way to tell for certain which direction of error predominates.

To extend this reasoning a bit further, there is no reason to consider subjective partisanship (i.e., "party identification") to be sacrosanct. It seems quite plausible to us that policy preferences—and relative policy distances from candidates—may be both causes and consequences of party loyalties. Just as opinion leadership by party figures might cause some citizens (even perfectly rational ones) to change their policy preferences, we strongly suspect that some voters' policy preferences—especially those touching on economic, social welfare or racial issues—have some effect on their choice of party in the first place. And, indeed, we would argue that policy distances from particular candidates, who may or may not take positions exactly along the lines of older party cleavages (thus reinforcing or weakening traditional policy profiles of the parties), are likely to affect the strength, if not the direction, of subjective partisanship during a given election campaign. Scholars interested in the relationship between partisanship and policy orientations have typically assumed that causation worked exclusively in one direction between the two, usually from party to issues. They may thereby have inflated their estimates of the effects of party identification (Campbell et al., 1960).[6]

Even Jackson's (1975b) pathbreaking non-recursive model postulates that party affects policy preferences but not vice versa. Jackson (1975b) and Markus (1976) also rule out any possible influence of candidate evaluations upon policy preferences.

Finally, we must consider the possibility that voters' party loyalties may both affect and be affected by comparative candidate evaluations or intended votes during a particular campaign period. While most researchers have conceptualized partisanship as a sort of blind habit, a relatively long-term exogenous factor affecting vote choice, we expect that to some (perhaps modest) extent, preferences based on a candidate's character or policy stands will affect the intensity—and at times even the direction—of party affiliations. It seems to us an overinterpretation of the temporal stability of partisan attachments to assume that they are altogether impervious to candidate choices in ordinary elections. Candidates, after all, reflect credit or blame upon the parties that nominate them. Thus the many studies of party identification as a determinant of candidate evaluations or voting choices, from *The American Voter* onward, may have overestimated its effect by ignoring the opposite possibility (Campbell et al., 1960). The Michigan Tradition dies hard.

Nor is *The Changing American Voter* immune to this criticism (Nie, Verba and Petrocik, 1976). Comparisons between groups or candidates or over time are also subject to error because the biases in estimates are not necessarily constant from group to group or candidate to candidate or year to year.

We have made the sweeping claim that virtually all studies of policy orientations, partisanship and the vote . . . are subject to simultaneity bias and are potentially quite misleading. It is fair enough to ask whether we have anything constructive to add to this work of destruction.

The most appropriate way to handle the problem, we would argue, is through the use of non-recursive, simultaneous equation models which explicitly allow for the possibility of causal processes operating in both directions between variables (Johnston, 1972; Theil, 1971; Hanushek and Jackson, 1977; Duncan, 1975).[7] We can begin to apply such techniques to the voting problem by specifying the central set of variables which we believe to be mutually endogenous—that is, which reciprocally affect each other: comparative candidate evaluations, relative policy distance between the voter and candidates, and current subjective partisanship. We will continue to treat measures of reported vote as direct consequences of overall candidate evaluations.

The relationships postulated among these variables are diagrammed in Figure 13-1. Within the context of this model, we seek to investigate not only the effect of policy orientations upon the vote, but also five other processes of interest:

Figure 13-1   Reciprocal Casual Paths in a Non-Recursive Voting
Model

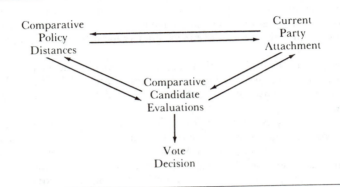

Source: Compiled by the authors.

namely, the reverse effect of overall candidate evaluations upon comparative policy distances, and the two-way linkages between current partisanship and policy distances as well as between party attachments and comparative candidate evaluations.

We cannot estimate any of the coefficients in Figure 13-1, as it stands, because the model is hopelessly underidentified. That is, there are only three empirically observable relationships among the central endogenous variables available to estimate the six causal processes of theoretical interest. Ordinary least squares regression is clearly not appropriate for estimating these causal paths since the required assumptions of independence between the regressors and error terms in each equation cannot be justified. To distinguish between the effects possibly operating in both directions between any two endogenous variables, we must bring additional information into the estimation process. The sort of information needed may be provided by a set of variables which are exogenous to the reciprocal processes specified in Figure 13-1—variables can be assumed (on theoretical grounds) to be unaffected by any endogenous variables, yet which have direct effects on some, but not all, of the endogenous variables (Fisher, 1966).

It is in the search for suitable exogenous variables that difficulties mount, for most of the pertinent social theory is either not very powerful or not universally accepted. The grounds for specifying that a given variable theoretically cannot affect or be affected by another are seldom overwhelming. The situation is worse than usual when one deals with psychological measurements or attitudinal variables, since practically any attitude might conceivably affect any other. There are times when we seem to be studying relationships between mush and slush.

Fortunately, however, it is possible to specify certain exogenous variables for our model with reasonable (and sometimes considerable) confidence, allowing us to identify several of the causal paths. Theory and past empirical research suggest, for example, that the party choices of voters' parents have a direct effect upon their own partisan proclivities, but do not affect their perceived policy distances or overall evaluations of the candidates, except insofar as they act through their own party affiliation. Parents' partisan commitments, therefore, can be specified as operating through uni-directional causal paths upon voters' partisanship only, and their direct effects excluded elsewhere in the model. This will help to identify the effects of voters' partisanship on their policy-oriented evaluations and their vote intentions.[8]

Similarly, we can with some confidence specify that voters' assessments of the character traits and personal qualities of the candidates (as measured by spontaneous responses to open-ended items about candidate likes and dislikes) should have direct effects upon overall comparative candidate evaluations, but should not be substantially affected by overall evaluations in return. In addition, we would argue that character and personality evaluations have no direct links to the voters' policy evaluations of candidates or to their current subjective partisanship, but rather that these effects are transmitted indirectly through the more general overall evaluations of candidates. Thus, the assumption of a recursive relationship from personal qualities assessments to overall candidate evaluations (and the concomitant exclusion of direct effects elsewhere in the model) allows identification of the causal paths from candidate evaluations to both partisanship and comparative policy distances.

Our confidence in this specification depends heavily upon our use only of specific, spontaneous comments about candidates' characteristics, which are far more likely to be causes than effects of candidate evaluations.

It is somewhat more difficult to specify variables which affect voters' comparative policy distances without also affecting the other endogenous variables in the system. We begin, however, by taking advantage of the fact that a number of the voters' background or demographic attributes—factors such as race, sex, age, income and education—affect policy proximities by initially affecting the voters' policy preferences. There is little question that voters' background characteristics are truly exogenous to the electoral process. But the question arises whether they also affect partisanship or general candidate evaluations directly, or whether their effects are transmitted entirely through perceived policy distances. We will assume the latter in our initial model and conduct some tests on the effects of that assumption below.

We have, now, a non-recursive model in which all hypothesized causal paths are identified:

$$
\begin{array}{l}
\text{Comparative Candidate Evaluations} = b_1 \text{Comparative Policy Distances} + \\
\qquad b_2 \text{Current Party Attachment} + b_3 \text{Personal Qualities Evaluations} + u. \qquad (1)
\end{array}
$$

$$\begin{matrix} \text{Comparative} \\ \text{Policy} \\ \text{Distances} \end{matrix} = b_4 \begin{matrix} \text{Comparative} \\ \text{Candidate} \\ \text{Evaluations} \end{matrix} + b_5 \begin{matrix} \text{Current} \\ \text{Party} \\ \text{Attachment} \end{matrix} +$$

$$b_6 \text{ Race} + b_7 \text{ Age} + b_8 \text{ Sex} + b_9 \text{ Education} + b_{10} \text{ Income} + u. \quad (2)$$

$$\begin{matrix} \text{Current} \\ \text{Party} \\ \text{Attachment} \end{matrix} = b_{11} \begin{matrix} \text{Comparative} \\ \text{Policy} \\ \text{Distances} \end{matrix} +$$

$$b_{12} \begin{matrix} \text{Comparative} \\ \text{Candidate} \\ \text{Evaluations} \end{matrix} + b_{13} \begin{matrix} \text{Father's} \\ \text{Party} \\ \text{Attachment} \end{matrix} +$$

$$b_{14} \begin{matrix} \text{Mother's} \\ \text{Party} \\ \text{Attachment} \end{matrix} + u. \quad (3)$$

Simply providing for identification of path coefficients does not guarantee adequate specification of the causal model, however, and we believe that additional exogenous variables must be included to overcome biases of a different sort. When important independent variables are omitted from any equation of the model, coefficients for the included variables will still be biased if, for whatever reason, the omitted and included variables are correlated. Several such variables are suggested by past research devoted to the individual equations of our model.

The literature on party identification points to five additional potential influences upon current subjective partisanship: the voter's sense of long-term, traditional involvement with a particular party; degree of consistency in party voting for president; religious preference; region of residence; and general ideological leaning. Some of these factors should carry greatest weight among voters whose party loyalties differ from those of their parents or who were not influenced in any partisan direction by their parents; others mediate parental influence.

For many voters, both the direction and strength of current partisanship may be expected to depend in part upon their degree of involvement with their chosen parties, considered either as reference groups to which loyalty is owed, or as information sources providing interpretations and evaluations of the political environment. We measured this sort of involvement by a net count of positive and negative comments which focus only on parties as traditional referents, wholly excluding both policy and candidate personality connotations: "I've just always been (or voted as) a Democrat," or "I like Nixon just because he's a good Republican."

An even stronger factor affecting current partisanship may be our measure of presidential voting consistency, which combines information about citizens' regularity of voting in presidential elections with data on whether they always supported a particular party for president.

In order to take account of socialization or information sources outside the family for those voters with neither a strong sense of partisan tradition nor a history of regular party voting, we included variables which classify citizens according to their region of residence (10-state South versus all other states) and their religious preferences (Catholics, Jews, Fundamentalist Protestants and those with no religious preference versus all others). Finally, for those voters whose partisanship derives from their view of the parties as purveyors of more or less coherent social and economic programs, we included a simple trichotomous classification of their ideological leaning based on their self-placement on the CPS closed-ended liberal/conservative scale. Rather than attempt to classify voters on this indicator with excessive (perhaps artificial) precision, we collapsed the seven points into a trichotomy of "pro-left," "pro-right" and neutral positions, combining voters who placed themselves at the mid-point with those who did not place themselves on the scale at all, as ideologically neutral.

To the five background variables exogenous to Comparative Policy Distances, we added a single additional measure—the same ideological classification included in the partisanship equation. Inclusion of so simple a classifying index allows us, without undue worry about reciprocal causation to estimate the extent to which voters, philosophical orientations not rooted in racial, sexual or socioeconomic differences may affect policy evaluations of the candidates. While attitudes are always suspect when used as exogenous variables, the high salience and stability of voters' self-classification as liberal or conservative to the moderate number of respondents who embrace such a label bolsters this specification. The direction of such a stance is considerably less subject to electoral influence than is the intensity of commitment.

The special nature of the Carter candidacy in 1976 raised the possibility of two additional factors which might have independent effects on comparative candidate evaluations, namely Carter's southern origins and his highly religious outlook. Therefore, we included in the equation for overall candidate evaluations two more exogenous variables. The first is the same indicator of region of residence which appears in the partisanship equation; the second is the dichotomous classification of citizens' religious preferences which also appears in the partisanship equation.

With the addition of these exogenous variables, our model may be described as diagrammed in Figure 13-2. Since each equation of the model includes overidentified paths, we estimated the standardized coefficients for the model using two-stage and three-stage least squares programs.[9] These estimates are also presented in Figure 13-2.

To us, the most striking aspect of the estimates in Figure 13-2 is the extent to which they differ from the corresponding coefficients obtained using simple recursive models. Comparative policy distances now appear to be the strongest single factor affecting intended votes, with a standardized, partial (3SLS) regression coefficient of .44. This estimate is greater than that produced by any of the multivariate recursive models examined above; it is roughly comparable in magnitude to the bivariate coefficient for the net policy comments measure, although it would be wrong to conclude that recursive models using comment counts necessarily give good estimates of policy voting generally, in all elections.

This major role played by policy orientations in the voting decision is, of course, very much in the spirit of rational-man spatial models. It is noteworthy that our estimation procedure, which takes explicit account of theory by using

Figure 13-2   Full Non-Recursive Voting Model with Overidentified
Structural Equations, 1976

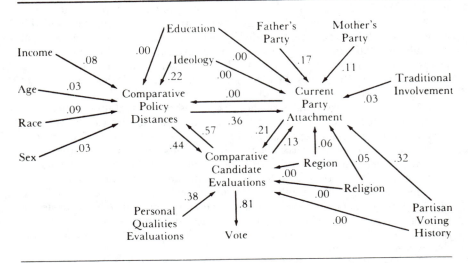

Note: Disturbance symbols and inter-correlations among exogenous variables have been omitted for the
sake of clarity.
Source: 1976 national election study, Center for Political Studies, University of Michigan.

policy proximity measures, reveals a greater extent of policy voting than do most
other methods. At the same time, however, evaluations of the candidates' personal
and leadership qualities run a close second in importance, with a standardized
coefficient of .38. Indeed, we cannot be sure that the policy effect was significantly
greater than that of candidate personality. Spatial models in their narrowest form,
postulating exclusively policy-oriented voting, are plainly inadequate. But we
would argue that this does not reflect badly on the citizenry. In a presidential
system, rational individuals must pay attention to leadership characteristics, if
only to ensure that their favored candidate is competent to carry out the promised
policy stands.

In 1976, citizens' party attachments had much less direct influence upon vote
intention than either policy orientations or evaluations of personal qualities. The
coefficient of .21 is lower than that for any of the recursive estimates presented
above. Party loyalties, in other words, had some independent effect on the vote—
again contrary to narrow notions of voter rationality, but not to a broader
conception. (Surely citizens are well advised to view the parties to some extent as
governing teams, with records of past performance which bear upon future
prospects. What V. O. Key called the "standing decision" to support one or
another party—subject, of course, to modification in the light of experience—is an
efficient and generally reliable aid in voting.) Yet our estimate indicates that

partisanship was by no means a straitjacket. It was clearly not the most important factor affecting the vote, as has been alleged of the 1950s and early 1960s.

Despite the special features of Carter's campaign, in 1976 the estimated coefficients for both region and religion did not differ significantly from zero. We suspect that this result follows from the fact that evaluations of personal qualities and current partisanship already take account of such effects. With these variables included in the candidate evaluations equation, the region and religion variables are superfluous.

Two important findings, which can emerge only from a non-recursive model like ours, concern the reciprocal effects of both intended votes and policy distances upon current partisanship. When all of the customary influences on the formation and maintenance of party attachments are allowed for, intended votes still show a modest independent effect (.13) on voters subjective partisanship. In 1976, then, partisanship was not an exogenous influence on the vote, impervious to other electoral stimuli. Instead citizens apparently alter their party loyalties when the parties nominate especially desirable or undesirable candidates, just as sensible voters would be expected to do. By ignoring this effect of overall evaluations of the presidential candidates upon partisanship, many scholars have overestimated the effects of party affiliation upon voting decisions.

What may be more surprising to some is the much stronger effect (.36) of comparative policy distances from the candidates upon party attachment. Conceptually, it seems logical enough that voters who see their policy interests served much better by one candidate than another might be inclined to consider themselves supporters of that candidate's party. The question arises, however, why such a judgment on policy grounds would not be translated into an overall positive evaluation of (i.e., an intention to vote for) that candidate, and only then go on to influence partisanship. The answer seems to involve the fact that policy judgments form only one of many independent dimensions of candidate evaluations; preference for one candidate on policy grounds does not guarantee a favorable evaluation overall. In fact, in 1976, over 15 percent of the survey respondents fell at the neutral or indifference point on our measure of comparative candidate evaluations. While 65 percent were classified as being closer to Carter on policy matters (35 percent closer to Ford), only 33 percent preferred Carter's personal and leadership qualities and 40 percent preferred Ford's. Thus even when comparative policy distances did not automatically lead to vote intentions, they appear to have influenced voters' feelings of attachment to the political parties.

For a given election, the overall magnitude of either of these endogenous effects on partisanship would depend, of course, upon citizens' partisan attitudes before the start of the campaign and upon their various evaluations of the nominees. The effects are not overwhelmingly large; we would not argue from these findings that major shifts of pre-existing party allegiances result from a campaign like that of 1976. The several variables which we specified as exogenous to current party attachment have significant (and in some cases, sizeable) coefficients, clearly indicating the presence of powerful stabilizing influences. The effects of parental socialization and of consistency in party vote for president, for example, no doubt serve to anchor some voters against the ebb and flow of campaign developments. Yet change in party attachment, whether through the weakening or strengthening of former ties, or by the creation of a sense of partisanship among new voters, clearly followed from evaluations of campaign stimuli. This finding, we hope, will help lay to rest the notion that partisanship can be treated as an unmoved mover in the analysis of voting behavior.

Perhaps the most theoretically important of all our estimates is the strong effect (.57) of overall candidate evaluations upon perceived policy distances. The existence of such an effect squarely controverts the assumptions of spatial models, which specify that voting decisions are the result of calculations of policy proximities or distances from the candidates, and that the policy preferences and perceptions of candidates' stands used in these calculations are independently arrived at. The evidence is clear that influence runs both ways: voters' evaluations of Carter's and Ford's policy stands were strongly conditioned by their overall judgments about the candidates. Those who generally favored Carter, let us say, tended to locate themselves and Carter close together on the policy scales; those who disfavored a candidate tended to place themselves and that candidate farther apart. This finding goes against the fixed-preferences and perfect-information assumptions widespread in economists' views of politics (and, for that matter, economics as well). It calls for considerable rethinking of some notions of electoral democracy.

At the same time, it would be quite erroneous to conclude that we have found voters to be irrational or deficient with respect to some democratic ideal. In the first place, the influence of candidate evaluations upon perceived policy distances from candidates encompasses a complex bundle of processes (projection, persuasion, rationalization), in which either voters' policy preferences or their perceptions of candidate stands are affected by their evaluations of the candidates. Some of these processes are useful or even essential to the workings of democracy; we cannot at present sort out which are operating. (To distinguish the effects on perceptions from those on preferences would require a four-equation model with two complicated nonlinear equations.) In the second place, most if not all of these processes are best understood as reactions by rational citizens to the problems of obtaining political information. To the extent that some reactions interfere with electoral democracy, much of the blame must fall upon the political environment and the kinds of information made available (or lacking), rather than upon the voters themselves.

It is quite possible—and compatible with our findings—that some voters who have no information about the candidates' policy stands, but who have developed a preference for one candidate (based on party ties or personal attributes) project their own preferred policy positions onto their favorite candidate, especially when pestered to answer survey questions about where candidates stand. In addition, there are no doubt voters for whom policy considerations are of sufficiently low salience that they blithely adopt as their own the policy prescriptions of whichever candidate they have come to prefer for non-policy reasons. Yet persuasion (i.e., a candidate's influence upon policy preferences) can take a much less causal form—a form equally compatible with our findings—when citizens listen to information and argument about policy and are genuinely convinced by a candidate they trust. In a complicated world of imperfect information, rational citizens must be open to persuasion.

Moreover, the existence of strong effects of policy orientations upon candidate evaluations suggests that few voters, if any, rely exclusively upon simple rationalization in arriving at their final evaluations of the presidential contenders' policies. It is much more likely that a given voter will have had at least some realistic notion of his or her comparative distances from the candidates which conditioned more general evaluations in the first place. Lacking perfect information, such voters might then combine what data they have on policy distances with party cues and judgments about the candidates' personal attributes into a preliminary comparative evaluation of the nominees, which they then may use to infer their ultimate net distance from the candidates over a wider range of policy areas. In this light, what at first seemed to be rationalization may in fact be rationality.

Again, we would emphasize that if voters make foolish and easily avoidable errors about candidates' policy stands (and no evidence yet establishes this to be so), this probably results as much from the obscurity and ambiguity of what candidates say as from limitations of citizens' cognitive processes (Page, 1978, Ch. 6).

All the findings we have discussed so far pertain to the 1976 presidential election. Both as a check on our methods and for its own substantive interest, we present in Figure 13-3 comparable estimates for 1972. All measures were constructed in precisely the same way as for 1976, and the series of alternative specifications used for testing purposes were identical.

Comparison of Figures 13-2 and 13-3 reveals many similarities in overall structure, especially in the effects of exogenous variables. This increases our confidence in the model and the estimation procedure. At the same time, the comparison uncovers some sharp differences, which are readily interpretable in terms of differences in the electoral environment. Plainly the Carter-Ford contest and the Nixon-McGovern campaign differed in ways which aroused dissimilar reactions among the voters.

As in 1976, we find in 1972 clear evidence of reciprocal causation between policy orientations and overall candidate evaluations. Many citizens voted on policy grounds, but many also were influenced in their assessment of policy distances by their overall evaluations of the candidates. As in 1976, the effect of candidate evaluations upon perceived policy distances (.81) appears slightly stronger than the effect in the opposite direction (.76), but this difference was much smaller in 1972 than in 1976 and is not statistically significant. No doubt the projection or rationalization of issue stands was relatively more difficult in the "clear choice" setting of 1972.

What stands out most strongly is the much greater magnitude of both roles of policy orientations (as both independent and dependent variables) in 1972. The Nixon-McGovern election was truly an issue-oriented affair; no other factor approached the importance of public policy orientations in affecting voting

Figure 13-3 Full Non-Recursive Voting Model with Overidentified Structural Equations, 1972

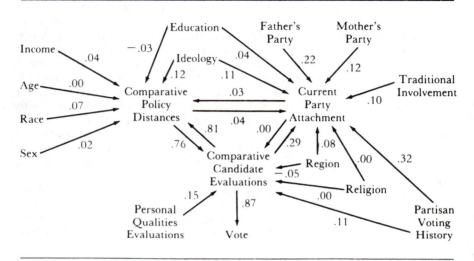

Note: Disturbance symbols and inter-correlations among exogenous variables have been omitted for the sake of clarity.
Source: 1976 national election study, Center for Political Studies, University of Michigan.

decisions. Indeed, this feature of the election was so marked that it can be discerned no matter how crudely the data are analyzed, as when we replicated for 1972 various simple recursive models. Yet, at the same time, the clarity of the choice on policy grounds evidently did not prevent a very substantial amount of alteration in perceptions of candidate stands and/or policy preferences in response to feelings about the candidates.[10]

The impact upon votes of citizens' evaluations of personal qualities was surprisingly low (.15) in 1972, suggesting that explanations of the vote which emphasize McGovern's allegedly poor judgment and personal instability as important direct factors are probably somewhat wide of the mark. According to our estimates, policy distances had an effect over five times as great as did reactions to the candidates' personal attributes. Still, this finding is not inconsistent with the possibility that the outcome of the election (as opposed to the total variance in voting decisions) was heavily influenced by judgments about the candidates' personal and leadership qualities. Calculations of Stokes-type net effects, which take account of the strongly anti-McGovern drift of this factor, indicate that it was quite important (Popkin et al., 1976).

Among the most noteworthy aspects of Figure 13-3 is the nearly total absence of any effect of party attachments upon the other two endogenous variables. Our estimates reveal that in 1972—quite unlike 1976—party loyalties played no part in the formation either of voting decisions or perceptions of closeness to the candidates on policy matters. McGovern dramatically dissociated himself from the Democratic party's mainstream; and, by the same token, the central core of the Democratic party abandoned McGovern to his own devices. Party *per se* had no independent effect at all on the vote. Furthermore, the absence of a significant effect of policy distances upon partisanship, together with the very strong impact of policy distances upon intended vote, indicates that the policy choices around which voting decisions revolved (the Vietnam War, urban unrest, campus disturbances, alternative life styles) cut across the grain of the older party cleavages.

There was, on the other hand, apparently some effect of intended votes upon partisanship. That is, although party loyalties did not affect votes, intended votes did affect partisanship—presumably because some Democratic defectors to Nixon felt their Democratic affiliations to be weakened. There are, however, some doubts about this finding. In spite of the moderate size of this coefficient (.29), the conventional significance test (which is asymptotically valid for two- and three-stage least squares estimation) indicates that it is not significantly different from zero at the .05 confidence level. Examination of the intermediate two-stage calculations reveals a high degree of collinearity between the "decontaminated" versions of the policy distance and candidate evaluations variables. This results in high standard errors of estimates for the respective coefficients (i.e., lowers their precision), which substantially raises the difficulty of disentangling the independent effects for these two variables. Since we presently lack any satisfactory way to deal with multicollinearity in the second stage of two-stage least squares, it is necessary to reserve judgment on the significance or insignificance of the 1972 impact of intended vote upon partisanship.

Among the exogenous factors in 1972, there are also some differences from 1976 related to the nature of the candidate pairings in those two years. For the most part, however, the exogenous variables—especially those which represent stable characteristics of respondents—exerted roughly comparable amounts of influence in both elections. In general, the overall structural similarity between the estimated models for 1972 and 1976 is an encouraging sign that the estimates are correct and not subject to vagaries of the estimation technique or arbitrary variations with independent data sets.

Thus the variation in the effects of ideological orientations is easily exhausted in terms of the differences in the kinds of policies at issue during the two campaigns. In 1976, policy debates tended to line up much more with older, New Deal notions of liberalism and conservatism than was the case in 1972. Our measure of ideological leaning (which relates most closely to voters' attitudes on New Deal type issues) therefore had a greater effect on policy distances in 1976 than in 1972. In addition, whereas in 1972 voters' ideological orientations affected both policy distances and party attachments directly, in 1976 the effects of ideology were passed entirely through policy distances, affecting partisanship indirectly via the path from policy distances to partisanship.

Changes in the pattern of effects for partisan voting consistency are of a similar nature. In 1972, party attachments had no discernible effect on comparative candidate evaluations. Yet the more consistently citizens had voted for the same party for president, the more likely they were to prefer that party's candidate to the opposition in 1972. Presumably it took a rather special kind of partisan attachment rooted in a firm history of voting support to make Democrats (independently of other factors) prefer McGovern to Nixon. In 1976, however, we find that the direct path from voting history to comparative evaluations no longer functioned. Again, controlling for other factors, voting history directly affected only current party attachments, with candidate evaluations being affected only indirectly.

Finally, it seems to us that the differences in the effect of personal qualities evaluations between the elections is largely due to the great differences in the intensity of the effects of policy issues in the two campaigns. Policy distances were so overwhelmingly important in 1972 that judgments about personal attributes were left with relatively little independent explanatory power.

Conclusions

The clearest implications of our findings concern errors inherent in recursive voting models. In the first place, researchers who rely on single-equation techniques simply fail to reproduce faithfully the underlying complexity of the electoral decision process. Beyond this, even if multiple equations are specified in elaborate hierarchical recursive models, the estimated coefficients are still subject to simultaneity bias.

This defect is most damaging when recursive models are used with variables (such as the policy distance measures) which are especially likely to have been influenced by the very factors of which they are presumed causes. Our results suggest that the use of such measures should be restricted to non-recursive simultaneous equation models and that only those estimation techniques appropriate for such models should be applied. Yet practically all studies of issue voting, party identification and the like have specified uni-directional causal relationships without having theoretical justification for doing so. Our findings indicate that the degree of error introduced by mis-specification and simultaneity bias in such models can be quite substantial.

Our most important empirical discovery involves the reciprocal causal paths between policy orientations and overall candidate evaluations. In both 1972 and 1976 there was a high degree of policy-oriented voting—considerably more than is revealed by some less powerful analytical techniques. The identification in both years of a substantial effect from intended votes to policy distances, as well, confirms what many theorists have suspected for some time: policy-based evaluations of presidential candidates are endogenous to the electoral process.

We have argued that the effect of intended votes upon policy distances is consistent with individual rationality, since it may be perfectly rational to be persuaded by a favored candidate's policy stands, or even to infer a candidate's positions on policies (and, hence, one's degree of proximity to them) from other characteristics. We have pointed out, however, that this is inconsistent with simple spatial models of voting behavior, in which preferences are assumed to be fixed, and perceptions of candidate stands are assumed to vary only randomly (if at all) among the electorate.

In addition, the estimates from our two data sets imply that the effect of partisanship on the vote varies considerably across elections, depending largely upon the nature of the candidate pairings and the extent to which current policy issues conflict or coincide with established party cleavages. When the policy debates of a campaign are such that the parties are seen to have relatively distinct and internally coherent positions, and when the presidential nominees are perceived as being reasonably typical representatives of their respective parties' interests and stands (as was largely the case in 1976), then voters' current party attachments may both affect and be affected by policy orientations and overall candidate evaluations. When these conditions are not met (and surely 1972 was a quintessential case where they were not), partisanship is isolated from the electoral process.

Further, when party loyalties do enter in, they do not function purely as fixed determinants of the vote; those loyalties can themselves be affected by attitudes toward the current candidates. Even short of major realignments, party affiliations are effects as well as causes in the electoral process.

We have contended that non-recursive simultaneous equation models are necessary in order to eliminate substantial, systematic biases from estimates based on cross-sectional data. At the same time, we must concede that the modeling procedures and estimating techniques we advocate are by no means free from specification problems. One of the chief difficulties is locating variables in existing data which are genuinely exogenous—that is, which are truly free from reciprocal influence by their target endogenous variables, and which can be excluded on persuasive theoretical grounds from having direct effects on certain other endogenous variables. In the search for plausible and identifiable specifications, researchers must be quite careful to state their theoretical justifications, and also to make clear, by the use of sensitivity testing, just what the consequences of alternative specifications would be.

Simultaneous equation analyses are, to an important extent, dependent for their success upon the decisions of those who design survey instruments and collect the data. If important variables are not measured or are measured poorly, one cannot place much confidence in empirical findings. By "important variables," we mean not only those of major theoretical and substantive interest, but also potential exogenous variables, some of which may be of little interest in themselves but which have the theoretical properties necessary to assist in estimation.

Lacking tailor-made measures, we have tried to exercise great caution in the specification of exogenous variables—choosing wherever possible items on which voters had fixed characteristics, or had reached established values prior to the campaign under study. Where this was not possible, e.g., in the cases of evaluations of candidates' personal qualities or of voters' ideological leanings, we sought constructs which approached the theoretical ideal as closely as possible. Our measure of personal qualities evaluations, for example, was operationalized so as to minimize the possibility that individual voters' scores would be affected by other factors, while maximizing the probability that they would reflect the true extent to which personal qualities evaluations formed the basis of the voter's electoral decision. We doubt that this construct perfectly satisfies all of the theoretical requirements of an ideal exogenous variable. We believe, however, that it is a defensible specification and that any biases introduced by this type of measure will be small indeed when compared with those resulting from single equation or recursive estimation. The estimates of effects from candidate evaluations to policy distances and partisanship, which depend heavily upon this specification, may be slightly inflated, but we are satisfied that they are very nearly correct.[11]

Future presidential elections will no doubt be accompanied by voter surveys of varying purposes and designs. The opportunities for further developments in non-recursive modeling remain open on a good many fronts. The refinement of existing exogenous measures, the use of panel studies and the incorporation of quasi-experimental designs in future surveys all offer possibilities for improvements in the analytical techniques advocated here. Even limited success in this direction will add far more to our understanding of voting behavior than will repetition of error-ridden, mis-specified models.

NOTES

1. See RePass (1976), Kessel (1972), Brody and Page (1972).
2. The term "recursive"—literally "running back"—is unfortunate, because it gives exactly the opposite of the correct impression. It does not actually describe relationships between variables, but refers to a property of the corresponding system of equations. It is probably too late to undo the confusion resulting from this usage.
3. Thermometer scores range between 0 ("very cold or unfavorable") through 50 ("no feeling at all for candidate") to 100 ("very warm or favorable"). In the 1972 survey, when thermometer questions were asked both before and after the election, we used average scores in order to reduce measurement error.
4. We experimented with a number of coding rules governing which comments to count as policy-oriented, ranging from the vague and general to only the most specific. Inclusion of vague comments led to a much larger, and probably inflated, relationship with candidate evaluations. The estimates reported here are all based upon a narrow, specific definition of policy concerns.
5. We presume linearity rather than the quadratic loss function specified by Davis et al. (1970) because we see the CPS seven-point scales, with their labeled endpoints but unlabeled interiors, as encouraging respondents to report positions and distances in utility units rather than objective policy units. If they do, the linear relationship with candidate evaluations follows directly from the rationality assumptions of spatial models. Observed relationships are very nearly linear.
6. A particularly misleading procedure is the "normal vote" technique. It does not attempt to give unbiased estimates of policy and party effects through regression analysis, but simply assigns the joint covariance of policy and party with the vote in two different extreme ways, so that the reader can choose between "long-term" and

"short-term" effects. Except by chance, neither of these magnitudes correctly estimates the extent of either policy preferences or party upon the vote (or of party or policy each upon the other); indeed, the technique does not even identify boundaries around the maximum or minimum possible effects. See Boyd (1972).

7. Time-series techniques offer an alternative way to sort out causal orderings, but even when time-series or panel data are available, they offer no panacea. In the first place, whether or not measurements are widely separated in time, there is danger in treating lagged variables as causes of current values of the same variables (e.g., party identification): error terms are often autocorrelated as a result of the omission of other factors (e.g., policy preferences) which affect both, and this biases estimates—usually upwards. To capture distinct stages in the development and change of cognitive elements, to ascertain what changes first, measurements might well have to be repeated almost instantaneously. Moreover, quasi-experimental measurements before and after exogenous events are likely to reveal more about the impact of those particular events than about the net mutual influences of different attitudes in the whole electoral process.

8. Since parents' party is measured in the CPS surveys by the respondent's report, it is conceivable that the reported party affiliation of parents is affected by respondents' partisanship through a conscious or unconscious desire to have it be the same (or different), or simply as an aid to faulty memory. Independent studies based on interviews with parents, however, indicate that the bias in the reports is probably not very serious for our purposes (Jennings and Niemi, 1968). This is particularly true since other proximate influences on partisanship reduce the importance of parents' party in our models.

9. The Statistical Analysis System (SAS) software package was used. The third stage offers improvements in the efficiency of estimates from the previous stage by taking account of the correlations among the equations in the system (Johnston, 1972). In this case, 3SLS estimates differed little from those at the second stage. All variables were standardized before computations were made.

10. In point of fact, the clarity of the choice in 1972, like that in 1964, actually left much to be desired. Nixon's policy utterances were vague throughout, and McGovern gradually retreated into ambiguity after taking unusually specific stands on the defense budget, income redistribution, and the like (Page, 1978).

11. Extensive sensitivity testing was conducted using a series of alternative specifications for each of the three equations. For example, personal qualities evaluations were tested for direct effects in both the partisanship and the policy distances equations, with negative findings. Similar testing showed that the potentially controversial specification of some demographic variables as affecting perceived policy distances but not (directly) partisanship, has surprisingly little effect upon the estimates among endogenous variables. In fact, so long as parental partisanship was included in the equation, none of the demographic variables was found to have significant effects upon current party affiliations. In the same vein, when our predictors of partisanship were inserted in the equations predicting overall candidate evaluations and policy distances, only those specified in our final models showed significant direct effects.

14. A DYNAMIC SIMULTANEOUS EQUATION MODEL OF ELECTORAL CHOICE

Gregory B. Markus and Philip E. Converse

There is no shortage of studies which focus upon the roles of candidate personalities, partisan leanings, and contemporary issues in affecting the outcomes of elections in the United States. The value of this research is obvious, but it is probably fair to say that too much attention has been paid to the relative importance of factors idiosyncratic to particular elections and not enough effort has been directed toward the development and evaluation of an integrated and generalizable behavioral model of the voter's calculus. The result has been an uncomfortable lack of fit between verbal theories of micro-level electoral dynamics and statistical models of that process.

The goal of this study is *not* simply predictive accuracy, nor the assessment of the "relative importance" of various predictors of the vote. Nor do we intend for this work to be interpreted narrowly as a study of a particular election. What follows is a self-conscious effort at developing a model which is verisimilar to the dynamic cognitive process underlying citizens' electoral decision making. To the extent that we are able to synthesize a scattered set of verbal hypotheses and pre-theories into a precise and testable quantitative structure, we shall consider the effort a success even before confronting a shred of empirical information. Should the data corroborate the hypothesized structure or provide insights into how it might be modified—so much the better.

The model to be presented and evaluated here has two major advantages over previous work: it explicitly embodies the simultaneous interdependence of perceptions and evaluations of political stimuli specific to a particular election; and it is a truly dynamic model in that it depicts how the campaign and the ultimate vote choice modify or reinforce prior orientations. The utility of the model will be assessed by examining its goodness of fit to the 1972-1976 panel data gathered by the Center for Political Studies. . . .

Freed from many of the earlier data limitations, this study builds on [earlier] work but offers some significant advances. First, the model incorporates recent

Source: *American Political Science Review* (1979) 73:1055-70. Reprinted with permission of the publisher.

thinking about the social psychological processes involved in policy-oriented voting. Second, the model is dynamic, explicitly taking into account not only the simultaneous interplay of political attitudes within the context of a single presidential campaign but also the longitudinal dependence of these attitudes from one election to the next. Among other advantages, a model in this longitudinal form can be given more satisfying specification than one tailored to synchronic measurement. This is so because useful exogenous variables are at hand in states and behaviors actually measured at earlier periods, rather than dredged up by recall. Thus we can say with considerable certainty that evaluations of Carter and Ford as presidential candidates in 1976 cannot have exerted causal influence on expressions of party identification or issue positions in 1972, and hence the latter are suitably exogenous to the nexus of attitudes in 1976. When all measurements are synchronic, it can of course be claimed that certain variables are likely to be exogenous, simply as a tactic to permit the identification of a non-recursive model. However, such arguments must always remain in the final analysis more or less suspect.[1] Our longitudinal data base substantially liberates us from this difficulty.

An Overview of the Model

The preeminence of the trilogy of party affiliation, issue orientations, and candidate personalities as determinants of electoral choice is firmly established in the literature, and the model to be developed here is generally in keeping with this perspective. As Figure 14-1 illustrates, however, we maintain that these factors are not linked directly to the vote.[2] Instead, their confluence yields a set of overall candidate evaluations, on the basis of which a choice is made. More specifically, the model posits that the citizen compares his or her summary evaluations of the candidates and votes for the one most preferred, provided the preference differential is reasonably large. However, the smaller the amount by which the voter prefers one candidate over others, the greater the influence of party loyalty in determining the final choice. For a two-candidate race at time t, the equation linking the probability of a vote for candidate 1 to candidate evaluations and party affiliation is:

$$\text{Cand.}_1 \text{ Vote}_t = a + b_1 (\text{Eval.}_{1t} - \text{Eval.}_{2t}) + (b_2 - b_3 \mid \text{Eval.}_{1t} - \text{Eval.}_{2t} \mid)ID_t + e_t \tag{1}$$

The first explanatory variable in Equation (1) is simply the difference in candidate evaluations, while the second term involves the absolute value of this difference and reflects the hypothesis that the impact of party ties on the individual electoral decision depends on the degree to which one candidate is preferred over the other. Note that when the evaluation differential is small, the amount by which the party identification coefficient is diminished is also small. On the other hand, if one candidate is preferred to the other by a sufficiently large margin, the coefficient for the impact of partisanship may be reduced close to zero. This aspect of the model is consonant with the spirit of the "Decision Rule" devised by Kelley and Mirer (1974) as well as with normative models of the voter's calculus. Its mathematical form is quite different, however.

It should be noted parenthetically that the model is addressed to the topic of choice among candidates and does not deal directly with the question of who votes and who does not. Implicit in this delimitation is the argument that these two concerns may indeed be fairly distinct from one another and, hence, separable for analytical purposes. This argument is made on the grounds that the decision to vote or not in a given election is determined for the most part by fairly stable attitudes toward the act of voting itself and is only secondarily affected by election-specific variables (candidates, issues, etc.). The stream of literature beginning with *The American Voter* and culminating most recently in the works of Riker and Ordeshook (1968) and Ferejohn and Fiorina (1975) supports this contention. As Campbell et al. (1960, p. 93) first put it, and as it has been demonstrated repeatedly since then, "Inquiry into the determinants of voting turnout is less a search for psychological forces that determine a decision made anew in each campaign than it is a search for the attitude correlates of voting and non-voting from which these modes of behavior have emerged and by which they are presently supported."

Issue Orientations

The difficulty with assessing the impact of issues on the voting decision is that perceptions of candidate stands on issues of the day may vary significantly from voter to voter. Some of this variation will be unsystematic, rising from the casual attention most voters pay to campaign information—or arising from the ambiguous nature of the information itself. Against this background of noise, however, how voters perceive candidate policy positions may depend systematically upon their own issue preferences and overall affective orientations toward the candidates. For instance, voters may "project" their own issue stands onto candidates they like on other grounds, and by the same token they may tend to cognize the policy stances of negatively evaluated candidates in such a way as to increase the issue-related distance between themselves and these candidates (Page and Brody, 1972; Brody and Page, 1972).

In addition to the projection hypothesis, there is also the possibility of "persuasion." If a citizen were to alter his or her issue positions to coincide with those of a favorably regarded candidate, then one might say that the voter had been persuaded by the candidate (Brody and Page, 1972). A form of reverse persuasion would occur if a voter changed his or her position so as to contrast it with that of a negatively evaluated contender for office.

Lastly, the summary evaluations of the candidates are likely to be simultaneously interdependent with an individual's own policy preferences and perceptions of candidate positions. Specifically, the hypothesis is that, other things equal, the candidate thought to be most proximate to one's own position in the issue space will be favored.

The projection hypothesis is modeled as follows:

$$\text{Perceived Cand. Stand}_t = \text{Actual Cand. Stand}_t +$$
$$b_1 \left(R\text{'s Stand}_{t-1} - \text{Actual Cand. Stand}_t \right) \text{Eval.}_t + e_t \qquad (2)$$

Figure 14-1   A Model of the Voting Decision

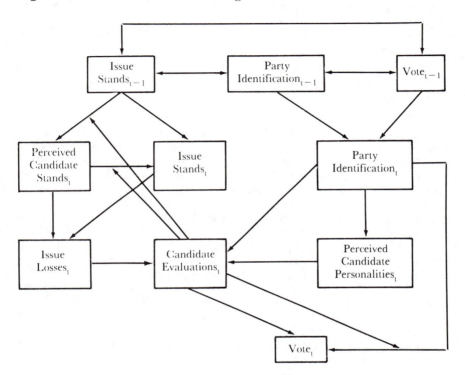

The equation implies that a voter will cognize a candidate's policy position in such a way as to decrease the issue distance between the voter and a positively evaluated candidate or to increase the distance from a negatively evaluated candidate. Since the voter may enter the campaign period with a set of policy preferences, the respondent's issue self-placements at $t - 1$ are incorporated into the equation.

The operationalization of the candidates' "actual" issue stands is problematic. One approach would involve content analysis of campaign speeches (Page and Brody, 1972). Or one might rely on the judgments of a panel of electoral experts. The method employed here is not so ambitious; we shall simply use the sample mean location of each candidate. This procedure is, of course, not without its shortcomings, and it may well be that these average placements do not correspond exactly to the candidates' "true" locations in the issue space. The mean placements nevertheless permit us to ascertain how an individual's perceived locations of the rivals for office differ from where the candidates were seen by the electorate as a whole.

The persuasion hypothesis is modeled for a two-candidate race according to Equation (3):

$$R\text{'s Stand}_t = a + b_1 R\text{'s Stand}_{t-1} + b_2 (\text{Perceived Cand.}_1 \text{ Stand}_t -$$
$$R\text{'s Stand}_{t-1}) \text{ Eval.}_{1t} + b_3 (\text{Perceived Cand.}_2 \text{ Stand}_t -$$
$$R\text{'s Stand}_{t-1}) \text{ Eval.}_{2t} + e_t \tag{3}$$

This equation represents the idea that a voter's issue orientations prior to the campaign may be modified as a function of the candidate's issue stands, as the voter sees them. That is, the voter will move toward a favored candidate's perceived position and/or away from that of a negatively evaluated candidate.

One might question the absence of party identification in Equation (3), particularly since some recent research has suggested an increasing alignment of issue opinions and partisan ties (RePass, 1971; Pomper, 1972). However, a closer examination of the proposed model in Figure 14-1 reveals that the specification does not imply a lack of relationship between partisanship and issue opinions. First, the *long-term* effect of party affiliation on policy preferences is captured in their correlation at $t - 1$. In addition, the *endogenous* influence of party ties on issue stances is posited to flow via the effect of such ties on candidate evaluations.

This specification is supported both empirically (Markus, 1976; Converse and Markus, 1979) and by theoretical considerations. With regard to the latter, the argument is that, within the course of a presidential campaign, issues become imbued with partisan qualities insofar as the partisan rivals for office come to be identified with particular policies. The candidates form the link between partisanship and intra-campaign change in policy-related attitudes.

Equation (4) is derived from the ideas underlying the loss function model of evaluation. It posits that the net candidate evaluation differential is a function of issue-based losses and losses (or, in the positive, gains) accruing from preferences in candidate personalities and partisan identification:

$$(\text{Eval.}_{1t} - \text{Eval.}_{2t}) = a + b_1 (\text{Loss}_{1t} - \text{Loss}_{2t}) +$$
$$b_2 (\text{Personality}_{1t} - \text{Personality}_{2t}) + b_3 \text{ID}_t + e_t \tag{4}$$

Candidate Personality

One would expect that, other things equal, Democrats will tend to prefer the personal traits of a Democratic candidate to those of a Republican office-seeker, and conversely for Republicans. The model, therefore, includes an equation which posits the difference in a citizen's ratings of the candidates' personalities to be a function of partisan ties:

$$(\text{Personality}_{1t} - \text{Personality}_{2t}) = a + b_1 \text{ID}_t + e_t \tag{5}$$

Party Identification

The party identification equation is structured to reflect the possibility that while partisanship is relatively stable through time, it may nonetheless be influenced by prior voting behavior. Thus although the vote is the ultimate dependent variable within the context of a single presidential election, from a dynamic perspective it may feed forward to influence the voter's future political orientations.[3] The model also permits the precursors of current partisanship to interact, with voters and nonvoters differing in terms of the relative stability of party identification through time:

$$ID_t = a + b_1 \text{ Demo. Vote}_{t-1} + b_2 \text{ Repub. Vote}_{t-1} + (b_3 + b_4 \text{ Voted}_{t-1})ID_{t-1} + e_t \tag{6}$$

Results

As mentioned earlier, the model of electoral choice was fitted against the CPS 1972-1976 panel data. These data contain information on a national sample of 1286 adult respondents interviewed in the periods immediately following the two presidential elections (see Miller et al., 1976; Miller and Miller, 1977; Converse and Markus, 1979).

Before detailing the results, we should make a few technical comments about our analytical methods. Because of the simultaneous nature of the system of equations, we employed two-stage least squares as an estimator, except in those instances where ordinary least squares estimation appeared justified. Lagged dependent variables were treated as predetermined with respect to the 1976 data, implying a lack of autocorrelation in the disturbances. Although this assumption is perhaps not fully warranted, it is not unreasonable, given the fairly long time lag between waves (cf. Hibbs, 1972). The assumption also finds support in some of our earlier analyses (Converse and Markus, 1979). Finally, the estimation proceeded in modular fashion from equation to equation, rather than being carried out initially for the structure as a whole, and thereby avoids the considerable attrition of case numbers that occurs when cases with missing data on as little as one of the totality of variables in the structure are deleted from any role in the estimation.

Party Identification

The party identification variable ranges in seven integer steps from -3 (Strong Democrat) to $+3$ (Strong Republican). For purposes of operationalization, the other variables in Equation (6) are coded in a binary fashion, denoting whether the respondent voted in 1972 and, if so, for the candidate of which party. Nonvoters are coded zero on all three binary variables.

Estimation of Equation (6) by ordinary least squares yields the following results (standard errors in parentheses):

$$ID_t = -.37 - .20 \text{ Demo. Vote}_{t-1} + .49 \text{ Repub. Vote}_{t-1} +$$
$$ (.07) \quad (.10) \phantom{\text{ Demo. Vote}_{t-1}} (.09)$$
$$ (.63 + .10 \text{ Voted}_{t-1})ID_{t-1} + e_t$$
$$ (.04) \quad (.05)$$

$$R^2 = .64; \ N = 1252.$$

Party identification is found to be very durable from one election to the next, a result consistent with work on these and other data. Also, as hypothesized, the relationship between prior and current partisanship is somewhat stronger among voters than among nonvoters (with an estimated coefficient of .63 + .10 = .73 for voters versus .63 for nonvoters in 1972). But while partisan attachments move relatively little from one election to the next, they are not completely immune to electoral forces, as demonstrated by the significant coefficients attached to the partisan voting variables.

The feedforward effect of electoral choice on party identification is displayed in Table 14-1, in which the coefficient estimates have been used to generate predictions of party identification at time t for different combinations of past identification and vote. The table shows that when partisanship is not reinforced by consistent electoral behavior, it may weaken. The predicted effect of a deviating vote in a single election is hardly dramatic; indeed, if it were, there would be reason to doubt the analysis. Nevertheless, the cumulative effects of a series of votes running counter to an individual's prior party ties might well lead to a conversion of partisan orientations at the individual level.

Issue Opinions

Five policy domains were selected for study here: social welfare, busing, government assistance to minority groups, tax reform, and women's rights. These issues were chosen because comparable items dealing with them were included in both the 1972 and 1976 Election Studies and because they were issues which were salient to many voters in 1976, as will be illustrated in a moment. For each policy domain, respondents were asked to place themselves and the major party candidates along a seven-point continuum with labeled endpoints.[4]

It is, of course, possible that the inclusion of other issues to the set of five might have altered the results of the analysis significantly, but we deem this unlikely. For one thing, the five issue domains appear to cover most of the public's major policy concerns in 1976. Our evidence for this statement is derived from an open-ended query in the 1976 interview regarding "the most important problem the country faces." Some degree of ambiguity is always inherent in mapping open-ended responses into fixed categories, but by our count over three-quarters of the answers directly concerned one or more of the five issues under study.

Perceptions of where the presidential candidates stood on the issues in 1976 varied with an individual's own policy preferences and affective orientations toward the contenders (see Table 14-2 [for two issues]). Generally, a citizen's placement of a favorably evaluated candidate along an issue continuum is positively associated with the individual's own preferred position on the seven-point scale. At the same time, the perceived location of a negatively evaluated candidate is inversely correlated with self-placement. This relationship is by no means invariant across issue domains and candidates, nor do average perceptions of candidate positions float unanchored across the entire seven-point range. Nevertheless, the tabular results display an unmistakable regularity. Table 14-2 does not, however, enable one to gauge the extent of persuasion or projection, since the pattern of association is consistent with either of these hypotheses—or a

Table 14-1 Predictions of Party Identification$_t$, by Prior Partisanship and Voting

Vote$_{t-1}$	Party ID$_{t-1}$						
	Strong Democrat	Demo-crat	Inde-pendent Democrat	Inde-pendent	Inde-pendent Repub-lican	Repub-lican	Strong Repub-lican
Nixon	−2.07 (D)	−1.34 (ID)	− .61 (ID)	.12 (I)	.85 (IR)	1.58 (R)	2.31 (R)
None	−2.25 (D)	−1.63 (D)	−1.00 (ID)	−.37 (I)	.26 (I)	.88 (IR)	1.51 (R)
McGovern	−2.76 (SD)	−2.04 (D)	−1.31 (ID)	−.58 (ID)	.15 (I)	.88 (IR)	1.61 (R)

Note: Mid-points between scale values were used as cut-points to generate the parenthesized category predictions.

Source: Equation (6), as estimated using data from the 1972-76 Center for Political Studies National Election Panel Study.

combination of them. We must turn to the simultaneous equation model for further explanation of the interdependencies exhibited above.

Table 14-3 presents the two-stage least squares estimates of the ten (two candidates x five issues) "projection" equations. The R^2 values associated with these equations are fairly low, but then this is not unexpected: probably most of the variation in perceptions of candidate stands is simply noise arising from the presidential office-seekers' strategy of obscuring their positions on specific issues—especially in 1976.[5] Nevertheless, in all instances save one, the regression coefficient reflecting the extent of projection is significant, hovering around an estimated value of .005. One way of interpreting this value is that it implies that for a very favorably evaluated candidate (i.e., one receiving a translated thermometer score near +50), up to 25 percent of any difference between the candidate's objective issue position and the respondent's favored position would be "projected away."[6] Another way of interpreting these estimates is illustrated in Table 14-4. In that table, predicted candidate placements have been calculated for various combinations of self-placements on the first two issues and feelings toward the candidates. By comparing these predictions with the actual mean scores in Table 14-2, one can see that the mathematically parsimonious projection equations yield aggregate profiles that are consistent with the observed findings.

The two-stage least squares estimates of the equations for voters' preferences on the five issues are presented in Table 14-5. The analysis indicates that issue opinions possess a durability which, although much less than that of party identification, is nonetheless quite significant.[7] There is also evidence of the persuasion or leadership effect with regard to three policy domains: welfare, minority groups, and tax reform. The presidential candidates apparently exerted

Table 14-2   Mean Candidate Issue Placement, by Self-Placement and Candidate Feeling Thermometer Score

	Social Welfare							
	Carter				Ford			
R's Location	Warm		Cool		Warm		Cool	
1 (Liberal)	2.2	(77)	4.8	(4)	3.4	(31)	6.2	(40)
2	2.5	(48)	3.9	(7)	3.6	(35)	5.9	(21)
3	2.8	(96)	3.4	(18)	3.9	(81)	5.4	(34)
4	3.2	(137)	3.0	(42)	4.1	(149)	5.3	(36)
5	3.8	(103)	2.5	(56)	4.4	(123)	5.0	(32)
6	3.5	(77)	2.2	(48)	4.5	(105)	4.2	(15)
7 (Conservative)	3.7	(87)	2.6	(77)	4.7	(142)	3.7	(28)
Grand Mean	3.2	(625)	2.6	(252)	4.3	(666)	5.2	(206)
eta-squared	.15		.13		.07		.27	

	Busing							
	Carter				Ford			
R's Location	Warm		Cool		Warm		Cool	
1 (Favor)	3.3	(28)	5.0	(3)	2.5	(10)	6.0	(20)
2	2.7	(27)	5.0	(2)	4.1	(21)	6.1	(8)
3	3.4	(18)	5.0	(2)	4.0	(16)	5.7	(6)
4	3.8	(44)	5.2	(12)	4.1	(39)	5.1	(19)
5	4.1	(32)	3.0	(11)	4.4	(36)	4.4	(14)
6	4.2	(79)	3.5	(35)	4.2	(105)	3.8	(22)
7 (Oppose)	4.2	(318)	3.3	(137)	4.5	(441)	3.3	(120)
Grand Mean	4.0	(546)	3.4	(202)	4.4	(668)	4.0	(209)
eta-squared	.06		.05		.03		.21	

Note: Cool feelings include feeling thermometer scores of 0-49 degrees. Warm feelings are scores of 51-100 degrees.
Source: 1976 Center for Political Studies National Election Panel Study.

very little influence upon public sentiments toward busing and women's rights, however.

These findings recall a pattern that emerged in our first cut at these data (Converse and Markus, 1979). In that study, the stability of opinion on various issues was found to be arrayed hierarchically, with attitudes on issues of a moral nature displaying a distinctively higher degree of temporal stability and hence apparently greater crystallization than did opinions on civil rights, domestic policy, and foreign affairs. It stands to reason that attitudes tied closely to one's

Table 14-3 Two-Stage Least Square Estimates for the Perceived Candidate Issue Position Equations

Issue	Candidate	Mean	Coefficient	Standard Error	N	R^2
Welfare	Carter	3.01	.007	.001	854	.08
	Ford	4.51	.006	.001	869	.02
Busing	Carter	3.84	.005	.001	701	.06
	Ford	4.26	.007	.001	848	.06
Minorities	Carter	3.18	.005	.001	773	.04
	Ford	4.00	.005	.001	813	.04
Tax Reform	Carter	3.32	.000	.000	735	.00
	Ford	4.40	.003	.001	685	.01
Women	Carter	3.20	.002	.001	711	.01
	Ford	3.37	.005	.001	748	.03

Source: 1972-76 Center for Political Studies Election Panel Study.

sense of morality would not be very susceptible to the influence of campaign debate, and that is precisely what we find here.

Lastly, since the dependent and persuasion variables from Table 14-5 are expressed in the same currencies as the dependent and regressor variables, respectively, in the preceding set of equations, the relative effects of projection and persuasion may be compared.[8] Upon doing so, one finds that with respect to both Carter and Ford the projection coefficients are larger than the corresponding persuasion values for all issues but one. The differences are by no means staggering, but they do suggest that projection is about 20 percent stronger than persuasion, on the average. One should bear in mind, however, that under certain circumstances—e.g., a new issue for which public opinion has not yet jelled—the influence of political leaders upon the electorate's policy preferences might be substantial.

Candidate Personalities

In 1976, respondents were asked to rate on a seven-point scale the degree to which each of the major candidates had "the kind of personality a President ought to have." The estimated equation linking the difference in ratings of Ford's and Carter's personalities to partisanship is (standard errors in parentheses):[9]

$$(\text{Ford Personality} - \text{Carter Personality}): = .20 + .60 \ ID_t + e_t$$
$$\qquad\qquad\qquad\qquad\qquad\qquad (.07) \quad (.04)$$

The equation accounts for 20 percent of the variation in the dependent variable (N = 1193), equivalent to a standardized regression coefficient of .44 for party identification. On the average, the personalities of both candidates were scored at about 1.4 on a -3 to $+3$ scale. The unstandardized coefficient

Table 14-4   Predicted Perceived Candidate Location for Various Combinations of Self-Placement and Candidate Feeling Thermometer Score

| | *Social Welfare* | | | | |
| | *Carter* | | | *Ford* | |
Respondent Position	*Warm*	*Cool*		*Warm*	*Cool*
1 (Liberal)	2.7	3.4		4.0	5.0
3	3.0	3.0		4.3	4.7
5	3.4	2.7		4.6	4.4
7 (Conservative)	3.7	2.3		4.9	4.1

| | *Busing* | | | | |
| | *Carter* | | | *Ford* | |
Respondent Position	*Warm*	*Cool*		*Warm*	*Cool*
1 (Favor)	3.5	4.2		3.7	4.8
3	3.7	3.9		4.0	4.5
5	4.0	3.7		4.4	4.1
7 (Oppose)	4.2	3.5		4.7	3.8

Note: Scores of −25 and +25 degrees were used to represent cool and warm feelings, respectively, on a translated feeling thermometer ranging from −50 to +50 degrees. The former values are virtually identical to the observed mean feeling scores for the two sets of respondents.

Source: Equation (2), as estimated using data from the 1972-76 Center for Political Studies National Election Panel Study.

estimates show Ford receiving a score about two points higher than Carter among Strong Republicans, however, and about 1.6 points below Carter among Strong Democrats.[10]

Evaluations of the Candidates

Equation (4) posits that a citizen's overall evaluations of the presidential candidates are formed from a mix of policy considerations, partisan predispositions, and beliefs about the personalities of the rivals for office. The operationalizations of the regressors in that equation are by now familiar, with the exception of the issue-loss component. The issue loss associated with each candidate was constructed as the average squared difference between the respondent's self-placement on each issue and his or her perceived location of the candidate. We used an average rather than a simple sum of squares because not all respondents could provide both a preferred policy and a candidate location for all five issues.

Table 14-5 Two-Stage Least Squares Estimates for the Voter Issue Position Equation

	Coefficient	Standard Error
Social Welfare		
Constant	2.59	.14
Issue Position$_{t-1}$	.47	.03
Carter Persuasion	.006	.001
Ford Persuasion	.006	.002
$R^2 = .29$ $N = 883$		
Busing		
Constant	2.35	.19
Issue Position$_{t-1}$	.61	.03
Carter Persuasion	.002	.001
Ford Persuasion	.003	.001
$R^2 = .40$ $N = 685$		
Minority Groups		
Constant	2.25	.14
Issue Position$_{t-1}$	.52	.03
Carter Persuasion	.004	.001
Ford Persuasion	.004	.002
$R^2 = .33$ $N = 764$		
Tax Reform		
Constant	2.54	.22
Issue Position$_{t-1}$	.40	.05
Carter Persuasion	.007	.002
Ford Persuasion	.004	.002
$R^2 = .16$ $N = 657$		
Women's Rights		
Constant	1.67	.16
Issue Position$_{t-1}$	.41	.05
Carter Persuasion	−.001	.002
Ford Persuasion	.001	.003
$R^2 = .21$ $N = 689$		

Source: Data from the 1972-76 Center for Political Studies National Election Panel Study.

This method weights each included issue equally, a procedure which appears to conflict with the notion that all issues may not be equally salient to the voter. A number of considerations render this approach less objectionable than it might seem, however. First, taken as a whole the five issues are salient ones, and the majority of respondents were able to locate themselves and the candidates on each of the issue continua. Moreover, issues that are utterly non-salient to a respondent are given a weight of zero, since both self and candidate placements

Table 14-6   Two-Stage Least Squares Estimates for the Evaluation
Differential Equation

	Unstandardized Coefficient	*Standard Error*	*Standardized Coefficient*
Constant	2.72	.77	
Ford−Carter Issue Loss	−1.34	.38	−.30
Ford−Carter Personality	6.26	.51	.43
ID_t	5.66	.64	.29
$R^2 = .67$ $N = 1013$			

Source: Data from the 1972-76 Center for Political Studies National Election Panel Study.

are required for the issue to be included in the loss calculus. Third, preliminary attempts to devise a weighting scheme based on open-ended and other responses actually led to a slight decrease in explanatory power for the regression equation. This came as little surprise, since a number of recent psychological studies have demonstrated that people are generally quite unreliable in assessing the relative importance of factors in determining their decisions (Nisbett and Wilson, 1977). Moreover, other work indicates that the choice of weights tends to make little difference in the ultimate predictions (Wainer, 1976; Dawes and Corrigan, 1974).

The two-stage least squares estimates for the candidate evaluation are displayed in Table 14-6. The analysis indicates that all three elements—issues, party, and personalities—were important determinants of feelings toward Ford and Carter. Taken together, these three variables account for two-thirds of the variation in the feeling thermometer differential for the presidential rivals.

The results suggest that the perceived personal qualities of the candidates weighed most heavily, at least in the direct-effect sense, in determining the public's overall evaluations of Ford and Carter. The standardized coefficient for the personality differential variable equals .43, and the unstandardized coefficient implies nearly a 40-point difference (6.26 x 6) in the thermometer scores of candidates rated at opposite extremes of the presidential personality scale.

Issues and party ties were about equally important in terms of their direct effect on candidate evaluations, with standardized coefficients of −.30 and .29, respectively. Keeping in mind that the issue loss differential can range from +36 (favoring Carter) to −36 (favoring Ford), note that the unstandardized coefficient for that variable implies that for each unit increase in Ford's loss value relative to Carter's, the voter's thermometer difference (Ford−Carter) decreased by a little more than one degree, other variables held constant. At the same time, the coefficient for party identification indicates a 20-degree differential favoring Ford among Strong Republicans and a 14-degree contrast favoring Carter among Strong Democrats, *ceteris paribus*.[11]

The fairly modest standardized coefficient for party identification might be somewhat puzzling, given the crucial role that partisanship has been assumed to play in electoral behavior. It is important to remember, however, that in addition to its direct impact on candidate evaluations, party affiliation also exerts a substantial *indirect* influence via its effect upon perceptions of candidate personalities. When this indirect influence is combined with the direct effect, it yields an "effects" coefficient of .29 + .43(.44) = .48, larger than the standardized coefficient for either candidate personalities or issue proximities (see Figure 14-2). This latter value may be more in line with intuitive judgments—and prior evidence—about the impact of partisanship on candidate evaluations. Moreover, under some circumstances party identification may play a significant role in determining the electoral decision quite apart from its influence on feelings toward the candidates, as we shall see in a moment.

The Vote Decision

Least squares estimation of the vote choice equation generates the following results (standard errors in parentheses):[12]

$$\text{Ford Vote} = .506 + .009 \text{ (Ford Eval.} - \text{Carter Eval.)}$$
$$(.010) \quad (.0004)$$
$$+ (.141 - .0025 \mid \text{Ford Eval.} - \text{Carter Eval.} \mid)ID_t + e_t$$
$$(.009) \quad (.0002)$$

The regression analysis lends clear support to the hypothesized vote choice equation. All coefficients have the expected signs and are many times larger than their associated standard errors. The R^2 value for the equation equals .64 (N = 884), but because of the dichotomous nature of the dependent variable, the best measure of goodness of fit is provided by the fact that the equation correctly predicts respondents' votes 90 percent of the time.[13]

Moreover, it can be shown that the direct intrusion of party identification in influencing the vote choice when there is relative indifference in candidate evaluations is the only case in which prior variables in the model affect the vote, save indirectly through the comparative candidate evaluations. That is, the addition of other model variables, including most notably the issue losses and personality ratings, to the simple vote choice regression equation based on differential candidate evaluations and party identification, leads to virtually no increase in predictive accuracy. As a further test, we applied the estimated equation to the data from the 1972 wave of the panel to ascertain its predictive accuracy with regard to the Nixon-McGovern contest.[14] The result was that 97 percent of the voters were correctly classified, a very satisfactory result given that the coefficient estimates are based on an entirely different set of data. Indeed, the predictive accuracy might seem to be *too* good, but the explanation is simply that evaluations of Nixon and McGovern tended to be more disparate than those for Ford and Carter, and hence electoral choice was more predictable than in 1976.

The values of the coefficient estimates possess some charming qualities. For instance, the constant term implies a virtual 50-50 split in the vote of Independents who evaluated the two candidates equally. Furthermore, if one simulates an election wherein net short-term partisan forces (i.e., the evaluation differential) are zero and inserts the sample mean for the party identification

Figure 14-2 Candidate Evaluations Segment of the Model of
Electoral Choice

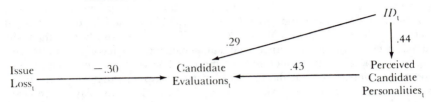

Source: Based on the regression estimates outlined in the text.

variable, the prediction (interpreting the result in aggregate terms) is a 46 percent vote for the Republican candidate—precisely the value of the normal vote (Converse, 1966b).

Note that the direct impact of party identification upon the vote decision depends upon the size of the candidate evaluation differential. When both candidates are evaluated identically, each step toward the Republican end of the partisan continuum increases the predicted dependent score (roughly, the probability of voting for Ford) by .14. Once the difference in candidate evaluations reaches about 55 degrees, however, the predicted direct effect or partisanship on the vote is virtually nil, as indicated by its small coefficient: $.141 - .0025(55) = .003$.[15] Although the direct influence of party ties on the vote decision would be negligible under these circumstances, their indirect effect, i.e., their prior impact on the candidate evaluations themselves, nevertheless remains appreciable.

The relative effects of candidate evaluations and party identification on the choice between presidential contenders is illustrated in Table 14-7. As displayed there, the predicted probability of a Ford vote ranges from .00 for Strong Democrats, with a 50 degree evaluation differential favoring Carter, to 1.00 for Strong Republicans, with an equally large pro-Ford difference. The table also illustrates the varying impact of party identification, depending on the contrast in candidate evaluations: when the differential is large, the probability entries do not vary much across partisan categories; if the evaluation differential is within the bounds ±20 degrees, however, the residual impact of partisanship on electoral choice is more potent.

Conclusions

From a substantive point of view, a model is something more than the sum of its parts. We may therefore conclude by moving from an examination of the separate equations comprising the model to a brief summary and discussion of its broader implications.

Table 14-7 Predicted Probability of a Ford Vote, by Party Identification and Candidate Evaluation Difference

	Party Identification						
Differential	Strong Democrat	Democrat	Independent Democrat	Independent	Independent Republican	Republican	Strong Republican
(Pro-Carter) −50	.00	.02	.04	.06	.07	.09	.10
−40	.02	.06	.11	.15	.19	.23	.27
−20	.05	.14	.24	.33	.42	.51	.60
−10	.07	.18	.30	.42	.53	.65	.76
0	.08	.22	.37	.51	.65	.79	.93
10	.25	.36	.48	.60	.71	.83	.94
20	.41	.50	.60	.69	.78	.87	.96
40	.74	.78	.83	.87	.91	.95	.99
(Pro-Ford) 50	.91	.92	.94	.96	.97	.99	1.00

Source: Equation (1), as estimated using the 1972-76 Center for Political Studies National Election Panel Study.

Perhaps most importantly, the hypothesized model of electoral choice has fared rather well against the 1972-1976 panel data. No alterations in the posited specification were indicated. To the contrary, a number of R^2 values approach what must be their upper bounds, given normal sampling error and other idiosyncratic sources of noise.

The analysis affirms the crucial role of candidates in the dynamics of electoral choice. Candidate evaluations have been shown to be a primary determinant of the vote, with policy considerations and even partisan orientations affecting the vote either exclusively or largely through the way they help to shape feelings toward the presidential rivals. The candidates also mediate the flow of campaign stimuli toward the cognitive predispositions comprising the citizen's network of political beliefs: they serve as the primary vehicle through which policy debate takes on partisan coloration, and through their determining influence on the vote, feelings toward the candidates even act dynamically in at least a small degree to modify or reinforce standing party ties. In the American system of elections, the choice is ultimately between competing candidates.

The fact that comparative candidate assessments are the most potent proximal determinant of the vote decision should not, however, lead us to overlook the causally prior impacts of issues and parties on these assessments. Policy considerations were shown to be significant in determining voters' evaluations of the 1976 presidential candidates. Some of these manifest linkages between issues and candidates turned out to be modestly circular in one sense or another. Thus, for example, a degree of "projection" was uncovered, whereby voters reporting issue positions of candidates they already liked would shade these perceptions toward the issue positions the voter already preferred, while assuming that disliked candidates must have more sharply dissimilar positions. In the same causal nexus it was possible to isolate a persuasion effect as well, whereby the voter appeared to be shifting his or her own reported issue position to conform more closely with that of a preferred candidate, or to distinguish it more sharply from that perceived for a disliked candidate. The persuasion effect was less strong in these data than the projection effect, and furthermore showed signs of variation by type of issue. For issues like school busing or women's rights, where there is independent evidence of sharp crystallization of public feeling, any persuasion effect is negligible. It is chiefly on issues where voters are less personally exercised that the policy position of candidates can sway their admirers' views of the issue.

However intriguing and plausible these side effects may be, the estimates we have derived from the model make clear that they remained no more than side effects in 1976. The policy differences consensually perceived to exist between the candidates, coupled with prior differences in voter positions on these issues, had a noteworthy effect on voters' comparative assessments of the candidates, and through these invidious assessments, the policy terms ultimately left their mark on final voting decisions.

Similarly, the model helps to delineate more clearly than did prior work the important function of partisan predispositions in the processes leading to a voting choice. Earlier investigations limited to static data bases have often tried to assess the relative role of parties, issues and candidates by assigning each a single ultimate regression weight, leading to comparisons which take on the flavor of a simplistic horse race. Viewing the formulation of a voting decision in terms which are more explicitly processual may rob us of such a simple "final score," but may yield redeeming satisfactions due to greater verisimilitude.

In such process terms, the causal role of partisanship appears to be particularly important for two reasons. First, party identifications are much more stable in the intermediate term than other elements in the model. If the game were redefined as one of predicting a voting decision on the basis of political attitudes examined eight years before election day, there would be little contest: the identity of the candidates would be utterly unknown at such remove, some issues to become important later would also be unknown, and voter attitudes on other more abiding issues would be subject to considerably greater flux in the interim.

The second reason shows up clearly in the structure of the model and hinges on the fact that the party component is unique in the way it intrudes at multiple points in the process. Partisan predispositions may be outweighed by other model terms at particular stages, as other research on a static base has shown, but these loyalties keep coming back as determinants while the vote decision process unrolls. For example, Figure 14-2 suggested that neither issues nor partisanship were as important in their direct effects upon ultimate comparisons between the candidates as were simple judgments of their personalities. However, the very same figure makes clear that reactions to candidate personalities have already been shaped by prior partisan predispositions, so that there is an indirect path from party to candidate evaluations which is of imposing proportions in itself, quite apart from the direct path also depicted. Or at a later point, partisanship again enters the model significantly in influencing the final vote when the voter has trouble making sharp affective discriminations between the candidates.

In the same vein, given the durable nature of these loyalties over lengthy periods of time (Converse and Markus, 1979), it may well be that prior partisanship has also intruded at stages too early for adequate representation in our model. Thus, for example, we located an edge of "persuasion" whereby the voters' issue locations were mildly affected by the issue positions perceived for liked and disliked candidates. If such candidate persuasion exists, then it would not be at all surprising if there were an earlier *party* persuasion term of entirely parallel structure accounting for some of the party-relatedness of issue positions at our first time point, yet which is exogenous to our model as presented. Such party persuasion would presumably be operative in the first stages of issue emergence, and hence likely to have more impact on the distribution of attitudes in the electorate than do candidates who arrive on the scene after such issue positions have become at least modestly crystallized.

In short, then, while partisan predispositions are unlikely to dominate the process completely at given stages where the candidates are being assessed, these loyalties appear to make repeated inputs of substantial magnitude throughout the process.

We believe that the model as presented is an integrated and generalizable one that captures most of what is important as voters face elections involving candidate competition. The model could be enlarged to become more general still. It could, for example, add considerations of turnout, representing the fact that voting and nonvoting are for the most part habitual differences, but capturing those margins of turnout variance that are in fact current and dynamic responses to the specific election configuration, such as the likely diminution in turnout that may accompany feelings of sheer disgust about *both* candidates. The model could also be extended more deeply in time, explicating the genesis of the relationships between prior issue positions, prior party loyalties, and prior votes.

Perhaps the most important consideration to keep in mind is that whereas we have used data from the specific period 1972-76 for estimation of model parameters and assessment of general fit, the model per se should be seen as a shell, or a vessel, designed to apply to a wide range of specific elections. Estimates of specific parameters would naturally vary across types of elections, or for specific elections of the same series over time. To seize an example which is too obvious, for candidate elections which are truly non-partisan in fact as well as intent, the coefficients representing the various points of impact of the party term in the model would by definition fall to zero.

It is this conditional variation from one election to another that becomes of subsequent interest to understand. The present model is thus a satisfying vehicle for providing the kinds of parameter estimates that seem to express the voting calculus well in any special case.

NOTES

1. A common tactic with models tailored to static data is to depend on recall of earlier states for exogenous variables. Thus, for example, recall of parental partisanship may be used as an exogenous variable on grounds that current political attitudes cannot act backward causally in time to affect parental partisanship in an earlier period. When no other longitudinal information is available, such an assumption is better than nothing. However, this assumption ignores the possibility that *current* recall of earlier parental partisanship can itself be contaminated by currently evolving political attitudes.

2. In Figure 14-1 we are adopting the convention that an arrow leading to another arrow denotes an interaction or mediating effect. In addition, when the simultaneous equation form of Figure 14-1 is presented, the coefficients and error term in each equation will be subscripted only with respect to that equation (i.e., the constant term for such equation is simply a, the error term is e_i, etc.). The purpose is to keep the notation simple, and it should cause no confusion to the reader.

3. It is important to keep in mind here, as elsewhere in the model equations, that we are less making an assertive assumption that prior votes *do* influence party identification, than merely building a model structure which permits such effects to be discriminated *if they exist*. Earlier recursive models of the Goldberg (1966) type were obliged to proclaim by assumption that these reverse effects of vote on party identification did not exist, at least within the time frame of the model. We do not make a contrary proclamation that such effects *do* exist, since a given testing of the model in a special case might show the relevant coefficients to be zero.

4. The text of the issue items may be found in the CPS 1976 National Election Study codebook, available from the Inter-University Consortium for Political and Social Research.
5. Correlations are also probably depressed by the presence of error arising from imprecise instrumentation and the stochastic nature of the latent attitudes being measured (Converse, 1970; Achen, 1975; Converse and Markus, 1979).
6. Multiplication of the .005 average coefficient estimate by the thermometer score of 50 yields the 25 percent figure. The translated thermometer used in estimating Equations (2) and (3) ranges from −50 to +50 degrees.
7. See Converse and Markus (1979) for a further discussion of the relative stabilities of political outlooks.
8. We prefer the unstandardized coefficients to standardized ones because the equations are nonlinear in the variables, rendering the usual interpretation of standardized coefficients problematical (Allison, 1977). Moreover, since standardized coefficients are by definition variance-sensitive, comparisons of their values across equations— even linear ones—can lead to misinterpretations.
9. The equation was estimated by ordinary least squares, which assumes a lack of correlation between the disturbances in the party identification and personality differential equations. The consequence of this assumption being incorrect would be to overstate the impact of the independent variable. Given the plausibly moderate value of the coefficient estimate, the assumption appears not to have been grossly unreasonable.
10. The predicted dependent variable value is .20 + .60(+3) = 2.0 for Strong Republicans and .20 + .60(−3) = −1.6 for Strong Democrats.
11. For Strong Republicans, the expected thermometer differential is 2.72 + 5.66(+3) = 19.70; for Strong Democrats it is 2.72 + 5.66 (−3) = −14.26.
12. Both two-stage least squares (2SLS) and ordinary least squares (OLS) estimators were originally employed. Although the methods yielded similar coefficient estimates, the OLS values are preferred here because they yield fewer predictions outside of the allowable 0-1 range and because the 2SLS residuals were only modestly correlated with residuals elsewhere in the system, thus permitting the more efficient OLS estimation. The 2SLS estimates (with standard errors parenthesized) are:

$$\text{Ford Vote} = .503 + .011 \text{ (Ford Eval.} - \text{Carter Eval.)}$$
$$(.012) \quad (.001)$$
$$+ (.157 - .0036 \mid \text{Ford Eval.} - \text{Carter Eval.} \mid)ID_t + e_t$$
$$(.019) \quad (.0007)$$
$$R^2 = .65; \ N = 753.$$

13. Respondents with estimated dependent variable scores >.50 were predicted to have voted for Ford, while those with estimated values ≤.50 were classed as Carter voters.
14. This prediction to the 1972 presidential vote refers, of course, to the vote choice equation taken alone. The full model being presented could not be estimated for 1972 separately, for lack of prior panel data in that year.
15. In 1976, 15 percent of all respondents saw no difference in their overall evaluations of the candidates. One half of the sample had evaluation differentials of 25 degrees or less, and nearly 90 percent are included in the ±55 degree span.

PART IV: CONGRESSIONAL ELECTIONS

15. WHAT DETERMINES
THE CONGRESSIONAL VOTE?

Congressional voting has become one of the liveliest areas of electoral research. Three forces converged to create this focus on congressional voting. First was the stream of research on the effects of the economy and presidential popularity, especially controversial because work with aggregate data initially found very weak support in survey studies. Second was a seeming decline in the number of closely contested seats in the House of Representatives, a decline that proved to be difficult to explain. Third was the involvement of congressional scholars in a new set of mass surveys sponsored by the National Election Studies; the survey in 1978 was the first since 1958 to focus on congressional candidates rather than on concerns derived from presidential election studies.

Each of these forces spawned controversy and a good deal of research. Fortunately, progress in the form of relatively firm conclusions was made, though of course some controversy and some unanswered questions remained. Most of the research could be summarized around the theme of "district level variables versus national political forces" (Jacobson and Kernell, 1981, p. 17).

Congressional Elections as National Events

Those who see legislative elections as basically national events generally stress at least one of three interpretations of these elections: they are partisan affairs where only party identification matters, they are referendums on the incumbent executive's job performance, or they are rewards or punishments for the status of the economy. The local incumbent and challenger are treated as virtually nonentities in these formulations, since the election result is viewed as depending on circumstances beyond their control.

The original emphasis on the role of partisanship in congressional elections is due to a 1958 study by the Michigan Survey Research Center. Stokes and Miller attempted to study the 1958 congressional elections as they had studied the presidential elections of the 1950s, but to their dismay they found that voters often could not even recall the names of the candidates and that issues did not play a part in the evaluations of the candidates the citizens did know. Chapters 16 and

17—short excerpts from two of their articles—summarize their evidence and forcefully state their conclusion. If candidates and issues played a small role in the election, then partisanship was paramount, having the same large impact on the vote that it had on presidential voting. Campbell (1960) was able to use this result to construct an explanation of the loss of seats in Congress that the president's party has invariably suffered in midterm elections: that fewer partisan voters who show up to vote in presidential elections and swing on the basis of short-term considerations to one presidential candidate (and then support his party's ticket for lower offices) are the ones who do not bother to vote at the off-year elections, thus cutting both turnout and the congressional vote for the president's party. Regardless of whether or not one finds this "surge and decline" explanation convincing, survey evidence is clear that party identification is a major correlate of congressional voting.

Still, the partisanship interpretation did not satisfy many scholars. They felt that some issues were of importance—economic issues in particular. And they felt that one candidate was relevant—the incumbent president. One long series of studies, based on analysis of aggregate data, dealt mostly with economic variables, including changes in unemployment levels, real income, and the rate of inflation, although some of the contributions also suggested the relevance of overall satisfaction with the president's performance. The series began with an article by Gerald Kramer (1971), in which he showed that a number of economic variables are related to the total congressional vote over the period 1896-1964.[1] A large number of criticisms and reformulations ensued.[2] For example, Bloom and Price's (1975) analysis suggested that the president's party is hurt by bad economic times but not helped by good times. Later, Hibbing and Alford (1982) found a relationship between economic conditions and U.S. Senate voting, and Lewis-Beck and Bellucci (1982) extended such analyses to legislative voting in France and Italy. This series is one of the factors that led to a growing corpus of work on economic influences more generally, both here and abroad (Niemi and Weisberg, 1992, chapter 9). Altogether this work—both the congressional series and the presidential—leaves little doubt that "election outcomes are in substantial part responsive to objective changes occurring under the incumbent party, where for congressional elections incumbency refers to the president" (Kramer, 1971, p. 140).

The impact of the national economy, along with the added factor of presidential performance, was most compellingly stated in a work by Tufte (1978), part of which is reprinted here as Chapter 19. Tufte used only two variables, Gallup's presidential approval rating and the yearly change in real disposable personal income per capita, and yet his model achieved an extremely close fit with congressional election figures. Perhaps more than any other work, Tufte's analysis strongly suggested that congressional elections were national phenomena, responding to the national economy and to the performance of the president. This left little room for the candidates themselves, but as noted, early survey work on congressional voters suggested that the candidates were hardly known by the voters anyway.

For a time, the problem with the "economic and presidential popularity" theory was that it could not be directly confirmed by survey-based work. This was especially true of economic factors. Among others, Fiorina (1978) searched diligently for evidence that individual voters considered economic factors in deciding how to vote and came up largely empty-handed (see also Kuklinski and West, 1981; Brown and Stein, 1982). The presumed impact of presidential popularity received somewhat greater support, but even here the results were mixed. Kernell (1977) showed that those who disapproved of the president's performance voted for candidates of their party less often than those who approved of the president's performance even when party identification was controlled. Yet the evidence for 1974—when presidential popularity plummeted—did not suggest a strong connection with congressional voting (Jacobson and Kernell, 1981, p. 10). and Ragsdale's (1980) multivariate analysis suggested that presidential evaluations are of no consequence once other relevant variables in addition to partisanship are controlled.

For quite some time, then, there was an impasse. Aggregate studies appeared to show that the performance of the economy and the president were highly predictive of congressional voting behavior, but survey work could find little supporting evidence. Fortunately, a resolution emerged. Indeed, there now appear to be three distinct ways of reconciling these differences.[3]

One reconciliation came from the work of Kinder and Kiewiet (1981), in which the authors argued that personal economic grievances were not related to congressional voting but that judgments about the national economy were related to both voting and party identification. Though it was not made clear in the series of aggregate studies (since there was no reason to clarify it), the underlying assumption seemed to be that individuals voted their own pocketbooks. For example, those who were unemployed during a Republican administration tended to vote Democratic. This kind of economic voting is what could not be found in survey studies. But Kinder and Kiewiet found that collective (what they called "sociotropic") economic judgments—concern, for example, about unemployment nationally, irrespective of one's own employment status—were a crucial determinant of congressional voting, not to mention presidential voting and party identification. While there remained some debate about just how personal economic factors determine political behavior, the findings about collective judgments afforded one reconciliation of the aggregate-versus individual-level debate.[4]

A second resolution to this debate came from the realization that positive aggregate effects without individual-level effects are not statistically incompatible. For one thing, if only a portion of the electorate is influenced by economic variables and no other factors vary between elections in a systematic, nationwide fashion, this may translate into a rather strong relationship at the aggregate level. More significantly, Kramer (1983) demonstrated that the effects of changes in economic conditions over time might not be picked up by the typical individual-level, cross-sectional analysis. In each of two cross-sectional studies (from different years), there might be little relationship between economic well-being and the vote. Yet between these years there might be a large shift in well-being and a corresponding shift in the vote. The time series would show a strong relationship, but not the cross-section. Kramer also extended his argument to investigations such as Kinder and Kiewiet's, and essentially the same argument could apply to the effects of presidential popularity. Thus there could be largely methodological explanations for the apparent conflict between the aggregate and individual-level studies.

Yet a third way of resolving the apparent conflict involved an important new element in studies of congressional voting—namely, the behavior of elites, or what has come to be known as the "strategic politicians" argument (Jacobson and Kernell, 1981). Elections may have something of a self-fulfilling quality because of the behavior of incumbent representatives, potential candidates, and contributors. As Fiorina (1978, p. 440) put it:

> Take 1974, for example. Everyone expects a Republican disaster. Thus serious Republican candidates wait for a more propitious time before seeking office (or a move to a higher office), and Republican incumbents find voluntary retirement more attractive than usual. Meanwhile Republican contributors hesitate to invest funds in an apparently lost cause. Thus, the Republican ticket is composed of underfinanced cannon fodder. In contrast, the Democrats have a plentitude of enthusiastic candidates lavishly financed by those who know a good investment when they see one.

The beauty of this story is that if elites make their decisions on this basis, congressional and other elections can reflect national forces such as the state of the economy and presidential popularity even if voters do not base their decisions on those factors.[5]

Before departing from this theme of congressional elections as national events, we should note that the existence of a partisan factor is compatible with the other theories discussed so far. Tufte's formulation of the economic and presidential popularity theory, for example, was actually modeled so as to predict the deviation from the long-term or expected vote for Congress (as opposed to the actual congressional vote), where the long-term vote can easily be construed to be the underlying partisanship of the electorate. And while party identification may have declined as a factor in the 1970s as the number of Independents rose, it remained an almost universal finding in survey studies that party plays a major role in voting (including congressional voting, as in Hinckley, 1980a, esp. pp. 456-57; Kuklinski and West, 1981, pp. 441-42; Fiorina, 1981c, p. 556), further supporting the argument that congressional elections are best viewed as national political events.

Congressional Elections as Local Events

Simultaneously, incumbency was increasingly seen as an important factor in congressional elections, although for a time the significance of this for congressional election theories was not altogether clear. The facts of the matter were first observed in the early 1970s, especially in an influential article by Mayhew (1974b) on the "vanishing marginals," a portion of which is reprinted here as Chapter 18. It had long been known that a large proportion of House incumbents win reelection; what Mayhew noted was that beginning in the mid-1960s, the margin of victory tended to increase. Hence, candidates from marginal (that is, competitive) districts were vanishing.

Several plausible hypotheses were put forward to explain this change. One was that redistricting had somehow made representatives' districts safer. This hypothesis soon appeared to be unsupported by the evidence (Ferejohn, 1977). Another possible explanation was that as partisanship declined as a voting cue because of the decline in the number of partisans in the mid-1960s, voters substituted incumbency as a kind of necessary guide to voting in these relatively low-information elections. However, as Fiorina (1977a, p. 26) pointed out, this explanation also fails to account for some of the observed evidence.

What turned out to be particularly important about the vanishing marginals observation was the emphasis it placed directly on the congressional candidate. It was not enough to look at the state of the economy or the popularity of the president; who the candidate was made a difference as well. In fact, it soon was apparent that focusing only on one candidate factor, incumbency, was itself too narrow a viewpoint. The recognition that the individual candidates are an important factor in congressional elections left the door open to all sorts of new insights. But there was still one obstacle. The traditional view of voters, based largely on the 1958 Michigan election study, noted earlier, was that they know little about the candidates. How could the particular candidates be important if voters did not even know who they were? Thus, in explaining the role of incumbency, an attack also had to be made on this traditional view of the congressional voter.

Perhaps the most forceful onslaught against this traditional view was made in a book by Thomas Mann (1978). Mann began by pointing out that much had been made of the fact that many voters could not even recall the names of the congressional candidates. He demonstrated, however, that far more individuals could recognize their names than could spontaneously recall them. Moreover, voters were often able to evaluate candidates. Contrary to the traditional view that "to be perceived at all is to be perceived favorably" (Stokes and Miller, 1966), both positive and negative evaluations were made. Finally, these evaluations were based on policy concerns to a greater degree than the traditional view suggested. While it was true that few constituents had any detailed information about representatives' voting records or policy stands, Mann presented several kinds of information suggesting that voters were often aware of general ideological positions and/or other pertinent characterizations of the candidates.[6]

Mann's argument went beyond these points, however. In fact, what may be his most persuasive evidence is the fact that there is variety across congressional districts on almost any statistics cited. To take but one example, his survey showed that on average about 25 percent more respondents recognized the incumbent than the challenger. But this figure varied from −2 percent (that is, the challenger was actually better recognized) to +52 percent. Thus, to lump together all incumbents or all of any other category is to fail to see the oftentimes sizable variety across supposedly similar constituencies.

Mann's results were based on special (and not necessarily representative) surveys conducted in 1974 and 1976. However, the basic thrust of his work was substantiated by results of the 1978 CPS election study and other research.[7] Mann himself, in collaboration with Wolfinger, made many of the same points in an analysis of the 1978 study. Their work actually covers so many of the points discussed here, that we reprint it as Chapter 20.

Further support for Mann's position was found by Hinckley. In a brief survey of post-1978 work, she reported that *"voters' evaluations of the congressional candidates, House and Senate, have a major influence on the vote,* separate from incumbency and party . . ."* (1980b, p. 643). No one has replicated Mann's analysis of the range of various statistics, but Jacobson's (1981) methodological commentary on the 1978 study made the point that important variations in candidate (especially challenger) quality existed in that year. Likewise, one of the major distinctions now made between the two houses of Congress is that "there are *two* candidates competing in the [Senate] contests" (Hinckley, 1980a, p. 458; see also Abramowitz, 1980). Challengers in Senate campaigns are usually quite well known, but House challengers are of variable quality and often "invisible."

Results showing greater-than-anticipated voter awareness of congressional candidates in general, combined with greater visibility of House incumbents compared to challengers, go a long way toward explaining the vanishing marginals problem. Challengers in recent House elections have been a weak lot; therefore incumbents, being well known and liked, often roll over their opponents with relative ease. But it is not due to some mysterious incumbency effect or simply the substitution of incumbency for party as a voting cue. Incumbency itself was found to contribute little to electoral margins (Hinckley, 1980a, pp. 457-58; Jacobson, 1981, pp. 234-37). What matters is "the very favorable public images members of Congress acquire and the much more negative images—if any— projected by their opponents" (Jacobson, 1981, p. 237).

This explanation for the incumbency advantage naturally raised a further question: why are incumbents so well known and liked? Attempts to answer that question have led to some controversy, but disagreement or not, discussions of the question seem to revolve around behavior of the candidates themselves, thereby adding to the view of congressional elections as local phenomena.

One answer to the question why incumbents are so popular is that incumbents make considerable and effective use of all the resources at their command. Some of these are fairly traditional: the franking privilege, free transportation to and from their constituencies, personal staffs that can be used for self-promoting activities, and so on. Even in these traditional areas there has been tremendous growth in recent years (Jacobson, 1983, pp. 31-36). About all this there is little disagreement. Fiorina (1977b) went a step further, however, and argued that constituency service—casework—accounts for a good deal of the favorable image of incumbents. Here the evidence is generally positive (for example, Epstein and Frankovic, 1982; Yiannakis, 1981) though not entirely so. In one study directed specifically to this question, the authors could find no support for the hypothesis (Johannes and McAdams, 1981). Controversy over that analysis suggests at a minimum that the matter depends to some degree on the theorizing about the processes involved and consequently on the specification of the equations used to test for effects. There is also some suggestion that, as in the study of economic factors, individual-level data may need to be supplemented by other kinds of evidence (Powell, 1982).[8]

The role of constituency service was also looked at in studies abroad. Cain, Ferejohn, and Fiorina (1984), for example, looked at the question in the British House of Commons and concluded that constituency service plays a role there as well. Thus, even in that more party- and leader-oriented system, legislative elections are to some degree local events.

One other answer has also been given to the question of incumbency popularity. This answer stems from Jacobson's observation that *"the more incumbents spend, the worse they do"* (Jacobson, 1978, p. 472). It is not, of course, that money chases away votes. It is simply that many incumbents face weak challengers and consequently win with only small expenditures. Those who face stiff challenges must defend themselves with larger amounts of money. Sometimes they lose, leading to the observation above. Admittedly, this explanation has an element of circularity. It says that incumbents are popular because of weak challengers. How do we know they are weak challengers? Because they win so few votes. Nevertheless, the explanation and the evidence indicate that incumbents are not *always* more visible and well liked. Given a sufficiently strong challenger supported by enough money, the incumbency advantage can be overcome. But some factors—perhaps congressional public relations efforts and casework—make it sufficiently difficult to challenge an incumbent such that strong candidates are often unavailable. In any event, it is the candidates that make the difference.

Conclusion

It was folly in the 1980s, as it would be today, to argue that there is no disagreement among congressional researchers. Indeed, we have indicated that there are differences of opinion among supporters of each of the major traditions. Supporters of the economic and presidential popularity theory disagree at a minimum over the precise working of the theory and sometimes over whether there are any effects at all. The work on national versus personal economic factors is still fairly new, and only recently has their been some closure on this matter (Markus, 1988). There is also some disagreement and uncertainty regarding the local-events interpretation of congressional elections. The role of constituency service, for example, remained an unsettled matter, and the degree of policy voting (or the content and meaningfulness of candidate evaluations) is still a matter of some debate. And Fiorina (1981a) raised fundamental questions about how much change has really occurred.

In spite of these controversies, progress has been made in understanding congressional voters and elections. Neither the national nor the local events interpretation has a lock on the truth. To say that both explanations are correct is more than a face-saving compromise, however. As we discussed at some length earlier, the two interpretations are not incompatible. Elites and voters alike are influenced by the economic situation and by presidential popularity, and if our interest is in studying national swings, we would do best to focus on these factors. At the same time, the variations across congressional districts, convince us that it makes a difference who the candidates are and what they do. If our interest is in particular congressional races, we would do well to focus on factors related to the candidates themselves. Moreover, the strategic politicians theory provides a linkage between the two levels. That is, the national context sets up the possibility that the local campaign will be heavily contested, but the nature of the contest depends as well on local circumstances (for example, whether there is someone who could be a strong challenger).

It is perhaps appropriate to conclude on a normative note. It is fashionable to decry contemporary elections as somehow inadequate and failing. Blame may be attributed to political structures (especially the Electoral College and the very lengthy primary system for nominating presidential candidates), the behavior of elites (they are too self-centered and ambiguous, or the best ones don't run), or voters (they know too little or are too easily swayed by politicians). While some degree of cynicism is appropriate, since we should never be complacent about our political situation, we think that the contemporary balance between national and local factors is better than is often thought to be the case. The increasing local-level influence (or perhaps the awareness of long-standing local-level influence) rescued the voter from the status of an automaton guided unthinkingly by party identification, economic circumstances, and the behavior of the president. Evaluations of candidates are perhaps based too much on constituency service, but the influence of the national economy and of presidential actions (not to mention limited evaluation of the policies of representatives themselves) suggest that policy and ideology are not irrelevant. Thus, the greater insight into congressional elections afforded by the past decade of studies encourages us to think not only that we are making progress in the discipline, but also that the structure and conduct of congressional elections remains a very meaningful exercise.

NOTES

1. Atesoglu and Congleton (1982) updated his results.
2. A good, two-page summary and list of references is found in Fiorina (1978).
3. Similar conflicting results have appeared in work on German voters. Baker et al. (1981, pp. 96-99) reviewed these studies and suggested resolutions of the differences similar to what we discuss here.
4. Some contradictions could be found, however. In 1981, for example, Kiewiet (1981) observed that between 1958 and 1978, "it seems clear that voters' perceptions of national economic problems have come to have virtually no impact upon their voting decision in congressional elections" (p. 458).
5. The strategic politicians theory has been very popular (see Niemi and Weisberg, 1992, chap. 14).
6. Fiorina (1981a) raised the interesting methodological question of whether congressional voters in the 1970s and 1980s really are that different from 1950s voters. New and altered questions in 1978 make it appear on the surface as if respondents in that year

were more informed than respondents in the 1958 congressional study. Yet a careful, though necessarily inclusive comparison indicates that the differences may not be as widespread or as dramatic as sometimes suggested.

7. A dissenting note with respect to voters' knowledge of candidates' policy positions is found in Hurley and Hill (1980).

8. Fowler, Stonecash, and Carrothers (1982) argue that casework is not a factor in state legislatures.

FURTHER READINGS

Determinants of Voting for Congress

Thomas E. Mann, *Unsafe at Any Margin: Interpreting Congressional Elections* (Washington, D.C.: American Enterprise Institute, 1978). Emphasizes insecurity of congressional incumbents despite the well-known incumbency advantage.

Barbara Hinckley, "The American Voter in Congressional Elections," *American Political Science Review* (1980) 74:641-50. Summarizes results from the 1978 National Election Study.

Gary C. Jacobson and Samuel Kernell, *Strategy and Choice in Congressional Elections,* 2d ed. (New Haven, Conn.: Yale University Press, 1983). Full statement of their theory of strategic decision making by candidates and potential candidates.

Keith Krehbiel and John R. Wright, "The Incumbency Effect in Congressional Elections: A Test of Two Explanations," *American Journal of Political Science* (1983) 27:140-57. Partisan dealignment does not account for safer congressional seats.

Economic Effects on Congressional Voting

Gerald H. Kramer, "Short-Term Fluctuations in U.S. Voting Behavior," *American Political Science Review* (1971) 65:131-43. Original statement of the relationship between the state of the economy and voting behavior.

D. Roderick Kiewiet, *Macroeconomics and Micropolitics: The Electoral Effects of Economic Issues* (Chicago: University of Chicago Press, 1983). Electoral effects of economic issues are less consistent for congressional than for presidential voting.

Effects of Constituency Service

Morris P. Fiorina, *Congress, Keystone of the Washington Establishment* (New Haven, Conn.: Yale University Press, 1977, 1989). Strong statement of the constituency service role of representatives.

John R. Johannes and John C. McAdams, "The Congressional Incumbency Effect: Is It Casework, Policy Compatibility, or Something Else?" *American Journal of Political Science* (1981) 25:520-42. Questions the effects of constituency service.

Diana E. Yiannakis, "The Grateful Electorate: Casework and Congressional Elections," *American Journal of Political Science* (1981) 25:568-80. Casework is important, especially for swaying the challenger's supporters.

Bruce E. Cain, John A. Ferejohn, and Morris P. Fiorina, *The Personal Vote* (Cambridge, Mass.: Harvard University Press, 1987). Concludes that constituency service plays a role in the more party- and leader-oriented British House of Commons.

Effects of Constituency

Morris P. Fiorina, *Representatives and Roll Calls* (Lexington, Mass.: Lexington Books, 1974). Formal analysis of constituency electoral characteristics and their impact on voting in Congress.

Samuel H. Barnes, *Representation in Italy* (Chicago: University of Chicago Press, 1977). Attitudes and linkages between voters, communal councillors, and parliamentary deputies.

Christopher H. Achen, "Measuring Representation," *American Journal of Political Science* (1978) 22:475-510. Pitfalls of the correlation coefficient for measuring representation.

Philip E. Converse and Roy Pierce, "Representative Roles and Legislative Behavior in France," *Legislative Studies Quarterly* (1979) 4:525-62. Differing roles taken by legislators in France.

Lynda W. Powell, "Issue Representation in Congress," *Journal of Politics* (1982) 44:658-78. Reevaluates the impact of constituency on legislative behavior.

Financing of Congressional Elections

Gary C. Jacobson, *Money in Congressional Elections* (New Haven, Conn.: Yale University Press, 1980). The role of money in congressional elections, especially for nonincumbents.

_____, *The Politics of Congressional Elections,* 3d ed. (New York: Harper Collins, 1992). Overview of work on all aspects of congressional elections.

16. PARTY GOVERNMENT AND
THE SALIENCY OF CONGRESS

Donald E. Stokes and Warren E. Miller

... Great stress should be laid on the fact that the public sees individual candidates for Congress in terms of party programs scarcely at all. Our constituent interviews indicate that the popular image of the Congressman is almost barren of policy content. A long series of open-ended questions asked of those who said they had any information about the Representative produced mainly a collection of diffuse evaluative judgments: he is a good man, he is experienced, he knows the problems, he has done a good job, and the like. Beyond this, the Congressman's image consisted of a mixed bag of impressions, some of them wildly improbable, about ethnicity, the attractiveness of family, specific services to the district, and other facts in the candidate's background. By the most reasonable count, references to current legislative issues comprised not more than a thirtieth part of what the constituents had to say about their Congressmen.

The irrelevance of legislative issues to the public's knowledge of Representatives is underscored by the nature of some primary *determinants* of saliency. ... Although our investigation has given a good deal of attention to communication factors and to characteristics of Congressmen and constituents themselves that determine the probability a given Congressman will be known to a given constituent, this interplay of causes cannot be explored very deeply here. However, it *is* noteworthy in the present discussion that many factors increasing the saliency of candidates are unlikely to enhance what the public knows about their stands on issues. An excellent example is sex. Both for incumbents and non-incumbents, a candidate property that is related to saliency is gender; one of the best ways for a Representative to be known is to be a Congress*woman*. How irrelevant to policy issues this property is depends on what we make of the causal relation between sex and salience. The fact of being a woman may make a candidate more visible, but a woman may have to be unusually visible (as a Congressman's widow, say) before she can be elected to the House, or even become a serious candidate. If the first of these inferences is even partially right,

Source: *Public Opinion Quarterly* (1962) 26:531-46. Reprinted with permission of the University of Chicago Press.

Table 16-1 Influence of "Friends and Neighbors" Factor on Saliency of Candidates for Voters[a] (in percent)

	Incumbent Candidate Lives in		Nonincumbent Candidate Lives in	
Voter Is	*Same Community as Voter (N = 269)*	*Other Community than Voter (N = 414)*	*Same Community as Voter (N = 304)*	*Other Community than Voter (N = 447)*
Aware of candidate	67	45	47	22
Not aware of candidate	33	55	53	78
Total	100	100	100	100

[a] Metropolitan and large urban districts, for which the notion of the candidate living outside the voter's community has no clear meaning, are excluded from the analysis.

the salience of the candidate is not likely to be in terms of positions taken on legislative issues.

Given the number of women who run for Congress, the role of sex may seem a trivial example to demonstrate the irrelevance of issue stands to saliency. However, the same point can be made for a much wider set of districts by the greater saliency of candidates who live in the constituent's home community. . . . As the entries of Table 16-1 show, dividing a nationwide sample of constituents according to whether they live in the same community as their Congressman or his opponent produces marked differences of saliency. The "friends and neighbors" effect made familiar by studies of primary voting in one-party areas has a counterpart in voting for Representatives throughout the country, apart from the large metropolitan areas.[1] And despite the fact that localism is found here in the context of as tightly party-determined an election as any in American politics, the irrelevance of local appeal to legislative issues is probably as great as it is in the wide-open, one-party primary. . . .

NOTE

1. See Key (1949, pp. 37 ff.). We have demonstrated the "friends and neighbors" effect in terms of candidate salience because of our interest in the policy content of candidate perceptions. However, owing to the impact of salience on the vote, living in the same community with the candidate has a clear effect on voting as well.

17. CONSTITUENCY INFLUENCE IN CONGRESS

Warren E. Miller and Donald E. Stokes

... Of the three conditions of constituency influence, the requirement that the electorate take account of the policy positions of the candidates is the hardest to match with empirical evidence. Indeed, given the limited information the average voter carries to the polls, the public might be thought incompetent to perform any task of appraisal. Of constituents living in congressional districts where there was a contest between a Republican and a Democrat in 1958, less than one in five said they had read or heard something about both candidates, and well over half conceded they had read or heard nothing about either. And these proportions are not much better when they are based only on the part of the sample, not much more than half, that reported voting for Congress in 1958. Even of the portion of the public that was sufficiently interested to vote, almost half had read or heard nothing about either candidate.

What the voters "knew" was confined to diffuse evaluative judgments about the candidate: "he's a good man," "he understands the problems," and so forth. Of detailed information about policy stands not more than a chemical trace was found. Among the comments about the candidates given in response to an extended series of free-answer questions, less than 2 percent had to do with stands in our three policy domains; indeed, only about three comments in every hundred had to do with legislative issues of *any* description.

This evidence that the behavior of the electorate is largely unaffected by knowledge of the policy positions of the candidates is complemented by evidence about the forces that *do* shape the voters' choices among congressional candidates. The primary basis of voting in American congressional elections is identification with party. In 1958 only one vote in twenty was cast by persons without any sort of party loyalty. And among those who did have a party identification, only one in ten voted against their party. As a result, something like 84 percent of the vote that year was cast by party identifiers voting their usual party line. What is more, traditional party voting is seldom connected with current legislative issues. As the party loyalists in a nationwide sample of voters told us what they liked and disliked about the parties in 1958, only a small fraction of the comments (about 15 percent) dealt with current issues of public policy.

Source: *American Political Science Review* (1963) 57:45-56. Reprinted with permission.

18. CONGRESSIONAL ELECTIONS: THE CASE OF THE VANISHING MARGINALS

David R. Mayhew

Of the electoral instruments voters have used to influence American national government few have been more important than the biennial "net partisan swing" in United States House membership. Since Jacksonian times ups and downs in party seat holdings in the House have supplied an important form of party linkage.

The seat swing is, in practice, a two-step phenomenon. For a party to register a net gain in House seats there must occur (a) a gain (over the last election) in the national proportion of popular votes cast for House candidates of the party in question. That is, the party must be the beneficiary of a national trend in popular voting for the House. But there must also occur (b) a translation of popular vote gains into seat gains. Having the former without the latter might be interesting but it would not be very important. . . .

The foregoing is a preface to a discussion of some recent election data. The data, for the years 1956-1972, suggest strongly that the House seat swing is a phenomenon of fast declining amplitude and therefore of fast declining significance.

The data are presented in Figure 18-1, an array of 22 bar graphs that runs on for five pages. If the pages are turned sideways and read as if they were one long multi-page display, the graphs appear in three columns of nine, nine, and four. It will be useful to begin with an examination of the four graphs in the right-hand column.

Each of the four right-hand graphs is a frequency distribution in which congressional districts are sorted according to percentages of the major-party presidential vote cast in them in one of the four presidential elections of the years 1956-1968.[1] The districts are cumulated vertically in percentages of the total district set of 435 rather than in absolute numbers. The horizontal axis has column intervals of five percent, ranging from a far-left interval for districts where the Democratic presidential percentage was 0-4.9 to a far-right interval where the percentage was 95-100. Thus the 1956 graph shows that the

Source: *Polity* (1974) 6:295-317. Reprinted with permission of the publisher.

Figure 18-1 Frequency Distributions of Democratic Percentages of the Two-Party Vote in House Districts

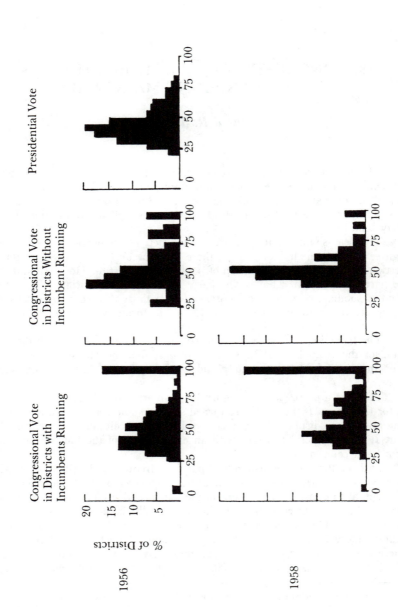

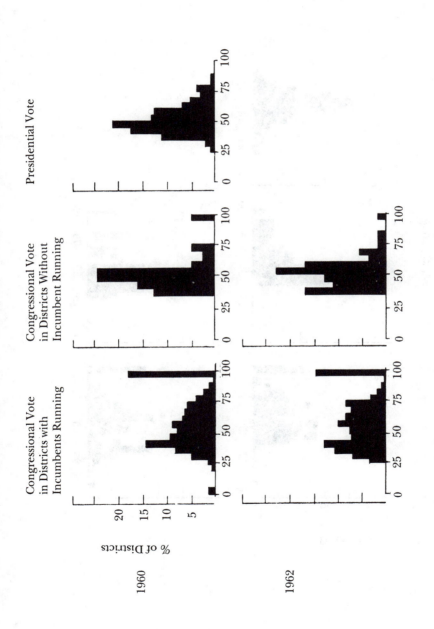

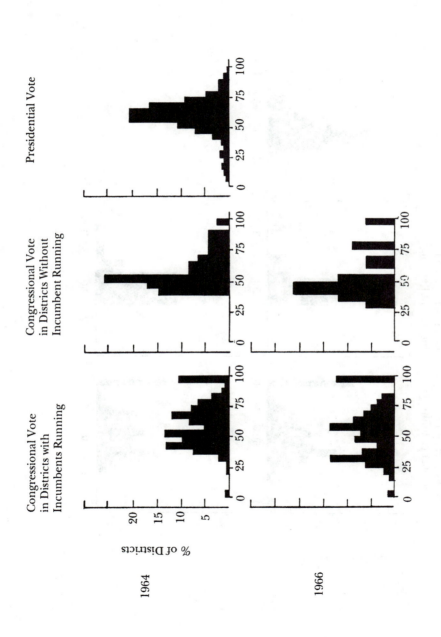

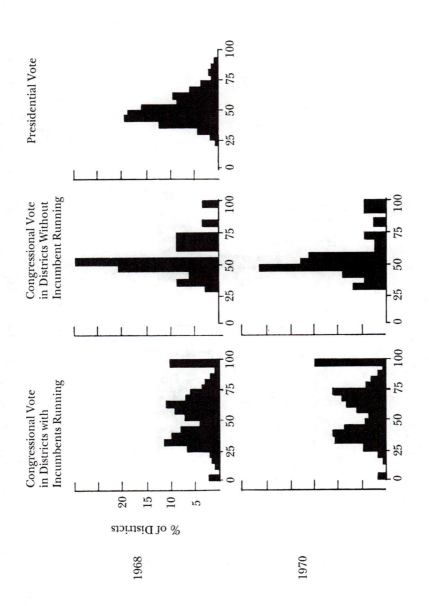

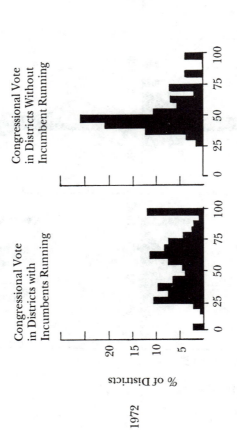

Congressional Vote
in Districts with
Incumbents Running

Congressional Vote
in Districts Without
Incumbent Running

% of Districts

1972

Stevenson-Kefauver ticket won 50 to 54.9 percent of the major-party vote in about 7 percent of the districts (actual district N = 30) and a modal 40 to 44.9 percent of the vote in about 20 percent of the districts (actual N = 87).

In themselves these presidential graphs hold no surprises; they are presented for the purpose of visual comparison with the other data. The presidential mode travels well to the left of the 50 percent mark in 1956 and well to the right in 1964, but the four distributions are fundamentally alike in shape—highly peaked, unimodal, not far from normal.

The center and left columns give frequency distributions, organized on the same principles as the four presidential graphs, in which House districts are sorted according to percentages of the major-party House vote cast in them in each of the nine congressional elections in the years 1956-1972. But for each House election there are two graphs side by side. For each year the graph in the left column gives a distribution of returns for all districts in which an incumbent congressman was running, the center column a set of returns for districts with no incumbents running.

The center graphs, the "open seat" distributions, are erratically shaped because the N's are small. The number of House districts without incumbents running averages 43 (about a tenth of the membership) and ranges from 31 (in 1956) to 59 (in 1972); there is no discernible upward or downward trend in the series. With allowances made for erratic shape these nine "open seat" distributions are much alike. All are highly peaked and centrally clustered. In 1958 and 1968 nearly 30 percent of the readings appear in the modal interval (in both cases the 50-54.9 percent Democratic interval). Over the set of nine elections the proportion of "open seat" outcomes falling in the 40-59.9 percent area ranges from 54.8 percent to 70.2 percent, the proportion in the 45-54.9 percent area from 29.0 percent to 50.1 percent. All of which imparts the simple and obvious message that House elections without incumbents running tend to be closely contested.

The nine graphs in the left-hand column give distributions for districts with incumbents running.[2] Thus in 1956 about 9 percent of districts with incumbents running yielded returns in the 45-49.9 percent Democratic interval. In some of these cases the incumbents were Democrats who thereby lost their seats; in any of these nine graphs the election reading for a losing incumbent will appear on what was, from his standpoint, the unfortunate side of the 50 percent line. In an Appendix [not included here] the nine data sets are disaggregated to show where in fact incumbents lost.

Immediately visible on each of these incumbency graphs is the isolated mode in the 95-100 percent interval, recording the familiar phenomenon of uncontested Democratic victories—mostly in the South. But, if these right-flush modes can be ignored for a moment, what has really been happening in the contested range is far more interesting. In 1956 and 1960 the distributions in the contested range are skewed a little to the right, but still not far from normal in shape. In the 1958 and 1962 midterm years the distributions are somewhat flatter and more jagged.[3] In 1964 and 1966 they appear only tenuously normal. In 1968, 1970, and 1972 they have become emphatically bimodal in shape. Or, to bring in the uncontested Democratic seats again, the shape of incumbency distributions has now become strikingly trimodal. Thus in the 1972 election there was a range of reasonably safe Republican seats (with the 25-29.9 percent and 35-39.5 percent intervals most heavily populated), a range of reasonably safe Democratic seats (peaked in the 60-64.9 percent interval), and a set of 44 uncontested Democratic seats.

The title of this paper includes the phrase, "The Case of the Vanishing Marginals." The "vanishing marginals" are all those congressmen whose election percentages could, but now do not, earn them places in the central range of these incumbency distributions.... For some reason, or reasons, it seems to be a lot easier now than it used to be for a sitting congressman to win three-fifths of the November vote....

NOTES

1. At the time of writing no comparable figures were yet available for the 1972 election. Dealing with the 1968 returns by calculating percentages of the major-party vote poses obvious problems—especially in the South—but so does any alternative way of dealing with them. Congressional district data used in Figure 18-1 were taken from *Congressional Quarterly* compilations.

2. ... Districts with two opposite-party incumbents running against each other [were excluded]. There were 16 of these throw-in cases over the period....

3. On balance it can be expected that distributions will be more centrally clustered in presidential than in midterm years, for the reason that presidential elections enroll expanded electorates in which disproportionate numbers of voters violate district partisan habits in their congressional voting. See Kabaker (1969).

19. ECONOMIC AND POLITICAL DETERMINANTS OF ELECTORAL OUTCOMES: MIDTERM CONGRESSIONAL ELECTIONS

Edward R. Tufte

Outcomes of midterm elections appear as a mixture of the routine and the inexplicable. In every off-year congressional election but one since the Civil War, the political party of the incumbent president has lost seats in the House of Representatives, falling back from its gains won in the presidential election two years before. V. O. Key (1964, pp. 567-68) suggested that midterm ballots were not produced by an electorate responding in any consistent fashion to economic or any other measurable factors:

> Since the electorate cannot change administrations at midterm elections, it can only express its approval or disapproval by returning or withdrawing legislative majorities. At least such would be the rational hypothesis about what the electorate might do. In fact, no such logical explanation can completely describe what it does at midterm elections. The Founding Fathers, by the provision for midterm elections, built into the constitutional system a procedure whose strange consequences lack explanation in any theory that personifies the electorate as a rational god of vengeance and of reward.

The diagnosis of midterms as non-elections, as non-referendums, and as merely the routine swing of the electoral pendulum against the in-party became the standard textbook wisdom, as well as an example of something that political scientists knew and professional politicians did not (Campbell, 1960, 1964; Key, 1964, pp. 568-69). Many politicians and journalists read the midterm vote as the electorate's evaluation of how well the incumbent administration had done during the two years since its inauguration (Kernell, 1977).

Most recently students of politics have come to agree with the politicians' view of midterms as referenda. Kramer reported in his 1971 paper that short-run changes in economic conditions accounted for about 60 percent of the variance in the ups and downs of the national vote; the electorate was more likely to favor the party of the incumbent president in congressional elections when economic times

Source: *Political Control of the Economy* (Princeton: Princeton University Press, 1978), pp. 106-15. Copyright 1978 by Princeton University Press. Reprinted by permission of Princeton University Press.

were good in the year before the election and to move toward the out-party in less prosperous times.[1] Then the reality of the 1974 midterm congressional election, so clearly a negative referendum on the Republican presidency and the slumping economy, made difficult the continued maintenance of the textbook interpretation.

I will consider the contributions of three factors determining the partisan division of the national congressional vote:

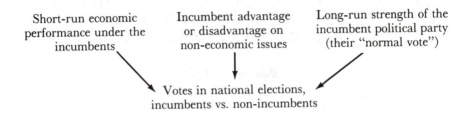

Short-run economic performance under the incumbents

Incumbent advantage or disadvantage on non-economic issues

Long-run strength of the incumbent political party (their "normal vote")

Votes in national elections, incumbents vs. non-incumbents

The *incumbent party* is taken as the party of the president rather than as the party controlling the House. Since no other targets other than local ones present themselves in off-year elections, it is reasonable to expect that voters upset by the performance of the president will take their dissatisfaction out on the congressional candidates of the president's party (cf. Stokes and Miller, 1962). Arseneau and Wolfinger (1973) found evidence that "the public image of Congress is rather undifferentiated and, moreover, assessments of the two parties' performance are likely to be determined predominantly by evaluation of the president rather than Congress . . . congressional candidates are likely to suffer or benefit from voters' estimates of how well the president has been doing his job." Further evidence is reported in Piereson (1975) and Kernell (1977).

The measure of *short-run economic conditions* will be the election-year change in real disposable income per capita (ΔE). Since it is "real"—that is, in constant dollars—inflation is discounted. And since it is "disposable," ΔE represents the election-year change in after-tax income.

The measure of the *public's evaluation of incumbent performance on non-economic issues* for midterm elections will be the standard Gallup Poll question: "Do you approve or disapprove of the way President _____ is handling his job as president?"[2]

The measure of the *outcome of the election* will be the share of the nationwide vote won by congressional candidates of the president's party relative to the long-run strength of that party. The long-run, average strength of the incumbent party is taken as the average of the vote that the party has won over the eight preceding elections. This standardization (measuring how each election deviates from a long-run average) is important in the case of congressional elections mainly because of the persistent Democratic advantage. For if the incumbent president is a Democrat and his party receives, say, 52 percent of the vote, that is a relative defeat since the Democrats usually win about 54 percent of the nationwide congressional vote. On the other hand, 52 percent of the congressional vote for the Republicans would be a spectacular victory.

Table 19-1 shows the data for elections from 1946 to 1974. In equation form, the referendum model of midterm outcomes is:

$$
\begin{array}{c} \text{Standardized vote} \\ \text{loss by} \\ \text{president's} \\ \text{party in the midterm} \end{array}
= \beta_0 + \beta_1
\begin{array}{c} \text{Yearly} \\ \text{change in} \\ \text{economic} \\ \text{conditions} \end{array}
+ \beta_2
\begin{array}{c} \text{Presidential} \\ \text{Popularity} \end{array}
$$

The idea is that the lower the approval rating of the incumbent president and the less prosperous the economy, the greater the loss of support for the president's party. Table 19-2 shows the multiple regression estimating the model's coefficients. The fitted equation indicates that:

—A change of one percentage point in the growth of real disposable income per capita in the year before the election is associated with a national change of 0.6 percentage points in the midterm vote for the congressional candidates of the president's party (Figure 19-1).
—A change in presidential popularity of 10 percentage points in the Gallup Poll is associated with a national change of 1.3 percentage points in the national midterm vote for congressional candidates of the president's party.

The model fits well and the observed effects are strong.[3] A year of prosperous growth (say a 3.0 percent increase in real disposable income) compared to a mild recession (a decline of 1.0 percent) is worth an extra 2.5 percent of the vote, which would typically translate into an extra 20 to 30 seats in the House of Representatives. That is about the same as the difference between having a presidential approval rating of 60 percent and 40 percent. In midterm elections, the party of a popular president in prosperous times will win from 40 to 60 congressional seats more than the party of an unpopular president in times of economic recession.

These estimates of the electoral effect of changes in real disposable income growth and presidential approval rating help us to assess the impact of each factor in the 1974 midterm. When President Ford came into office in August 1974, Republican chances increased substantially. Ford's approval rating was initially 71 percent; Nixon's had been running in the low twenties in the months before he resigned. This 50 percent shift in presidential approval translated, according to the model, into about 6 percent of the national congressional vote. Then came the pardon of Nixon, and Ford's ratings fell 20 points, costing the Republicans about 2.5 percent of the congressional vote. The economic decline of 1974 played an even more important role in creating the Democratic surge. During that election year, real disposable income per capita dropped by 2.3 percent. Compared to the 1970 midterm year, when real disposable income had increased by 3.0 percent per capita, the 1974 economic drop-off cost Republican congressional candidates about 5 percent of the vote.

Survey interviews conducted during the 1974 campaign confirm the inter-

Table 19-1 Midterm Elections, 1946-1974

Year	V_i Nationwide Midterm Congressional Vote for Party of Incumbent President	N_i^8 Mean Congressional Vote for Party of Incumbent President in 8 Prior Elections	$Y_i = V_i - N_i^8$ Standardized Vote Loss $(-)$ or Gain $(+)$ by President's Party in Midterm Election	P_i Gallup Poll Rating of President at Time of Election	ΔE_i Yearly Change in Real Disposable Income Per Capita
1946	45.27%	Democratic 52.57%	−7.30%	32%	−2.6%
1950	50.04%	Democratic 52.04%	−2.00%	43%	5.9%
1954	47.27%	Republican 49.77%	−2.50%	65%	−0.6%
1958	43.60%	Republican 49.75%	−6.15%	56%	−0.5%
1962	52.64%	Democratic 51.75%	0.89%	67%	2.6%
1966	51.33%	Democratic 53.20%	−1.87%	48%	3.9%
1970	45.77%	Republican 46.54%	−0.77%	56%	3.0%
1974	41.38%	Republican 46.17%	−4.51%	55%	−2.3%
1978		Democratic 54.40%			

Table 19-2 Midterm Congressional Elections: Multiple Regression

$$Y_i = \beta_0 + \beta_1(\Delta E_i) + \beta_2 P_i + u_i$$

	Regression Coefficient and Standard Error	Simple Correlation with Midterm Loss
Yearly change in real disposable income per capita (ΔE)	$\hat{\beta}_1 = .622$ .166	.72
Presidential approval rating (P)	$\hat{\beta}_2 = .132$ .044	.58
$\hat{\beta}_0 = -10.74$		
$R^2 = 0.825$		

pretations based on the aggregate model. The Democratic vote ran 11 percentage points higher than normal among those who thought the government was doing a poor job on economic policy, whereas those who liked government efforts at economic management voted only one percent more Democratic than normal. For a majority of voters, economic issues influenced their decision more than the remains of Watergate.[4]

An equation forecasting the 1978 midterm results from solving the fitted equation of Table 19-2 and substituting in the normal Democratic vote (N^8 for 1978 is 54.40 percent):

Nationwide congressional
vote for Democrats $= 43.66 + .622(\Delta E) + .132(P),$
in 1978 midterm election

where ΔE is the percentage change in real disposable income per capita over the 12 months right before the election and P is the president's approval rating (in the Gallup Poll) in September-October 1978. Both P and ΔE are known in advance of the election. For previous midterms, the forecasts from the model have been as accurate as pre-election polls predicting vote. Over a range of values of P and ΔE, the predicted 1978 Democratic congressional vote is:

		Change in real disposable income per capita		
		0%	+2%	+4%
Gallup Poll approval rating	40%	48.9%	50.2%	51.4%
	50%	50.3%	51.5%	52.8%
	60%	51.6%	52.8%	54.1%

Since the Democrats won 57.3 percent of the congressional vote in 1976, it is likely that they will lose at least several percentage points of that vote in 1978, unless the economy is booming (a gain in ΔE of around 6 percent) and the president's approval rating equals past highs (65 to 70 percent).

Figure 19-1   Election-Year Economic Performance and the
Vote in Midterm Congressional Elections

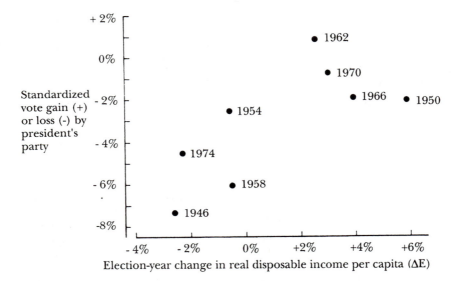

The vote cast in midterm congressional elections, then, is a referendum on
the performance of the president and his administration's management of the
economy. Although the in-party's share of the vote almost invariably declines in
the midterm compared to the previous on-year election, the magnitude of that loss
is substantially smaller if the president has a high level of popular approval, if the
economy is performing well, or both.[5]

NOTES

1. Kramer (1971). A data error in this paper is corrected in its Bobbs-Merrill reprint
   (PS-498); see also Goodman and Kramer (1975). Other studies dealing with the effects
   of aggregate economic conditions on the national vote are reviewed in Edward R. Tufte,
   "On the Distribution of Published R²: Consequences of Selection of Models and
   Evidence," manuscript, 1977. The recent work includes Arcelus and Meltzer (1975);
   Bloom and Price (1975); Fair (1975); Fair (1976); Kramer and Lepper (1972); Lepper
   (1974); Meltzer and Vellrath (1975); Stigler (1973); and Tufte (1975). For France, see
   Rosa and Amson (1976).
2. The approval rating itself is slightly contaminated with perceptions of how well the
   economy is performing. Most studies have found a weak-to-moderate relationship
   between approval ratings and economic conditions. It appears, however, that in times
   when economic issues become increasingly salient to the electorate, the approval ratings

become more closely connected to short-term economic fluctuations. Normally the approval ratings bounce around month by month in response to non-economic events, particularly foreign policy issues, which move so much more quickly—in the headlines at least—than the relatively glacial pace of the national economy. The yearly drift in the ratings, however, is likely to be affected by the course of the economy. Stimson's findings that the ratings are high at the beginning and at the end of the presidential term might be explained by the election-inspired upswings of the economy that occur near the end of the four-year term and spill over to the beginning of the next. See Stimson (1976). In contrast, see Bruno S. Frey and Friedrich Schneider, "Economic and Personality Determinants of Presidential Popularity," manuscript, 1977.

3. Two-thirds of the residual sum of squares comes from the 1958 election, when the Democrats won 56.4 percent of the vote despite the model's prediction of 53.9 percent.
4. *ISR Newsletter,* Institute for Social Research, University of Michigan (Summer 1976), 6-7; and Arthur H. Miller and Richard Glass, "Economic Dissatisfaction and Electoral Choice," manuscript, 1976.
5. The midterm model is developed in additional substantive and technical detail in Tufte (1974, pp. 139-46) and Tufte (1975). Those presentations contain further statistical validations of the model. Some slight data errors in the previous versions have been corrected here.

20. CANDIDATES AND PARTIES IN CONGRESSIONAL ELECTIONS

Thomas E. Mann and Raymond E. Wolfinger

During the first generation of research on voting behavior, scant attention was paid to congressional elections. In the 1970s scholars interested in congressional elections quickly exhausted the analytic possibilities of data from the principal source of nationwide sample surveys, the biennial National Election Studies of the University of Michigan Center for Political Studies. Their research provided some interesting findings but also pointed to a need for more and better survey items to explain the gaps and contradictions in the existing state of scholarly understanding.

The Michigan CPS study of the 1978 elections included a number of new questions about public perceptions of congressional candidates and incumbent members of Congress; for the first time scholars have data with which to find valid answers to some of the fundamental questions about how members of Congress are elected. In this chapter we will exploit the new data source to provide answers to these questions: What do voters know about congressional candidates? How do voters decide between candidates? Why are House incumbents so successful at getting reelected by wide margins? Why do Senate incumbents fare less well? How are elections won or lost?

The 1978 National Election Study

The unusually widespread scholarly interest in the 1978 congressional elections stems from the availability of a distinctly new data set rather than from any unusual features of the results. The outcome of the election can be briefly summarized. The Democratic party maintained the majority status in both houses that it has enjoyed without interruption for over two decades. The national net Republican gain in the House of Representatives of 2.8 percent of the votes and 3.4 percent of the seats was modest by midterm election standards, but not wholly unexpected, given several mitigating factors: the absence of presidential

Source: *American Political Science Review* (1980) 74:617-32. Reprinted with permission of the publisher.

coattails in 1976 (Jimmy Carter ran behind 270 of the 292 Democrats elected to the House in that year); Carter's partial and temporary recovery in the opinion polls following his Middle East Camp David summit meeting; and the electoral advantage of incumbency. Twenty-four House incumbents seeking reelection were defeated—5 in the primaries and 19 in the general election—leaving 94 percent successful. Incumbency was a less obvious advantage in the Senate, where 10 of the 25 senators seeking reelection were defeated—three in the primaries and seven in the general election.[1]

The 1978 elections witnessed the continuation of three additional trends that have been present for several successive elections. First, turnout declined to a postwar low of 35.1 percent. Second, David Mayhew's (1974b) vanishing marginals vanished even further. In 1978, 76 percent of all House races contested by an incumbent were won by a margin of 60 percent or more. Third, the growing insulation of House incumbents from defeat has not led to stability in membership. To the contrary, 18 percent of the House were replaced following the 1978 elections. When added to the shifts following the 1974 and 1976 elections, this means that half the members of the 96th Congress were not in office when Richard Nixon resigned from the presidency. This is equally true for the Senate, where 20 new members entered following the 1978 election and where 49 are in their first term. The answer to this seeming paradox is obvious: retirement has replaced defeat as the primary source of turnover and the number of retirements has been rising since 1972. Once again, 1978 was no exception to this pattern—49 representatives and 10 senators declined to seek reelection. Both figures are as high as any in modern times.

The 1978 National Election Study is the first nationwide survey in 20 years to include more than the most basic questions concerning congressional elections. A better sense of the opportunities as well as the limitations of working with this new data set can be gained by looking at [table not shown], which presents the number of respondents, voters, districts and states in the 1978 sample. . . .

If one has a special interest in races where the outcome is not a foregone conclusion, the sample's limitations are more pronounced. As we indicated above, 24 percent of all House incumbents seeking reelection won with margins of less than 60 percent, which is matched almost perfectly in the sample with 18 "marginal" races out of 77 incumbent-contested races. Although the sample was right on target in this respect, the number of voting respondents in these districts is small for most analytic purposes (178, of whom 170 are major party voters). Moreover, there is a clear incumbent bias in the voting reports of these respondents. While challengers in all marginal districts averaged 46 percent of the actual vote, less than 35 percent of all the respondents in the sample of these districts reported a vote for the challenger. Any interpretation of the public's view of challengers in competitive districts must take this discrepancy into account.

Actually, an over-report of the vote for incumbents in the sample is not limited to marginal districts. In the universe of districts in which they faced opposition, incumbents won 66 percent of the major-party vote; yet in the CPS sample of these districts 79 percent of the vote was reportedly cast for incumbents.

Only one of the 19 districts in which incumbents were defeated fell within the sample; by chance, we would have expected four or five. We cannot expect the sample to represent such districts; nor would their inclusion have altered substantially the figures for the entire sample. Nonetheless, it is worth observing that a politically and analytically important type of district is under-represented in the sample.

The Senate sample poses much more serious problems. There is no purposive sample of Senate races; what we have is a by-product of designing a national sample of noninstitutionalized adults and of congressional districts. . . . We think it best to use the Senate figures for only the simplest comparisons with the House. This chapter primarily concerns voting in House elections.

The Importance of Party

Because members of Congress are less familiar than the president to most voters, it is easy to accept the proposition that party identification is a far more important determinant of congressional than of presidential voting. This notion can be evaluated by examining Table 20-1, which displays the proportion of voters in every House and presidential election from 1956 through 1978 who were pure Independents, people who identified with a party and voted for that party's candidate, and people who identified with one party and voted for the candidate of the other party.[2]

The first observation to be made is the marked increase in defection in presidential elections in 1968 and 1972, and then the equally sharp return in 1976 to the same modest levels of defection that were found during the 1950s. The trend toward weakening party lines that was so widely discussed in literature based on the 1968 and 1972 elections may well have reflected the candidacies of George Wallace and George McGovern rather than any secular movement in the strength of party loyalties (Nie et al., 1976).

Second, and more interesting for our present purposes, is the continuous increase in the proportion of congressional voters who defect. In 1956, just 9 percent of all those people casting a ballot in a House contest voted for the other party's candidate, compared with 15 percent of presidential voters. The proportion of House defectors crept up slowly and steadily in virtually every election since 1956. Until the most recent elections, however, defection was always lower than in presidential races, and so the contrast between presidential and House voting remained consistent with the proposition that ignorance about House candidates led to greater party-line voting than in presidential balloting, where public familiarity with the candidates produced more defection. But more recently the continued increase in House defection combined with a return to party-line presidential voting to reverse the previous relationship. In 1976, just 15 percent of presidential voters defected; by 1978, a substantially larger number of House voters—22 percent—identified with one party and voted for the other party's candidate. This reversal, whether temporary or permanent, is sufficiently damaging to the conventional wisdom to require further investigation.

Table 20-1   The Composition of the Vote in Presidential and House Elections, 1956-1978 (Percent)

	House Elections			Presidential Elections		
	Party-Line Voters [a]	*Defectors* [b]	*Pure Inde-pendents*	*Party-Line Voters* [a]	*Defectors* [b]	*Pure Inde-pendents*
1956	82	9	9	76	15	9
1958	84	11	5			
1960	80	12	8	79	13	8
1962	83	12	6			
1964	79	15	5	79	15	5
1966	76	16	8			
1968	74	19	7	69	23	9
1970	76	16	8			
1972	75	17	8	67	25	8
1974	74	18	8			
1976	72	19	9	74	15	11
1978	69	22	9			

[a] Party identifiers who vote for the candidate of their party.

[b] Party identifiers who vote for the candidate of the other party.

Source: National Election Studies, Center for Political Studies, University of Michigan.

Incumbency as an Electoral Force

Defection has not increased in a politically neutral manner. Cover and Mayhew (1977) found that the proportion of defections in favor of House incumbents rose substantially after 1970 and accounted for over three-quarters of all votes cast against party lines in House races. Even in 1974, when national tides ran strongly against the Republican party and 36 Republican representatives were defeated, 74 percent of all defections favored the incumbent. By 1978, challengers received only 11 percent of the defections; two decades earlier the comparable number was 43 percent.[3] These findings suggest that the secular decline in party-line voting observed in Table 20-1 reflects the greater ability of incumbents to attract votes from people who identify with the other party.

The relationship between party, incumbency and vote choice in the 1978 elections can be seen more directly in Table 20-2. Party and incumbency together appear to be an almost unbeatable combination in House elections. Only 5 percent of the voters (19 respondents) who belonged to the same party as their incumbent representative (hereafter called "incumbent partisans") voted for the challenger. When party and incumbency are in conflict, the latter appears as the more powerful electoral force. By contrast, incumbency has a somewhat weaker influence in Senate voting.

Table 20-2　Vote for House and Senate, by Party Identification and Incumbency, 1978 (Percent)

	Party Identification of Voter		
	Incumbent's Party	Independent	Challenger's Party
Vote for House			
Incumbent	95	79	54
Challenger	5	21	46
n =	(407)	(72)	(277)
Vote for Senate			
Incumbent	89	64	31
Challenger	11	36	69
n =	(179)	(36)	(179)

Source: 1978 National Election Study, Center for Political Studies, University of Michigan.

Before exploring the source of this incumbency advantage, we believe it is worth introducing here a theme to which we return later. The figures reported in the last paragraph are national averages, and they reflect the overwhelming advantage incumbents enjoy nationally. Yet House elections are held in individual congressional districts and the relative influence of party and incumbency may vary from one district to another. One study based on surveys in a number of congressional districts (most of which were in the "marginal" range at one point or another during the last six years) found that some challengers attracted as many as 20 percent of the votes of incumbent partisans, while some incumbents received only 14 percent of the support of challenger partisans (Mann, 1978). Of course, these examples are not representative of districts generally, but no discussion of voting in congressional elections is complete without a consideration of when and how challengers make the best showing against incumbents. Without this understanding, we are in no position to learn the conditions under which change might occur. But with only 19 incumbent partisans voting for challengers in the 1978 data set, there is no variance to investigate. Nonetheless, this need not prevent us from looking for processes of individual decision making that, when certain conditions change, might produce very different results.

　　The source of the increased incumbency advantage that was registered in the 1960s has been a puzzle to scholars. David Mayhew (1974a) originally suggested three possible explanations: (1) incumbents benefited from favorable redistricting that increased the number of majority partisans in their districts; (2) incumbents gained political support by becoming more adept at advertising, credit-taking, and position-taking; and (3) incumbents benefited fortuitously from the erosion of party loyalties—incumbency replaced party as a voting cue. Mayhew did not explicitly mention a fourth possibility, not unrelated to his third, that the visibility and attractiveness of challengers decreased during this time.

Cover (1977) and Ferejohn (1977) have shown that redistricting does not account for the increased advantage of incumbency, although doubtless there are particular cases where redrawing district lines made incumbents safer. Investigation of the second and third explanations has been constrained by the lack of adequate data on public perceptions of congressional candidates. Cover (1977), Ferejohn (1977) and Nelson (1978) all show that the increase in incumbents' electoral advantages was not accompanied by any increase in the proportion of the population who could recall their names, which suggested that incumbency provided a voting cue unmediated by public awareness of the incumbent. The same conclusion came more directly from Nelson's finding that many voters defected to incumbents whose names they could not recall. This implausible possibility can now be safely dismissed, as we will soon see. But unraveling the other two possibilities—that incumbents are better known and/or better liked now than before, or that the advantage in visibility and reputation long held by incumbents, although not increased, now translates more profitably into votes because party ties are weaker—has been frustrated by the lack of appropriate recognition and reputation measures during the decade when the advantage increased. While we can never adequately investigate this period of change, we can begin to describe more accurately what the public knows about incumbents and challengers today.

Candidate Familiarity

Incumbents are better known than their opponents. Scholars have generally said that incumbents enjoy more "name recognition," and point to repeated findings that incumbents are known to about twice as many people as challengers. What the surveys invariably measure however, is not name *recognition* but name *recall*. The Michigan CPS question in 1974 was: "Do you happen to remember the names of the candidates for Congress—that is, for the House of Representatives in Washington—that ran in this district last November?" Of course, it is far more difficult to recall someone's name without help than it is to recognize a name when it is encountered. Many voters unable to recall the names of their representatives or challengers can nevertheless recognize the names when presented with them, which is the situation they face in the voting booth (Mann, 1978). It seems reasonable to expect, then, that the apparent existence of an incumbent electoral advantage without public knowledge of the incumbent reflects a faulty measure of knowledge, not an ability to impress voters without their conscious awareness.

The 1978 Michigan study for the first time included a true measure of name recognition, one that resembled (although not exactly) the situation voters face in the polling place. This was done with the "candidate thermometer," which elicited responses to a number of public figures, including all major party congressional candidates as well as several national political celebrities. For each person on the list of more than 20 names, the respondents could indicate they did

Table 20-3 Candidate Recognition Among Voters in Contested Races, House and Senate, 1978 (Percent)

	Recognize and Rate	Recognize, but not Rate	Don't Recognize
House			
Incumbents (n = 754)	93	4	3
Challengers (n = 754)	44	19	37
Open seat candidates (n = 116)	72	20	8
Senate			
Incumbents (n = 408)	96	3	1
Challengers (n = 408)	86	7	7
Open seat candidates (n = 158)	88	8	5

Source: 1978 National Election Study, Center for Political Studies, University of Michigan.

not recognize the name, that they recognized but could not rate the person, or that they recognized and rated the person. The thermometer thus measures both name recognition and affect toward the person. Table 20-3 shows the percentage of voters in contested races who recognized and rated the House and Senate candidates, those who claimed to recognize but could not rate the candidate, and those who confessed they could not recognize the candidate.

We see that House incumbents are almost universally recognized by voters in their districts, while the names of challengers are familiar to just under two-thirds of the voters. The lead of incumbents over challengers is more pronounced when we use a more stringent standard of recognition—both recognizing and rating the candidate. Open-seat candidates are substantially more visible than those who challenge incumbents, confirming the general view that open seats are more hotly contested than incumbent-held seats. The contrast with the Senate is instructive, with a caveat for the peculiar nature in the Senate sample. Senate challengers are almost as invisible to the electorate as Senate incumbents, probably reflecting both more serious efforts by the opposition and the publicity that comes automatically to a statewide challenger.

Although most voters know the names of challengers and almost all are familiar with the incumbent, this discrepancy alone does not explain the incumbent advantage. Incumbents' very high victory rate is not fully explained by their greater name familiarity. Challengers have an uphill fight even when the voters know them. This is revealed in Table 20-4, which displays defection by incumbency, party identification, and name recognition. Voters who belong to the incumbent's party are almost sure to vote for the incumbent. Even the handful who do not recognize their representative's name have only a one-in-seven chance of defecting. By the same token, the challenger whose name is known to the incumbent's partisans wins only 7 percent of their voters—and loses fully 46 percent of his or her own partisans. The challenger is better off being recognized,

Table 20-4   Party Defection by Incumbency and Candidate Recognition, 1978 House Elections (Percent)[a]

| | *Voter Recognizes*[b] | | | |
| | Incumbent | | Challenger | |
Party Identification	Yes	No	Yes	No
Incumbent's party	4	14	7	3
n =	(366)	(29)	(161)	(243)
Challenger's party	57	15	46	63
n =	(257)	(20)	(145)	(132)

[a] The entry in each cell is the percentage of voters with the indicated characteristics who defected.
[b] Defined as able to rate candidates on thermometer from 0-100.
Source: 1978 National Election Study, Center for Political Studies, University of Michigan.

but visibility alone is not enough. Thus we must move beyond simple name recognition in order to understand the advantages of incumbency and the opportunities for challengers.

Candidate Reputation

The 1978 National Election Study interview schedule gave respondents several opportunities to evaluate the congressional candidates in their district and state. Responses to these questions are all consistent with the proposition that as a class, incumbents are well regarded by their constituents. Table 20-5 shows the percentage of voters who rated the candidates on the feeling thermometer as positive, neutral, negative, or unknown. Almost three-fourths rated the incumbent positively, while less than a fifth made similar evaluations of the challenger.

One can better understand the advantage of incumbency in House elections by contrasting these figures with those for candidates in open House seats and for Senate incumbents and challengers. In the latter cases, the standing of the non-incumbents is relatively high and the gap between the two candidates is relatively narrow.

In addition to thinking highly of incumbents' personal qualities, most voters also feel that their representative is doing a good job. The two sorts of assessments are not always similar. (Sometimes the public combines generalized admiration for a political figure and a low assessment of performance. Jimmy Carter and Gerald Ford come immediately to mind.) Table 20-6 presents the job ratings of House members by party identification and the amount of defection at each category of performance assessment. These figures confirm the well-known point that individual members are highly esteemed despite the public's critical view of Congress as an institution (Fenno, 1975). Nearly two-thirds of all voters think

Table 20-5 Voters' Feelings About Candidates, 1978 (Percent)

	Feeling Thermometer Evaluation			
	Positive	*Neutral*	*Negative*	*Can't Rate: Don't Recognize*
House				
Incumbents (n = 754)	73	10	9	7
Challengers (n = 754)	17	18	9	56
Open-seat candidates (n = 116)	50	13	9	28
Senate				
Incumbents (n = 408)	61	15	20	4
Challengers (n = 408)	48	17	20	15
Open-seat candidates (n = 158)	58	16	14	12

Source: 1978 National Election Study, Center for Political Studies, University of Michigan.

their representative is doing a "good" or "very good" job, and a mere 4 percent have a distinctly unfavorable view. As we would expect, these assessments are affected by party identification; the incumbent's partisans are more enthusiastic than members of the other party. The more important finding, however, is that half the challenger's partisans have a favorable view of the incumbent's

Table 20-6 Incumbent Job Ratings and Defection by Voters in House Elections, 1978 (Percent)

	Rating of Incumbent's Performance					
	Very Good	*Good*	*Fair*	*Poor*	*Very Poor*	*Don't Know*
Percent of all voters rating incumbent	20	44	22	3	1	10
Percent defecting from:						
Incumbent's party	0	4	12	—	—	8
n =	(113)	(180)	(68)	(3)	(2)	(38)
Challenger's party	89	75	35	11	—	21
n =	(28)	(114)	(83)	(19)	(4)	(29)
Percent of Independents voting for challenger	0	11	27	—	—	30
n =	(7)	(36)	(15)	(3)	(1)	(10)

Source: 1978 National Election Study, Center for Political Studies, University of Michigan.

Table 20-7 Favorable Comments About House Candidates, Party
Identification, Incumbency, and Defection, 1978 (Percent)

| | Incumbent | | Challenger | |
	Same Party	Other Party	Same Party	Other Party
Percent liking something about the candidate	71	56	20	6
n =	(407)	(277)	(277)	(407)

	Yes	No	Yes	No	Yes	No	Yes	No
Percent defecting	2	12	72	30	16	63	20	3

Note: "Yes" and "no" refer to whether the respondent likes anything about the candidate in the given category.
Source: 1978 National Election Study, Center for Political Studies, University of Michigan.

performance, and only 8 percent say the incumbent is doing a "poor" or "very poor" job.

The relationship between job assessment and defection is about as strong as we could expect, particularly in light of the handful of incumbent partisans who defected. Incumbents lost no votes at all from members of their own party who say they are doing a "very good" job, and very few from those who rate them "good" or "fair." The numbers are much more striking among challenger partisans, whose support for the incumbent ranges from 89 to 11 percent, depending on their evaluation of his performance. Support for the challenger among pure Independents is similarly related to the incumbent's job rating.

A final measure of candidate affect comes from the open-ended questions asking respondents if there is anything they like and dislike about the Democratic and Republican House candidates. Predictably, voters' party affiliations shape their answers. Whether incumbents or challengers are the object of the query, the incidence of favorable comments is about 15 percentage points higher among their own partisans. This modest difference is overshadowed by the far stronger relationship of incumbency to favorable assessment, as Table 20-7 shows. Only a fifth of the voters in the challenger's party had anything good to say about the challenger, while three times as many of them expressed favorable opinions about the incumbent in the other party.

The consequences of these assessments for the vote can be seen in the bottom line of Table 20-7. This shows both the importance of candidate image in congressional voting decisions and incumbents' vastly greater success in creating favorable impressions. Differences in defection rates in this table are more pronounced, especially for challengers, than those associated with simple name recognition (Table 20-4). Thus the advantage of incumbents reflects more than just their ability to get their names before the public. It seems likely, moreover, that defection rates would be less loaded toward incumbents if more challengers could make themselves favorably known to voters.

Two final notes on the open-ended comments about the candidates. First, the number of respondents who disliked something about the incumbent or the challenger was relatively small—18 percent for the former, 12 percent for the latter—but higher, particularly for the incumbent, than appeared on either the feeling thermometer or the job rating. Second, the content of the open-ended remarks was highly personalized, with very few references to party, ideology, or issues. Voters appear to judge candidates, and incumbents in particular, on the basis of their perceived character, experience, and ties to the local community. Issues and ideology are subordinated to these personal and particularistic concerns.

Candidate Preference

The evidence presented above makes clear that voting in congressional elections is strongly associated with evaluations of the candidates. Yet up to this point we have analyzed vote choice only as it relates to the assessment of a single candidate. A more likely decision process is for the voters to evaluate both candidates at the same time and to choose the more attractive one. It is possible that a number of voters who rate the challenger positively have an even higher opinion of the incumbent. The reverse is less likely in view of the challenger's lower visibility, but it is possible. In order to deal with this possibility, we must include comparative candidate preferences, not just individual candidate ratings.

Table 20-8 displays the vote for incumbent and challenger by party identification and candidate preference, following a format developed by Richard Brody (1976) for the study of presidential elections. Candidate preference is determined by the relative ranking of the incumbent and challenger on the feeling thermometer. "Don't recognize" and "can't rate" responses are treated as neutral; in cases where one candidate is not recognized or rated, feelings toward the other candidates are decisive. A respondent who does not recognize the challenger but who rates the incumbent negatively is coded as preferring the challenger.

The figures in Table 20-8 confirm the appropriateness of the candidate preference model for congressional voting: 94 percent of all respondents who prefer the incumbent vote for the incumbent; 88 percent of all respondents who prefer the challenger vote for the challenger. In cases where neither candidate is preferred, party identification is the best predictor of the vote, although incumbents fare better among challenger partisans in this situation than we might expect. This is probably best explained by our coding conventions—incumbents who were recognized but rated as neutral on the thermometer were treated the same as challengers who were not recognized, although the former have an edge in recognition.

With the data in Table 20-8 we can divide the vote for incumbents and for challengers into four categories: votes consistent with both party identification and candidate preference, those consistent with candidate preference only, those consistent with party identification only, and those consistent with neither. The

Table 20-8 Vote in 1978 House Election by Party Identification and
Candidate Preference

Candidate Preference[a] and Vote	Party Identification							
	Incumbent's Party		*Independent*		*Challenger's Party*		*Total*	
	N	*%*	*N*	*%*	*N*	*%*	*N*	*%*
Prefer incumbent								
Incumbent	258	99	31	91	103	84	392	94
Challenger	2	1	3	9	20	16	25	6
Prefer neither								
Incumbent	123	95	25	81	45	47	193	75
Challenger	7	5	6	19	50	53	63	25
Prefer challenger								
Incumbent	7	41	1	14	2	3	10	12
Challenger	10	59	6	86	58	97	74	88
Total								
Incumbent	388	95	57	79	150	54	595	79
Challenger	19	5	15	21	128	46	162	21

[a] Determined by the relative ranking of the incumbent and challenger on the feeling thermometer.

Source: 1978 National Election Study, Center for Political Studies, University of Michigan.

results of this exercise, displayed in Table 20-9, demonstrate that routine party support not backed up by express preference for the party's candidate provides a small part of incumbents' total support (22 percent), and a substantially larger part for that of challengers (43 percent). This reflects the failure of most challengers to build a substantial personal following. Yet, overall, most party-line votes are accompanied by a preference for the party's candidate; when partisanship and candidate preference conflict, voters are likely to defect from their party.

This analysis of candidate preference is, of course, colored by the relatively low visibility and standing of challengers in our national sample. The 17 cases in the lower left-hand cell of Table 20-8—where incumbent partisans prefer the challenger—are not sufficient to produce confidence in our finding that candidate preference for challengers will override partisanship to the detriment of incumbents. As additional support for our conclusion, therefore, we refer readers to a similar investigation based on surveys in a sample of generally competitive districts (Mann, 1978). That study confirms the ability of more visible and attractive challengers to garner the support of substantial numbers of incumbent partisans.

Table 20-9   Relationship of Party Identification and Candidate Preference to Each Candidate's Total Vote, House, 1978 (Percent)

Vote Consistent With:	Incumbent	Challenger
Party ID and candidate preference	44	36
Candidate preference only	23	10
Party ID only	22	43
Neither[a]	12	11
	100	100
n =	(595)	(162)

Note: Numbers may not add due to rounding.

[a] Vote is consistent with neither party identification nor candidate preference.

Source: 1978 National Election Study, Center for Political Studies, University of Michigan.

Why Incumbents are Well Known and Well Liked

We have argued that voting in a congressional election primarily involves choosing between competing candidates; party plays an important role for some voters in determining whether a candidate is attractive and in providing guidance for voters who lack information about the candidate, but it is secondary to the images of the candidates themselves. Incumbents have an enormous advantage over challengers, not because the voters' decision rules are rigged in their favor, but rather because they are more visible and more attractive. Why are members of Congress in such a desirable position?

The data in Table 20-10 move us a long way toward an explanation. Each figure in this table represents the percentage of all voters who had the designated form of contact with incumbents, challengers, or open seat candidates, in the House and Senate. When contrasted with the image of relative anonymity that appeared in the 1958 study of congressional elections (Stokes and Miller, 1966) the figures in this table, especially for incumbents, are staggering. Only 10 percent of all voters had no form of contact with the House incumbent. Almost a fourth met their representative personally, while nearly three-fourths had seen press coverage about him or her via the print media and/or television. By contrast, only 44 percent of these voters had any type of contact with the challenger. The gap between incumbent and challenger is greatest in mail contacts, which probably reflects the enormous advantage members of the House enjoy in blanketing their districts with mass and specialized mailings. The prohibition on franked (free) mass mailings by representatives for 60 days before an election evidently does not ease the effects of this perquisite of office.

The more one examines Table 20-10, however, the less impressive one finds the argument that the inherent advantages of office adequately explain incum-

Table 20-10 Voter Contact with House and Senate Candidates, 1978 (Percent)

Form of Contact	House Incum-bent	House Chal-lenger	House Open Seat	Senate Incum-bent	Senate Chal-lenger	Senate Open Seat
Any type	90	44	73	94	82	88
Met personally	23	4	14	9	5	9
Saw at meeting	20	3	13	10	5	13
Talked to staff	12	2	13	6	4	9
Received mail	71	16	43	53	32	47
Read about in a newspaper, magazine	71	32	57	73	63	78
Heard on radio	34	15	28	45	37	49
Saw on TV	50	24	48	80	70	78
Family or friend had contact	39	11	26	—	—	—
$n =$	(756)	(756)	(121)	(409)	(409)	(158)

Source: 1978 National Election Study, Center for Political Studies, University of Michigan.

bents' greater visibility. Candidates for open House seats reached a far larger share of voters than challengers did, and in many types of contact were nearly as successful as incumbents. One way or another, open-seat candidates reached 73 percent of the voters, compared to 90 percent for incumbents and 44 percent for challengers. The putative advantages of office are even less evident in Senate races, where voters have nearly as much contact with challengers and open-seat candidates as with incumbents. (Amount of contact is measured by numbers of voters reached, not the number of separate interactions.)

We believe that House incumbents benefit more from the scarcity of serious challenges than from the perquisites of office. Evidence on this point can be found in the data on House and Senate campaign expenditures displayed in Table 20-11. We assume that budgets are a reliable index of total campaign effort, particularly for non-incumbents who must pay for many services that are free to sitting members. The generous spending of candidates for open House and Senate seats helps explain our earlier findings about their visibility to the electorate. In races contested by incumbents, however, the campaign effort and consequently, we believe, the visibility of challengers varies enormously. Just over 70 percent of these elections were won by an incumbent with more than 60 percent of the vote. These campaigns were low-budget productions on both sides. The spending was even more lopsided than the voting, with challengers being outspent three-to-one by the victorious incumbents. Budgets were far larger in the 90 House races decided by smaller margins, particularly for the challengers, who spent an average five to six times as much as their counterparts in non-competitive races.

Table 20-11   Mean Campaign Expenditures in House and Senate Races, 1978

All Races	*House*	*Senate*
Open-seat candidates	$201,049	$ 820,787
$n =$	(111)	(25)
Incumbents	111,557[a]	1,341,942[b]
$n =$	(377)	(22)
Challengers	72,373	697,766
$n =$	(309)	(21)

Incumbent-Contested Races by Election Outcome	*House*		*Senate*	
	Incumbent	*Challenger*	*Incumbent*	*Challenger*
Incumbent won with 60% or more of vote	$ 93,218	$ 32,564	$ 453,772	$ 47,346
$n =$	(287)	(219)	(7)	(6)
Incumbent won with less than 60% of vote	161,856	156,445	2,496,484[c]	992,831
$n =$	(71)	(71)	(8)	(8)
Incumbent lost to the challenger	200,607	217,083	908,348	918,054
$n =$	(19)	(19)	(7)	(7)

[a] Includes 68 uncontested races.

[b] Includes 1 uncontested race.

[c] Without the $7.5 million spent in Jesse Helms' narrowly successful reelection campaign in North Carolina, this figure would be $1.8 million.

Source: Computed by authors from Federal Election Commission data presented in *Congressional Quarterly Weekly Report,* September 29, 1979.

The pattern is similar in Senate contests—challengers in the closer races spend vastly more than challengers who are defeated decisively—but the frequencies are quite different. Most Senate challengers are big spenders and run competitive races, while the vast majority of House challengers have small budgets and even smaller chances of winning.

The absence of serious challenges to most House incumbents surely owes something to their public standing and their resourcefulness in exploiting the advantages inherent in their office. We suspect that many decisions not to wage a major challenge involve other factors as well, including the vitality of the local opposition party, the high cost of a serious campaign, the difficulty of raising enough money, and some degree of satisfaction with the incumbent among local interests. Moreover, some House districts have such a lopsided division of Republicans and Democrats that members of the minority party have little chance of winning under any circumstances. This is seldom true of Senate races because statewide constituencies generally are more evenly balanced between the two parties.

Table 20-10 also confirms other bits of conventional wisdom about House-Senate differences. Senators and those aspiring to the office are much more likely than their House counterparts to communicate with the electorate via broadcast media, especially television. Doubtless this reflects the better fit between statewide constituencies and television audiences. In contrast, many congressional districts are such a small portion of a metropolitan television viewing area that their representatives' activities are not very newsworthy. And when the media audience is so large, advertising becomes prohibitively expensive for a candidate who wants to reach only a fraction of it. Also, senators are bigger celebrities than representatives, a result of their smaller number and differences between the impersonal House and the Senate's star system.

The electoral payoff of contact with the voters can be seen from Table 20-12. Among voters who had contact only with incumbents, challengers lose 72 percent of their partisans and attract but 2 percent of the incumbent's partisans. Defection among challenger partisans is 26 percent lower among voters who have had contact with both candidates and 40 percent lower than the handful of respondents who have had contact with neither candidate. These latter results point to the importance of efforts by both incumbent and challenger.

In the face of these striking findings on the extent of candidate contact with voters, the increased advantage of incumbency clearly is not a result only of the errand boy or ombudsman activities of House members (Fiorina, 1977b). Responses to a battery of questions on citizen-initiated contact with representatives let us assess more directly the electoral consequences of these activities. One-fifth of the voting respondents said that they had contacted their representative or someone in the representative's office—to express an opinion, to seek information, or to seek help with a problem, in roughly equal proportions. Virtually everyone received a response, and the vast majority were very satisfied with that response. Yet defection rates between those who contacted their representative's office and those who did not are almost identical. (Actually, the absence of a difference for all voters masks a partisan difference: Democratic incumbents do slightly better among those voters who *have not* contacted their office, while Republican incumbents do slightly better with those who *have* contacted their office.) If we look at just those respondents who wrote to seek help with a problem, we find that a large majority are incumbent partisans; and of the 19 challenger partisans who fell into this category, 11 voted for the incumbent, producing a defection rate identical to that of all challenger partisans in the sample. In other words, responding to constituent requests paid no special vote dividend for House members in 1978.

While the direct payoff for constituent service may have been limited, a reputation for service appears to have been more valuable. Many voters who have not themselves made requests of their congressmen know others who have, and this latter phenomenon is more strongly related to the vote. Moreover, a third of the voters believe their representative would be "very helpful" if asked to help with a problem, and this reputation for service garners the vote of almost 80

Table 20-12   Defection in 1978 House Elections, by Contact with Incumbent and Challenger (Percent)

	Contact with:			
Defection from:	*Both Candidates*	*Incumbent Only*	*Challenger Only*	*Neither Candidate*
Incumbent's party	8	2	—	8
n =	(155)	(213)	(0)	(38)
Challenger's party	46	72	—	32
n =	(145)	(103)	(1)	(28)
Support for challenger among Independents	29	7	—	—
n =	(34)	(30)	(1)	(6)

Source: 1978 National Election Study, Center for Political Studies, University of Michigan.

percent of the challenger partisans. It is very likely that congressmen build a reputation for service in a variety of ways, exploiting vehicles for mass publicity without limiting themselves to direct servicing of constituent requests. In any case, the reach of other forms of contact with voters extends considerably beyond the constituent service domain.

One final note on additional ingredients in the positive image of incumbents. Richard Fenno (1978) has demonstrated that House members adopt a diversity of "home styles" in presenting themselves in their districts. Some members are highly issue-oriented in their discussions with constituents while others stress their personal identification with the district and make few references to substantive issues. In either case, however, Fenno believes that the result of such encounters with House members is an impression of their personal qualities rather than specific information on their issue positions or voting record. This proposition is confirmed by responses to items in the 1978 study that deal with the member's voting record or positions on issues. Only 15 percent of all voters remembered how their representative voted on any bill in the past couple of years. Fewer than half could say whether they generally agreed or disagreed with the way that representative voted in Washington. In either case, there was very little disagreement with the representative's actions, and the consequent loss in votes was trivial. These data strike a heavy blow at the argument that House members are likely to accumulate enemies because they must take visible stands on many controversial issues. Indeed, only a fraction of all comments about incumbents concern their positions on issues, and the vast majority of these are favorable.

There is somewhat wider awareness of the general ideological posture of representatives—80 percent of voters could place themselves on a liberal-conservative scale and 63 percent could place their congressman. However, only 26 percent were able to classify the challenger. Most ideological descriptions are

Table 20-13 Party Defection, by Ideological Distance of Voters from House Candidates (Percent)[a]

	Voter's Ideological Position		
Party Identification	*Closer to Incumbent*	*Equidistant from Candidates*	*Closer to Challenger*
Incumbent's party	2	6	50
$n =$	(54)	(18)	(10)
Challenger's party	58	57	15
$n =$	(12)	(21)	(40)

[a] Includes only voters who classified their own ideological position and that of the two candidates.

Source: 1978 National Election Study, Center for Political Studies, University of Michigan.

accurate; Democrats are seen as predominantly liberal, Republicans as conservative. We can gauge the importance of ideological proximity voting by looking at those voters who could place themselves and the two candidates on the scale— roughly a fourth of all voters. Table 20-13 displays the level of defection in House elections by the ideological distance of voters from the incumbent and challenger. The entries confirm the presence of proximity voting, but the sparse number of cases in each cell, particularly those where party and proximity conflict, demonstrate how minimal its effect is.

It would be a mistake, however, to conclude that issues and roll-call voting have no importance for congressional elections. The low salience of issues may reflect in part the efforts of the incumbent to avoid being dramatically out of step with district sentiment. In order to preserve a favorable public image, incumbents may act to forestall vociferous criticism on policy grounds. Incumbents must state positions on issues to satisfy local groups that are important for endorsements, campaign contributions, and volunteers. House members realize that the best way of ensuring their continued reelection is to discourage serious opposition. This requires making peace with those in the district who might otherwise underwrite a vigorous challenge. Finally, most politicians operate at the margin, not at the base. A loss of two or three percent of the vote as a result of a vote or a position taken on an issue will give them pause. Thus the small numbers of cases in Table 20-13 are not conclusive evidence against the proposition that taking positions on issues could affect the outcome of some House elections, and that the prospect of such an influence may well constrain members of Congress.

Midterm Elections as Referendums on Presidential Performance

Several scholars have presented evidence that voting in congressional elections is affected by public assessment of the president's performance.

Members of the president's party who like the job the president is doing are less likely to vote for a House candidate of the other party. By the same token, people in the other party who like the way the president is behaving in office are more likely than their fellow-partisans to vote for a congressional candidate in the president's party (Arseneau and Wolfinger, 1973; Kernell, 1977). Using aggregate data, Tufte argues that the size of the losses sustained by the president's party in midterm elections depends on his popularity and how the economy is fairing (1975, 1978). Actually, this latter theory predicts only changes in the partisan division of the national vote for the House of Representatives, either from the preceding presidential year or from some standardized measure of the normal midterm vote. Consequently, at the individual level, we should expect to see its effect only at the margin. And in a year like 1978, when the national swing was less than 3 percent, we should find little evidence of voting in reaction to the president's performance. Moreover, since incumbency seems to insulate House members of the president's party somewhat from adverse judgments of the president's performance (Nelson, 1978), we might expect that the rising electoral effects of incumbency would reduce the referendum effect.

Table 20-14 shows how voting for the House varied according to respondents' judgments of President Carter's performance. Twenty-six percent of Democrats who disapproved of his performance defected, compared to 22 percent of those Democrats who liked his White House record. Republicans who liked the job Carter was doing voted for Democratic House contenders at a rate of 29 percent, compared to 21 percent for Republicans who disapproved. While these differences are minuscule compared to those based on the relative attractiveness of the congressional candidates discussed earlier, they are sufficient to account for the national shift that was observed in 1978. The bottom half of Table 20-14 demonstrates that differences in defection rates are somewhat larger when more refined measures of presidential performance are used.

This finding in no way contradicts a major conclusion of this chapter—that in deciding how to cast their ballots, most voters are influenced primarily by the choice of local candidates. But if we want to explain changes in the national division of the vote from one election to another, especially when those shifts are substantial, we must turn our attention to national forces. How the national swing then translates into swing at the district level and swing in the number of seats, and how important these national forces seem to candidates contesting in local districts, are other questions entirely.

Conclusion

Recent congressional elections can no more be accurately viewed as reflecting standing party decisions than can presidential elections. Most voters have sufficient information about at least one and often both of the candidates to base their decision on something other than party loyalty. Scholars have underestimated the level of public awareness of congressional candidates primarily because of faulty measures. Voters are often able to recognize and evaluate individual candidates without being able to recall their names from memory. At the same

Table 20-14 Two Measures of Carter's Job Performance and Voting in House Elections (Percent)

House Vote	Democrats Approve	Democrats Disapprove	Independents Approve	Independents Disapprove	Republicans Approve	Republicans Disapprove
Democrat	78	74	51	47	29	21
Republican	22	26	49	53	71	79
	100	100	100	100	100	100
n =	336	98	45	19	106	185

House Vote	Democrats[a] Very Good	Good	Fair	Poor	Republicans[a] Good	Fair	Poor	Very Poor
Democrat	87	78	73	72	24	27	20	14
Republican	13	22	27	28	76	73	80	86
	100	100	100	100	100	100	100	100
n =	45	168	214	24	41	169	75	28

[a] There were too few Democrats giving "very poor" and Republicans giving "very good" ratings to be included in the table.

Source: 1978 National Election Study, Center for Political Studies, University of Michigan.

time, the content of these evaluations is both thin and highly personalized, with little apparent ideological or issue content.

Incumbents are both better known and better liked than challengers, which accounts for their obvious electoral advantage. No one activity of incumbents—such as the much-heralded ombudsman role on behalf of their constituents—is solely responsible for their popularity. A variety of activities that bring them to the attention of the voters in their districts pay handsome electoral dividends. Yet it is inaccurate to portray congressional voting as simply favorable or unfavorable (but mostly favorable) decisions on the incumbent. Equally important are the public visibility and reputation of the challenger. Most voters make their decision between candidates by judging which one they like better, not by pulling the party lever or turning automatically to the incumbent. In most districts the challenge to incumbents is so inconsequential that the largely favorable images of incumbents prevail. In a much smaller number of districts, challengers stage a strong enough campaign to make the task of choosing between candidates a meaningful exercise. The advantage of incumbency in House elections—in contrast to Senate elections—is enhanced by the absence of a serious challenge and the greater likelihood of a lopsided partisan balance in the smaller and more homogeneous House constituency. The explosion of congressional perquisites has enabled House members to communicate with their constituents far more frequently and directly; and the absence of meaningful party competition at the district level coupled with traditional patterns of local press reporting (Robinson, 1980) works against alternative sources of (negative) information about the incumbent.

Finally, public assessments of the president provide a national dynamic to congressional voting, but the effect is modest compared to the salience of the local choices.

These findings raise as many new questions as they answer old ones. One of us has begun to explore how the conditions of election and reelection outlined here influence the way members of Congress behave in Washington (Mann, 1978, 1980). We won't repeat those arguments. Instead, we conclude with a comment on the research agenda of those who study congressional elections.

If most elections to the House are won for lack of a contest, and the evidence for this is impressive, then we need to know much more about the conditions under which a serious challenge is waged. Incumbent popularity among the voters is certainly an important deterrent to potential opponents and to those who might underwrite their campaign. When an incumbent looks popular, the most attractive candidates are unlikely to waste their time and credibility in a challenge against apparently heavy odds. The same consideration probably keeps contributors' checkbooks closed. Yet local leaders are likely to take other factors into consideration as well, such as the incumbent's record on legislative matters of great interest to them. Fenno reports that incumbents consciously strive to forestall serious opposition. We need to know more about what they do to accomplish that objective, and how these efforts are reflected, if at all, among the mass public. These and other questions relating to the recruitment of candidates and the mobilization of resources should lead us to supplement national samples with surveys of leaders and of contribution patterns at the district level. If most incumbents win reelection before the campaign begins, we should start to find out what happens between elections. . . .

NOTES

1. Two of the three senators defeated in the primaries were short-term appointees filling vacant seats, as was one of the seven who lost their seats in the November election.
2. People who initially call themselves Independents and then (in response to the follow-up question) admit that they lean toward one or the other party think and vote like outright identifiers with that party rather than like people who insist that they are Independents (Keith et al., 1977). Therefore we have classified these Independent Democrats and Independent Republicans with the relevant party here and throughout this chapter.
3. Because the 1978 CPS sample over-reported the national vote for incumbents, defections favoring challengers probably were somewhat higher in 1978.

PART V: PARTY IDENTIFICATION

21. HOW MEANINGFUL IS PARTY IDENTIFICATION?

It has long been recognized that a person's vote does not depend solely on the candidates and issues of the current election. The formerly strong tendency of southern Americans to vote Democratic year after year (the solid South), the strong association of blacks with the Democratic party since the New Deal of the 1930s, and numerous other examples of persistent regional, linguistic, and religious differences both here and abroad attest eloquently to the existence of a long-term component in voting. Early American voting studies (for example, Lazarsfeld, Berelson, and Gaudet, 1944) and many past and recent studies of voting in Europe treat group attachments such as those mentioned above as this stabilizing element. However, our current understanding of voting behavior was very heavily influenced by the University of Michigan researchers' emphasis on party identification as the most important long-term factor. Their question wording and the distribution of party identification from 1952 through 1982 is given in Table 21-1.

The critical insight of the Michigan researchers (Campbell, Gurin, and Miller, 1954; Campbell, Converse, Miller, and Stokes, 1960), partially reprinted here as Chapter 22, consisted of two points. First, just as people identify with religious, racial, and ethnic groups, so do they identify with political parties. Second, parties, like other groups, tend to be quite stable in terms of what they stand for, so that partisanship was appropriately viewed as a long-term component of the political system. In particular, partisanship persists even when people vote contrary to their usual beliefs, as when many Democrats "defected" to Dwight Eisenhower in the 1950s and many Republicans voted for Lyndon Johnson in 1964. However, partisanship was also important because its influence went beyond its *direct* effects on the vote. As portrayed in *The American Voter* (Campbell, Converse, Miller, and Stokes, 1960), party identification affects the other major determinants of the vote—attitudes toward the issues and attitudes toward the candidates. Republican identifiers are more likely to agree with Republican leaders on the issues and to look favorably on Republican candidates. In part this is because partisanship serves a screening function, as citizens selectively perceive political information to the benefit of their preferred party.

Table 21-1 Party Identification in the United States, 1952-1982

	1952	1956	1960	1964	1968	1972	1976	1980	1982
Strong Democrat	22	21	20	27	20	15	15	18	20
Weak Democrat	25	23	25	25	25	26	25	23	24
Independent Democrat	10	6	6	9	10	11	12	11	11
Independent	6	9	10	8	11	13	15	13	11
Independent Republican	7	8	7	6	9	10	10	10	8
Weak Republican	14	14	14	14	15	13	14	14	14
Strong Republican	14	15	16	11	10	10	9	9	10
Apolitical	3	4	2	1	1	1	1	2	2
Democratic Presidential Vote	44%	42%	50%	61%	43%	38%	50%	42%	
Republican Presidential Vote	55	57	50	38	43	61	48	52	

Note: The classification is based on the following question series: "Generally speaking, do you usually think of yourself as a Republican, a Democrat, an Independent, or what? (If partisan:) Would you call yourself a strong (Republican/Democrat) or a not very strong (Republican/Democrat)? (If not partisan:) Do you think of yourself as closer to the Republican or Democratic Party?"

Source: Computed from data collected in the 1952-1982 Center for Political Studies/National Election Studies election surveys, University of Michigan.

Republican identifiers are more likely to listen to Republican candidates and to news and advertisements favorable to Republicans; also, they are more likely to interpret whatever they hear as favorable to Republicans.

Acceptance of the party identification concept was sufficiently strong that most commercial polls, such as the Gallup Poll, now regularly measure the number of Republican and Democratic partisans, and even small fluctuations are subject to journalistic analysis. But later work led researchers to wonder just how meaningful party identification is. In the United States, concern initially grew from questions about the stability of partisanship and the degree to which it is affected by short-term forces. As researchers tried to transport the concept to other nations, doubt arose over occasionally low levels of partisanship and was compounded when partisanship seemed to be no more stable than voting behavior. In addition, researchers have raised the question: is party identification being measured correctly? In the first part of this chapter, we will look carefully at the challenges being raised against the notion of partisanship as a universally stable and meaningful component of the vote. Then we will review the evidence in favor of the party identification concept as well as responses to the criticisms. Finally, the closing section will address the methodological questions.

Party Identification as Transitory and Meaningless

The first challenge to the importance of partisanship came from what was taken to be a serious decline in identification with the parties in the United States during the mid-1960s. This decline was emphasized most dramatically in *The Changing American Voter* (Nie, Verba, and Petrocik, 1976), a part of which is reprinted here as Chapter 23. In contrast to *The American Voter*, Nie et al. found that fewer citizens considered themselves strong partisans in the 1960s and 1970s than in the 1950s, and more considered themselves independents. In addition, more partisans voted for the "other" party, people increasingly voted split tickets rather than voting for candidates of only one party for every office, and presidential candidates were less often evaluated in terms of their party affiliation than in terms of their personal characteristics. Overall, the frequency and the ties of partisanship were weakening. These changes suggested to many researchers that partisanship was no longer such an important part of the voting equation.

The decline in partisanship in the United States also suggested that it is less stable than it first seemed to be, at both the aggregate and the individual level. True, the aggregate stability of party identification was considerable, even in the 1960s and 1970s. Still, there were hints of susceptibility to short-term forces, as when a party's strength fell in years that its presidential candidate suffered a disastrous defeat (such as 1964 for the Republicans and 1972 for the Democrats). More important was the considerable increase in independence in the 1960s and 1970s (Nie et al., Fig. 23-1). Not only did this indicate volatility of public attitudes, but it was literally a movement away from identification with the parties. Also, panel studies showed there was even greater change in individual partisanship that was inevitably concealed in the aggregate figures by compensating changes in opposite directions, with the greatest shifts involving movement into and out of political independence (Converse, 1966a; Dreyer, 1973; LeDuc, 1981).

Evidence of the instability of partisanship led to the possibility that it was not totally long term but was affected by short-term factors. The early causal models of the vote decision (Schulman and Pomper, 1975), which attempted to derive the separate impact of partisanship, candidate orientation, and issue position on the vote, assumed that party identification was strictly long term in its effects. By contrast, later analyses—most notably that by Page and Jones (Chapter 13), but also one by Jackson (1975b)—allowed for the possibilities of reciprocal causation and found a rather considerable effect of issue and candidate evaluations on current party affiliation. The view of partisanship as subject to short-term influences is most clearly apparent in the research of Fiorina, a portion of whose work is reprinted here as Chapter 24. Fiorina sees partisanship as a running tally of retrospective evaluations, based not only on socialization and historical effects, but also on evaluations of current political happenings. He points out that there is a considerable degree of continuity in party evaluations. But the fact that partisanship is constantly being tested with information about current politics considerably alters the almost totally static view sometimes gleaned (perhaps erroneously) from the writings of the Michigan researchers.

Another challenge to the meaningfulness of partisanship came when studies in other countries revealed widely differing levels of party identification, with much less identification with parties in some countries than in the United States. Researchers sometimes concluded that left/right identifications were more important in those countries than party identification (Percheron and Jennings, 1981; Inglehart and Klingemann, 1976; van der Eijk and Niemöller, 1983).

The final challenge to the view of partisanship as stable and meaningful asked whether party identification is really distinct from the vote, at least outside of the United States. If partisanship is a long-term identification, then it need not change when people switch their votes from one election to the next. Indeed, most change should be of that form, with partisanship staying the same even when one's vote changes, as is true in the United States. However, analysis for other countries suggests this is often not the case.

The Butler and Stokes (1969) study, *Political Change in Britain,* was the first to report that party identification might be less stable in other countries than in the United States, particularly when people do not vote for their own party. (It was still quite stable in Britain, but less so than in the United States.) They explain the national differences by referring to ballot differences: Americans develop party loyalties as they vote for several different offices at the same election, while British citizens cast a vote for only a single office and so are less likely to distinguish between their current party and their current vote. Subsequently, Thomassen's (1976) analysis of Dutch data, excerpted here as Chapter 25, had a major impact; Thomassen found that people in the Netherlands are actually less stable in partisanship than in vote. (Compare in Table 25-3 the 10 percent of Dutch respondents who voted the same way in 1971 and 1972 but changed their partisanship, and the 6 percent who changed their vote while maintaining their partisanship.) From this Thomassen concluded that party identification in the Netherlands is actually affected by the vote rather than being causally prior to it as in the United States. This severely limits the utility of the concept of party identification in that country. Later data from Sweden (Holmberg, 1981, p. 177) showed a similar pattern there. LeDuc's (1981) analysis of four countries (the United States, Britain, the Netherlands, and Canada) found that changes in party identification were typically two to three times as great in other countries as in the United States. A quarter or more of the respondents altered their partisanship in no more than a five- or six-year period. And as noted, the stability of partisanship compared to the vote was unusual in the United States.

The extent to which partisanship moves with the vote is so great in some countries, especially West Germany and the Netherlands, that analysts for those countries have frequently dismissed the concept of party identification as irrelevant for them (see, for example, Thomassen, 1976, and the references cited in Baker, Dalton, and Hildebrandt, 1981, pp. 195-98). Some analysts have salvaged the concept by rejecting the direction component while retaining the strength component (Holmberg, 1981), but this seriously erodes the value of the concept. The original notion was that one could obtain a measure of people's predispositions toward the parties independently of their current votes. This may remain true for some individuals (for example, strong identifiers) and in some countries (especially the United States), but in many cases it is unlikely that a measure of partisanship tells us anything different from a measure of how people voted.

Thus, what began as a modest questioning of the view that partisanship was fully stable in the United States and that it was equally important abroad led to major attacks on the meaningfulness of partisanship in voting. An increasing number of studies argued that it is affected by short-term forces in the United States and is not distinct from the vote in other nations, positions that undermine the utility of the party identification concept as a long-term component in models of the vote decision. Many (and possibly most) analysts, however, still find party identification a useful concept, because they feel that other evidence shows party identification to be reasonably stable.

Party Identification as Stable and Meaningful

The responses to the several challenges presented above are based on some early data as well as later analyses. We shall begin with the American case and move on to the challenges in other countries. First, the level of stability of partisanship is considerable, even if it is not perfect. There is some ebb and flow, of course, in Table 21-1, but the Democratic lead in partisanship remained intact from 1952 to 1982. In spite of minor fluctuations and even the considerable growth in independence, it is clear that the overwhelming majority of Americans still identifies with (or at least feels closer to) one of the major parties and that the Democrats remain the more popular party.[1]

Further support for the stability of partisanship is found in individual-level data. Across a panel study in which the same respondents were interviewed in

1956, 1958, and 1960, very few respondents changed from Republican to Democrat, or vice versa (Converse, 1966a). Similarly, the report by Converse and Markus in Chapter 8 emphasizes the stability of partisanship in the 1970s panel. Early multiyear panel studies in other countries likewise found minimal change across waves (Butler and Stokes, 1969), though Thomassen's research clearly shows there is greater change in some countries.

As originally viewed by the Michigan researchers, the only significant change in party identification over time (except for critical periods such as the 1930s) involves strength of partisanship, with people becoming stronger partisans as they age (Campbell, Converse, Miller, and Stokes, 1960, pp. 161-69). Similar life-cycle effects were found in other countries (Converse, 1969). A lively debate developed on the existence of such a life-cycle effect in the United States when Abramson's (1975) inspection of "cohort data" failed to find the expected increases in partisan strength. (Cohort data follow a birth cohort through time, for example, comparing the partisanship in 1964 and 1968 of those who were born between 1940 and 1947, instead of just comparing 21- to 24-year-olds in the two years.) Converse (1976), however, conceding that events of the mid-1960s caused a modest general retreat from parties, argued that strength increased with age, at least for the "steady state" period of 1952-1964. The life-cycle effect is undoubtedly small, but this merely indicates that stability was greater than anticipated.[2]

The early research also found party identification to be highly stable across generations, especially when compared with other attitudes (Jennings and Niemi, 1968). And again, similar stability was found in early studies of other countries, such as the Butler and Stokes (1969, chap. 3) study of Britain. Later analysis shows that respondents' reports that their partisanship is the same as their parents' must be discounted since respondents frequently misperceive their parents' partisanship (Niemi, 1974). This problem is avoided in studies based on actual interviewing of parents and offspring (Jennings and Niemi, 1974, 1981), which show frequent slippage across generations into and out of the Independent category but little switching from one party to the opposite party.

As to the effect on party identification of short-term political factors, the question is not *whether* it is affected but how much. Some studies claim a large effect, but two studies, while explicitly recognizing that partisanship can be affected by short-term influences, found that the effect is not great. In their dynamic analysis of the 1972-1974-1976 panel study, Markus and Converse (Chapter 14) show that partisanship is weakened when a person votes for the other party, but "the predicted effect of a deviating vote in a single election is hardly dramatic" (p. 146). Markus' (1982) analysis of the 1980 panel study provides comparable evidence. In this instance he observed the effect on partisanship in one wave of candidate ratings in the previous wave. Partisanship remained highly stable, with only a modest effect in the latter part of the campaign. One could argue, however, that these studies still do not adequately test the short-term hypothesis. For example, Markus and Converse model current party identification as affected by prior partisanship, which is affected by issues, but current party identification is not directly affected by current issues or by candidate factors. Thus, they *assume* partisanship to be long term, which accounts in part for their finding only small short-term effects. Because of sensitivity to such assumptions, different models are obtaining and probably will continue to obtain different results as regards the importance of short-term effects on partisanship. Minimally, stability may be less than once thought, but the extent of susceptibility to short-term considerations should not be overstated. Even Fiorina's explicit effort to model partisanship as a summary of past influences had to cope with the considerable stability of the measures.

Turning to the challenges from other countries, the differences in the extent of politicization across countries can be seen as a logical result of differences in the countries' histories. Converse and Dupeux (1962) provided the initial recognition that one has to adjust one's understanding of and expectations about partisanship in accordance with a country's history and its present politics. They found that identification with a party was less common in France than in the United States in the late 1950s, and accounted for the difference by arguing that intergenerational transmission in the two nations proceeded from different initial levels of parental partisanship. Thus, the transmission process was similar across nations, but France started with a much lower level of partisanship in the parents' generation, which led to a lower level of partisanship in the generation being studied. Percheron and Jennings (1981) disagreed with the specific argument of Converse and Dupeux, arguing that what is transmitted in France is not identification with a specific party so much as position on an ideological dimension. Yet this does not destroy the meaningfulness of partisan feelings, so long as one realizes that what appears to be important in France is not one's precise party but one's identifications with left or right tendencies.[3]

Similar points are relevant for studies of other countries. Converse (1969), for example, incorporated different political histories in an explanation of differing levels of partisanship in the five-nation (United States, Britain, Italy, West Germany, and Mexico) study of Almond and Verba (1963). In Germany and Italy, identification tended to increase with age, as was the case in the United States and Britain, except that identification was especially low for the age groups most affected by the fascist experience in those countries. Mexico showed a more radical departure from the common relationship between age and partisanship, but this can be accounted for by the fact that Mexican women were unable to cast a presidential vote until a year before the survey was conducted. Sani (1976) and Barnes (1977, chap. 5) also found differences in intergenerational transmission of partisanship in Italy, but they were able to explain the differences by reference to the strong family, organizational, and community ties of Italians. Overall, data from multiple countries make it clear that partisanship will not always be at a uniform level across countries, nor will there be identical relationships with age and other variables. In many of these cases, however, the differences can be explained in terms of democratic experiences, the party system, and other national characteristics.

The final challenge to the notion of meaningful partisanship is in some ways the most serious. If party identification does not "travel" as a concept to other countries, then the logical status of partisanship as a useful concept for the United

States would next have to be re-evaluated. The attack on this basis has been most severe from Dutch (chap. 25) and West German (Kaase, 1976) sources. The Dutch case might be discounted since relationships could be different in a nation with a dozen political parties. As regards the German case, Norpoth (1978) emphasized the prosaic problem of translating questions from one language to another and found that many of the apparent differences were the result of which survey questions were used. Still, looking at more comparable partisanship questions led him to conclude that "durable party attachments are common, though not ubiquitous in the West German electorate" (p. 55). Baker, Dalton, and Hildebrandt (1981) also found that party identification is an appropriate concept for West Germany, although they used party thermometers to construct their measure.[4]

Finally, even if the direction component of partisanship is identical to vote choice in some countries, the strength of partisanship is still a meaningful concept. In Britain, for example, where partisanship and the vote move in tandem to a greater degree than in the United States, Särlvik and Crewe (1983) showed that strong identifiers behave differently from those weakly identified with a party. Likewise, Holmberg (1981, chap. 10) showed differences by strength of identification in Sweden. All this suggests that party identification remains a vital concept in the United States and probably also in many other nations. Party identification may not be as stable as was once thought, but this view is that it is sufficiently stable to be treated as a long-term component of the vote.

Measurement Questions: Is Party Identification Being Measured Correctly?

Research has not been limited to analysis of the stability and universality of partisanship. Studies have begun to question how party identification should be conceptualized and measured. The reconsideration began when Petrocik (1974), excerpted here as Chapter 26, called attention to some "intransitivities" in the usual party identification scale. One would expect strength of partisanship to be monotonically related to many other variables, but this was not so in every instance. In many elections, for example, independent leaners were more likely to vote for their preferred party than were weak partisans.

Why might independent leaners behave in a more partisan fashion than weak partisans? One explanation is that independent leaners are actually "closet partisans" who do not wish to admit their partisanship. Brody's (1977) analysis of the 1956-1958 and 1972-1974 panel data supported this position, as did Miller and Miller's (1977) report on the 1976 American national election study. Yet this explanation does not account for all the results since Petrocik and others have found instances in which the leaners behave as other Independents.

Shively (1977) offered a second possible explanation: that the leaners were really Independents who were reporting how they were planning to vote in the election. The leaners would show up as politically involved in Petrocik's analysis since they were the Independents who were interested enough to vote; at the same time, they would vote for their party more often than weak identifiers since they were responding to the party identification question on the basis of their planned vote. The result of Shively's critical test was that, as expected, leaners more often than partisans changed their party identification when they switched their vote. However, the number of respondents underlying this test is too small to be definitive. And the explanation does not account for the large proportion of leaners who vote for the other party (Miller and Miller, 1977).

The explanation with the most serious potential for our treatment of partisanship is that independence may be a separate dimension from partisanship. The Weisberg chapter (27) summarizes the evidence in favor of this interpretation. Separate dimensions minimally mean that some people can be both partisans and Independents while other people are neither (see Table 27-2). Petrocik's intransitivities can then be explained in that some independent leaners are more partisan than are some weak identifiers, even though they call themselves Independents since they are also more independent than are the weak identifiers (Valentine and Van Wingen, 1980). Also, Weisberg's Table 27-7 shows that people who consider themselves neither partisans nor Independents disproportionately fall into the weak identifier category. Consequently, weak partisans might be more partisan than leaners if both categories were purged of people who actually consider themselves neither. Other studies have also given support to a multidimensional interpretation. Katz (1979) analyzed partisan change over American and British panel studies, using multidimensional scaling to place partisan categories closer together the more respondents switch from one category to another. He found that two dimensions—a direction dimension (Republicans versus Democrats in the United States) and an intensity dimension (partisans versus Independents)—were required to handle the change patterns. Jacoby's (1982) analysis of college students' rank orders of their preferences for the different partisan categories (strong Republican, weak Republican, and so on) found that a third of the sample had preferences that were consistent with a two-dimensional space similar to Katz's, with the other two-thirds fitting the conventional unidimensional scale.

A basic problem in deciding among these explanations is that the standard party identification measure assumed unidimensionality rather than testing for it. However, the 1980 American national election study included several new partisanship questions that were designed to test the multidimensional model and to explore what the traditional party identification questions have been measuring. The Weisberg chapter uses some of these questions to support the multidimensional interpretation. Dennis (in work presented at conferences in the early 1980s and later published in Dennis, 1988) has also extensively analyzed the new partisanship questions, finding three basic components: partisan direction, party system support (Democrats and Republicans are both highly supportive of the party system, while Independents are low on this component), and political involvement (people who are both Independents and partisans are especially high on this component, while those who are neither are especially low). Both Dennis and Weisberg (1983) used the 1980 questions to construct and test new party support and closeness typologies.[5]

Once the possibility of multidimensionality of partisanship and independence is recognized, it is also necessary to consider whether there should be separate dimensions for reactions to different political parties. Reactions to the Democratic and Republican parties need not be opposites of one another, as Weisberg argues in Chapter 27. Related ideas have been suggested by other researchers. In particular, Maggiotto and Piereson (1977) have examined the "hostility hypothesis" that defection from one's own partisanship depends on one's evaluation of the opposition party. They found that evaluation of the opposition party indeed has an independent impact on the vote. (See also Smidt, 1975a, 1975b, 1981; Guynes, n.d.; Guynes and Perkins, n.d.; Wattenberg, 1982.) Additionally, Weisberg (1982) showed that attitude toward a party is the prime variable affecting feelings toward its candidates, with party identification and attitudes toward the other party having little added impact. This suggests a model of partisanship in which the citizen has an identification with each party, based partly on socialization experiences with that party and partly on later satisfaction or dissatisfaction with that party's performance over the years. This model is similar to that which Fiorina offers at the beginning of Chapter 24, except that identification with one party need not be the negative of identification with the other party.

This multidimensional approach may also be useful in treating partisanship in other countries. Indeed, the first discussion of partisanship to emphasize the citizen's reaction to each party separately was Crewe's (1976) discussion of "negative partisanship" in Britain. Crewe found it useful to distinguish four types of partisans: "polarized," who are very strongly for their own party and very strongly against the other party, "loyal," who are very or fairly strongly for their own party but are not very strongly against the other party, "negative," who are not very strongly for their own party but are very strongly against the other party, and "apathetic," who are not very strongly for their own party and not very strongly against the other party.

Canadian researchers have also found it useful to adopt a multidimensional measure of partisanship. Clarke et al. (1979) developed a typology of partisanship based not only on intensity (very strong, fairly strong, weak), but also on whether or not the party choice is consistent at federal and provincial levels and whether or not it has been stable over time. Strong, stable, consistent partisans are most likely to report always having voted for the same party, while those who "deviate" on all three characteristics are least likely to do so.[6]

As we move toward countries with even larger numbers of parties, we might anticipate ever more complex patterns of partisanship. The Dutch party system may be the epitome of this extreme, with 18 parties having won seats in the lower house of parliament (the Second Chamber) from 1945 to 1981 and high points of 14 parties winning seats in 1971 and 1972. It is perhaps not surprising then that van der Eijk and Niemöller (1983) found that close to half the party adherents actually identified with multiple parties. These multiple identifications were consistent ideologically, as when two-fifths of the adherents of both the small right-wing Calvinist religious fundamentalist parties also identified with the other of these parties. Multiple identification based on ideological proximity may be an entirely appropriate response to a fragmented party system and may make the concept of partisanship appropriate where it would not otherwise be.

All in all, it is still too early to draw firm conclusions about these measurement questions. The traditional U.S. party identification question and scale do very well for many purposes, and we have the advantage of a lengthy time-series of their values. Yet they may confound strength of partisanship with independence, so that new measures might be more useful in dealing with party system support and political involvement. The examples of Britain, Canada, and the Netherlands suggest that it is worth extending the treatment of separate reactions to different parties and of multiple partisanship to more party systems. But this should not be read as saying that the case for the multidimensionality of partisanship has been proven. For example, an article by McDonald and Howell (1982) challenges the multidimensional interpretation of American partisanship and Fiorina (p. 261) forcefully argues that the traditional measure can still be used. Clearly these measurement issues remain a topic of dispute.

Conclusion

If there was little questioning of the concept of party identification in the years after it was first introduced, by the mid-1980s there seemed to be no end to the questioning of it. There were disagreements over the nature and measurement of partisanship—disagreements that continue today. In part, the question is whether the American treatment of partisanship is useful for studying other countries, but also we ask how we should understand partisanship in the United States itself.

This controversy certainly cautions us about exporting concepts from voting behavior research in one country to studies of other countries. Once a new concept is developed, there is a natural tendency to rush out and try to apply it everywhere. Unfortunately, that may not always work. For one thing, it may be impossible to develop comparable questions in different languages. But the larger problem is that there are meaningful differences between political systems, and these differences may affect the application of concepts across nations. Even if we expect human behavior to be everywhere similar, the differences in political systems and ballot choices yield differences in the stimuli to which citizens react when they vote, and these in turn yield behavioral differences. In particular, there are enough unique factors in the American political system to ensure that some concepts developed for the United States may not apply equivalently abroad. At the same time, we should not dismiss problems in applying a concept cross-nationally as irrelevant to the United States. Thus, the problems found in transporting the party identification concept abroad helped alert researchers to the possible theoretical and measurement problems in the American data.

In the end, does the nature of partisanship have real political effects? We think so. If partisanship is solely long-term identification, then political change is likely to occur only at glacial speeds. On the other hand, if partisanship is responsive to short-term factors, then there is a potential for dramatic change that the analyses of the last 30 years have not noticed. This is a very real difference, not only for political scientists but also for practitioners—the politicians who must decide whether the public's partisanship tightly limits the vote for their party or whether it is worth trying to exploit new issues to bring about large voting change. This is a theme to which we will return in the next section of this book, where we examine different interpretations of contemporary political developments.

Looking back, the questioning of the measurement and stability of partisanship during the late 1970s and early 1980s was only a beginning. The standard measure of party identification survived these challenges, but the literature reviewed here led to a virtual explosion of work on these topics during the mid- and late-1980s. In particular, there has been further sharp probing of question wording effects, the treatment of independents, and over-time stability at individual and aggregate levels. In any case, partisanship has remained of such crucial theoretical importance that it continues to be worth intense examination.

NOTES

1. Partisanship appears to be such a useful baseline that Converse (1966b) developed the notion of a "normal vote" to describe the results of a hypothetical election in which long-term party identification predominates and short-term issue and candidate factors are negligible. Taking into account both the greater number of Democratic identifiers and the fact that Democrats are less likely to vote than Republicans are, Converse found that the "normal vote" was about 53-54 percent Democratic and 46-47 percent Republican. Those results were for the 1950s, but Miller's (1979) recomputation of the normal vote for the 1960s and 1970s produced virtually identical results. Achen (1979) has demonstrated the existence of a bias in the use of these normal vote estimates to determine the importance of issues.

2. Abramson (1979) questioned the strengthening of party identification even during the 1952-1964 period; he argued that changes in overall figures were due to the development of partisan feelings among blacks. (See also Converse, 1979.) Claggett (1981) has argued quite persuasively that some of the differences between Converse and Abramson are due to their ignoring an important distinction between acquisition of partisanship (moving from independent to partisan) and intensification of partisanship (moving from weak partisan to strong partisan), with the two having different dynamic processes.

3. Partisanship in France was later explored in much more detail. See Converse and Pierce (1986) and the references cited therein.

4. Similarly, although party identification in Britain is closer to the vote than in the United States, Särlvik and Crewe (1983) found the concept useful in their study of British voting in the 1970s. In addition, Cain and Ferejohn (1981) showed that the earlier Butler and Stokes result was partly due to their keeping Liberals in the British analysis while omitting Independents from the American data.

5. Weisberg (Chapter 27) uses also an alternative measure of partisanship based on thermometer ratings. However, McDonald and Howell (1982) show that this measure is less stable and reliable than the conventional measure, suggesting that it is more susceptible to short-term electoral forces than the traditional measure. If so, Weisberg's party difference measure is not an appropriate validating measure.

6. Another interpretation of the inconsistent partisanship between federal and provincial levels in Canada is offered by Blake (1982), who viewed it as rational when a person's favorite party at one level of government is not a serious contender at another level. For example, since the Conservative party is very weak at the provincial level in British Columbia, it is entirely reasonable for a voter to be Conservative at the federal level but Social Credit in provincial politics. From this perspective, dual loyalty may not be so much a matter of inconsistency as a case of multiple identification due to different party systems. There is some evidence of dual partisanship in the United States as well, especially in the South (Jennings and Niemi, 1966; Hadley, 1983).

FURTHER READINGS

The Normal Vote

Philip E. Converse, "The Concept of a Normal Vote," in *Elections and the Political Order,* ed. Angus Campbell, Philip E. Converse, Warren E. Miller, and Donald E. Stokes (New York: Wiley, 1966). Development of the normal vote concept.

Christopher H. Achen, "The Bias in Normal Vote Estimates," *Political Methodology* (1979) 6:343-56. Normal vote analysis is misspecified.

Age Effects on Partisanship

Philip E. Converse, *The Dynamics of Party Support* (Beverly Hills, Calif.: Sage, 1976). Partisan strength increases with age.

Paul R. Abramson, "Developing Party Identification," *American Journal of Political Science* (1979) 23:78-96. Partisan strength does not increase with age.

William Claggett, "Partisan Acquisition Versus Partisan Intensity," *American Journal of Political Science* (1981) 25:193-214. Reexamines aging effect while distinguishing between acquisition and intensification of partisanship.

Richard G. Niemi, G. Bingham Powell, Harold W. Stanley, and C. Lawrence Evans, "Testing the Converse Partisanship Model with New Electorates," *Comparative Political Studies* (1985) 18:300-22. Finds an effect of age that is independent of voting experience.

The Measurement of Partisanship

David C. Valentine and John R. Van Wingen, "Partisanship, Independence, and the Partisan Identification Question," *American Politics Quarterly* (1980) 8: 165-86. Party direction and independence as separate dimensions.

Martin Wattenberg, "Party Identification and Party Images: A Comparison of Britain, Canada, Australia, and the United States," *Comparative Politics* (1982) 14:23-40. Both positive and negative images of the parties are important.

Michael D. McDonald and Susan E. Howell, "Reconsidering the Reconceptualization of Party Identification," *Political Methodology* (1982) 8:73-91. Argues for a unidimensional interpretation of partisanship.

Usefulness of Party Identification in Other Countries

Lawrence LeDuc, "The Dynamic Properties of Party Identification: A Four-Nation Comparison," *European Journal of Political Research* (1981) 9:257-68. Uses panel data to show differences in partisan stability, by itself and in comparison with voting behavior, across four countries.

Warren E. Miller, "The Cross-National Use of Party Identification as a Stimulus to Political Inquiry," in *Party Identification and Beyond*, ed. Ian Budge, Ivor Crewe, and Dennis Farlie (London: Wiley, 1976). Defense of the party identification concept.

The Decline of Partisanship in the United States

Jerrold G. Rusk and Helmut Norpoth, "Partisan Dealignment in the American Electorate: Itemizing the Deductions since 1964," *American Political Science Review* (1982) 76:522-37. Decomposition of the increase in Independents into generational and period effects.

Martin P. Wattenberg, *The Decline of American Political Parties, 1952-1988* (Cambridge, Mass.: Harvard University Press, 1991). Major trend is increasing neutrality toward the parties, not alienation from them.

The Socialization of Partisanship

M. Kent Jennings and Richard G. Niemi, *The Political Character of Adolescence* (Princeton, N.J.: Princeton University Press, 1974). Reports of independent interviews with high school seniors and their parents.

M. Kent Jennings, Klaus R. Allerbeck, and Leopold Rosenmayr, "Generations and Families: General Orientations," in *Political Action*, ed. Samuel Barnes, Max Kaase et al. (Beverly Hills, Calif.: Sage, 1979). Reports of interviews with adolescents and parents in five countries.

Russell J. Dalton, "Reassessing Parental Socialization: Indicator Unreliability versus Generational Transfer," *American Political Science Review* (1980) 74:421-31. A multiple-indicator approach to studying intergenerational agreement.

M. Kent Jennings and Richard G. Niemi, *Generations and Politics: A Panel Study of Young Adults and Their Parents* (Princeton, N.J.: Princeton University Press, 1981). Shows increasing divergence between young adults and parents.

22. THE IMPACT AND DEVELOPMENT
OF PARTY IDENTIFICATION

Angus Campbell, Philip E. Converse, Warren E. Miller, and Donald E. Stokes

... A general observation about the political behavior of Americans is that their partisan preferences show great stability between elections. Key speaks of the "standing decision" to support one party or the other, and this same phenomenon soon catches the eye of any student of electoral behavior. Its mark is readily seen in aggregate election statistics. For virtually any collection of states, counties, wards, precincts, or other political units one may care to examine, the correlation of the party division of the vote in successive elections is likely to be high. Often a change of candidates and a broad alteration in the nature of the issues disturb very little the relative partisanship of a set of electoral units, which suggests that great numbers of voters have party attachments that persist through time.

The fact that attachments of this sort are widely held is confirmed by survey data on individual people. In a survey interview most of our citizens freely classify themselves as Republicans or Democrats and indicate that these loyalties have persisted through a number of elections. Few factors are of greater importance for our national elections than the lasting attachment of tens of millions of Americans to one of the parties. These loyalties establish a basic division of electoral strength within which the competition of particular campaigns takes place. And they are an important factor in assuring the stability of the party system itself.

The Concept and Measurement of Party Identification

Only in the exceptional case does the sense of individual attachment to party reflect a formal membership or an active connection with a party apparatus. Nor does it simply denote a voting record, although the influence of party allegiance on electoral behavior is strong. Generally this tie is a psychological identification, which can persist without legal recognition or evidence of formal membership and even without a consistent record of party support. Most Americans have this sense of attachment with one party or the other. And for the individual who does, the strength and direction of party identification are facts of central importance in accounting for attitude and behavior.

Source: Excerpted from *The American Voter*, New York: Wiley, 1960, chaps. 6,7.

In characterizing the relation of individual to party as a psychological identification we invoke a concept that has played an important if somewhat varied role in psychological theories of the relation of individual to individual or of individual to group. We use the concept here to characterize the individual's affective orientation to an important group-object in his environment. Both reference group theory and small-group studies of influence have converged upon the attracting or repelling quality of the group as the generalized dimension most critical in defining the individual-group relationship, and it is this dimension that we will call identification. In the present chapter the political party serves as the group toward which the individual may develop an identification, positive or negative, of some degree of intensity.

The importance of stable partisan loyalties has been universally recognized in electoral studies, but the manner in which they should be defined and measured has been a subject of some disagreement. In keeping with the conception of party identification as a psychological tie, these orientations have been measured in our research by asking individuals to describe their own partisan loyalties. Some studies, however, have chosen to measure stable partisan orientations in terms of an individual's past voting record or in terms of his attitude on a set of partisan issues. Thus Republican and Democratic identifiers are sometimes defined as those who vote consistently for the same party and "independents" as those who do not. The fact that a definition of this sort serves many practical and scholarly purposes underscores the immense influence of party identification in motivating behavior. But we feel that such a definition blurs the distinction between the psychological state and its behavioral consequences. We have not measured party attachments in terms of the vote or the evaluation of partisan issues because we are interested in exploring the influence of party identification on voting behavior and its immediate determinants. When an independent measure of party identification is used it is clear that even strong party adherents at times may think and act in contradiction to their party allegiance. We could never establish the conditions under which this will occur if lasting partisan orientations are measured in terms of the behavior they are thought to affect.

Our measurement of party identification rests fundamentally on self-classification. Since 1952 we have asked repeated cross sections of the national population a sequence of questions inviting the individual to state the direction and strength of his partisan orientation.[1] The dimension presupposed by these questions appears to have psychological reality for virtually the entire electorate. The partisan self-image of all but the few individuals who disclaim any involvement in politics permits us to place each person in these samples on a continuum of partisanship extending from strongly Republican to strongly Democratic. We use the word "continuum" because we suppose that party identification is not simply a dichotomy but has a wide range of intensities in each partisan direction. In practice this range has to be represented by relatively few points, but we have devised our measures to preserve as much of the true variability as possible. The sequence of questions we have asked permits those of strong Republican or Democratic allegiance to be distinguished from those of

Table 22-1 The Distribution of Party Identification

	October 1952	September 1953	October 1954	April 1956	October 1956	November 1957	October 1958
Strong Republicans	13%	15%	13%	14%	15%	10%	13%
Weak Republicans	14	15	14	18	14	16	16
Independent Republicans	7	6	6	6	8	6	4
Independents	5	4	7	3	9	8	8
Independent Democrats	10	8	9	6	7	7	7
Weak Democrats	25	23	25	24	23	26	24
Strong Democrats	22	22	22	19	21	21	23
Apolitical, don't know	4	7	4	10	3	6	5
Total	100%	100%	100%	100%	100%	100%	100%
Number of Cases	1614	1023	1139	1731	1772	1488	1269

weaker identification with one of the parties. Moreover, it allows us to distinguish the Independents who lean toward one of the parties from those who think of themselves as having no partisan coloration whatever.

The measure these methods yield has served our analysis of party identification in a versatile fashion. To assess both the direction and intensity of partisan attachments it can be used to array our samples across the seven categories shown in Table 22-1, which gives the distribution of party identification in the electorate during the years from 1952 to 1958. By treating Independents as a single group we may reduce seven categories to five. By suppressing, too, the distinction between strong and weak partisans we have a three-point scale showing only the direction of partisanship. And by "folding" the measure of party identification at its central point we have a scale showing only the strength of this psychological tie to party.

In using these techniques of measurement we do not suppose that every person who describes himself as an Independent is indicating simply his lack of positive attraction to one of the parties. Some of these people undoubtedly are actually repelled by the parties or by partisanship itself and value their position as Independents. Certainly independence of party is an ideal of some currency in our society, and it seems likely that a portion of those who call themselves Independents are not merely reporting the absence of identification with one of the major parties.

Sometimes it is said that a good number of those who call themselves Independents have simply adopted a label that conceals a genuine psychological commitment to one party or the other. Accordingly, it is argued that a person's voting record gives a more accurate statement of his party attachment than does his own self-description. Our samples doubtless include some of these undercover partisans, and we have incorporated in our measure of party identification a means of distinguishing Independents who say they lean toward one of the parties from Independents who say they do not. We do not think that the problem of measurement presented by the concealed partisan is large. Rather it seems to us much less troublesome than the problems that follow if psychological ties to party are measured in terms of the vote.

This question can be illuminated a good deal by an examination of the consistency of party voting among those of different degrees of party identification, as is done in Table 22-2. The proportion of persons consistently supporting one party varies by more than sixty percentage points between strong party identifiers and complete Independents. For the problem of the undercover partisan, the troublesome figure in Table 22-2 is the 16 percent of full Independents who have voted for the candidates of one party only.[2] The importance of this figure diminishes when we remember that some of these persons have voted in very few presidential elections and could have supported one party consistently because of the way their votes fell, free of the influence of a genuine party tie.

A simple test of this hypothesis is made in Table 22-3 by separating persons who have come of voting age for a greater number of elections. Plainly, the length of time a person has had to develop a variable voting record influences the

Table 22-2   Relation of Strength of Party Identification to Partisan Regularity in Voting for President, 1956

	Strong Party Identifiers	Weak Party Identifiers	Independents Leaning to Party	Independents
Voted always or mostly for same party	82%	60%	36%	16%
Voted for different parties	18	40	64	84
Total	100%	100%	100%	100%
Number of cases	546	527	189	115

Note: The question used to establish party consistency of voting was this: "Have you always voted for the same party or have you voted for different parties for president?"

likelihood that he will report that he has voted for the candidates of more than one party, whatever the strength of his party identification. But among complete Independents the proportion of people thirty-five years old or older who could reasonably be called concealed party identifiers is now reduced to 11 percent. A detailed inspection of these cases shows that a number of these individuals have voted in relatively few elections and have had little opportunity to form an inconsistent voting record. When the frequency of voting turnout is considered, the proportion of extreme Independents who have voted only for the candidates of one party is not greater than we would expect it to be by chance alone.

If Table 22-3 suggests that we will describe relatively few genuine partisans as Independents by using self-classification to measure party attachments, it also suggests some of the difficulties of trying to use voting behavior to measure psychological identifications with party. The number of votes an individual may cast in a lifetime is small. In the early years of adulthood a person has voted too few times to give a sure indication of party allegiance; and if the individual seldom goes to the polls through the middle and later years, we have no better indication of his allegiance. And for the sensitive task of indicating *change* in these psychological identifications a simple record of behavior is clearly inadequate.

The measurement of party identification in the period of our research shows how different a picture of partisan allegiance voting behavior and self-description can give. Despite the substantial Republican majorities in the elections of 1952 and 1956, the percentages of Table 22-1 make clear that the Democratic Party enjoyed a three-to-two advantage in the division of party identification within the electorate in these same years.[3] Moreover, Table 22-1 documents the stability of this division of party loyalty in a period whose electoral history might suggest widespread change. Except for the shifting size of the group of respondents refusing to be assigned any position on the party scale, there is not a single variation between successive distributions of party identification that could not be laid to sampling error.

Table 22-3   Relation of Strength of Party Identification to Partisan
Regularity in Voting for President, by Age Groups, 1956

Age	Strong Party Identifiers	Weak Party Identifiers	Independents Leaning to Party	Independents
21 to 34				
Voted always or mostly for same party	91%	78%	60%	33%
Voted for different parties	9	22	40	67
Total	100%	100%	100%	100%
Number of cases	104	120	53	21
35 and above				
Voted always or mostly for same party	80%	55%	26%	11%
Voted for different parties	20	45	74	89
Total	100%	100%	100%	100%
Number of cases	440	405	136	93

The constancy of partisanship in the nation at large in these years implies a good deal of constancy in individual identifications with party. This implication is a loose one since the percentages of Table 22-1 show only the absence of net change in this interval of time. The similarity of these distributions may conceal a substantial volume of compensating change. To show conclusively that this is not the case we would need to have data collected through time on the party attachments of individual people. But the great stability of partisan loyalties is supported, too, by what we can learn from recall data about the personal history of party identification. We have asked successive samples of the electorate a series of questions permitting us to reconstruct whether an individual who accepts a party designation has experienced a prior change in his party identification. The responses give impressive evidence of the constancy of party allegiance.

The fact that nearly everyone in our samples could be placed on a unitary dimension of party identification and that the idea of prior movements on this dimension was immediately understood are themselves important findings about the nature of party support within the electorate. In view of the loose, federated structure of American parties it was not obvious in advance that people could respond to party in these undifferentiated terms. Apparently the positive and negative feelings that millions of individuals have toward the parties are the result of orientations of a diffuse and generalized character that have a common psychological meaning even though there may be a good deal of variation in the way party is perceived. . . .

Party Identification and Political Involvement

Evidently no single datum can tell us more about the attitude and behavior of the individual as presidential elector than his location on a dimension of psychological identification extending between the two great parties. Yet our discussion of the impact of party identification should not close without some consideration of the relation of party allegiance to the dimension of political involvement. It is not accidental that the individual's general partisan orientation and the extent of his involvement in politics, either of which may influence a wide set of attitudinal and behavioral characteristics, are related to each other. Although our causal understanding of this relation is far from sure, the fact of association is clear enough: the stronger the individual's sense of attachment to one of the parties, the greater his psychological involvement in political affairs.

The association is easily missed in popular accounts of electoral behavior.[4] The ideal of the Independent citizen, attentive to politics, concerned with the course of government, who weighs the rival appeals of a campaign and reaches a judgment that is unswayed by partisan prejudice, has had such a vigorous history in the tradition of political reform—and has such a hold on civic education today—that one could easily suppose that the habitual partisan has the more limited interest and concern with politics. But if the usual image of the Independent voter is intended as more than a normative ideal, it fits poorly the characteristics of the Independents in our samples. Far from being more attentive, interested, and informed, Independents tend as a group to be somewhat less involved in politics. They have somewhat poorer knowledge of the issues, their image of the candidates is fainter, their interest in the campaign is less, their concern over the outcome is relatively slight, and their choice between competing candidates, although it is indeed made later in the campaign, seems much less to spring from discoverable evaluations of the elements of national politics.

These differences may be illustrated in terms of two measures of involvement. When those of strong partisan identifications are compared with those who call themselves Independents, the partisan tends both in his interest in the campaign and his concern over the outcome to be more involved than the political Independent. What is more, a further division of the Independent group would show in each case that those who refused to say they were closer to one party or the other are even less involved than other Independents. It is of course true ... that some of the Independents in our samples are highly involved. But these individuals are rare enough that the characteristics of Independents as a group are widely different from those suggested by the familiar stereotype.

It is by no means clear what causal interpretation should be given the association of strength of party identification and degree of political involvement found in the interviews taken at single points in time. For the moment we may suppose that a person's location on either of these fundamental dimensions will influence his locations on the other. The individual who has a strong and continuing involvement in politics is more likely to develop a commitment to one or the other of the major parties. And the individual who has such a commitment is likely to have his interest and concern with politics sustained at a higher level. But we may suppose, too, that the relation of partisanship and involvement is to be explained in part by common antecedents. Discovering what it is in the individual's life experience that could account both for his party allegiance and his political involvement leads naturally to a consideration of the development of party identification.

The Development of Party Identification

Identification with political parties, as we have seen, is an attachment held widely through the American electorate with substantial influence on political cognitions, attitudes, and behavior. We may now turn our inquiry toward an exploration of the circumstances from which party identification itself may be thought to spring. This will carry us backward in the life experience of the individual citizen and into the political history of our society.

Origins of Party Identification

When we examine the evidence on the manner in which party attachment develops and changes during the lifetime of the individual citizen, we find a picture characterized more by stability than by change—not by rigid, immutable fixation on one party rather than the other, but by a persistent adherence and a resistance to contrary influence.

Early Politicization.   At the time we meet the respondents of our surveys they have reached the minimum voting age, and most of them are considerably beyond it. The only information we can obtain about their political experience in their pre-adult years depends on their recall. Hyman's (1959) review of the literature on "political socialization" brings together the available data to extend our understanding of this important stage of political growth. It is apparent from his presentation that an orientation toward political affairs typically begins before the individual attains voting age and that this orientation strongly reflects his immediate social milieu, in particular his family.

Our own data are entirely consistent with this conclusion. The high degree of correspondence between the partisan preference of our respondents with that which they report for their parents my be taken as a rough measure of the extent to which partisanship is passed from one generation to the next.[5] This correspondence is somewhat higher among those people who report one or both of their parents as having been "actively concerned" with politics than among those whose parents were not politically active. If we make the reasonable assumption that in the "active" homes the political views of the parents were more frequently and intensely cognized by the children than in the inactive homes, we should of course expect to find these views more faithfully reproduced in these children when they reach adult years. In contrast, we find that persons from inactive

Table 22-4   Intergenerational Resemblance in Partisan Orientation, Politically Active and Inactive Homes, 1958

Party Identification of Offspring	One or Both Parents Were Politically Active			Neither Parent Was Politically Active		
	Both Parents Were Dems.	Both Parents Were Reps.	Parents Had No Consistent Partisanship	Both Parents Were Dems.	Both Parents Were Reps.	Parents Had No Consistent Partisanship
Strong Dem.	50%	5%	21%	40%	6%	20%
Weak Dem.	29	9	26	36	11	15
Independent	12	13	26	19	16	26
Weak Rep.	6	34	16	3	42	20
Strong Rep.	2	37	10	1	24	12
Apolitical	1	2	1	1	1	7
	100%	100%	100%	100%	100%	100%
Number of cases	333	194	135	308	187	199

homes, especially those with no clear political orientation, tend strongly toward non-partisan positions themselves. For a large proportion of the electorate the orientation toward politics expressed in our measure of party identification has its origins in the early family years. We are not able to trace the history of these families to find an explanation of why the homes of some people were politically oriented and others were not. Such homes appear to exist in all social strata, less frequently in some than others of course.

The Persistence of Partisanship.   The extent to which pre-adult experience shapes the individual's political future may be judged from the constancy with which most people hold to the partisan orientation they have at the time they enter the electorate. We find a number of evidences of this in our data, aside from the fact of parent-child relationship shown in Table 22-4. When we ask people to recall their first presidential vote, for example, we discover that of those who can remember their first vote for president two-thirds still identify with the same party they first voted for. A majority (56 percent) of these presidential voters have never crossed party lines; they have always supported their party's candidate.

A direct assessment of the stability with which the average citizen holds to his political orientation may be obtained from his report on whether he has ever identified himself differently than he does at present. The picture is generally one of firm but not immovable attachment (Table 22-5). The greatest mobility is found among those people whose party attachment is weakest, the strongly

Table 22-5 Stability and Change in Party Identification, 1956

	Strong Dem.	Weak Dem.	Ind. Dem.	Ind.	Ind. Rep.	Weak Rep.	Strong Rep.
Have not changed from one party to another[a]	93%	89%	69%	68%	55%	74%	85%
Were Rep., changed to Dem.	7	11					
Were Rep., changed to Ind.			13	10	8		
Were Dem., changed to Ind.			18	22	37		
Were Dem., changed to Rep.						26	15
Number of cases	364	397	108	145	144	250	261

[a] Included here may be some people who moved from an Independent position to one of the parties. Our interview does not permit us to isolate such cases.

identified are least likely to have changed sides.

It is apparent from these various pieces of evidence that identification with political parties, once established, is an attachment which is not easily changed. Not all members of the electorate form strong party attachments, however, and they make up a sufficiently large proportion of the population to permit the short-term influence of political forces associated with issues and candidates to play a significant role in determining the outcome of specific elections. Even strong identifiers are not impervious to such influences and occasional cataclysmic national events have had the power to produce substantial realignment in long-standing divisions of political sentiment. . . .

NOTES

1. The initial question was this: "Generally speaking, do you think of yourself as a Republican, a Democrat, an Independent, or what?" Those who classified themselves as Republicans or Democrats were also asked, "Would you call yourself a strong (Republican, Democrat) or a not very strong (Republican, Democrat)?" Those who classified themselves as Independents were asked this additional question: "Do you think of yourself as closer to the Republican or Democratic Party?" The concept itself was first discussed in Belknap and Campbell (1952).
2. In this discussion we assume that the concealed partisan is less likely to distort his voting record than his description of his party attachment; that is, we assume that what the undercover partisan values is chiefly the designation "Independent." To the extent this is untrue, the analysis of voting consistency by strength of party identification fails to enhance our understanding.

3. Because Republican identifiers voted with somewhat greater frequency than Democratic identifiers in these years, the Democratic edge in party allegiance was slightly less among voters.

4. But it has been found by other investigators of voting behavior. See Berelson, Lazarsfeld, and McPhee (1954, pp. 25-27) and Agger (1959).

5. There are obvious weaknesses is this measure. Some of our respondents had undoubtedly carried an "inherited" party identification into early adulthood but had changed by the time we interviewed them.

23. THE DECLINE OF PARTISANSHIP

Norman H. Nie, Sidney Verba, and John R. Petrocik

Perhaps the most dramatic political change in the American public over the past two decades has been the decline of partisanship. As we have seen party affiliation was the central thread running through interpretations of American politics in the 1950s and 1960s. Citizen attitudes on issues appeared to be only slightly related one to another, and they were unstable enough over time to suggest that a high proportion of citizens had no meaningful issue positions. But party affiliation was a stable characteristic of the individual: it was likely to be inherited, it was likely to remain steady throughout the citizen's political life, and it was likely to grow in strength during that lifetime.[1]

Even more important, party affiliation was connected to other political phenomena. For the citizen, his sense of identification with a party was a guide to behavior; citizens voted for their party's candidates. It was a guide to understanding the political universe; candidates and issues were evaluated in party terms. Parties were objects of affective attachment; citizens expressed positive feelings about their parties. And those citizens with partisan affiliation were the most active and involved citizens; partisanship appeared to be a force mobilizing citizens into political life. Partisanship gave continuity and direction to the political behavior of citizens and to American electoral life.[2]

The weakening of partisanship has been documented many times in the works of political scientists such as Gerald Pomper, Walter Dean Burnham, and Jack Dennis.[3] Much of the data we present in this chapter parallels theirs and will not be new to the student of the subject. It is, however, important to lay out the variety of ways in which the decline of partisanship has been manifested in order to connect these varied changes with other trends we shall discuss. The situation can be summarized as follows: (1) Fewer citizens have steady and strong psychological identification with a party. (2) Party affiliation is less of a guide to electoral choice. (3) Parties are less frequently used as standards of evaluation. (4) Parties are less frequently objects of positive feelings on the part of citizens. (5) Partisanship is less likely to be transferred from generation to generation.

Source: *The Changing American Voter*, enlarged ed., Harvard University Press. Copyright © 1976, 1979 by the Twentieth Century Fund. Reprinted with permission of Twentieth Century Fund.

Figure 23-1   Partisan Affiliation, 1952-1974

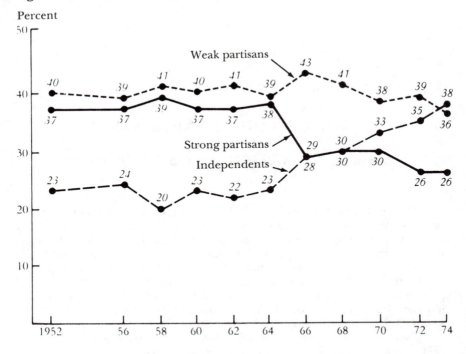

Some Data on Partisanship

Party Identification

Figure 23-1 traces over time the proportion of the population that strongly identifies with one of the political parties, the proportion that weakly identifies with a party, and the proportion that professes independence of the parties. From 1952 to 1964 the proportions remain remarkably stable: a little more than a third of the populace is strongly partisan and a slightly larger group is weakly partisan. The remaining fifth of the population is Independent. The stability of these figures through 1964—despite the wide swings in popular vote from the strong Eisenhower victory of 1956, through the close 1960 race, to the Johnson sweep in 1964—represent convincing evidence of the continuity of partisanship.

From 1964 through 1974, however, the situation changes. The proportion of strong identifiers drops while the proportion of Independents rises. By 1974 only about one out of four Americans can be considered a strong partisan while 38 percent are Independent. Note also that among those who identify with a political party from 1952 through 1964, about equal numbers consider themselves weak and strong partisans. By the 1970s those who consider themselves partisans are more likely to be weak than strong partisans. The figures indicate a clear erosion of the strength of party affiliation in the American public.[4]

Party and the Vote

In 1956 party identification was the key to the vote. Despite the large number of Democrats who crossed party lines to vote for Eisenhower, 83 percent of those Americans with a party identification voted consistent with that identification in the presidential election; about 90 percent voted consistent with that identification in the congressional elections.

Consider the data in Figure 23-2 which show the proportion of party identifiers who did not vote for the candidate of their party in the elections from 1952 to 1974. The proportion defecting from their party in presidential elections was quite similar from 1952 to 1964, again a stability worth stressing given the heterogeneity of those elections. The defection rate in 1968 was substantially higher (largely a reflection of George Wallace's candidacy) and stayed high in 1972. In 1968 and 1972, more than one out of four party identifiers voted for the presidential candidate of the opposition party. If the group of identifiers who abandoned their party in 1972 to vote for the opposing presidential candidate (they are 17 percent of all voters[5]) is added to the 34 percent who are Independents in that year, one finds that 51 percent of the voting population are not guided by a party affiliation. They either vote against their own party's candidate, or they are Independent with no party ties to guide them.

Presidential voting figures, however, are hard to interpret since they are heavily dependent on the noncomparable exigencies of the particular race. The extent to which the division of the vote is influenced by the characteristics and appeal of the presidential candidates, for example, is well known. The defection rates in other races, therefore, may be essential to interpreting the erosion of party support. The proportion of defectors in both House and Senate elections also rises, especially toward the end of the period. There tends to be somewhat more defection in presidential years because of the pull of the presidential candidates and because the electorate is larger and contains more voters with weak party ties (Campbell, 1960). For this reason, off-year elections may provide clearer data on the role of party. We have plotted the off-year elections separately, and they show a pattern of change similar to that of the presidential elections. Compare 1958 with 1974, for instance. The defection rate in Senate and House elections almost doubles.[6]

Lastly we can look at the defection rates for state and local elections. The defection rates are in general higher in these races since we consider a voter to be a defector if he did not vote the straight party ticket in state and local elections— that is, even one defecting vote for one of the many offices in the election makes one a defector. The number of voters not voting a straight ticket in state and local elections remains more or less steady from 1952 through 1960. From then on, it

Figure 23-2 Proportion of Party Identifiers Voting for Candidate of Other Party, 1952-1974

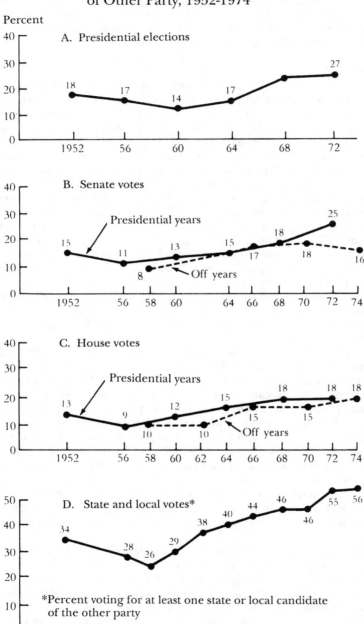

rises sharply. By 1974 more than half of those voting report abandoning their party at least once.

The data for the nonpresidential elections are compelling evidence of the weakening of party ties. Presidential elections depend heavily on the particular candidates. In congressional and local elections where candidates are less well known, party should be more important.[7] Yet there is a clear decline in the importance of party on all political levels. Clearly, citizens no longer depend as heavily as they once did on party labels in deciding their vote. They more easily switch to the candidate of the opposition party. To look at the data another way, in 1956 the correlation between party identification and House vote was .72; between party identification and Senate vote it was .68. By 1972 these correlations had fallen to .55 and .47, respectively.[8]

The data on split ticket voting are summarized in Figure 23-3, which shows the proportion of the population that reports voting a straight party ticket and the proportion that reports split ticket voting. Among the latter group we distinguish between those who vote a straight ticket except for the presidential vote and those who report some ticket splitting at the subpresidential level since the latter form of ticket splitting may represent a more significant break in partisanship.

There is little variation in the proportion who split their ballot only on the presidential vote. The proportion remains small throughout the period. What does change substantially is the proportion of voters who vote a straight ticket. Of course this change is reflected in the proportion who split their ballots below the presidential level. The high points of straight ticket voting are 1956 and 1960. Split ticket voting was greater in 1952 and returns to that level in 1964; in 1968 and 1972 it increases even further. The data summarize what has been shown thus far: the 1956 and 1960 elections were high points of party attachment.

The data are particularly striking when one remembers that these are defection rates for those who profess affiliation with a party. Over time the proportion with such self-identification has fallen. One would think that those who remain attached to one or the other of the parties would be those whose commitment was stronger, the less committed having moved into the Independent ranks. Yet even among the increasingly smaller group of party identifiers one finds party affiliation playing a smaller role in determining the vote.[9]

The change in the strength of party ties from the 1950s to the beginning of the 1970s is also apparent in the constancy of party voting from election to election. In each of the elections from 1952 to 1972, respondents were asked whether they always voted for the same party in presidential elections. In 1952, one-third of the voters reported that they had not always voted for presidential candidates of the same party. By 1972, the situation had changed drastically. Over half of the voters reported that their presidential vote had not been constant in party terms (Figure 23-4, dotted line).

The proportion of citizens who are inconstant in their vote—sometimes voting for the presidential candidate of one party, sometimes for the other—can be expected to rise with the rise in the proportion of Independents in the population. Their votes are more likely to move from party to party. But even those who still

Figure 23-3   Straight and Split Ticket Voting, 1952-1972

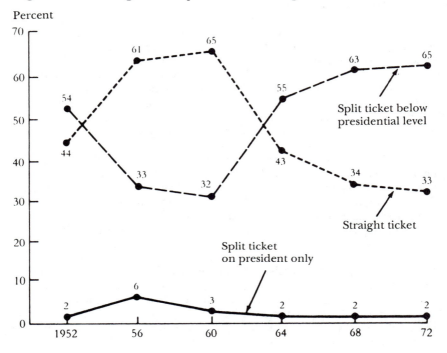

consider themselves to be partisans are more likely to switch their votes from party to party. The solid line in Figure 23-4 reports the proportion of inconstant presidential voters only for those with a party affiliation. The inconstancy of presidential voting has increased even among those who have maintained their affiliation. In 1952, only one out of four party identifiers reported inconstancy in the vote. By 1972, almost one out of two identifiers said that they did not always vote for the same party.

The identifiers in the later years—1968 and 1972—ought to be a "hard-core" of partisans since so many of the weaker partisans have taken to considering themselves Independents. But even the hard-core group is weakening in the steadiness with which it follows the party line when it comes to the presidential vote.

Party and Candidate Evaluation

It is clear from these data that citizens are less frequently guided by partisan affiliation in the choice of the candidate for whom they will vote. One can observe

Figure 23-4   Percent Reporting They Have Not Always Voted for the Candidate of the Same Party in Presidential Elections: All Voters and Partisan Identifiers, 1952-1972

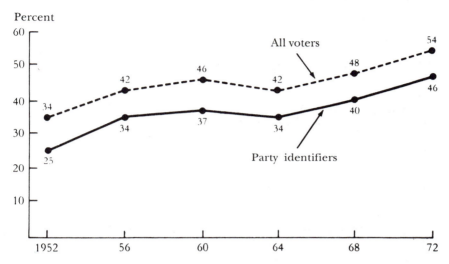

this in a somewhat different way by considering what it is that respondents like or dislike about the candidates in presidential races.[10] As noted earlier, almost half of the electorate mentions the party affiliation of the candidate as one reason for liking or disliking a candidate: "He is a good Democrat," and so forth. Figure 23-5 shows the proportion that use partisanship as an evaluative standard for candidates from 1952 to 1972. In 1952, 46 percent of the voters cite a party reason for candidate preference. The percentage goes down in 1964 but up again in 1968. By 1972, that figure has dropped to 24 percent. And the proportion of citizens who evaluate both candidates in party terms—they like their own candidate because of his party and dislike the opponent because he is affiliated with the opposition—had fallen even more precipitously, from 12 percent to 2 percent.[11]

The decline in the use of party as an evaluative standard is not merely a function of the larger proportion of the populace who have no party ties. The frequency with which candidates are preferred or rejected because of their party ties has declined, even among those who identify with one of the parties. The data on the use of partisan characteristics of the candidate as a basis for evaluations of the candidate add an important separate confirmation of the erosion of the importance of party. The candidate evaluation questions are open-ended. They elicit whatever standards of evaluation the

Figure 23-5 Proportion of Citizens Mentioning the Candidate's
Party Affiliation as a Reason for Liking or Disliking Him,
1952-1972

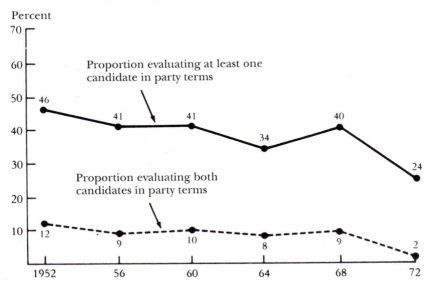

respondent has in his mind. When party is mentioned it is mentioned
spontaneously. The fact that the frequency of such spontaneous mentions
declines so rapidly is further evidence that the political centrality of the political
party has declined.

Citizen Affection for the Parties

Perhaps the clearest evidence of the erosion of support for the parties
is found in Figure 23-6. In each of the election years, the SRC has
asked respondents what they like and what they dislike about each of
the parties. Earlier, answers to these questions were used to assign respondents to one or another level of conceptualization. These responses can
also be used to measure the extent to which respondents have positive
or negative views about the parties. Respondents can mention a number
of things they like about each party and a number of things they dislike.
We compared the rate of positive and negative references. In 1952 we find
that most respondents fall in a category we called "partisans": they say
on balance more positive than negative things about their own party and on
balance are either negative or neutral about the opposition. Sixty-four percent

Figure 23-6 The Decline in Positive Evaluation of Parties, 1952-1972

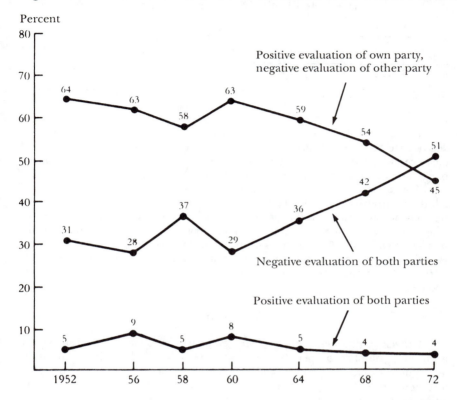

Percent

Positive evaluation of own party, negative evaluation of other party

Negative evaluation of both parties

Positive evaluation of both parties

of the population falls into this category. An additional 5 percent says positive things about both parties. The remaining 31 percent of respondents are considered nonsupporters of the party system: they are either negative about both parties, negative about one and neutral about the other, or have no opinion about either.

Figure 23-6 shows what happens to the proportion of these various types of party supporters. The small group that likes both parties remains low throughout the period. More striking is the decline in the partisans and the rise in the nonsupporters. In the elections of the 1950s those who were positive about their own party and combined that with negative or neutral views about the opposition outnumbered those who supported neither party by more than two to one. By 1972 more Americans were either hostile or neutral toward the political parties than were supporters of one or the other parties.

Table 23-1   Proportion of Partisan Identifiers Who Report Changing
Their Party Identification During the Previous Four Years,
1952-1974

1952	1956	1958	1960	1964	1968	1970	1972	1974
3	5	2	3	4	3	3	5	4

In sum, the data show a dramatic decline of partisanship during the two decades we have been tracing. The decline is apparent across a wide range of measures. Citizens are less likely to identify with a party, to feel positively about a party, or to be guided in their voting behavior by partisan cues.

The loosening of party ties, however, is not manifested in a switch of allegiance from one of the major parties to the other. In the SRC studies, respondents are asked if they have switched parties. Table 23-1 shows the proportions who report switching allegiance from one party to the other in the previous four years. As one can see, the proportion is small and remains small even during the period of rapid erosion of partisanship in the late 1960s and early 1970s.[12] The trend appears to be away from parties, not from one party to another. . . .

Conclusion

Citizen affiliation with the major political parties has been looked at from a number of perspectives: party as a psychological identification, as a guide to electoral choice and candidate evaluation, and as an object of affection. In each case, the data confirm a decline in the attachment of the citizenry to the political parties. Party affiliation, once the central thread connecting the citizen and the political process, is a thread that has certainly been frayed.

However, these changes in the depth and stability of partisan attachment have confirmed one of the conclusions of the early studies that stressed the centrality of partisanship. Partisanship does appear to be a long-term, habitual commitment of individuals. For those in the late 1960s with fully developed and long-term partisan identifications, the erosion of party support is not nearly as dramatic as it is for those with a less firmly rooted party attachment. The data on recent changes [not shown in this excerpt] make clear that some political events can interfere with the development through the life cycle of that long-term commitment. Such events seem to have been powerful in recent years because they have not only retarded the acquisition or development of a party preference, but they have also reduced the significance of party affiliation for those who remain identified with a party. Citizens who identified with a party are less guided by their affiliation in the seventies than they were in the fifties.

NOTES

1. See Campbell, Gurin, Miller (1954); Campbell, Converse, Miller, and Stokes (1960); Campbell, Converse, Miller, and Stokes (1966); Converse (1969); Converse (1964), especially 238-40 where the stability of party preference is compared to the stability of other political attitudes; Hyman (1959); Jennings and Niemi (1968).

2. The concept of party identification and the linkages between that identification and electoral behavior was first systematically elaborated by Belknap and Campbell (1952). The utility and power of the concept of psychological attachment to political parties as a property separate from voting or voting intentions was fully elaborated in Campbell and others (1954; 1960). In Campbell and others (1966), the authors demonstrate how this variable, along with actual voting patterns, can be used to understand the nature of elections and the flow of the voting in American society. For the centrality of party identification as a systemic as well as individual concept in American politics see Prewitt and Nie (1971, pp. 479-502).

3. For excellent overviews, parallel to our own, see Dennis (1975) and Pomper (1975, chap. 2). The decline of partisanship is presented in historical perspective in Burnham (1970).

4. This overview of national trends conceals many variations hidden within the data—the South differs from the North, young from old, and so on.

5. That is, they are 27 percent of the party identifiers, but only 17 percent of the voters.

6. For an analysis of the declining importance of party in Senate elections see Kostroski (1973).

7. On the other hand, it is not obviously wrong to assume that the factor of personal recognition does play a considerable role in voting for lower level offices. The "friends-and-neighbors" factor in local voting can be a significant determinant of the outcome of local elections. In a lower level election an individual's reputation can be more important to many voters than his party. The invulnerability of some public officials in otherwise competitive states, counties, and cities can only be attributed to the recognition and positive personal evaluations these officials enjoy. Certainly this is one of the factors which go into giving incumbent politicians an advantage. For some illustrations of the variable importance of party see Stokes and Miller (1966).

8. The correlations reported here are Pearson product moment correlations.

9. There is little evidence that weak partisans have become Independents over the preceding years. Our conclusions about this party change rest upon data which show that most of the change in party identification depends upon the introduction of new populations into the electorate in the last twenty years. Since there does seem to be some small abandonment of party affiliation, however, remaining strong partisans constitute a group which has not relinquished their party loyalties in spite of the relatively great disfavor into which parties have fallen.

10. For early demonstrations of the importance of these feelings see Campbell, Gurin, and Miller (1954); Campbell, Converse, Miller, and Stokes (1960); Campbell and Stokes (1959); Stokes, Campbell, and Miller (1958); Stokes (1966). More recent use of these measures to account for voting choice include RePass (1971) and Kelley and Mirer (1974).

11. The decline between 1968 and 1972 may be partly attributable to a change in coding for the 1972 study, but the decline through 1968 leads us to believe that it cannot be completely attributed to coding.

12. The data on recalled switch of parties is quite consistent with a more direct measure of party switching derived from the panel study of voters conducted by the SRC in

1956, 1958, and 1960. If one cross tabulates the party allegiance of voters in 1956 with their allegiance in 1960, one finds that 4 percent report allegiance to one party in 1956 and to the other in 1960. Computed from data in Pierce and Rose (1974, p. 633). For a fuller discussion of the panel data and some recent analyses that seem to contradict this point see Appendix 4 [of Nie, Verba, and Petrocik].

24. EXPLORATIONS OF A POLITICAL THEORY OF PARTY IDENTIFICATION

Morris P. Fiorina

For some two decades the concept of party identification dominated research on American voting behavior as well as accounts of the electoral process premised on that research. A generation of scholars learned to "control" the most commonsensical relationships for party identification and upon doing so often concluded that common sense was in error. Those more concerned with the operation of democratic political processes than with applied psychology resigned themselves to the search for the second, third, and nth most important determinants of voting choice.

But while it is fair to say that party identification has played a dominant role in research on voting behavior, it is necessary to add that the nature of that dominance has changed over time. Revolutions—intellectual as well as political—may consume their children. For perhaps a decade the concept of party identification stood unchallenged. It provided the "natural" structure for electoral research. During the most recent decade, however, party ID has increasingly become a target of critical studies. At first hesitantly, then more boldly, revisionists have attacked the old conceptual fortress. That they have only managed to loosen a few stones testifies to the continued strength of that structure.[1]

In chapter 4 [of Fiorina, 1981b] I offered a political theory of party ID, one based on a running tally of retrospective evaluations of party promises and performance. This chapter develops that theory more fully and confronts it with data from the two CPS panel studies. Before presenting that analysis, however, I will briefly examine the concepts of party identification past and party identification present. What was it originally thought to be? How, if at all, has recent research changed our view of what it is? Rhetoric aside, let us briefly consider the nature of the evidence.

Source: *Retrospective Voting in American National Elections*, New Haven: Yale University Press, 1981. Copyright © 1981 by Yale University Press. Reprinted with permission of the publisher.

The Concept of Party Identification According to Campbell, Converse, Miller and Stokes

The Michigan researchers Campbell, Converse, Miller, and Stokes (1960, p. 121) defined identification as "the individual's affective orientation to an important group-object in his environment." Given the numerous possible ways of conceptualizing long-term party affiliations (Key's standing decision, for one), what was the basis for the decision to ground party ID in psychological group theory rather than in some alternative conceptual framework? The answer appears to lie in the characteristics of the long-term party affiliations uncovered in the surveys.

There was first the fact that party ID was highly stable. Relying on analysis of a recall question, Campbell, Converse, Miller, and Stokes (1960, p. 150) reported that only 20 percent of the sample had changed party ID during their lifetime, although this refers to a simple three-way categorization rather than to the full party ID scale. Second, there was the fact that assumption of a party ID did not appear to be a concomitant of citizenship or a political coming of age: As later research (Hyman, 1959; Hess and Torney, 1967) verified, party ID appeared to develop early in life[2] and well prior to the development of policy preferences, or indeed policy awareness. Moreover, party ID appeared to strengthen with length of affiliation (Campbell, Converse, Miller, and Stokes, 1960, pp. 161-165; Converse, 1969). These characteristics put one in mind of a religious affiliation. Children learn that they are Catholics or whatever long before they have any understanding or appreciation of church dogma—if they ever do. But for many, the process of maturation brings inclusion in church-related social networks that typically evoke emotional attachments on the part of their members.

The capstone to the preceding line of thought no doubt came from the presumed relationship between party ID and the formation of the partisan attitudes that incorporate the short-term forces of politics. Although recognizing that objective events and conditions could lead to the modification of party ID (Campbell, Converse, Miller, and Stokes, 1960, pp. 133-35, 165), Campbell, Converse, Miller, and Stokes (1960, p. 135) concluded, "In the period of our studies the influence of party identification on attitudes toward the perceived elements of politics has been far more important than the influence of these attitudes on party identification itself." Again, acceptance of dogma follows affiliation rather than vice versa. We are given a picture of party ID as stable, affectively based, and relatively impervious to change except under extremely stressful conditions such as major depressions (Campbell, Converse, Miller, and Stokes, 1960, p. 151).

As one reads the relevant chapters of *The American Voter,* one is struck by the careful, cautious tone of the discussion. Caveats abound, and one feels that revisionist political scientists have not always played fair in their attribution of positions to Campbell, Converse, Miller, and Stokes. Yet that same reading also reveals how sparse the data underlying the Michigan conception of party ID actually were. The evidence for stability came from a recall question that is now

Table 24-1   Stability of Party Identification in 1956-60 SRC Panel Study

	1956-58	*1958-60*
Category stable[a]	84.2	85.8
Strength stable	54.3	56.1
Weighted *n*	1,222	1,723

[a] Moves to or from "pure independence" from any other position are treated as categorical (i.e., interparty) change. This produces somewhat higher categorical change estimates than those of Dobson and St. Angelo, who treat moves to and from independence as intraparty, and Brody, who treats moves to independence as interparty but eliminates initial independents from his analysis.

Source: The data are drawn from pre-election surveys in 1956 and 1960 and the 1958 post-election survey. (The party ID item was not included in the 1956 post-election survey.)

treated with considerable skepticism (Brody, 1977, p. 23, n. 13). The aforementioned quotation on the primacy of party ID over partisan attitudes is introduced as a "judgment" and is followed (p. 135) by the remark that "our conviction on this point is rooted in what we know of the relative stability and priority in time of party identification and the attitudes it may affect" and a bit later (p. 136) by the admission that "our statement of causal priorities is in the end an inference." It is both a tribute to Campbell, Converse, Miller, and Stokes and a commentary on the rest of our discipline that such judgments, convictions, and inferences went almost unquestioned for a decade, even given the general availability of a data set whose contents raise fundamental questions about the prevailing conception of party ID.

The Revisionist Critique

Not all political scientists uncritically accepted the prevailing view of party ID during the 1960s, but those who did not had little direct evidence to justify their skepticism.[3] The basis for a serious revision came when scholars turned to an examination of the 1956-58-60 SRC Panel Study. Although the panel had been used to study attitude stability by various scholars (Converse, 1964), its significance for the examination of the prevailing conception of party ID was not fully realized until the 1970s. Then revisionist scholars pointed out some rather surprising results. Far from changing "glacially" at the individual level, party ID showed considerable fluctuation. As seen in Table 24-1, during the two-year periods of the panel, about 15 percent of the respondents (the exact number depends upon how independents are treated) changed *categories* (Democrat, Independent, Republican) on the party ID scale and more than 40 percent of the panel changed at least one place on the full seven-point scale. This was hardly what the prevailing view had led researchers to expect.

Dreyer (1973) suggested that most of the change on the panel could be dismissed as response error. When they were queried at two-year intervals, is it surprising that some previously strong identifiers might report presently weak

Table 24-2 Stability of Party Identification in the 1972-76 CPS Panel Study

	1972-74	1974-76
Category stable	80.2	82.0
Strength stable	50.4	54.5
Weighted *n*	1,576	1,155

Source: The data are drawn from pre-election surveys in 1972 and 1976 and the 1974 post-election survey. (The party ID item was not included in the 1972 post-election survey.)

identifications, or vice versa? But various other analyses (Dobson and Meeter, 1974; Dobson and St. Angelo, 1975; Brody, n.d.) concluded that random fluctuation was not a sufficient explanation for the panel's instability; real change of a systematic nature appeared to be evident.

Very recently the subfield of electoral behavior has come into possession of a second panel study. Its contents are quite consistent with the earlier panel. Consider Table 24-2. If anything, party ID is marginally less stable in the later panel than in the earlier one. On the basis of such data, Brody (1977) cautions that party ID should be treated only as a nominal variable, suggesting that the three-point categorization captures whatever long-term component exists but that the full seven-point scale appears hopelessly polluted by the effects of short-term forces.

Change over two- or four-year periods may fail to shake the strongest proponents of the traditional view. They could point out, for example, that a portion of the change is more apparent than real in that some changers come "home" to their original ID after a brief flirtation with the opposition or a brief spat with their own party (Butler and Stokes, 1974). A lot can happen in four years. Consider, then, the observations of Macaluso (n.d.). In the 1960 SRC Election Study the party ID items appeared in both the pre- and post-election surveys, thus yielding a short panel covering a span of at most four months. More than 10 percent of more than 1,700 respondents shifted categories on the party ID scale (see Table 24-3), and fully 40 percent of the respondents shifted at least one position on the full seven-point scale. Meier (1975) reports similar shifts (20 percent on the categorical scale, 40 percent on the seven-point scale) for a local National Opinion Research Center (NORC) panel study in 1972. All in all, it seems difficult to maintain the position that party ID is a deep-seated, stable characteristic of individuals that changes at only a "glacial" rate.

With the scent of blood in the air, the revisionists made the logical leap. Why does party ID change? If change is systematic, then in principle it is explainable. Brody and Macaluso show that changes in party ID relate to short-term forces— attitudes toward candidates, issues, and political conditions. Just as a religious affiliation learned at a parent's knee may give way when one later runs afoul of some particular dogma, so a socialized, affective party ID may crumble in the face of short-term political forces.

Table 24-3 Stability of Party Identification Pre- and Post-election Measurements in the 1960 SRC Election Study

	Pre-Post Election
Category stable	86.7
Strength stable	59.5
Weighted n	1,768

Findings like the preceding are positive in the sense of expanding our specific knowledge, but so far as general explanations go, they leave us in a state of uncertainty. To previous evidence that party ID shapes the interpretation of political events and conditions, we now add equally suggestive evidence that such events and conditions modify party ID. Can we ever sort out the causal links? On purely statistical grounds, the answer is probably no, unless the funds become available for panel studies more ambitious than heretofore imagined. An alternative option is to construct more complex theories than those previously accepted, to ascertain whether the empirical regularities we now possess can be subsumed under those theories, and to test any new propositions those theories produce. In other words, a purely empirical effort to pin down the "real" place of party ID in a dynamic model of electoral choice is probably chimerical. All we can do is work toward ever-superior models of voting choice. The models must provide the causality, while the data should keep us from going too far astray.

The enterprise that follows reflects the preceding point of view. In chapter 4 [of Fiorina, 1981b] we proposed a model of party choice based on cumulations of retrospective evaluations. Part of that model was defined as the basis of party ID. The remainder of this chapter explores the empirical evidence in light of that definition.

Party ID as a Running Tally of Retrospective Evaluations

In chapter 4 [of Fiorina, 1981b] we defined party ID as the difference between an individual's past political experiences with the two parties, perturbed by a factor, γ, that represents effects not included directly in an individual's political experiences (e.g., parents' party ID). To repeat the definition,

$$PID(\Theta) = (PPE(\Theta) - PPE(\Psi) + \gamma)$$
$$PID(\Psi) = -PID(\Theta)$$
$$PID = \text{independent if } PID(\Theta) = PID(\Psi) = 0$$

Past political experiences (PPE), of course, are simply the voter's subjectively weighted retrospective evaluations formed while observing the postures and performances of the contending parties during previous election periods.

Based on the preceding theoretical development, the statistical model we use to explain *present* party ID is

$$PID_p = \gamma + \sum_{i=1}^{p} B_i RE_i + u_p, \tag{1}$$

where RE_i is a vector of retrospective evaluations for period i, B_i is the associated vector of coefficients, and u_p is an error term. Owing to the additive structure of the model, equation 1 can be decomposed to

$$PID_p = PID_{p-1} + B_p RE_p + (u_p - u_{p-1}), \tag{2}$$

which is estimable with the panel data previously discussed. Before proceeding to those estimations, however, I would like to emphasize two features of the proposed model of party ID.

First, the model provides an explicit *political* basis for party ID. When a citizen first attains political awareness, the socialization influences summarized by γ may dominate party ID. But as time passes, as the citizen experiences politics, party ID comes more and more to reflect the events that transpire in the world. Granted, those events may not be interpreted exactly the same by all individuals, but why should they be? As human beings we do not perceive ball games, concerts, lectures, or anything else in exactly the same way, either. But that is not to deny the realities underlying our divergent perceptions. Party ID as modeled here reflects evaluations of party activities.

Second, the model provides an explicit mechanism for change in party ID. The traditional conception of party ID suggests that change in identification is a step function of political evaluations: up to a certain severity they have no impact on party ID, while beyond that they shake an individual loose from an existing identification. Clearly, the model we are using allows party ID to vary continuously. As new evaluations form, an individual's identification may wax and wane. Indeed, given that Great Depressions don't happen all that frequently, the pattern of change we would expect is precisely that present in the CPS panel studies: considerable variation in strength of party ID but much less indication of major (i.e., categorical) shifts. Furthermore, any categorical shift that does occur should be disproportionately composed of those whose previous party ID was near the turning point (independent) of the scale. And this, of course, is exactly what happens empirically.

Here is an appropriate place to address a matter that has provoked considerable debate in the literature: the purported relationship between length of affiliation with a party and strength of party ID.[4] If a model like the one proposed here is accurate, the length-strength relationship is probably an artifact. To elaborate, if the parties favor the same sides of various socioeconomic cleavages over time, and if citizens find themselves in the same socioeconomic circumstances over time, then one would expect most citizens consistently to evaluate one party as preferable to the other, which according to our model will produce a continuously strengthening party ID. To the extent that affiliation with a party proxies this kind of consistency in evaluation, an empirical relationship between length of affiliation and strength of affiliation will arise, but there is nothing particularly lawlike about that relationship. If the parties are inconsistent over time, or if social mobility is exceptionally high, or if new issues regularly arise, citizens' PID may fluctuate randomly around some initial level (γ) and neither strengthen nor weaken over time. The length-strength correlation may occur in some countries at some times (U.S., 1930-65) but not in other countries (e.g., India) or at other times (U.S., 1965-) even though the same model applies in all cases (Eldersveld, 1973; Converse, 1976). One must differentiate the general features of a model from the specific values its elements assume at particular times and places.

Finally, a disclaimer. The model allows latitude for a variety of processes to produce a party ID. For example, referring to expression 4-5', we could have "responsive" party identifiers, those for whom $\alpha_{j-1} < \alpha_j$, $\forall_j \leq p$. For such individuals, increasingly distant political experiences become increasingly less important as time passes. But then again, we could have "traumatized" party identifiers for whom α_j increases with $|U_{j+1} - U_j|$. Such individuals may never forget Hoover's depression or Sherman's march to the sea. Other possibilities exist as well. But we will be unable to examine such subtleties in the analyses that follow. All we have is party ID at time ($p - 1$) and a few retrospective evaluations from the present (pth) period. We can check to see if certain types of citizens are more sensitive than others to recent events and conditions, but the numerous possible processes at work are hidden in PID_{p-1}.

The 1956-58-60 SRC Panel Study

In the final section of chapter 2 [of Fiorina, 1981b] we presented summary analyses that related various retrospective evaluation items to the vote. This section uses the items listed in table 2.11 [of Fiorina, 1981b] to account for modifications in party ID across the 1956-58-60 SRC Panel Study. These items—financial situation, avoiding war, foreign dealings, and domestic conditions—are all treated as simple retrospective evaluations. I will report two analyses covering the shifts in party ID from 1956-58 and 1958-60, each of which is performed for both the seven-point and three-point versions of the party ID measure.

To account for party ID in 1958, we wish to estimate a model like the following:

$$PID_{1958} = \alpha + b_1 PID_{1956} + b_2 \text{(financial situation same)} + b_3$$
$$\text{(financial situation better)} + b_4 \text{(foreign dealings so-so)} + b_5$$
$$\text{(foreign dealings good)} + b_6 \text{(domestic affairs same)} + b_7$$
$$\text{(domestic affairs better)} + b_8 \text{(head always employed past}$$
$$\text{two years).}$$

The preceding specification includes a constant term, although none appears in equation 2—there it is incorporated in PID_{p-1}. Given that our indicators of retrospective evaluations are dummy variables, however, the constant term incorporates all the excluded categories. In addition, the preceding specification includes a coefficient on PID_{p-1}, though expression 2 implicitly constrains that coefficient to be one. There are two reasons not to impose the constraint. First, PID_{p-1} is replaced by an instrument (see below) with a scale not comparable to PID_p. Second, the changes in party ID are measured over two-year intervals, but the retrospective evaluations often refer to "during the past year" or leave the time span of unspecified length. By freeing the coefficient on PID_{p-1}, we enable the specification to take account of such failures of "fit" among the right-hand-side variables.

The technique of estimation is a maximum likelihood probit procedure. . . . Although much has been written about the robustness of ordinary least squares (OLS) under violations of the traditional assumptions, there is no denying that applying OLS to a limited dependent variable results in biased estimates of the standard errors of estimated coefficients. As a consequence, hypothesis tests involving the coefficients are undependable. Given that the significance of particular coefficients is of crucial concern to this analysis, the trouble and expense of the probit procedure appear justified.

A second complication is apparent from a glance back at equation 2. In decomposing PID_p into $(PID_{p-1} + RE_p)$ we obtain a new error term, $(u_p - u_{p-1})$, which, of course, is correlated with PID_{p-1}.[5] This situation might produce biased and inconsistent estimates if we took no remedial action. When using linear regression, the standard remedy for such a problem is a two-stage procedure that first estimates a "purged" variable, PID^*_{p-1}, that then substitutes for the offending variable, PID_{p-1}. An analagous procedure exists for probit analysis. And while the two-stage probit estimates do not have all the desirable properties of the two-stage least squares estimates, they do have the important property of consistency (Heckman, 1978; Nelson and Olson, 1978; Amemiya, 1979). Thus, the estimates in the party ID equations are two-stage probit coefficients. Following Jackson (1975a), the purged version, PID^*, of PID is obtained from an analysis in which party ID serves as the dependent variable in an equation with various socioeconomic and demographic characteristics as independent variables. The predicted values, PID^*, are then used as input for the second stage of the analysis. (Appendix B [of Fiorina, 1981b] contains the details of the first-stage analysis.) Briefly, the data yield no surprises. Party ID is strongly associated with religion, region of residence, union membership, and father's party ID. Occupation and age relate less strongly—but significantly—to party ID, while a variety of other socioeconomic and demographic variables show little by way of genuine association with party ID. The retrospective variables (financial situation, avoiding war, and domestic progress) also relate significantly to party ID. Table 24-4 presents summary statistics on the 1956 and 1958 instruments. The latter are somewhat better, so the analysis of party ID change across the 1958-60 waves rests on firmer statistical foundations than that of change across the 1956-58 waves.

Table 24-4   Party ID Instruments, 1956-60 Panel Study

Instrument to Replace	$\hat{R}^2$	Rho (Predicted v. actual party ID)
1956 Seven-point scale	.26	.46
1956 Three-point scale	.32	.42
1958 Seven-point scale	.41	.61
1958 Three-point scale	.51	.56

Note: 1956 n = 1,362. 1958 n = 1,738.

Tables 24-5 and 24-6 contain results that lend considerable credence to the conception of party ID as a running tally of retrospective evaluations. In each case the coefficient of the party ID instrument is quite large and significant: present party ID of course relates strongly to past party ID. But note also the importance of recent retrospective evaluations in accounting for temporal change in party ID. The dependent variable is coded from strong Democrat to strong Republican or from Democrat to Republican. Thus, satisfaction with the incumbent Republican administration should result in movement toward the Republican end of the scale. This is indeed what happens. Republican identification increases significantly among those who believe that the domestic situation has improved, that foreign dealings have gone well, and that our chances of avoiding war have declined. In fact, even a so-so or ambiguous situation seems to be associated with an increase in Republican identification.[6] The financial situation and unemployment variables usually have the right sign, but their effects appear to be smaller and statistically less precise.

The differences between the 1958 and 1960 party ID analyses are in line with the conventional picture of those campaigns. In 1958 the generalized domestic affairs item has an effect considerably stronger than the generalized foreign affairs item, and the latter is the sole foreign affairs indicator in the analysis, while three domestic affairs items must compete. In 1960 the relative effects of both foreign affairs items are much stronger, although the domestic affairs item still has the largest coefficient. Even though the worst of the recession had passed, perhaps Kennedy's talk of "getting this country moving again" kept domestic affairs in the spotlight.

As explained in Appendix A [of Fiorina, 1981b], in probit analysis one cannot discuss the effects of a particular variable in isolation. How much any given variable affects the dependent behavior depends on the values taken on by other variables in the equation. Thus, in order to convey to the reader some indication of the range of effects represented in Tables 24-5 and 24-6, I will examine some hypothetical cases. Consider five individuals, the first with a score on the 1958 party ID instrument equal to the mean of the respondents (μ = .83) included in the analysis, the second and third individuals with scores one standard deviation (σ = .84) above and below the mean, respectively, and the fourth and fifth with scores two standard deviations above and below the

Table 24-5   1958 PID as a Function of 1956 PID and Recent Retrospective Evaluations, Two-Stage Probit Estimates

	Seven Point	Three Point
Financial situation—better	.06	.12
Foreign dealings—gone well	.23***	.31***
Domestic affairs—better	.54***	63***
Financial situation—same	.08	.11
Foreign dealings—so-so	.14	.23*
Domestic affairs—same	.27***	.31***
Foreign dealings—don't know	.24**	.20*
Domestic affairs—don't know	.45***	.40***
Head not unemployed in past two years	.11	.19
1956 PID**	1.01***	1.02***
Constant	−.75***	−.88***
$\hat{R}^2$	.32	:39
rho	.52	.48
n	1,062	1,062

*$p < .10$.   **$p < .05$.   ***$p < .01$.

mean, respectively. This gives us a set of individuals whose prior party identifications range from very strong Democratic to fairly strong Republican. To make things simple, let us consider the effects of (a) uniformly favorable retrospective evaluations (financial situation, domestic affairs, chances of avoiding war "better," foreign dealings "gone well," and employed); (b) mostly neutral retrospective evaluations ("same" on the four items, employed); and (c) uniformly unfavorable retrospective evaluations ("worse" on the four items, unemployed). Predicted 1960 party ID (from Table 24-6, column 1) for each of the five individuals for each of the three conditions is shown below.

	1960 Retrospective evaluations		
1958 ID	Unfavorable	Neutral	Favorable
Average −2σ	Strong Democrat	Strong Democrat	Weak Democrat
Average −σ	Strong Democrat	Weak Democrat	Independent
Average	Weak Democrat	Independent Democrat	Weak Republican
Average +σ	Independent Democrat	Independent Republican	Strong Republican
Average +2σ	Independent Republican	Weak Republican	Strong Republican

Two things are evident from the hypothetical cases. First, retrospective evaluations can play a major role in moving individuals up and down the party identification scale, though we have deliberately structured the examples so that all the retrospective evaluations work in concert. In the less consistent real world, the observed effects will seldom be so powerful as those illustrated above; still, the

Table 24-6 1960 PID as a Function of 1958 PID and Recent Retrospective Evaluations, Two-Stage Probit Estimates

	Seven Point	*Three Point*
Financial situation—better	.01	−.04
Foreign dealings—gone well	.41**	.45**
Avoiding war—better chance	.42**	.49**
Domestic affairs—better	.58**	.65**
Financial situation—same	−.03	−.02
Foreign dealings—so-so	.20*	.34**
Avoiding war—same chance	.12*	.20*
Domestic affairs—same	.19**	.23*
Foreign dealings—don't know	.06	.00
Avoiding war—don't know	.02	.21
Domestic affairs—don't know	.12	.14
Head not unemployed in past two years	.18*	.09
1958 PID**	.76**	.82**
Constant	−.40**	−.62**
$\hat{R}^2$	.41	.53
rho	.63	.61
n	1,316	1,316

* $p < .05$.   ** $p < .01$.

potential is clearly there. Second, the more partisan an individual, the less responsive his or her reported partisanship will be to retrospective evaluations, although, as the latter cumulate over time, even strong identifiers may eventually cross the threshold of their category. . . .

All in all, Tables 24-5 and 24-6 present a compelling picture: party ID responds to the recent performance of the party in power via a citizen's formation of retrospective judgments. This finding is wholly in accord with the concept of party identification developed in chapter 4 [of Fiorina, 1981b]. Of course, other concepts of party ID are also compatible with these tables. Consider, for example, a Bayesian theory in which past (present) identification reflects a citizen's prior (posterior) distribution of party positions and retrospective judgments reflect the samples of information he or she has acquired in the process of proceeding from prior to posterior.[7] Such a theory is a live competitor. We can never hope to "prove" *the* one correct theory, but the important point concerns what theories can be dismissed. And it appears that we can safely eliminate any theory positing that party ID is either devoid of political content or impervious to change. Granted, party ID may not reflect an elaborate ideology or a wealth of detailed information about current public policies, but at least it reflects the political experiences of the citizen. And while party ID might remain empirically stable for long periods of time, that stability only reflects the empirical consistency of political experiences with previous identification, not the resistance of the latter to change. The underlying theoretical dependence of current party ID on political events and conditions remains.

To this point I have not mentioned the fact that Tables 24-5 and 24-6 contain parallel analyses using both the three- and seven-point measures of party ID. The reason is that it apparently doesn't matter. Whether one looks at column one or two in the tables, the conclusion is the same: change in party ID is predictable from knowledge of an individual's perceptions of recent political events and conditions. Earlier we took note of Brody's then-radical conclusion that the three-category version of the party ID measure captures the presumed long-term essence of a psychological party affiliation, while the seven-place measure is hopelessly "polluted" by short-term forces. If anything, Brody's conclusion is too conservative. The second columns of Tables 24-5 and 24-6 clearly indicate that the categorical measure too is significantly affected by at least one type of "short-term force"—retrospective evaluations. Empirically, we may not see very much by way of categorical change—few political events are sufficiently noteworthy to reverse the sign of a strong Democrat's or Republican's party identification, but over time, movement across the categorical divides appears to follow the same patterns as up-and-down movements in strength of party ID.

At the least, the preceding analysis should give pause to those who would use party ID as a simple "control" of the same order as income, occupation, religion, or race. Variables like the latter nearly always can be treated as purely exogenous in one's analysis: they affect the political behavior of interest but are not themselves affected by it. Party ID is a different matter. It is both cause and consequence of some kinds of political behavior. To take it purely as the former may lead to statistical misspecification and substantive error.[8] At least, that is the import of the analysis of the 1950s panel study.

The 1972-74-76 CPS Panel Study

The major difference between the 1950s panel and the 1970s panel is the presence in the latter of mediated retrospective evaluations such as presidential performance, government economic performance, and the Nixon pardon. Otherwise, this section simply repeats the preceding section with a later data set. Again, the analysis employs party ID instruments estimated from a variety of demographic variables and retrospective evaluations. . . .

In 1974, only evaluations of Ford's performance and his pardon of Nixon appear to be important factors in the temporal transformation of party ID. The estimates for 1976 party ID are quite similar to those for 1974. Again evaluations of Ford's performance and his pardon of Nixon play a clear and important role in modifying past party ID, though the relative importance of the two reverses as the pardon recedes in time and the length of Ford's incumbency increases. Evaluations of the administration's performance on inflation and unemployment also appear to bear some relationship to changes in party ID between 1974 and 1976. But again, simple retrospective evaluations relate weakly and inconsistently to temporal change in party ID. . . .

What is the general conclusion to be drawn [for 1974 and 1976]? On the one hand, they reinforce the conclusion drawn from Tables 24-5 and 24-6: party ID waxes and wanes in accord with a citizen's evaluations of the recent performance of the party in power. Yet on the other hand, there is a major difference between the two sets of [years]. In [1958 and 1960] we see party ID changing in response to evaluations of general *conditions*—international tension, the domestic situation, personal unemployment, and so forth—whereas in [1974 and 1976] we see party ID changing principally in response to evaluations of *people*—Ford and Nixon. One might reasonably suspect that past party ID contributes a great deal to those very evaluations, thus producing a spurious link between them and current party ID. When general conditions rather than political personalities are at issue, the question of spuriousness is much less worrisome.

Throughout the preceding chapters we have treated mediated retrospective evaluations (MREs) gingerly, always admitting the possibility that they do not represent what they seem to on their face. Now, with the interpretation of [1974-1976] hanging in the balance, we must come to grips with MREs. That is the task of the next chapter [of Fiorina, 1981b]. In order to write a conclusion to this chapter, however, I must offer a preview of the next. We will see that MREs definitely reflect previous party ID, but we will see as well that they just as definitely reflect simple retrospective evaluations. They appear to play the kind of intervening role hypothesized in Figure 4.1 (see chapter 4 [of Fiorina, 1981b]). While one should not interpret them as purely objective judgments, one cannot interpret them as purely subjective rationalizations, either. In light of those findings, I am reasonably sanguine about the interpretation of [1974-1976]; like Tables 24-5 and 24-6, they indicate that a citizen's party ID waxes and wanes in accord with his/her perceptions of societal conditions, political events, and the performance of incumbent officeholders.

A final caveat. In the preceding pages, conclusions about the nature of party ID have been stated firmly and often. But I will now emphasize a point deliberately understated in the chapter, namely, the empirical continuity of party ID. As Tables 24-5 and 24-6 and [the data from 1974-1976] clearly show, present party ID does relate very strongly to previous party ID. There is a pronounced element of continuity, probably enough to merit the shorthand of "habit" or "standing decision." We should never go so far as to deny the existence of some notion of party identification, to treat it as a mere summary for an individual's issue preferences, for example. The tables in this chapter simply support what many of us have believed without adequate evidence all along: there is an inertial element in voting behavior that cannot be ignored, but that inertial element has an experiential basis; it is *not* something learned at mommy's knee and never questioned thereafter.

Addendum: Some Methodological Observations on the Traditional Party ID Measure

. . .[T]he probit procedure assumes that we observe only the ordinal reflection of an underlying cardinal variable. The observed categories are hypothesized to correspond to intervals on the underlying variable, intervals determined by $(n - 1)$ "thresholds" if there are n observed categories. The program of McKelvey and Zavoina provides estimates of these thresholds, normalized so that the lowest one is set at zero. These thresholds, of course, are of interest in their own right in that they provide estimates of the size of, and distance between, the ordinal categories with which we must work.

Most researchers who work with the seven-point party ID measure treat it as an equal-interval scale. That is, before doing their statistical analyses, they code an individual's party ID from -3 to 3 or from 0 to 6. Table 24-7 raises serious doubts about such practices. Let us ignore the strong-identifier categories, which are of infinite length. This is a property of the normal distribution, which matters only if one or more right-hand-side variables is unbounded. Otherwise, there will be some lower (higher) point beyond which no one's party ID scores are predicted to lie. (Theoretically, there is no particular reason to bound party ID scores.) The remaining five categories, on the other hand, are of determinate length, and here we can make relative comparisons. Let us take the 1958 and 1960 estimates first. In each of these years we see that the weak Republican and weak Democratic categories are of comparable length, but they are two and one-half to four times longer than any of the three independent categories. In the 1974 and 1976 data, the weak Democratic and weak Republican categories are again of similar length, but now they are less than twice the length of each of the three independent categories. Put another way, in 1958 independents, broadly defined, occupied a portion of the scale roughly 85 percent as long as that occupied by the weak identifiers. In 1976 broadly defined independents occupied a portion of the scale roughly 150 percent as long as the weak identifiers.

Table 24-7 suggests two conclusions. First, the seven-point party ID measure is not an equal-interval scale. Consequently, analyses that treat it as such may be misleading.[9] Second, the seven-point measure is not invariant over time; there is considerable movement in the relative sizes of the categories. Thus, diachronic analyses, which treat party ID as an equal-interval scale, may be doubly misleading. The relationship between party ID and some aspect of political behavior might appear to change over time when actually it is the measure that is changing.

As long as we are on the subject of methodological caveats about previous research using the party ID measure, we might as well consider a caveat that potentially applies to this research. Table 24-7 reflects the assumption that party identification is one-dimensional: the probit procedure presumes an underlying cardinal dimension, which we observe only imperfectly as a series of ordered categories. (The unidimensional assumption, of course, is also implicit in treatments of party ID as an equal-interval scale.) Very recently, however, scholars (Valentine and Van Wingen, 1980; Weisberg, 1980) have suggested that responses to the traditional party ID items may require a two-dimensional representation, one measuring attitudes toward the parties, the second measuring attitudes toward "independence." The evidence thus far is sketchy. In evaluating this line of work Kessel (1980, p. 231) notes the strong association between the

Table 24-7 Estimated Locations of Thresholds Between Party ID Categories

	1958	1960	1974	1976
Strong Democrat				
	.00	.00	.00	.00
Weak Democrat				
	.75	.84	.77	.89
Independent Democrat				
	.95	1.04	1.27	1.29
Independent				
	1.18	1.32	1.66	1.66
Independent Republican				
	1.38	1.62	2.18	2.12
Weak Republican				
	2.10	2.34	2.95	2.88
Strong Republican				

Note: In 1958, .75 marks the boundary between those predicted to be weak Democrats and those predicted to be independent Democrats. In 1976, 2.88 marks the boundary between those predicted to be weak Republicans and those predicted to be strong Republicans, and so on.

traditional ordinal scale and the two-dimensional classification, suggesting, "We can continue to use the traditional classification with the caveat that it is an imperfect reflection of more complex attitudes about partisanship and independence."

I am fully in agreement with Kessel's conclusion, and I would append to it the sentiment that we should not let methodology run away with substance. The *concept* of party identification developed by the Michigan group *is* one-dimensional—a bipolar scale anchored by two opposing reference groups. Independents are just that, people who have no particular identification with either party, not those who positively identify with "independence." Similarly, the reconceptualization of party ID proposed in this chapter *is* one-dimensional—the weighted utility difference between past experiences with two parties. Independents are just people who have done equally badly or equally well at the hands of the parties. If the traditional means of *measuring* party ID ("Generally speaking, do you . . .") turns out to elicit multidimensional responses, we have two choices. The obvious one is to clean up the measure. The less obvious one is to reconceptualize party ID as a multidimensional phenomenon including such strange notions as affect toward "independence." [10]

The theory I have proposed is a theory of individual responses to the attitudes-toward-the-parties dimension (if there is more than one) of the traditional ordinal measure. If this measure, in fact, is forcibly combining two dimensions, then replications of my analyses using a purer, one-dimensional measure should yield results even stronger than those reported in this chapter.

NOTES

1. The reader may find it interesting to examine the treatments of party identification in the current American government texts. There the traditional orthodoxy reigns supreme.
2. By fourth grade in New Haven, according to Greenstein (1969).
3. For example, using mostly the aggregate distributions of party ID and the recall item about change in previous identification, Kessel (1968, pp. 302-08) argues that party ID is at least somewhat responsive to short-term forces.
4. For a review of the debate from the standpoint of one of its principal protagonists, see Converse (1976).
5. Recall that PID_{p-1} would be written as

$$\gamma + \sum_{i=1}^{p} B_i RE_i + u_{p-1}$$

6. Usually, one drops the "don't knows" from the analysis, but there are quite a number of them on the foreign-dealings, domestic affairs, and avoiding-war items, so retaining them (easily done in a dummy variable formulation) significantly increases the number of cases usable for estimation.
7. For one illustrative use of such a model, see Zeckman (1979).
8. Regrettably, some of my earlier work is vulnerable to this charge. See Fiorina (1978).
9. When using party ID as a right-hand-side variable, the preferred course would be to represent the seven-point scale by a set of six dummy variables. When using party ID as a left-hand-side variable, the preferred course would be to utilize probit, logit, multiple discriminant, or some other appropriate statistical procedure.
10. This is not to say that "attitudes toward independence" do not exist, not that they are unimportant, only that it is questionable whether they belong under the concept of "party identification."

25. PARTY IDENTIFICATION AS A CROSS-NATIONAL CONCEPT: ITS MEANING IN THE NETHERLANDS

Jacques Thomassen

. . . It is of interest to test the validity of the concept of party identification on Dutch data. . . . These data [are] derived from a three-wave panel study that covers three successive elections, the provincial elections in 1970, the parliamentary elections in 1971 and the parliamentary elections in 1972. A nationwide random sample ($N = 1,838$) was interviewed in 1970. Because of panel mortality this number was reduced to 1,266 in 1971 and to 972 in 1972. Full panel data are available for 834 respondents. In all three panel waves party identification was measured by this set of questions:

> Many people think of themselves as adherents of a certain party, but there are also people who do not.
>
> Do you usually think of yourself as an adherent of a certain party? *(If yes:)* Which party do you like best?
>
> Some people are strongly convinced adherents of their party. Others are not so strongly convinced. Do you belong to the strongly convinced adherents of your party or do you not? *(If not an adherent?)* Is there any party that you are closer to than the others? *(If yes:)* Which?

These questions are as similar as possible to the SRC questions. . . .

The Stability of Party Identification

An essential property of party identification is its long-term stability. On the one hand, the time between our first and last panel wave is too short to prove long-term stability. On the other hand, if we were to find that party identification is not even stable over such a short time, we can be sure that there is not long-term stability either. There is not objective criterion to define how stable party identification should be, especially not in a time of realignment. However, if party identification is a lasting psychological attitude towards a party that is relatively

Source: *Party Identification and Beyond,* Ian Budge, Ivor Crewe, and Dennis Farlie, eds. London: John Wiley & Sons, 1976. Reprinted with permission of John Wiley and Sons Limited.

Table 25-1 Stability of Party Identification and Vote Preference

	Stable Vote Preference	*Stable Party Identification*
1970-1971	80.3%[a]	76.1%
1971-1972	77.7%	74.6%
1970-1972	71.1%	62.6%

[a] i.e. 80.3% of the people who voted both times voted for the same party in both elections.

insensitive to short-term factors and does not completely define the vote, it should be more stable than vote preference. Even in a time of realignment one should expect that party identification changes at a slower pace than vote preference.

In Table 25-1 the stability of party identification is compared with the stability of vote preference. Party identification is clearly less stable than vote preference. In all three combinations of the panel waves the turnover of party identification is higher than the turnover of vote preference. . . .

Now that we have found that party identification is less stable than vote preference, we should ask the question whether party identification is something more than an expression of volatile positive feelings toward a certain party at a particular moment, feelings caused by exactly the same circumstances that determine the vote. If this should prove to be the case it is very likely that party identification and vote preference are measuring one and the same phenomenon: the preference for a particular party at a certain moment.

Party Identification and Vote Preference

If party identification and vote preference are measuring the same phenomenon, party identification loses one of its most important functions. In the United States party identification has become such an invaluable analytical concept, precisely because it offers the opportunity to distinguish short-term factors from long-term influences. This made it possible to determine the role of candidates and issues in each election.

A distinction between long-term forces (party identification) and short-term forces can be made only when party identification and vote preference are really different concepts. A perfect congruence between party identification and vote preference means that the two are conceptually the same. It could mean that in a particular election no short-term factors are at work and that therefore everybody is voting according to this party identification. The more deviations there are between party identification and vote preference, the greater the role of short-term influences would be.

Counter-evidence to the hypothesis that there is no conceptual difference between party identification and vote preference is presented in Table 25-2. In all three years about 9 percent of all voters with a party identification voted for a

Table 25-2   Consistency of Party Identification and Vote Preference, Controlled for Strength of Party Identification

	1970	*1971*	*1972*
Strong adherents	98.3%[a]	98.5%	96.1%
Weak adherents	92.3%	92.9%	92.2%
Leaners	83.9%	86.5%	86.9%
Total	90.9%	91.7%	91.2%

[a] i.e. of the strong adherents who voted in 1970 98.3% voted for the party they identified with.

different party than the one they identified with. This percentage is lower than any comparable figure in the United States. . . .

Party Identification and Vote Preference: Causal Sequence

The theory of party identification is very clear on the causal sequence of party identification and vote preference. Party identification is defined as a lasting psychological attachment towards a party, the relationship between party identification and vote preference being described as the relation between "the psychological state and its behavioral consequences" (Campbell et al., 1960, p. 122). Goldberg observes that a causal model in which party identification is causally prior to vote preference indeed fits data on American voting behavior (Goldberg, 1966). . . .

. . . Butler and Stokes have shown that party identification changes more often in Britain than the United States. Their conclusion is based upon a comparison of the relation between stability of party identification and the stability of vote preference in Britain and the United States among the same respondents over three time-points (Butler and Stokes, 1969, pp. 41-2). In both countries party identification was found to be more stable than vote preference, although there was more stability in the United States (92 percent) than in Britain (83 percent). There were a limited number of voters who changed their vote as well as their party identification, although in Britain this percentage was twice as high (13 percent) as in the United States (6 percent). In both countries the percentage of people who changed their vote preference but not their party identification was higher than the percentage who changed their party identification but not their vote preference. However, in the United States the difference was much more marked than in Britain. In the United States the ratio was 8:1, in Britain 2:1, which suggests that in Britain party identification is much less independent of vote preference than in the United States.

Table 25-3 presents similar data for The Netherlands. Stable vote preference means that a respondent voted for the same party in 1970, 1971 and 1972. Stable party identification means that a respondent identified with the same party in all three panel waves. There is a dramatic difference between the Dutch data

Table 25-3 Stability of Party Identification and Vote Preference in Three Dutch Elections

| | | Vote Preference | | |
		Stable	Not Stable	Total
Party	Stable	61	6	67
Identification	Not stable	10	23	33
	Total	71	29	100%

and the British and the American data. Not less than 23 percent of all the voters in this table changed their party identification as well as their vote preference at least once. (We did not go into the question of whether these changes were symmetric). The most striking finding in this table is the difference between the upper right-hand and the lower left-hand cells. While only 6 percent of the respondents change their vote preference without changing their party identification, 10 percent change their party identification without changing their vote preference. This finding is the exact opposite of what was found in Britain and in the United States. . . .

These findings very strongly suggest that party identification is not causally prior to the vote, but simply a reflection of the vote and therefore causally posterior to the vote. . . .

26. AN ANALYSIS OF INTRANSITIVITIES IN THE INDEX OF PARTY IDENTIFICATION

John R. Petrocik

. . . A common expectation underlying wide use of the index of party identification is that there is an increase in general political involvement and partisan behavior as one compares independents with leaners, leaners with the weakly identified, and the weakly identified with the strongly identified.

This expectation, however, is not always met. For many variables against which one might plot partisanship the result would not be monotonic. As shown in Figure 26-1, which follows on page 268, only two of the ten variables examined are monotonically related to partisanship. The unexpected finding is that leaning independents are higher on several of the factors than those who are weak party identifiers. That is, the ascending order is not: independents, leaners, weakly identified, and strongly identified; but, instead: independents, weakly identified, leaners, and strongly identified.[1]

The data are unequivocal. The general expectation of monotonicity in the relationship between partisanship and political involvement (the rubric under which the variables in Figure 26-1 are discussed) cannot be supported. Only two of the ten expectations are clearly met. Leaners are less likely to vote a straight ballot and less likely to feel strongly about one party over the other than are identifiers; but they are higher than weak identifiers on all other measures of political involvement. . . .

NOTE

1. This pattern existed in the data across all of the election studies examined: 1952, 1956, 1960, 1964, 1968, 1970, and 1972. The data presented in the paper are the pooled results of a parallel analysis of the data from each sample.

Source: *Political Methodology* (1974) 1:31-47. Reprinted with permission of Butterworth-Heinemann.

Figure 26-1　Intransitivities in the Index of Party Identification

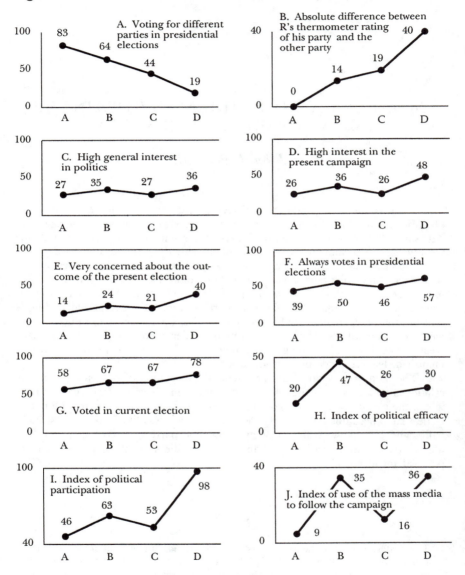

Note:　A = independents, B = leaners, C = weak partisans, D = strong identifiers.

27. A MULTIDIMENSIONAL CONCEPTUALIZATION OF PARTY IDENTIFICATION

Herbert F. Weisberg

Contemporary theories of American voting behavior give a prominent position to the role of psychological attachment to a political party in structuring the individual citizen's voting decision. Not only does partisanship affect one's vote, but also it affects one's attitudes toward the issues and candidates, which, in turn, affect one's vote.[1] In recent years, however, the meaning, importance, and measurement properties of party identification have been subject to an increasing challenge.[2] This chapter reexamines the concept and the measure from a dimensional perspective. Simply stated, the argument made here is that party identification involves separate attitudes toward several distinct objects—political parties generally, the Republican party, the Democratic party, and political independence—so a multidimensional view of party identification is required, rather than the traditional unidimensional view. This multidimensional perspective particularly affects our understanding of strength of identification and of political independence, accounting for incongruities on these topics which have recently been discovered.

This chapter begins with a reexamination of the concept of party identification and the survey questions used to measure it. Evidence from the biennial national election surveys taken by the University of Michigan's Center for Political Studies will be introduced, with special emphasis on the new partisanship questions asked in the January-February wave of their 1980 election study.[3]

The Dimensions of Party Identification

Dimensional Models of Partisanship

... The ... usual view of party identification in the United States is as a single dimension (to be denoted as P^1) with strong Republican identification at

Source: *Political Behavior,* Vol. 2, No. 1, 1980, by permission of Plenum Publishing Co.

Figure 27-1   The Seven-Point Party Identification Scale

Strong Democrats	Weak Democrats	Independents Leaning to Democrats	Pure Independents	Independents Leaning to Republicans	Weak Republicans	Strong Republicans

one end, strong Democratic identification at the opposite end, and political independence in the middle (see Figure 27-1). This approach makes a series of strong assumptions that have never been explicitly tested: (a) that independence is the midpoint of a Republican-Democratic continuum, (b) that Republican and Democratic identification are opposites of one another, and (c) that opposition to political parties is equivalent to independence. These assumptions can be relaxed in a number of different ways, yielding a series of alternative dimensional models of party identification.

In particular, political independence may be a separate object with which citizens can identify rather than merely a neutral midpoint of a Republican-Democratic scale. In fact, citizens could identify with independence regardless of whether or not they are neutral with respect to the two parties. This suggests a two-dimensional interpretation of party identification (to be denoted as P^2): one dimension ranging from Republican to Democrat with neutral in the middle, and the other dimension ranging from independent to not very independent (see Figure 27-2).[4]

Furthermore, Republican and Democratic identification need not be as diametrically opposed as the standard treatment assumes. It is possible for citizens to identify with both parties (or to identify negatively with both parties)—and citizens with such views may or may not identify with independence. This leads to a three-dimensional interpretation of party identification (to be labeled P^3): one

Figure 27-2   Two Dimensions of Partisanship and Independence

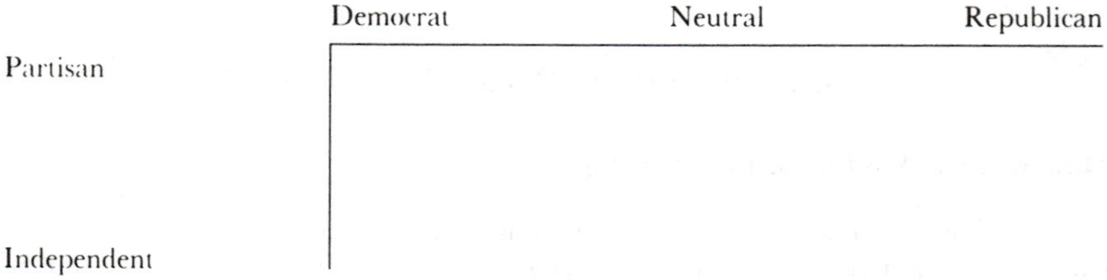

	Democrat	Neutral	Republican
Partisan			
Independent			

Figure 27-3 Three Dimensions of Party Identification

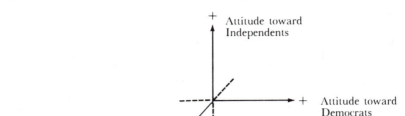

dimension measuring attitude toward the Republican party, another measuring attitude toward the Democratic party, and the third measuring attitude toward political independence (Figure 27-3).[5] These three dimensions need not be orthogonal to one another. The degrees of correlation among the P^4 dimensions are best regarded as parameters that can change over time. Negative correlations might be expected immediately after a party realignment, while the correlations might actually be positive during a dealignment.

What is most difficult is to decide how to introduce attitudes toward political parties generally into this spatial presentation. Viewing this as a fourth dimension allows people to like independence and the party system, as well as dislike both, and it allows people to like their favorite party and political parties generally, as well as dislike their preferred party and political parties generally. It is probable that this fourth dimension would be correlated with the others: positively with attitude toward the Republican party and toward the Democratic party, but negatively with attitude toward independence.

The choice among these dimensional perspectives can directly affect our understanding of voting behavior. For example, the growth in Independents since the 1950s takes on a very different meaning when independence is seen solely as a matter of neutrality between the parties than when it can also mean a positive attraction toward independence or a negative repulsion from the party system, but these distinct meanings are blurred in the conventional P^1 view of partisanship. Similarly, the usual finding of increased strength of partisanship as a citizen ages (Converse, 1976) takes on a very different meaning when it is realized that the usual unidimensional P^1 interpretation combines three aspects that are separate in P^3—how much the person likes his own party, how much more the person likes his party than the opposite party, and how much the person likes political independence—and that it might be that only one of these three aspects really changes with aging. . . .

New Evidence on the Dimensionality of Partisanship

An initial test of the standard unidimensional interpretation can be obtained by examining responses to the "party thermometers" included in the national election studies since 1964.[6] Respondents are asked to rate "Republicans" and "Democrats" on a 100 degree thermometer scale, where 100° means very warm feelings toward the group, 50° is a neutral response, and 0° represents very cool feelings. A unidimensional interpretation would imply a very negative correlation between ratings of Republicans and Democrats. Instead, the correlation has ranged from mildly negative to zero: −.38 in 1964, −.18 in 1968, .02 in 1972, .01 in 1976, and −.17 in the January-February 1980 wave (where the stimuli were changed to "the Republican party" and "the Democratic party").[7] These correlations suggest that attitudes toward the two parties are separate dimensions (separated by an angle of something like 90-110 degrees) and not a single dimension.

A further test is provided by the 1980 election study which asked respondents to rate the Republican party, the Democratic party, and "people who call themselves political independents" on the thermometer (see Table 27-1). Under a unidimensional interpretation (Coombs, 1964, chapter 5), Republicans at one end of the dimension would be closer to Independents than to Democrats at the opposite end of the dimension, and so should rate Independents higher than Democrats. Similarly, Democrats at one end of the dimension would be closer to Independents than to Republicans at the opposite end of the dimension, and so should rate Independents higher than Republicans. However, of the respondents who liked either the Republican party or the Democratic party the most, and who gave different ratings to the three groups, only 37 percent preferred Independents to the opposite party. Partisans do not seem to view Independents as being in the middle of a partisanship dimension.

The 1980 study also included a thermometer measure on attitudes toward "political parties, in general." The "political parties" and "political independents" thermometers have a trivial .11 correlation. Not only do some partisans dislike independents and some independents dislike partisans, but also many citizens like both partisans and independents, and many other citizens dislike both. Thus, independence is more than a dislike of parties. The average correlation between the "political independents" thermometer and the Republican and Democratic party thermometers is .04, with a tendency for people who like Independents to like the Republican party more and the Democratic party less.

Additionally, the 1980 study asked respondents a new set of partisanship questions, including "do you think of yourself as a supporter of one of the political parties, or not?" and "do you ever think of yourself as a political independent, or not?" The correlation between these two new items would be −1.0 if party support and independence were mutually exclusive conditions as the standard unidimensional approach assumes. Instead, the correlation was −.13, showing these are separate dimensions. As Table 27-2 shows, 16 percent of the sample considered themselves both party supporters and Independents. Only

Table 27-1 Frequencies of Preference Orders Based on Thermometer Ratings of the Democratic Party, the Republican Party, and Political Independents, January-February 1980

Preference Orders	
Compatible with Democratic-Republican-Independent Dimension:	
DIR	15%
IDR	14
IRD	10
RID	13
Total	52%
Not Compatible with Democratic-Independent-Republican Dimension:	
DRI	31%
RDI	17
Total	48%

Note: Preference orders are listed in first choice, second choice, third choice order. The total number of respondents with untied preference orders is 507. If each possible preference order on three alternatives were equally likely, two-thirds of the preference orders would be consistent with a single dimension.

56 percent of the sample consider themselves just party supporters or just Independents. The evidence suggests that the public interprets political independence as more complex than the absence of identification with a party.

Perhaps the most unexpected finding reported here is that a quarter of the respondents consider themselves neither party supporters nor Independents. One would expect that this large group has had unusual difficulty responding to the traditional party identification questions. Presumably these people do not think of politics in partisan terms and probably have little to do with politics, but further exploration is required.

Table 27-2 Party Support by Independence, January-February 1980 ($N = 954$)

Do you think of yourself as a supporter of one of the political parties?	Do you ever think of yourself as a political independent?		
	Yes	*No*	*Total*
Yes	16.4%	29.5%	45.8%
No	26.3	27.9	54.2
Total	42.7%	57.3%	100.0%

The results reported in this section do not determine definitively the proper dimensional interpretation of party identification, though they suggest that four (sometimes correlated) dimensions are involved. In any case, the results severely challenge the traditional unidimensional conception of partisanship. . . .

Alternative Partisanship Scales

The high correlations reported in the literature between the seven-point party identification scale and other variables might be viewed as evidence that the standard party identification scale is unidimensional. Even if the "true" partisanship space were multidimensional, the standard scale might compress that multidimensional space into a single dimension fairly faithfully, particularly if most respondents were located along a straight line in that multidimensional space. However, an alternative explanation of the high correlations in the literature should be considered: that the seven-point scale is just highly related to a more unidimensional measure of the partisan continuum. Exploration of this possibility requires examination of some alternative partisanship scales, particularly as to their relationship with criterion variables such as the vote decision.

Whereas the seven-point party identification scale has often been described as the best or most efficient single predictor of voting decisions (Converse, 1975, pp. 127-28), recent research has shown that it is not monotonically related to presidential vote (Keith et al., 1977; Miller and Miller, 1977).[8] Specifically, for the years 1964 to 1976, an average of 79 percent of independent leaners voted for their party, compared to only 74 percent of weak identifiers. This deviation from monotonicity fits the argument that the seven-point scale is not unidimensional. Furthermore, this deviation suggests that combining responses to the three party identification questions into the standard scale does not necessarily properly order respondents in terms of their partisan strength. . . . An alternative measure of partisanship would have to perform better in this regard, particularly in terms of predicting the vote.

A fully appropriate P^3 indicator of the partisan continuum is the *party difference:* how much more the person likes the Republican party than the Democratic party. The best operationalization of this in the Center for Political Studies surveys is obtained by subtracting the feeling thermometer for Democrats from that for Republicans. The Pearson r correlations between the seven-point party identification scale and the party difference in the 1964-1976 studies ranged from .55 to .76, indicating that the measures are highly related but not equivalent. Table 27-3 shows the relationship between party identification and the party difference score. The mean party difference score is not always even monotone with the party identification scale, with a problem again for the weak partisan and leaning independent category ordering.

If the P^3 model is correct, the party difference measure would account for the vote better than the seven-point scale does. To provide a sufficient number of cases in each category for a test, the party difference measure has been collapsed into five categories: strong Republicans (31 to 100), weak Republicans (1 to 30), neutrals (0), weak Democrats (−30 to −1), and strong Democrats (−100 to

Table 27-3 Average Party Difference Value by Party Identification, 1964-1976

Party Identification Category	1964	1968	1972	1976	Average
Strong Republicans	42.1	40.6	23.0	26.3	33.0
Weak Republicans	18.5	19.6	13.9	8.8	15.2
Leaning Republicans	14.7	20.9	6.4	6.4	12.1
Pure Independents	− 0.2	5.6	− 0.1	− 3.2	0.5
Leaning Democrats	−20.2	− 9.4	−12.6	−11.8	−14.0
Weak Democrats	−23.2	−14.3	−10.9	−15.4	−16.0
Strong Democrats	−48.6	−40.2	−30.5	−30.1	−37.4
Proportion of variance explained (η^2)	53.2	50.5	32.0	38.7	43.6

−31). Since having one-third of the sample in the neutral category necessarily detracts from the relationship, a seven-category version of this measure has also been devised, making use of the party identification question to break the neutral category into Republican neutrals, pure neutrals, and Democratic neutrals. The party difference measures have monotonic relationships with vote (see Table 27-4). Table 27-5 shows the proportion of variance in presidential vote explained by each of the partisanship measures for the 1964-1976 presidential elections. The party difference measures consistently explain the vote better than does the party identification scale.

The party difference may have the greater relationship with the vote, but party identification could still help account for some of the variance that the party difference leaves unexplained. This possibility can be examined by checking whether party identification affects the vote within categories of party difference, and vice versa. Table 27-6 displays the 1976 vote by combinations of categories on the two partisan variables. Within party identification categories (the columns), party difference has a definite effect—even if one ignores the cells with under ten cases. However, within categories of party difference (the rows), party identification has a minimal effect—except for the neutral category where party identification retains a strong influence on the vote. Party identification seems to have little added impact upon the vote once party difference is taken into account (and would have less were there a probe asking neutrals to which party they felt closer). Furthermore, much of the effect of party identification seems due to its relationship with the party difference.[9]

Two more party direction scales are available in the January-February 1980 election study. First, respondents were asked:

> In your own mind, do you think of yourself as a supporter of one of the political parties, or not? (If yes,) which political party do you support? On this scale from 1 to 7 where 1 means "not very strongly" and 7 means "very strongly,"

Table 27-4 Republican Vote Proportion of Two-Party Vote by Partisanship, 1976

Party Difference	% Republican Vote	% of Sample
Strong Republicans (31 to 100)	100	5
Weak Republicans (1 to 30)	94	17
Republican Neutrals (0; Republican PID)	79	14
Pure Neutrals (0; Pure Independent PID)	62	11
Democratic Neutrals (0; Democratic PID)	39	16
Weak Democrats (-30 to -1)	10	24
Strong Democrats (-100 to -31)	3	13
Total		100

please choose the number that describes how strongly you support the (Republican/Democratic) Party.

With appropriate manipulation, this question series leads to a *party support* scale ranging from -7 for strong Republican support to -1 for weak Republican support to 0 for not supporting either party to $+1$ for weak Democratic support to $+7$ for strong Democratic support. Second, respondents were asked:

(If no on the party support question above), do you ever think of yourself as closer to one of the two major political parties, or not? (If a party supporter on the original question or if yes on the above closeness question,) here is a scale from 1 to 7 where 1 means feeling very close to the Republican Party and 7 means feeling very close to the Democratic Party. Where would you place yourself on this scale?

Table 27-5 Proportion of Variance in Two-Party Presidential Vote Accounted for by Alternative Partisanship Measures, 1964-1976

	1964	1968	1972	1976	Average
Seven-point party identification scale	43.5[a]	49.4	28.0	41.6	40.6
Five-category party difference measure	47.1	53.6	42.0	49.9	48.2
Seven-category party difference measure	49.1	59.0	45.4	54.7	52.0

[a] Cell entries are eta-squares.

Table 27-6 Republican Proportion of Two-Party Vote by Party Difference and Party Identification, 1976

Party Difference	Party Identification						
	Strong Dem.	*Weak Dem.*	*Lean Dem.*	*Pure Indep.*	*Lean Rep.*	*Weak Rep.*	*Strong Rep.*
Strong Rep.	100%	100%	100%	100%	100%	100%	100%
	(1)	(5)	(2)	(2)	(9)	(21)	(56)
Weak Rep.	71	91	71	100	96	93	97
	(11)	(17)	(7)	(12)	(62)	(92)	(115)
Neutral-Rep.					83	73	92
					(87)	(100)	(25)
Neutral-Indep.				62			
				(127)			
Neutral-Dem.	23	43	39				
	(29)	(118)	(78)				
Weak Dem.	4	11	10	15	40	20	
	(113)	(144)	(68)	(17)	(13)	(20)	
Strong Dem.	2	5	0	9		0	
	(106)	(76)	(22)	(12)		(4)	

Note: Values in parentheses are numbers of cases.

This leads to a *party closeness* scale from 1 for very close to the Republican Party to 7 for very close to the Democratic Party, with a code of 4 for those not feeling closer to either major party.

We do not yet know how these two new scales perform in comparison with the standard seven-point scale or the party difference measure. After the 1980 election, it will be possible to check which best predicts the presidential vote and other variables of interest. It is clear that these two new scales are highly correlated with one another and with the two older measures (with intercorrelations ranging from .67 to .78). Yet much of this high correlation is due to their all doing a good job of separating Republicans from Democrats. How they differ in dealing with strength of partisanship and with independence will be examined in the following section.

The analysis of this section certainly does not render the standard seven-point scale useless. On the contrary, it has contributed much to our understanding of political behavior and it has a substantial relationship with vote choice, even if the party difference has a somewhat stronger relationship with presidential vote. Apparently the distribution of citizens across P^3 has been such that the seven-point scale transforms the three-space into a single partisan dimension with minimal violence. The party difference may be a somewhat better measure for some purposes, but the differences are small. Given the greater simplicity of the more familiar P^1 representation, it would be foolish to move to a multidimensional representation unless that provided real theoretical and substantive gains. However, before prematurely accepting the conventional scale as adequate, it is essential to consider its measurement of strength of partisanship and independence.

A New Understanding of Independence

If the multidimensional conceptualization is correct and there are multiple dimensions of party identification, then there are also multiple components of strength of partisanship. These several components of strength of partisanship in P^2 and P^3 are thoroughly confounded with one another in P^1. Not only does unbundling these components lead to a far richer conceptualization of partisanship, but it offers an intriguing explanation of the problems with the conventional party identification measure that have recently been demonstrated in the literature. The most obvious difficulty is that independence and strength of partisanship have been measured by the same questions in the Center for Political Studies surveys. Independence is orthogonal to the party dimensions in P^2 and P^3, so these are separate concepts that should be measured separately.

In P^3 there are actually three basic components of strength of identification: the "intensity" with which people like their own party, the degree to which they like their own party more than the other party ("extremity"), and their attitude toward political "independence." These separate meanings are indistinguishable in P^1. For example, strong partisans are viewed as intensely liking their own party, being extreme in preferring their own party over the opposite party, and being least independent. The usual four-point strength of identification scale (strong identifier, weak identifier, independent leaner, pure independent) measures all of the meanings simultaneously in P^1. The three basic strength components are more separate in P^3. For example, people who intensely like one party might strongly prefer their own party over the other party or might like the two parties about equally, and they might be favorable or unfavorable toward independents. No single strength of partisanship measure suffices in P^3; separate measures of the three components are necessary.

These different aspects of strength of identification can be operationalized from the feeling thermometers and the new partisanship questions in the 1980 election study. The intensity with which a person likes his/her own party can be measured by the maximum of the thermometer ratings given to the Republican and Democratic parties, as well as from folding the party support scale described in the previous section into a scale ranging from $+7$ for strong support of one's own party to $+1$ for weak support of one's own party and zero for not supporting either party. The degree to which the person likes his/her own party more than the other can be measured by the absolute values of the difference between the thermometer ratings given the two parties, as well as from folding the party closeness scale described in the previous section into a scale ranging from $+7$ for very close to one's own party to $+4$ for equally close to the two major parties. Attitude toward independence can be measured by the thermometer rating of political independents, as well as from a new strength of independence question in the 1980 study:

Do you ever think of yourself as a political independent, or not? (If yes,) on this scale from 1 to 7 (where 1 means "not very strongly," and 7 means "very strongly"), please choose the number that describes *how strongly* independent in politics you feel.

(Respondents not thinking of themselves as independents were assigned the value of zero on this scale.) Additionally, the thermometer rating of "political parties, in general" in the 1980 study gives a measure of antiparty system views.

The Standard Partisan Strength Scale

The 1980 data can be used to examine what the standard four-point (strong identifier, weak identifier, independent leaner, pure independent) strength of identification scale actually measures. To determine this, the standard scale was regressed on measures of the different aspects of partisan strength discussed above. Multiple regression analysis shows that the standard scale best taps relative closeness to one's own party as against the opposite party ($\beta = .37$; $r = .61$; measured by the folded party closeness scale) and partisan intensity ($\beta = .36$; $r = .61$; measured by the folded party support scale). The contribution is smaller for strength of independence ($\beta = .19$; $r = -.30$; measured by the strength of independence scale). Strength of antiparty feelings (measured by the "political parties" thermometer item) has been dropped from this equation because its coefficient was insignificant. Altogether, these aspects account for just half of the variance in the standard strength of identification scale, so that half of its variance remains unexplained. It is particularly important to note that the standard measure is least related to strength of independence and of antiparty feelings. These are important aspects of strength of identification which are not captured adequately by the standard scale.

A possible objection to this analysis is that strength of independence may itself just be a composite of the other aspects of strength of identification. However, multiple regression analysis shows that not to be the case. Only 3 percent of the variance in strength of independence is accounted for by the folded party closeness scale, the folded party support scale, and the "political parties" thermometer item. Independence appears to be very different from these other aspects of strength of identification.

To compare further the standard four-point scale with some of the new measures, Table 27-7 shows the relationship between the standard strength scale and the new party support and independence questions. Both row and column percentages are shown, as it is interesting to trace through this table in both directions. Many of the findings are obvious, such as that strong partisans nearly always think of themselves as party supporters. But some findings are surprising, such as that a fifth of strong partisans think of themselves as Independents as well as party supporters. Nearly half of the pure Independents really don't consider themselves either party supporters or Independents, suggesting that the standard party identification question series does not give them a good opportunity to describe their position.[10] Weak partisans scatter across all four categories in fairly

Table 27-7   Partisan Strength by Party Support and Independence, January-February 1980

	Partisan Strength			
	Strong	*Weak*	*Leaner*	*Pure Independent*
A. *Column Percentages*				
Party supporter only	67%	31%	1%	2%
Both party supporter and independent	19	21	16	2
Only independent	3	17	57	49
Neither	11	31	26	46
Total percent	100	100	100	99
Number of cases	(241)	(369)	(194)	(140)
B. *Row Percentages*				
Party supporter only	58%	40%	1%	1%
Both party supporter and independent	30	49	19	2
Only independent	2	26	44	28
Neither	10	45	20	25
Total percent	100	100	100	100
Number of cases	(280)	(156)	(250)	(258)

equal proportions, suggesting that the weak partisan category is unusually diverse in the nature of its partisanship. Table 27-7B shows that people who consider themselves neither party supporters nor Independents tend to be classified as weak partisans on the standard partisan strength scale, again emphasizing that these citizens who do not accept either partisan or independent labels are not handled well by the standard partisan questions.

   This set of results helps to explain why empirical studies of the correlates of independence and of strength of partisanship typically obtain weak and even inconsistent results (Petrocik, 1974; Keith *et al.,* 1977; Van Wingen and Valentine, 1979). In particular, Petrocik (1974) shows that the conventional four-point strength of identification scale is not monotonically related to other variables which are supposed to be related to strength of identification, with the weak partisans and independent leaner categories often out of their proper order. The dimensional perspective provides an explanation of this anomalous "intransitivity." The usual strength of identification scale is not measuring any concept purely. It synthesizes several related concepts, but this may muddy up its relationship with any other variable that would be expected to have a tidy relationship with one of the components of partisan strength. . . .

A New View of Independents

All in all, the standard partisanship and strength scales do measure important concepts, though there may be better measures for each of the concepts. However, the situation for independence is very different— the standard measures simply do not satisfactorily measure political independence. This calls into question the entire set of empirical findings about the nature of political independents, as well as the literature describing the consequences for the party system of the recent apparent growth in the numbers of independents.

The nature of independents can be examined in the 1980 study, although there are not very many criterion variables in the January-February wave. First, it turns out that people who consider themselves both party supporters and independents are unusually high on a number of measures, including interest in the campaign, talking about the candidates, expecting to vote in the fall election, past voting frequency in presidential elections, and education. People who consider themselves neither party supporters nor independents are unusually low on these same five variables.

Second, strength of independence is also correlated with many of these variables. The usual strength of partisanship measure finds that strong partisans are higher than independents on interest in the campaign, caring about the presidential election outcome, expecting to vote in the fall election, and past voting frequency in presidential elections. However, most of these relationships reverse for strength of independence, with strong independents being higher than nonindependents on interest in the campaign, talking about the candidates, expecting to vote in the fall election, and past voting frequency.

Perhaps the most important result has to do with education. When the election studies first began to study partisanship, one of the surprising results was that independents are not more educated than partisans. This is seen by the small correlation ($\tau_b = .07$) in the 1980 study. This relationship changes dramatically when strength of independence is examined. Strong independents are better educated than weak independents and nonindependents, with a τ_b of .21. In percentage terms, 36 percent of those with college education are strong independents (positions 5-7 on the scale) compared to only 15 percent of those without a high school diploma, while 42 percent of those with college education do not ever think of themselves as independents compared to 76 percent of those without a high school diploma.

These results already begin to suggest that our entire understanding of independence must be revised. Political independence appears to be a complex topic, with many different types of respondents being combined as independents in the standard scales. A more careful examination of independence is likely to show meaningful differences among these different types. Once independence is better understood, the meaning of the "Independent" response to the party identification questions of the past thirty years will also be better understood, and much of the findings and literature of that period may have to be reinterpreted.

Conclusions

A multidimensional conceptualization of party identification has been developed in this chapter. The empirical evidence is limited, but it does suggest that the usual unidimensional interpretation is incorrect. In particular, the usual strength of identification measure so confounds different components of partisan strength that past studies have not been able to study validly the nature of political independence. The new survey questions should lead to better measurement of the full concept of partisanship. Party identification has been the keystone of our understanding of voting behavior. With a little work to bolster its underpinnings, we may find that the concept is even richer and more important than we realized.

NOTES

1. The concept was first discussed by the Michigan researchers in Belknap and Campbell (1952). The question itself was first presented and analyzed in *The Voter Decides* (Campbell, Gurin, and Miller, 1954), where it was treated as a coequal of issue orientation and candidate orientation. It was considered the most important population grouping in Campbell and Cooper (1956), but it was *The American Voter* (Campbell, Converse, Miller, and Stokes, 1960) that pioneered in treating it as the central theoretical concept in the study of voting behavior. By the publication of *Elections and the Political Order* (Campbell, Converse, Miller, and Stokes, 1966), it had been conceptualized as the long-term component of the vote decision which could be used to construct an estimate of a "normal vote" (Converse, 1966b). Knoke (1976) provides a fine treatment of its social bases, while Fiorina (1977a) gives an excellent treatment of its rational basis.

2. The controversy regarding the stability of party identification is reviewed in Niemi and Weisberg (1976, chapter 17), as is the debate as to its relative importance in affecting the vote (Niemi and Weisberg, 1976, chapter 9). Descriptions of important changes since the 1950's in the importance of party identification are given in Burnham (1970), Ladd and Hadley (1978), Nie, Verba, and Petrocik (1976), and Pomper (1975). The use of party identification outside of the United States is severely attacked in *Party Identification and Beyond* (Budge, Crewe, and Farlie, 1976). The most important responses by the Michigan researchers are Miller (1976) and Converse (1975a, 1976). Additionally, measurement problems have been central in papers by Petrocik (1974), Brody (1977), Keith *et al.* (1977), Miller and Miller (1977), Shively (1977), Van Wingen and Valentine (1979) and Katz (1979), which will be referred to later in this chapter.

3. The data have been made available by the Inter-university Consortium for Political and Social Research, which bears no responsibility for the analysis and interpretation presented here.

4. The P^2 model is closely related to Van Wingen and Valentine (1979), whose work first led me to question the dimensional basis of partisanship. A P^2 display format is also used in Nie, Verba, and Petrocik (1976, p. 216ff). Katz (1979) develops a different two dimensional interpretation of party identification, with a strength dimension orthogonal to P^1.

5. This approach is related to the work of Randall Guynes and Jerry Perkins and of Corwin Smidt, but its development here is more so based on generalizing the P^2 approach of John Van Wingen and David Valentine on the basis of my memorandum for the Conference on Party Identification sponsored by the National Election Studies in Tallahassee, Florida on February 23-24, 1978.

6. The party thermometers have been analyzed from a different framework in Maggiotto and Piereson (1977).

7. The stimuli were changed in 1980 to provide less ambiguous referents. The 1979 research and development pilot study conducted by the National Election Studies tried both the group (Republicans) and party (Republican party) versions, and no systematic differences could be found in the responses to the different stimuli. This seems to be a situation where an intellectual case can be built for expecting response differences, but the stimuli differences are too small to affect the mass public.

8. Congressional vote is monotone with party identification, even though presidential vote is not. In any event, party identification is not monotone with one of the most important dependent variables in voting research.

9. An alternative explanation of the better fit for the party difference is that it may measure a more short-term attitude than does the party identification question, as shown by its lower stability in the 1974-76 panel study, an overtime correlation of .61 compared to .83 for the standard party identification scale. This alternative explanation deserves further attention as later work explores measures of party identifications more thoroughly.

10. The Center for Political Studies convention of coding respondents without a party preference as pure Independents further complicates this relationship.

PART VI: HISTORICAL PERSPECTIVES

28. HISTORICAL CHANGES IN VOTING BEHAVIOR

Party politics is always in flux. One party does better in a given election than it did in the last, while another loses some support. Some social groups support a party a bit more than they did at the last election, others a bit less. The issues on which a party ran previously are resolved or forgotten and new ones arise to take their place. But most of this change is minor and temporary, just part of the inevitable ebb and flow of politics. Sometimes, however, the change is larger and more permanent, demarcating new eras of political history. Understanding these critical changes is important; it is impossible to remember or record, much less to interpret, everything that occurs, even if we limit ourselves to events related to voting behavior. Some categorization is essential.

The importance of understanding the past, of course, is more than just a matter of reconstructing history. Understanding patterns of historical change helps us interpret contemporary political trends and decide whether current partisan change is highly transitory or relatively permanent. In this chapter, we review the debates over interpretation of electoral trends from the early days of the United States through the 1930s with some attention as well to the way in which elections were conducted and to citizen participation and political thinking (especially regarding strength of partisanship). Studying historical trends is fascinating and insightful in its own right, but it also provides the concepts and context necessary to understand the debates over the nature of partisan change since the 1930s (Niemi and Weisberg, 1992, Chap. 19).

Controversy over changes in parties and elections concerns both the extent of change—which ones were most meaningful—and the causes of those changes. Disagreements about contemporary developments are often intense, as we have seen throughout this volume. No less controversial, however, are changes earlier in our history. As we learned about voting behavior from contemporary survey research, researchers began to wonder whether the same patterns of opinions and behavior characterized the voters in earlier electoral periods. For example, was turnout higher or lower? Was the electorate more or less informed than at present? Was partisanship in the nineteenth century stronger than at present?

At times the disagreements are especially vexing because of the paucity of relevant data, though some analysts have been quite inventive in their use of historical material.

The Realignment Concept

How does electoral change occur? Initially, scholars simply assumed that each time control of the presidency changed from one party to another there had been a meaningful change in American partisan politics. It became apparent, however, that this approach overemphasized minor shifts that lacked historical significance while not giving sufficient emphasis to those changes that had lasting effects. The historian Arthur Schlesinger (1939) sought to remedy this by proposing a cyclical theory in which there was a shift from the liberal direction to the conservative side or back again every sixteen years. Yet even the sixteen-year change was on the short-term side, and Schlesinger's theory did not relate such change to the behavior of the electorate.

In 1955 V. O. Key introduced the notion of a realigning election. While the term has taken on a number of meanings, it seems always to include the notion of durable partisan change, such as the realignment of strength between Republicans and Democrats during the 1930s or the replacement of one major party by another in the late 1850s. When political scientists studying individual-level survey data began to regard partisanship as stable both across and within generations, they also accepted the notion of party realignments to account for the significant aggregate changes that occur once every generation or so.[1]

As it turns out, it is difficult to define realignments objectively, so political historians who have applied the concept to American electoral history often disagree about precisely when realignments have occurred. There is most agreement that realignments occurred around the elections of 1828, 1860, 1896, and 1932. When that was first noticed in the 1960s, the periodicity in these dates was observed, and a further realignment was anticipated in the mid-1960s. We shall not discuss the post-1932 period here, but the regularity of previous realignments remains of interest.

An intriguing question is how this periodicity arises—indeed, why there should be any regularity at all to the tempo of major electoral changes. An ingenious answer is provided by Beck, in an article reprinted in Chapter 31. This paper helps tie together the matter of issues, stability and change in individual partisanship, and the role of long-term components in electoral behavior. The argument revolves around the way in which people learn about political conflicts and the length of time that it takes for a new generation (which does not think of politics in the same way as those who lived through an earlier realigning era) to come of age. Although the specific details concerning generational lengths are imprecise, the concept is seminal because it suggests new ways to tie together notions of political socialization and realignment.

Beck also describes how politics changes as the years pass since the last realignment. His theory implies a movement away from parties in the later stages of a realignment cycle. This movement away from parties has since been denoted as "dealignment" and occurs when large numbers of people become independents and when large numbers of partisans begin to split their tickets between the two parties. Thus the decline of partisanship that Nie, Verba, and Petrocik discussed in Chapter 23 can be viewed as evidence in favor of dealignment. A new realignment could then occur, but only if some major issue came about which ignited partisan change. The debate as to whether realignment or dealignment occurred in the 1960s and since will be described in *Controversies in Voting Behavior.*

Despite the widespread sense of some periodicity in partisan change and Beck's innovative explanation of an electoral connection, a great deal of recent controversy has centered around the realignment concept. Is it a useful way of viewing American electoral history? The answer depends in part on how one defines realignment. If one thinks of realignment exclusively as a shift from an electoral majority for one party to an electoral majority for the other of two continuing parties, it is indeed a narrow concept and fits only a few historical moments. But other definitions are possible, and in *Controversies* we devote considerable attention to the question of what constitutes a realignment—or, adopting a broader term, what constitutes a critical election. We shall do so primarily by focussing on interpretations of post-New Deal changes, especially those of the 1960s and beyond.

Focussing only on earlier years, however, leaves considerable room for disagreement. First, there is controversy over whether there was a realignment in the 1820s (or possibly the 1830s). Second, there is controversy over the nature and long-term implications of the realignment of the 1890s. Third, there is controversy over the causes of the realignment of the 1930s, along with some disagreement over its timing. We shall take up each of these controversies in turn.

The Early Period: Prealignment or Realignment?

On the broad outlines of early party history there is considerable agreement. Parties formed on a national basis in the 1790s, especially with competition between the Federalist and Democratic-Republican parties over the presidential elections of 1796 and 1800. Development was uneven across the states, particularly in states newly admitted to the Union. It was initiated by factional conflict in the national administration and then in Congress, and while electoral conflict soon developed, there was no mass participation of the variety seen later in the nineteenth century. After 1815 the Federalist party was considerably weakened— "by 1824 the remnants of the first party system possessed some vitality in only five states" (McCormack, 1967, p. 94). Conflict was renewed with the election of Andrew Jackson in 1828; there were clear sectional differences in the vote, and participation soared, climbing to about 55 percent of the eligible electorate. Party development was uneven and somewhat episodic, but it became widespread by the mid-1830s with competition between the Whig party and the Democrats (the successor party to the Democratic-Republicans). Participation again rose substantially, to about 80 percent in 1840.

How to characterize this development is more problematic. For a generation of scholars in both political science and history, it has been customary to call the period from 1792 to about 1824 the first party system and that from 1828 to about 1860 the second party system (see, for example, Chambers and Burnham, 1967; Kleppner, 1979). As with later periods, there is ambiguity about the endpoints. Did the first system, for example, end as early as 1815? Others, however, have taken issue with the characterization of the earliest period as a party system (Formisano, 1981; Silbey, 1991),[2] and Silbey (1991) characterizes the entire period prior to 1838 as the "prealignment" era.

There is much more agreement that a realignment occurred in the 1850s with the demise of the Whig party and its replacement by the Republican party and with the shift from intersectional rivalry to regionally based parties. Political scientists have paid scant attention to this period, though historians have written extensively on party development in the 1850s (see, for example, Kleppner, 1979; Gienapp, 1987). There is, not surprisingly, some disagreement about the exact timing of the realignment (see pp. 337-38).

In part the question of prealignment versus alignment/realignment in the first half of the nineteenth century hinges on definitional matters, as noted above. Certainly, what happened in the 1820s was not identical to what occurred in the 1850s. And in neither of these periods was the change simply a matter of which of two existing parties commanded a majority. In any event, general agreement exists that the parties and their electoral connections underwent major changes sometime in the late 1820s and the 1830s and again in the late 1850s. Future work with the realignment concept as well as further analyses of the period— especially if more extensive analyses of the electorate are possible—may help resolve questions of timing and nomenclature.

The 1890s: Electoral or Institutional Change?

The current competition between the Republican and Democratic parties dates back to the 1850s, but political historians largely agree that a party realignment occurred in the 1890s. The balanced party competition from the 1860s to 1892 was replaced with Republican dominance from 1896 to 1932. The economy turned sour after Democrat Grover Cleveland's inauguration in 1893, and public support for the Democratic party fell sharply. The South had become Democratic after the Civil War (which southerners blamed on Lincoln's Republicans), and William Jennings Bryan's populist appeals on behalf of the Democrats in 1896 put northern cities firmly into the Republican camp. The result was an era of Republican dominance in presidential elections that was broken only when the party split in 1912. Yet these partisan changes were only part of the massive political changes taking place in those years.

As we saw in Chapter 4, contemporary survey studies have highlighted the inattentiveness to politics of large numbers of citizens. In contrast, if we are to believe historical accounts, politics was very different a century ago. How did politics differ in the nineteenth century, and when and why did things change? This was the question raised in 1965 by Burnham's seminal article, "The Changing Shape of the American Political Universe." In this article, a portion of which is reprinted here as Chapter 29, Burnham noted the intensity of partisanship in the last century and described 1896 as a watershed year in which there began a decline of party that has continued right up to the present time. Among other things, Burnham reported that after 1896 there was a decline in voting turnout, an increase in split-ticket voting, much less voting in off years than during presidential elections ("drop-off"), a tendency to vote only for the highest offices on the ballot ("roll-off"), and greater partisan vote swing between elections.

Aside from the question of what behavioral changes have occurred is the interpretation of change. Burnham saw the decline of competition between the parties, as well as other changes, such as in Supreme Court rulings, as a lessening of the alternatives open to voters. The leaders of the industrial revolution, in effect, stole the electoral system away from the people without doing away with the procedures and traditions of a democratic system. This capture of the electoral system by the elite led to the beginning of the decline of the party system. With the importance of their decisions greatly reduced, voters gradually became alienated and came to regard their participation as relatively meaningless. Party loyalties similarly became weaker.[3] Burnham saw these changes as progressing throughout the twentieth century, leading eventually to "the end of parties" in the current era, a point we shall discuss further in *Controversies*.

Alternative interpretations have also been made. Jensen (1971) and Kleppner (1970, 1979) emphasize the role of religious, cultural, and ethnic variables in the latter part of the nineteenth century. Jensen in particular attributes the changes in the 1890s to William McKinley, suggesting that McKinley brought an end to the religious battles of the previous years and introduced a politics of pluralism in which a broad coalition of interests could all benefit by working together to achieve electoral success. Importantly, as Rusk (1974, p. 1038) points out, Jensen "sees the consequences of the 1896 election as good, not bad," with McKinley "dampening and eventually stopping the religious wars by ousting them from the party and starting a new pluralist politics in which groups learn to bargain, compromise and get along with one another." [4]

In general, the view we have of nineteenth century politics is one of intense political and strongly partisan conflict. One might cite a great deal of statistical and other evidence in addition to the high turnout (McGerr, 1986). Jensen (1968; see also 1980), for example, provides a delightful account. Newspaper statistics are so numerous that it is difficult to know which figures to select, but that "329 cities in 1880 (roughly speaking all those above 7,000 population) possessed five or more newspapers" conveys the right impression (p. 6). In regard to political discussions, Jensen (p. 17) cites the 1892 election in Indiana, in which "the two parties held 5,000 schoolhouse meetings in the last week of the campaign alone." As something of a surprise, he notes that "by 1880 statewide polls [though not of the modern kind] were common, and critical battlefields were surveyed two and three times during a campaign. Less specifically, but equally powerfully, Gienapp (1982) notes that "politics seems to enter into everything."

This view of the nineteenth century electorate and of the changes in the

1890s has not gone unchallenged. There are at least two sources of disagreement. First, some would argue over the magnitude of change, questioning claims about the nature of the nineteenth century electorate. Second, some would argue that the important changes had to do with the nature of election and voting procedures, and that changes to parties were secondary.

Taken at face value, the figures cited by Burnham make it incontrovertible that a major decline in turnout occurred at the end of the nineteenth century. However, the reliability of those turnout figures is not an easy matter to establish. As Converse (1972) has pointed out, the absence of personal registration systems and the party-printed unofficial ballots opened the way to a variety of forms of fraud, including "repeating votes" and "voting the graveyard." That such fraud existed is not in question, but whether it seriously inflated turnout records is another matter.

By its nature, a corruption explanation is difficult to evaluate. Corrupt practitioners are hardly likely to leave a clearly traceable record, and one must be very careful in interpreting verbal, even if contemporary, descriptions of the phenomenon.[5] Thus, there is always room for some doubt, but most historians who have examined the question thoroughly are convinced that fraud is unlikely to explain the very high turnout in the nineteenth century, and that the elimination of that fraud is unlikely to explain the sharp declines after 1896.[6]

Perhaps even more controversial than questions about the extent of change in the post-1896 electorate are the explanations for that change. In addition to changes in electoral alignments and partisan strength, the 1890s and early 1900s saw major changes in the mechanics of conducting elections. In particular, the official and secret ("Australian") ballot was widely introduced about that time, as were personal registration systems. Converse and Rusk argue that the trends that Burnham reported were due to such election reforms instead of being due to actions by the economic elite, or to a "decline of party." They attempt to prove their point by analyses of the timing and apparent effects of election reforms. The full set of analyses is found in a number of sources, but we have reprinted as Chapter 30 a portion of Rusk's paper on the Australian ballot reform as their most systematic analysis relating to this problem. Rusk attempts to show that the changes in ballot form made split-ticket voting feasible for the first time. During the prior period, political parties distributed their own ballots, so that it was all but impossible to split a ticket. Thus, the new ballot form led directly to an increase in the incidence of split-ticket voting, more or less depending on the exact type of ballot.

An analysis by Converse (1972) focuses on Burnham's other three indicators, particularly turnout. He argues that registration systems, which were most frequently introduced between 1890 and 1910, might explain the drop in turnout, not only by a significant reduction in the amount of fraud, but by the lack of voting of those who failed to register but who would have voted otherwise (and did vote before personal registration was required). Although more difficult to show, Converse argues that the increase in drop-off and even in partisan swings might also be accounted for by a reduction in fraud and by the imposition of registration. In addition, Converse investigates the initiators of the reforms and suggests that there was certainly no conscious manipulation of electoral reforms by a corporate elite trying to insulate itself from the mass population.[7]

A related element of the debate over decreased turnout involves the "expanding electorate" theory—the view that enfranchising a new group depresses overall turnout since many members of that new group (particularly older members who grew up in an era in which voting was not their business) will not vote immediately. This theory would explain the decline in turnout around 1920 by the implementation of women's suffrage. An analysis by Rusk and Stucker (1978) suggests that there was an immediate 10 percent decline in turnout associated with that reform. However, Kleppner concludes that "neither female enfranchisement by itself, nor even in additive combination with a continuation of the pre-1920 secular trend, adequately explains the observed turnout levels of the 1920s" (1982, p. 642), and that the decrease was due instead to the fact that "politics generally lacked its earlier intensity and strong voter stimulus" (1982, p. 643).

The debate over the 1890s realignment involves historical and institutional analysis, two areas which are too rarely explored in political science (though institutional analysis has become more common, as noted in *Controversies,* Chapter 13). To Converse and Rusk, changes in voting statistics need further interpretation only if they cannot be explained in terms of changes in the legal and institutional circumstances. Yet, for Burnham, the legal and institutional changes themselves have causes, and he argues that the changes were brought about by a capitalist elite that adopted reforms such as registration systems to weaken the opposition and capture control of the government. This same argument has been seen more recently in Piven and Cloward's (1988) *Why Americans Don't Vote.* It is an argument over historical causes of reforms, the extent of voting fraud in earlier periods of history, the value of legal and institutional explanations of political change, and the extent to which such change helps explain the current trends. It is a dispute over the condition of the American electorate—whether it is deteriorating or improving and how it arrived at its present state.

The 1930s: Mobilization or Conversion?

If the realignment concept is at all meaningful, it is applicable to the 1930s. Republican domination, which had been established in the 1890s, was broken by the successive elections of Franklin Delano Roosevelt and by the election of Democratic majorities in Congress. What is at issue with respect to the 1930s is not whether a realignment occurred, but the nature of the change processes during this period. The lack of agreement stems in part from the fact that the 1930s realignment took place before the advent of widespread, high-quality survey data.

The traditional assumption had been that the New Deal realignment was caused by large-scale movement of voters from the Republican party to the Democratic party. Andersen (1979) initiated the controversy with her reconstruction of New Deal partisanship based on 1950s survey reports about whether and when respondents changed their party support. She found little evidence of wholesale conversion from Republican to Democratic identification in the 1930s. She showed instead that large numbers of new voters were mobilized into the Democratic party at that time—both young, first-time voters and immigrants who had not previously voted (see also Chapter 31, pages 333-35). Andersen's argument is intriguing, as it suggests that for a large-scale realignment to take place, a large pool of nonmobilized citizens is required.

However, Andersen's evidence is not definitive. For one thing, respondents' recall of partisan change is known to be unreliable, even when they are reporting party change during the brief period of a panel study (Niemi, Katz, and Newman, 1980). Thus, it is interesting that Erikson and Tedin (1981) found that the *Literary Digest* polls taken in 1928 and the 1930s (which have reliability problems of their own) do not indicate that new voters were distinctively Democratic but instead give evidence of considerable partisan conversion in the established electorate.[8]

A recent analysis by Gamm (1989) suggests that both types of change occurred, but to varying degrees across different ethnic and other groups. Based on an intensive analysis of precinct data in Boston neighborhoods, Gamm found, for example, that Italian immigrants were extensively mobilized by the New Deal; there was little partisan change because those who had voted previously were heavily Democratic in the 1920s. Jews, on the other hand, changed their allegiance from the Republican to the Democratic party, though they were also more heavily mobilized during the 1930s. Jewish men were more often converted, women more often mobilized. Interestingly, Gamm is also able to show that large-scale changes in voting behavior occurred before big changes in registration, as we had expected but not been able to demonstrate heretofore.

Gamm's analysis also speaks to another, less heated debate about the Depression realignment. Key's (1955) discussion suggested that in some areas the realignment might best be dated as beginning in the 1928 election. With data on both registration and voting, Gamm is able to provide considerably greater insight into this matter. He argues that Bostonians were deeply affected by Al Smith and that in the 1928 election "a stunning number of those who were registered to vote that year actually cast ballots for president" (p. 189). At the same time, "only in the 1930s did registration data begin to more generally reflect the development of a new Democratic coalition" (p. 189). Nevertheless, the timing of the Depression realignment may have varied somewhat in different states, which serves to remind us that even national level political trends may play through differently in different regions and states.

When contemporary political scientists look to see whether a new realignment has occurred, they seem to use the 1930s realignment as their standard. The 1930s saw as sharp a realignment as could be obtained without the demise of one of the major parties, as had happened in the 1820s and 1850s. The 1930s also saw a shift from a distinctly Republican majority to a distinctly Democratic majority, whereas the 1890s realignment shifted merely from balanced political competition to Republican dominance. Thus, as Carmines, Renten and Stimson, (1984, p. 559) noted, the 1930s realignment might be atypical of future realignments, just as much as World War II proved to be atypical of later wars. Thus it is to be expected that there has been disagreement about the nature of electoral change since the 1930s and specifically about whether a later realignment has occurred or there has just been extended dealignment.

Conclusion

If studies of contemporary events yield the controversies discussed in the other sections of this book, it is perhaps not surprising that historical interpretations are also controversial. Nonetheless, an explanation of our political present requires an understanding of the political past, and predictions of the future must be based on an analysis of the events that led to the present. Such analysis must be not only historical, but also both institutional (as when Rusk investigates the effects of various reforms) and, ultimately, comparative.

What makes this sort of study so intriguing is that one cannot automatically assume that patterns of thought and events found in contemporary America necessarily occur either in other periods in our own history or in other countries. We hope to find consistent patterns, but the fact that a relationship exists at one time for one country does not mean it is universal.

Modern voting studies for the United States have developed a complex theory, one that has implications for earlier periods in history as well as for other countries. But the analysis of voting behavior cannot be limited either in time or in space if we are to achieve a broad-level theory. The historical analyses in this section begin to open up the time parameter. Simultaneously, scholars have been studying voting behavior in numerous other countries in order to determine the spatial limitations of our understanding of voting. Historians and comparative scholars are now using quantitative voting analysis to understand voting behavior at other points in time and space. This interest and their insights should pay off eventually in terms of a greater understanding of our own present. We cannot yet foresee the likely conclusions, though we are willing to place one bet with assurance—that controversies will remain, at least so long as elections are conducted.

NOTES

1. Realignments are usually seen as issue-based, with the realignment establishing the issues over which political competition occurs for the following decades. Sundquist (1983) gives an excellent account of ways in which the introduction of new, polarizing issues might bring about realignments.
2. Even Kleppner (1981, p. 13) says that "it is meaningful to speak of the period through the mid-1820s as an 'electoral era' only in a restricted sense of that term." Historians point out that until the Jacksonian era, political parties were largely elite organizations. Mass political parties were developed only in the 1820s and 1830s. See Silbey (1991) and sources cited therein.

3. See also McGerr (1986): "Northern leaders never joined the Southern upper class in disfranchising the poor by violence, intimidation, and legislation. . . . But the decay of political participation was not simply the accidental product of impersonal social forces undirected by human agency. The same class predicament that led the reformers to explore suffrage restriction brought them to attack partisanship and its supporting institutions. . . . Partisanship lay at the heart of popular politics; the weakening of the one undermined the other" (p. 209).

4. The story of the 1893-1894 Depression and of the 1896 election between McKinley and William Jennings Bryan, as well as an overview of geographical and other patterns of electoral change, are nicely told by Kleppner (1987).

5. Kleppner (1987, p. 169), for example, points out that turn-of-the-century reformers used the word "corruption" to mean what we might simply refer to as uninformed voting.

6. Of course, one can also argue that turnout figures are inflated owing to a variety of difficulties in estimating both the numbers voting and the numbers eligible to vote using nineteenth-century material. See the critical analysis by Ginsburg (1986) and the stinging rebuttal by Burnham (1986).

7. Burnham later accepted the suggestion that institutional factors did apparently play some role in the changes he observed, but he (1970, p. 90) argued that "the systemic factors at work during these periods were far broader in their scope and far heavier in their impact than any single change in the rules of the game or, in all probability, of all such things put together."

8. The story of the *Literary Digest* polls is widely cited as the example par excellence of the unreliability of nonscientific survey sampling. The poll correctly predicted the election results of 1924-1932. However, in 1936, when Gallup correctly forecast a Roosevelt victory on the basis of a small, randomly chosen sample, *Literary Digest* predicted a large win for Kansas governor Alf Landon on the basis of millions of nonrandomly selected respondents. One analysis of some of the sources of bias in the Literary Digest polls is found in Squire (1988). See also Cahalan (1989).

FURTHER READINGS

Historical Periods and Their Interpretations

Walter Dean Burnham, *Critical Elections and the Mainsprings of American Politics* (New York: Norton, 1970). Burnham's full analysis of historical trends in voting. The end of parties?

William N. Chambers and Walter D. Burnham, eds., *The American Party Systems* (New York: Oxford University Press, 1967, 1975). Review of party systems through U.S. history.

Jerome Clubb, William H. Flanigan, and Nancy H. Zingale, *Partisan Realignment* (Beverly Hills, Calif.: Sage, 1980). Empirical analysis of realignments in American history.

Philip E. Converse, "Information Flow and the Stability of Partisan Attitudes," *Public Opinion Quarterly* (1962) 26:578-99. Discusses the implications of absence of national media in nineteenth-century America.

V. O. Key, Jr., "A Theory of Critical Elections," *Journal of Politics* (1955) 17:3-18. Classic theoretical statement of realigning elections.

Paul Kleppner et al., *The Evolution of American Electoral Systems* (Westport, Conn.: Greenwood Press, 1981). Historical review of conflicts in American party systems.

Byron E. Shafer, *The End of Realignment? Interpreting American Electoral Eras* (Madison: University of Wisconsin Press, 1991). Essays pro and con on the utility of the realignment concept for studying both early and contemporary party history.

James Sundquist, *Dynamics of the Party System: Alignment and Realignment of Political Parties in the United States* (Washington, D.C.: Brookings, 1973, 1983). Historical and theoretical perspective on U.S. realignments.

The Late Nineteenth Century and the 1890s Realignment

Walter Dean Burnham, "Theory and Voting Research: Some Reflections on Converse's 'Change in the American Electorate,'" *American Political Science Review* (1974) 68:1000-23. Institutional ballot changes are not enough to explain the voting shifts Burnham discovered.

———, "Change in the American Electorate." In *The Human Meaning of Social Change,* ed. Angus Campbell and Philip E. Converse (New York: Russell Sage, 1972). Registration systems and vote fraud and their implications for nineteenth century turnout and voting.

Richard J. Jensen, *The Winning of the Midwest: Social and Political Conflict, 1888-1896* (Chicago: University of Chicago Press, 1971). Religious-ethnic bases of Midwest politics.

Paul Kleppner, *Continuity and Change in Electoral Politics: 1893-1928* (New York: Greenwood Press, 1987). Changes in voting patterns and in party politics during the 1890s realignment and subsequent period.

Paul Kleppner and Stephen C. Baker, "The Impact of Voter Registration Requirements on Electoral Turnout, 1900-16," *Journal of Political and Military Sociology* (1980) 8:205-26. Decline of turnout in late nineteenth and early twentieth centuries not exclusively due to changes in registration requirements or voter fraud.

J. Morgan Kousser, *The Shaping of Southern Politics* (New Haven, Conn.: Yale University Press, 1974). Effects of suffrage restriction on one-party dominance in the South.

Michael E. McGerr, *The Decline of Popular Politics: The American North, 1865-1928* (New York: Oxford University Press, 1986). A delightful, nonstatistical account of changes in political participation between the nineteenth and twentieth centuries.

Jerrold G. Rusk, "The American Electoral Universe: Speculation and Evidence," *American Political Science Review* (1974) 68:1028-49. Summary of the controversy Burnham initiated; new data on historical trends in the South and on women's suffrage.

The 1930s Realignment

Kristi Andersen, *The Creation of a Democratic Majority, 1928-1936* (Chicago: University of Chicago Press, 1979). Reconstruction of the dynamics of the New Deal realignment, emphasizing mobilization.

Robert S. Erikson and Kent L. Tedin, "The 1928-1936 Partisan Realignment: The Case for the Conversion Hypothesis," *American Political Science Review* (1981) 75:951-62. New Deal realignment is due to wide-scale conversion (opposite of Andersen's argument).

Gerald H. Gamm, *The Making of New Deal Democrats* (Chicago: University of Chicago Press, 1989). Detailed analysis of voting and registration in ethnically homogeneous precincts of New Deal era Boston.

29. THE CHANGING SHAPE OF THE AMERICAN POLITICAL UNIVERSE

Walter Dean Burnham

. . . The primary objective here is the preliminary exploration of the scope of changes since the mid-nineteenth century in turnout and other criteria of voting participation, and the possible substantive implications of such changes.

There is also a second objective. . . . [It is] a matter of some importance to ascertain whether and to what extent the basic findings of survey research about the present American electorate are actually relevant to earlier periods of our political history. . . .

I

Several criteria of voting participation have been employed in this analysis: (1) estimated turnout; (2) drop-off; (3) roll-off; (4) split-ticket voting; (5) mean partisan swing. Turnout, the most indispensable of these criteria, is also unfortunately the "softest." A number of errors of estimate can arise from the necessary use of census data. For example, interpolations of estimates for intercensal years can produce significant error when abnormally large increases or decreases in population are bunched together within a few years. Estimates of the alien component in the total adult male population must also necessarily remain quite speculative for the censuses from 1880 through 1900, and are impossible to secure from published census data prior to 1870. No doubt this helps explain why students of voting-behavior research have avoided this area. But we need not reject these admittedly imprecise data altogether, because of their imperfections, when secular changes in turnout levels and variabilities from election to election are of far too great a magnitude to be reasonably discounted on the basis of estimate error.[1]

Moreover, the other criteria employed in this study not only share a very similar directional flow over time, but are directly derived from the voting statistics themselves. Free from the estimate-error problem, they are ordinarily

Source: *American Political Science Review*, 59 (1965):7-28. Reprinted with permission of the publisher.

quite consistent with the turnout data.[2] What is called "drop-off" here is the familiar pattern of decline in the total vote between presidential and succeeding off-year elections. The drop-off figures usually presented below are reciprocals of the percentage of the presidential-year total vote which is cast in the immediately following off-year election. If the total vote for the two successive elections is the same, drop-off is zero; if the total vote in the off-year election exceeds that cast in the immediately preceding presidential election, drop-off is negative. Secular increases in the amplitude of drop-off could be associated with such factors as a declining relative visibility or salience of off-year elections, or with an increasing component of active voters who are only marginally involved with the voting process as such.

"Roll-off" measures the tendency of the electorate to vote for "prestige" offices but not for lower offices on the same ballot and at the same election. If only 90 percent of those voting for the top office on the ticket also vote for the lesser statewide office receiving fewest votes at the same election, for example, the roll-off figure stands at 10 percent. Secular increases in this criterion of voting participation could be associated with such variables as a growing public indifference to elections for administrative offices which might well be made appointive, or with a growing proportion of peripheral voters in the active electorate; or with changes in the form of ballots. Split-ticket voting has been measured rather crudely here as the difference between the highest and lowest percentages of the two-party vote cast for either party among the array of statewide offices in any given election. Zero on this scale would correspond to absolute uniformity in the partisan division of the vote for all offices at the same election. The amplitude of partisan swing is computed in this study without reference to the specific partisan direction of the swing, and is derived from the mean percentage of the two-party vote cast for either party among all statewide races in the same election. Both of these latter criteria are more directly related to changes in the strength of partisan linkage between voters and government than are the others employed in this study.

Two major assumptions underlie the use of these criteria. (1) If a secular decline in turnout occurs, and especially if it is associated with increases in drop-off and roll-off, we may infer that the active voting universe: (a) is shrinking in size relative to the potential voting universe; and (b) is also decomposing as a relative increase in its component of peripherally involved voters occurs. Opposite implications, of course, would be drawn from increases in turnout accompanied by decreases in these rough indices of voter peripherality. (2) If split-ticket voting and the amplitude of partisan swings are also increasing over time, we may infer that a decline in party-oriented voting is taking place among a growing minority of voters. Reductions in these criteria would suggest a resurgence of party-oriented voting.

A recent study by Angus Campbell (1960) tends to support the view that the above criteria are actually related to the component of marginal voters and voters with relatively weak partisan attachments in today's active electorate. Campbell argues that surge and decline in voting participation and in partisan distribution of the vote result from two major factors: the entrance into the active electorate of peripherally involved voters who tend to vote disproportionately for such beneficiaries of partisan surges as President Eisenhower, and then abstain from the polls in subsequent low-stimulus elections; and the temporary movement of core voters with relatively low levels of party identification away from their nominal party allegiance, followed by their return to that allegiance in subsequent low-stimulus elections. Campbell's study reveals that split-ticket voting in the 1956 election tended to be heavily concentrated among two groups of voters: those who voted Republican for President in 1956 and did not vote in 1958, and those who voted Republican in 1956 but Democratic in 1958—in other words, among those with peripheral involvement in the political process itself and those with borderline partisan commitments. Moreover, roll-off—the failure to vote a complete ticket in 1956—was heavily concentrated among the non-voters of 1958. It is also suggestive that the level of drop-off in Campbell's panel from 1956 to 1958, 23 percent, very closely approximates the level of drop-off as measured by the aggregate voting data (25.6 percent).

II

Even the crudest form of statistical analysis makes it abundantly clear that the changes which have occurred in the relative size and shape of the active electorate in this country have not only been quantitatively enormous but have followed a directional course which seems to be unique in the contemporary universe of democratic polities. In the United States these transformations over the past century have involved devolution, a dissociation from politics as such among a growing segment of the eligible electorate and an apparent deterioration of the bonds of party linkage between electorate and government. More precisely, these trends were overwhelmingly prominent between about 1900 and 1930, were only very moderately reversed following the political realignment of 1928-1936, and now seem to be increasing once again along several dimensions of analysis. Such a pattern of development is pronouncedly retrograde compared with those which have obtained almost everywhere else in the Western world during the past century.

Probably the best-known aspect of the changing American political universe has been the long-term trend in national voter turnout: a steep decline from 1900 to about 1930, followed by a moderate resurgence since that time. As the figures in Table 29-1 indicate, nationwide turnout down through 1900 was quite high by contemporary standards—comparing favorably in presidential years with recent levels of participation in Western Europe—and was also marked by very low levels of drop-off. A good deal of the precipitate decline in turnout after 1896 can, of course, be attributed to the disfranchisement of Negroes in the South and the consolidation of its one-party regime. But as Table 29-2 reveals, non-Southern states not only shared this decline but also have current turnout rates which remain substantially below nineteenth-century levels.

The persistence of mediocre rates of American voting turnout into the present political era is scarcely news. It forms so obvious and continuing a problem of our democracy that a special presidential commission has recently

Table 29-1   Decline and Partial Resurgence: Mean Levels of National
Turnout and Drop-Off by Periods, 1948-1962[a]

Period (Presidential Years)	Mean Estimated Turnout (%)	Period (Off-Years)	Mean Estimated Turnout (%)	Drop-Off (%)
1848-1872	75.1	1850-1874	65.2	7.0
1876-1896	78.5	1878-1898	62.8	15.2
1900-1916	64.8	1902-1918	47.9	22.4
1920-1928	51.7	1922-1930	35.2	28.7
1932-1944	59.1	1934-1946	41.0	27.8
1948-1960	60.3	1950-1962	44.1	24.9

[a] Off-year turnout data based on total vote for congressional candidates in off years.

given it intensive study. Two additional aspects of the problem, however, emerge from a perusal of the foregoing data. In the first place, it is quite apparent that the political realignment of the 1930's, while it restored two-party competition to many states outside the South, did not stimulate turnout to return in most areas to nineteenth-century levels. Even if the mere existence of competitiveness precludes such low levels of turnout as are found in the South today, or as once prevailed in the Northern industrial states, it falls far short of compelling a substantially full turnout under present-day conditions. Second, drop-off on the national level has shown markedly little tendency to recede in the face of increases in presidential-year turnout over the last thirty years. The component of peripheral voters in the active electorate has apparently undergone a permanent expansion from about one-sixth in the late nineteenth century to more than one-quarter in recent decades. If, as seems more than likely, the political regime established after 1896 was largely responsible for the marked relative decline in the active voting universe and the marked increase in peripherality among those who still occasionally voted, it is all the more remarkable that the dramatic political realignment of the 1930's has had such little effect in reversing these trends.

At least two major features of our contemporary polity, to be sure, are obviously related to the presently apparent ceiling on turnout. First, the American electoral system creates a major "double hurdle" for prospective voters which does not exist in Western Europe: the requirements associated with residence and registration. . . . Yet there are certain areas—such as all of Ohio outside the metropolitan counties and cities of at least 15,000 population—where no registration procedures have ever been established, but where no significant deviation from the patterns outlined here appears to exist. Finally, while it may well be true that the partial displacement by TV and other means of entertainment has inhibited expansion of the active voting universe during the past generation, it is equally true that the structure of the American voting universe—i.e., the adult population—as it exists today was substantially formed in the

Table 29-2   Sectionalism and Participation: Mean Turnout in Southern
and Non-Southern States in Presidential Elections, 1868-1960

Period	Mean Turnout: Eleven Southern States (%)	Period	Mean Turnout: Non-Southern States (%)
1868-1880	69.4	1868-1880	82.6
1884-1896	61.1	1984-1896	85.4
1900 (transition)	43.4	1900	84.1
1904-1916	29.8	1904-1916	73.6
1920-1948	24.7	1920-1932	60.6
1952-1960	38.8	1936-1960	68.0

period 1900-1920, *prior* to the development of such major media as the movies, radio and television. . . .

III

[In this section, Burnham discusses voting patterns in five states. We include the highlights of his analysis.] A decisive shift away from the stable and substantially fully mobilized voting patterns of the nineteenth century occurred in Michigan after the realignment of 1896, with a lag of about a decade between that election and the onset of disruption in those patterns (Table 29-3). . . .

The Michigan data have still more suggestive implications. Campbell's discussion of surge and decline in the modern context points to a cyclical process in which peripheral voters, drawn into the active voting universe only under unusual short-term stimuli, withdraw from it again when the stimuli are removed. It follows that declines in turnout are accompanied by a marked relative increase in the component of core voters in the electorate and by a closer approximation in off years to a "normal" partisan division of the vote (Campbell, 1960, pp. 401-4). This presumably includes a reduction in the level of split-ticket voting as well. But the precise opposite occurred as a secular process—not only in Michigan but, it would seem, universally—during the 1900-1930 era. Declines in turnout were accompanied by substantial, continuous increases in the indices of party and voter peripherality among those elements of the adult population which remained in the political universe at all. The lower the turnout during this period, the fewer of the voters still remaining who bothered to vote for the entire slate of officers in any given election. The lower the turnout in presidential years, the greater was the drop-off gap between the total vote cast in presidential and succeeding off-year elections. The lower the turnout, the greater were the incidence of split-ticket voting and the amplitude of partisan swing. Under the enormous impact of the forces which produced these declines in turnout and party competitiveness after 1896, the component of highly involved and party-oriented core voters in the active electorate fell off at a rate which more than kept pace

Table 29-3 Michigan, 1854-1962: Decay and Resurgence? (Percentages)

| Period | Mean Turnout | | Mean Drop-Off | Mean Roll-Off | Mean Split-Ticket Voting | Mean Partisan Swing | Mean % D of 2-Party Vote |
	Pres. Years	Off- Years					
1854-1872	84.8	78.1	7.8	0.9	0.8	3.2	43.9
1878-1892	84.9	74.9	10.7	0.8	1.6	2.2	48.0
1894-1908	84.8	68.2	22.3	1.5	5.9	4.7	39.6
1910-1918	71.4	53.0	27.2	3.0	9.8	4.1	40.4[a]
1920-1930	55.0	31.5	42.9	6.0	10.0	7.3	29.8
1932-1946	63.6	47.3	25.9	6.7	6.0	7.4	47.9
1948-1962	66.9	53.6	19.1	4.1	5.8	4.9	51.0

[a] Democratic percentage of three-party vote in 1912 and 1914.

with the progressive shrinking of that electorate's relative size. These developments necessarily imply a limitation upon the usefulness of the surge-decline model as it relates to secular movements prior to about 1934. They suggest, moreover, that the effects of the forces at work after 1896 to depress voter participation and to dislocate party linkage between voters and government were even more crushingly severe than a superficial perusal of the data would indicate.

Pennsylvania provides us with variations on the same theme (Table 29-4). . . . And a more detailed examination of turnout and variability in turnout below the statewide level raises some questions about the direct role of immigration and woman suffrage in depressing voter participation. . . .

It is frequently argued that declines in participation after the turn of the century were largely the product of massive immigration from Europe and of the advent of woman suffrage, both of which added very large and initially poorly socialized elements to the potential electorate (Tingsten, 1937, pp. 10-36; Merriam and Gosnell, 1924, pp. 26, 109-22). There is no question that these were influential factors. The data in [Burnham's Table 5] indicate, for example, that down until the Great Depression turnout was consistently higher and much less subject to variation in rural counties with relatively insignificant foreign-stock populations than in either the industrial-mining or metropolitan counties.

Yet two other aspects of these data should also be noted. First, the pattern of turnout decline from the 1876-1896 period to the 1900-1916 period was quite uniform among all categories of counties, though the rank order of their turnouts remained largely unchanged. It can be inferred from this that, while immigration probably played a major role in the evolution of Pennsylvania's political system as a whole, it had no visible direct effect upon the secular decline in rural voting participation. Broader systemic factors, including but transcending the factor of immigration, seem clearly to have been at work. Second, a very substantial fraction of the total decline in turnout from the 1870's to the 1920's—in some

Table 29-4   Voting Patterns in Pennsylvania, 1876-1962: Decline and Resurgence? (Percentages)

Period	Mean Turnout		Mean Drop-Off	Mean Roll-Off	Mean Split-Ticket Voting	Mean Partisan Swing	Mean % D of 2-Party Vote
	Pres. Years	*Off-Years*					
1876-1892	78.5	69.3	9.4	0.6	0.6	1.4	47.7
1894-1908	75.7	64.7	12.2	5.2	1.3	6.3	38.5
1910-1918	64.0	51.4	20.0	4.3	4.7	5.8	43.6[a]
1920-1930	50.4	39.5	28.0	5.2	8.9	7.1	32.8
1932-1948	61.5	51.9	14.9	2.2	1.4	6.1	49.0
1950-1962	67.5	56.3	12.2	1.8	3.1	3.3	49.3

[a] Combined major anti-Republican vote (Democrat, Keystone, Lincoln, Washington).

rural native-stock counties more than half—occurred *before* women were given the vote. . . .

A major finding revealed by survey research is that the "farm vote" is currently one of the most unstable and poorly articulated elements in the American electorate (Campbell et al., 1960, pp. 402-40). It is said that since rural voters lack the solid network of group identifications and easy access to mass-communication media enjoyed by their city cousins, they tend to be both unusually apathetic and exceptionally volatile in their partisan commitments. As rural voting turnout was abnormally low in 1948, its rate of increase from 1948 to 1952 was exceptionally large and—fully consistent with Campbell's surge-decline model—was associated with a one-sided surge toward Eisenhower. A restatement of the data in [Burnham's Table 5] lends strong support to this evaluation of the relative position of the rural vote as a description of the current American voting universe.

But the data strongly imply that virtually the opposite of present conditions prevailed during the nineteenth century. Such variables as education level, communications and nonfamily-group interaction were probably much more poorly developed in rural areas before 1900 than they are today. Not only did this leave no visible mark on agrarian turnout; it seems extremely likely that the nineteenth-century farmer was at least as well integrated into the political system of that day as any other element in the American electorate. The awesome rates of turnout which can be found in states like Indiana, Iowa and Kentucky prior to 1900 indicate that this extremely high level of rural political involvement was not limited to Pennsylvania. As a recent study of Indiana politics demonstrates, the primarily rural "traditional vote" in that state was marked prior to 1900 by an overwhelming partisan stability as well (Key and Munger, 1959, pp. 282-88).

Perhaps, following the arguments of C. Wright Mills (1956, pp. 298-324) and others, we can regard this extraordinary change in rural voting behavior as a

Table 29-5 Patterns of Voter Participation in Ohio, 1857-1962: Decline Without Resurgence? (Percentages)

Period	Mean Turnout		Mean Drop-Off	Mean Roll-Off	Mean Split-Ticket Voting
	Pres. Years	Off-Years			
1857-1879	89.0	78.4	9.7	0.6	0.5
1880-1903	92.2	80.5	11.2	0.8	0.6
1904-1918	80.4	71.2	9.2	2.5	3.3
1920-1930	62.4	45.8	24.1	7.9	9.9
1932-1946	69.9	49.1	27.2	7.6	6.5
1948-1962	66.5	53.3	19.0	8.2	11.1

function of the conversion of a cracker-barrel society into a subordinate element in larger mass society. . . .

The behavior of the Ohio electorate down to about 1930 closely paralleled the patterns displayed in its neighbor states, Michigan and Pennsylvania. Since then a marked divergence has been manifest (Table 29-5). . . .

The development of the voting universe in New York is more analogous to the situation in Ohio than in either Michigan or Pennsylvania (Table 29-6). . . .

Curiously enough, examination of the data thus far presented raises some doubt that the direct primary has contributed quite as much to the erosion of

Table 29-6 New York Voting Patterns, 1834-1962: Decline Without Resurgence? (Percentages)

Period	Mean Turnout (Pres. Years)	Mean Drop-Off	Mean Roll-Off	Mean Split-Ticket Voting	Mean Partisan Swing	Mean % D of 2-Party Vote
1834-1858	84.8	3.3	1.6	1.2	1.7	50.9[a]
1860-1879	89.3	7.9	0.4	0.6	2.6	50.1
1880-1898	87.9	10.4	1.2	1.6	5.0	50.5
1900-1908	82.5	8.3	1.1	2.2	3.7	47.2
1910-1918	71.9	10.9	5.1	3.3	3.8	46.2
1920-1930	60.4	17.3	5.5	9.5	8.3	49.6
1932-1946	71.3	22.5	4.9	3.4	3.2	53.2[b]
1948-1962	67.8	20.6	3.6	6.5	5.8	47.3[b]

[a] Elections from 1854 to 1858 excluded because of major third-party vote.

[b] The American Labor Party, 1936-46, and the Liberal Party, 1944-62, are included in Democratic vote when their candidates and Democratic candidates were the same.

Table 29-7   Voter Peripherality and Party Decay: Oklahoma, 1907-1962
(Percentages)

| Period | Mean Turnout (Off-Years) | Mean Drop-Off | Mean Roll-Off[a] | Mean Split-Ticket Voting[a] | State and Congressional Elections Uncontested by Republicans | |
					Percent	Mean N[b]
1907-1918	52.9	12.1	6.1	3.6	2.1	32
1922-1930	40.1	13.0	13.9	9.7	2.1	31
1934-1946	37.1	32.2	16.4	8.1	14.8	32
1950-1962	44.5	26.3	14.0	10.5	41.3	29

[a] Roll-off and split-ticket voting are computed for contested elections only.

[b] Mean number of state and congressional races in each off-year election.

party linkages as has been often supposed (Key, 1956, pp. 169-96). There seems to be little doubt that it has indeed been a major eroding element in some of the states where it has taken root—especially in states with partially or fully one-party systems where the primary has sapped the minority party's monopoly of opposition. But comparison of New York with our other states suggests the need for further concentrated work on this problem. After a brief flirtation with the direct primary between 1912 and 1921, New York resumed its place as one of the very few states relying on party conventions to select nominees for statewide offices, as it does to this day. Despite this fact, the post-1896 pattern of shrinkage in turnout and increases in our other indices of political dissociation was virtually the same in New York as elsewhere. . . .

The relatively recent admission of [Oklahoma] to the union naturally precludes analysis of its pre-1896 voting behavior. Even so, it is quite clear that the further back one goes toward the date of admission, the closer one comes to an approximation to a nineteenth-century voting universe. . . . The magnitude of drop-off and roll-off has become relatively enormous in Oklahoma since the 1920's, with a very slight reduction in both during the 1950-1962 period (Table 29-7). . . .

As Key has suggested, the direct primary has almost certainly had cumulatively destructive effects on the cohesion of both parties in such modified one-party states as Oklahoma. The rapidly spreading device of "insulating" state politics from national trends by holding the major state elections in off years has also probably played a significant role. Yet it seems more than likely that these are variables which ultimately depend for their effectiveness upon the nature of the local political culture and the socio-economic forces which underlie it. Pennsylvania, for example, also has a direct primary. Since 1875, it has also insulated state from national politics by holding its major state elections in off years. Yet since the realignment of the 1930's, both parties have contested every statewide office in Pennsylvania as a matter of course. Indeed, only very infrequently have elections for seats in the state legislature gone by default to one of the parties, even in bailiwicks which it utterly dominates. . . .

IV

The conclusions which arise directly out of this survey of aggregate data and indices of participation seem clear enough. On both the national and state levels they point to the existence and eventual collapse of an earlier political universe in the United States—a universe in many ways so sharply different from the one we all take for granted today that many of our contemporary frames of analytical reference seem irrelevant or misleading in studying it. The late nineteenth-century voting universe was marked by a more complete and intensely party-oriented voting participation among the American electorate than ever before or since. Approximately two-thirds of the potential national electorate were then "core" voters, one-tenth fell into the peripheral category, and about one quarter remained outside. In the four northern states examined in this survey the component of core elements in the potential electorate was even larger: about three-quarters core voters, one-tenth peripherals and about 15 percent non-voters.

In other ways too this nineteenth-century system differed markedly from its successors. Class antagonisms as such appear to have had extremely low salience by comparison with today's voting behavior. Perhaps differentials in the level of formal education among various groups in the population contributed to differentials in nineteenth-century turnout as they clearly do now. But the unquestionably far lower *general* level of formal education in America during the last century did not preclude a much more intense and uniform mass political participation than any which has prevailed in recent decades. Though the evidence is still scanty, it strongly implies that the influence of rurality upon the intensity and uniformity of voting participation appears to have been precisely the opposite of what survey-research findings hold it to be today. This was essentially a pre-industrial democratic system, resting heavily upon a rural and small-town base. Apparently, it was quite adequate, both in partisan organization and dissemination of political information, to the task of mobilizing voters on a scale which compares favorably with recent European levels of participation.

There is little doubt that the model of surge and decline discussed above casts significant light upon the behavior of today's American electorate as it responds to the stimuli of successive elections. But the model depends for its validity upon the demonstrated existence of very large numbers both of peripheral voters and of core voters whose attachment to party is relatively feeble. Since these were not pronounced characteristics of the nineteenth-century voting universe, it might be expected that abnormal increases in the percentage of the vote won by either party would be associated with very different kinds of movements in the electorate, and that such increases would be relatively unusual by present-day standards.

Even a cursory inspection of the partisan dimensions of voting behavior in the nineteenth century tends to confirm this expectation. Not only did the amplitude of partisan swing generally tend to be much smaller then than now,[3] but nationwide landslides of the twentieth-century type were almost non-existent.[4] Moreover, when the party did win an unusually heavy majority, this increase was usually associated with a pronounced and one-sided *decline* in turnout. Comparison of the 1848 and 1852 elections in Georgia and of the October gubernatorial and November presidential elections of 1872 in Pennsylvania, for example, makes it clear that the "landslides" won by one of the presidential contenders in 1852 and 1872 were the direct consequence of mass abstentions by voters who normally supported the other party.[5] Under nineteenth-century conditions, marked as they were by substantially full mobilization of the eligible electorate, the only play in the system which could provide extraordinary majorities had to come from a reversal of the modern pattern of surge and decline—a depression in turnout which was overwhelmingly confined to adherents of one of the parties.

This earlier political order, as we have seen, was eroded away very rapidly after 1900. Turnout fell precipitately from nineteenth-century levels even before the advent of woman suffrage, and even in areas where immigrant elements in the electorates were almost nonexistent. As turnout declined, a larger and larger component of the still-active electorate moved from a core to a peripheral position, and the hold of the parties over their mass base appreciably deteriorated. This revolutionary contraction in the size and diffusion in the shape of the voting universe was almost certainly the fruit of the heavily sectional party realignment which was inaugurated in 1896. This "system of 1896," as Schattschneider (1960, p. 81), calls it, led to the destruction of party competition throughout much of the United States, and thus paved the way for the rise of the direct primary. It also gave immense impetus to the strains of anti-partisan and anti-majoritarian theory and practice which have always been significant elements in the American political tradition. By the decade of the 1920's this new regime and business control over public policy in this country were consolidated. During that decade hardly more than one-third of the eligible adults were still core voters. Another one-sixth were peripheral voters and fully one-half remained outside the active voting universe altogether. It is difficult to avoid the impression that while all the forms of political democracy were more or less scrupulously preserved, the functional result of the "system of 1896" was the conversion of a fairly democratic regime into a rather broadly based oligarchy.

The present shape and size of the American voting universe are, of course, largely the product of the 1928-1936 political realignment. Survey-research findings most closely approximate political reality as they relate to this next broad phase of American political evolution. But the characteristics of the present voting universe suggest rather forcefully that the New Deal realignment has been both incomplete and transitional. At present, about 44 percent of the national electorate are core voters, another 16 or so are peripheral, and about 40 percent are still outside the political system altogether. By nineteenth-century standards, indices of voter peripherality stand at very high levels. Party organizations remain at best only indifferently successful at mobilizing a stable, predictable mass base of support.

The data which have been presented here, though they constitute only a small fraction of the materials which must eventually be examined, tend by and large to support Schattschneider's (1956, 1960, pp. 78-113) functional thesis of American party politics. We still need to know a great deal more than we do about the specific linkages between party and voter in the nineteenth century. Systematic research remains also to be done on the causes and effects of the great post-1896 transition in American political behavior. Even so, it seems useful to propose an hypothesis of transition in extension of Schattschneider's argument.

The nineteenth-century American political system, for its day, was incomparably the most thoroughly democratized of any in the world. The development of vigorous party competition extended from individual localities to the nation itself. It involved the invention of the first organizational machinery—the caucus, the convention and the widely disseminated party press—which was designed to deal with large numbers of citizens rather than with semiaristocratic parliamentary cliques. Sooner than the British, and at a time when Prussia protected its elites through its three-class electoral system, when each new change of regime in France brought with it a change in the size of the electorate and the nature of *le pays légal,* and when the basis of representation in Sweden was still the estate, Americans had elaborated not only the machinery and media of mass politics but a franchise which remarkably closely approached universal suffrage. Like the larger political culture of which it was an integral part, this system rested upon both broad consensual acceptance of middle-class social norms as ground rules and majoritarian settlement (in "critical" elections from time to time), once and for all, of deeply divisive substantive issues on which neither consensus nor further postponement of a showdown was possible. Within the limits so imposed it was apparently capable of coherent and decisive action. It especially permitted the explicit formulation of sectional issues and—though admittedly at the price of civil war—arrived at a clear-cut decision as to which of two incompatible sectional modes of social and economic organization was henceforth to prevail.

But after several decades of intensive industrialization a new dilemma of power, in many respects as grave as that which had eventuated in civil war, moved toward the stage of overt crisis. Prior to the closing years of the century the middle-class character of the political culture and the party system, coupled with the afterglow of the civil-war trauma, had permitted the penetration and control of the cadres of both major parties by the heavily concentrated power of our industrializing elites. But this control was inherently unstable, for if and when the social dislocations produced by the industrial revolution should in turn provide a grass-roots counterrevolution, the party whose clienteles were more vulnerable to the appeals of the counterrevolutionaries might be captured by them.

The take-off phase of industrialization has been a brutal and exploitative process everywhere, whether managed by capitalists or commissars (Kerr, Dunlop, Harbison, and Myers, 1960, pp. 47-76; Rostow, 1960, pp. 17-58). A vital functional political need during this phase is to provide adequate insulation of the industrializing elites from mass pressures, and to prevent their displacement by a coalition of those who are damaged by the process of capital accumulation. This problem was effectively resolved in the Soviet Union under Lenin and Stalin by vesting a totalitarian monopoly of political power in the hands of Communist industrializing elites. In recent years developing nations have tended to rely upon less coercive devices such as non-totalitarian single-party systems or personalist dictatorship to meet that need, among others. The nineteenth-century European elites were provided a good deal of insulation by the persistence of feudal patterns of social deference and especially by the restriction of the right to vote to the middle and upper classes.

But in the United States the institutions of mass democratic politics and universal suffrage uniquely came into being *before* the onset of full-scale industrialization. The struggle for democracy in Europe was explicitly linked from the outset with the struggle for universal suffrage. The eventual success of this movement permitted the development in relatively sequential fashion of the forms of party organization which Duverger (1959) has described in detail. In the United States—ostensibly at least—the struggle for democracy had already been won, and remarkably painlessly, by the mid-nineteenth century. In consequence, the American industrializing elites were, and felt themselves to be, uniquely vulnerable to an anti-industrialist assault which could be carried out peacefully and in the absence of effective legal or customary sanctions by a citizenry possessing at least two generations' experience with political democracy.

This crisis of vulnerability reached its peak in the 1890's. Two major elements in the population bore the brunt of the exceptionally severe deprivations felt during this depression decade: the smaller cash-crop farmers of the Southern and Western "colonial" regions and the ethnically fragmented urban working class. The cash-crop farmers, typically overextended and undercapitalized, had undergone a thirty-years' decline in the prices for their commodities in the face of intense international competition. With the onset of depression in 1893, what had been acute discomfort for them became disaster. The workers, already cruelly exploited in many instances during this "take-off" phase of large-scale industrialization, were also devastated by the worst depression the country had thus far known. Characteristically, the farmers resorted to political organization while the workers sporadically resorted to often bloody strikes. The industrializers and their intellectual and legal spokesmen were acutely conscious that these two profoundly alienated groups might coalesce. Their alarm was apparently given quite tangible form when the agrarian insurgents captured control of the Democratic Party in 1896.

But the results of that great referendum revealed that the conservatives' fears and the anti-industrialists' hopes of putting together a winning coalition on a Jacksonian base were alike groundless. Not only did urban labor *not* flock to William Jennings Bryan, it repudiated the Democratic Party on an unprecedented scale throughout the industrialized Northeast. The intensity and permanence of this urban realignment was paralleled by the Democrats' failure to make significant inroads into Republican strength in the more diversified and depression-resistant farm areas east of the Missouri River, and by their nearly total collapse in rural New England. The Democratic-Populist effort to create a coalition of the dispossessed created instead the most enduringly sectional political alignment in American history—an alignment which eventually separated the Southern and Western agrarians and transformed the most industrially advanced region of the country into a bulwark of industrialist Republicanism.

This realignment brought victory beyond expectation to those who had sought to find some way of insulating American elites from mass pressures without formally disrupting the pre-existing democratic-pluralist political structure, without violence and without conspiracy. Of the factors involved in this victory three stand out as of particular importance. (1) The depression of 1893 began and deepened during a Democratic administration. Of course there is no way of ascertaining directly what part of the decisive minority which shifted its allegiance to the Republican Party reacted viscerally to the then incumbent party and failed to perceive that Cleveland and Bryan were diametrically opposed on the central policy issues of the day. But contemporary survey findings would tend to suggest that such a component in a realigning electorate might not be small. In this context it is especially worth noting that the process of profound break with traditional voting patterns began in the fall of 1893, not in 1986. In a number of major states like Ohio and Pennsylvania the voting pattern of 1896 bears far more resemblance to those of 1893-1895 than the latter did to pre-1893 voting patterns. Assuming that such visceral responses to the Democrats as the "party of depression" did play a major role in the realignment, it would follow that the strong economic upswing after 1897 would tend to strengthen this identification and its cognate, the identification of the Republicans as the "party of prosperity."

(2) The Democratic platform and campaign were heavily weighted toward the interests and needs of an essentially rural and semi-colonial clientele. Considerably narrowed in its programmatic base from the farmer-labor Populist platform of 1892, the Democratic Party focused most of its campaign upon monetary inflation as a means of redressing the economic balance. Bryan's viewpoint was essentially that of the smallholder who wished to give the term "businessman" a broader definition than the Easterners meant by it, and of an agrarian whose remarks about the relative importance of farms and cities bespoke his profound misunderstanding of the revolution of his time. Silver mine owners and depressed cash-crop farmers could greet the prospect of inflation with enthusiasm, but it meant much less to adequately capitalized and diversified farmers in the Northeast, and less than nothing to the depression-ridden wage-earners in that region's shops, mines and factories. Bryan's appeal at base was essentially Jacksonian—a call for a return to the simpler and more virtuous economic and political arrangements which he identified with that by-gone era. Such nostalgia could evoke a positive response among the native-stock rural elements whose political style and economic expectations had been shaped in the faraway past. But it could hardly seem a realistic political choice for the enthnically pluralist urban populations, large numbers of whom found such nostalgia meaningless since it related to nothing in their past or current experience. Programmatically, at least, these urbanites were presented with a two-way choice only one part of which seemed at all functionally related to the realities of an emergent industrial society. With the Democrats actually cast in the role of reactionaries despite the apparent radicalism of their platform and leader, and with no socialist alternative even thinkable in the context of the

American political culture of the 1890's, the Republican Party alone retained some relevance to the urban setting. In this context, its massive triumph there was a foregone conclusion.

(3) An extremely important aspect of any political realignment is the unusually intense mobilization of negative-reference-group sentiments during the course of the campaign. 1896 was typical in this respect. Profound antagonisms in culture and political style between the cosmopolitan, immigrant, wet, largely non-Protestant components of American urban populations and the parochial, dry, Anglo-Saxon Protestant inhabitants of rural areas can be traced back at least to the 1840's. Bryan was virtually the archetype of the latter culture, and it would have been surprising had he not been the target of intense ethnocultural hostility from those who identified with the former. He could hardly have appeared as other than an alien to those who heard him in New York in 1896, or to those who booed him off the stage at the Democratic Convention—also in New York—in 1924. Moreover, his remarks about the Northeast as "the enemy's country"—anticipating Senator Goldwater's views about that region in 1964—could only intensify a broadly sectional hostility to his candidacy and deepen the impression that he was attacking not only the Northeast's industrializing elites but the Northeast itself. Both in 1896 and in 1964 this region gave every visible evidence of replying in kind.

As Schattschneider has perceptively observed, the "system of 1896" was admirably suited to its primary function. One of its major working parts was a judiciary which proceeded first to manufacture the needed constitutional restraints on democratic political action—a development presaged by such decisions as the Minnesota railroad rate case of 1890[6] and the income tax cases of 1894-1895[7]—and then to apply these restraints against certain sensitive categories of national and state economic legislation. Another of the new system's basic components was the control which the sectional alignment itself gave to the Republican Party, and through it the corporate business community, over the scope and direction of national public policy. Democracy was not only placed in judicial leading-strings, it was effectively placed out of commission—at least so far as two-party competition was concerned—in more than half of the states. Yet it was one of the greatest, if unacknowledged, contributions of the "system of 1896" that democratic forms, procedures and traditions continued to survive. Confronted with a narrowed scope of effective democratic options, an increasingly large proportion of the eligible adult population either left, failed to enter or—as was the case with Southern Negroes after the completion of the 1890-1904 disfranchisement movement in the Old Confederacy—was systematically excluded from the American voting universe. The results of this on the exercise of the franchise have already been examined here in some detail. It was during this 1896-1932 era that the basic characteristics associated with today's mass electorate were formed. . . .

[Burnham ends the article by asking whether the "visible drift away from party-oriented voting" and the "mediocre rates of turnout" of the twentieth century are signs of a contented electorate or of political alienation. Burnham clearly leans toward the latter interpretation.]

NOTES

1. In computing turnout data, note that until approximately 1920 the criteria for eligibility to vote differed far more widely from state to state than they do now. In a number of states west of the original thirteen—for example, in Michigan until 1894 and in Wisconsin until 1908—aliens who had merely declared their intention to become citizens were permitted to vote. Woman suffrage was also extended piecemeal for several decades prior to the general enfranchisement of 1920. The turnout estimates derived here have been adjusted, so far as the census data permit, to take account of such variations.
2. If one computes the off-year total vote of the years 1950-62 as a percentage of the total vote cast in the preceding presidential election, a virtually identical correspondence is reached with estimated off-year turnout as a percentage of turnout in the immediately preceding presidential year.

Year	Total Off-Year Vote as % of Vote in Last Presidential Year	Estimated Off-Year Turnout as % of Turnout in Last Presidential Year
1950	82.9	80.4
1954	69.2	67.5
1958	73.9	72.1
1962	74.4	73.6

3. Mean national partisan swings in presidential elections since 1872 have been as follows: 1872-92, 2.3 percent; 1896-1916, 5.0 percent; 1920-32, 10.3 percent; 1936-64, 5.4 percent.
4. If a presidential landslide is arbitrarily defined as a contest in which the winning candidate received 55 percent or more of the two-party vote, only the election of 1872 would qualify among the 16 presidential elections held from 1836 to 1896. Of seventeen presidential elections held from 1900 through 1964, at least eight were landslide elections by this definition, and a ninth—the 1924 election, in which the Republican candidate received 54.3 percent and the Democratic candidate 29.0 percent of a three-party total—could plausibly be included.
5. The total vote in Georgia declined from 92,203 in 1848 to 62,333 in 1852. Estimated turnout declined from about 88 percent to about 55 percent of the eligible electorate, while the Democratic share of the two-party vote increased from 48.5 percent in 1848 to 64.8 percent in 1852. The pattern of participation in the Pennsylvania gubernatorial and presidential elections of 1872 is also revealing.

Raw Vote	Governor, Oct. 1872	President, Nov. 1872	Absolute Decline
Total	671,147	562,276	−108,871
Democratic	317,760	213,027	−104,733
Republican	353,387	349,249	−4,138

Estimated turnout in October was 82.0 percent, in November 68.6 percent. The Democratic percentage of the two-party vote was 47.3 percent in October and 37.9 percent in November.

6. Chicago, Milwaukee & St. Paul Railway Co. v. Minnesota, 134 U.S. 418 (1890).
7. Pollock v. Farmers' Loan & Trust Co., 157 U.S. 429 (1895); (rehearing) 158 U.S. 601 (1895).

30. THE EFFECT OF THE AUSTRALIAN BALLOT REFORM ON SPLIT TICKET VOTING: 1876-1908

Jerrold G. Rusk

... The purpose of this study is to analyze the effects of one institutional property of the electoral system—the Australian Ballot reform—on the changing split ticket voting patterns of the American electorate in the 1876-1908 time period. A theory is advanced to predict the ways in which ballot might be expected to affect split ticket voting. The theory encompasses not only the comparative effects of the Australian Ballot and the earlier unofficial "party strip" ballot, but also the differential effects of the varying internal formats the Australian Ballot assumed in the several states. A test of this theory is then made—involving a comparison of mean split ticket scores for the various ballot conditions across states within election years and within states across election years. Results show that the basic theory is confirmed. A test of Walter Dean Burnham's (1965) alternate theory of voting behavior for this time period is also made, and it is shown to be largely unsubstantiated insofar as it is dependent on the ticket-splitting phenomenon. ...

The American Ballot System[1]

The Australian or "official" ballot was instituted in most states in the early 1890's. Massachusetts was the first to adopt it statewide in 1888[2] and, in less than eight years, approximately 90 percent of the states had followed suit. Rarely in the history of the United States has a reform movement spread so quickly and successfully. The example of Australia, which originated the Australian Ballot Law in 1856, and several other nations who adopted this law was sufficient to recommend the new system as a probable cure for the ills of the electoral administration of the time.

Before the introduction of the Australian Ballot, there was a separate ballot for each party called a "party strip" or "unofficial" ballot since it was prepared and distributed by the party instead of the government. Each party, in essence,

Source: *American Political Science Review*, 64 (1970): 1220-38. Reprinted with permission of the publisher.

made up its own ballot, listing only its candidates, and had "party hawkers" peddle it to the voters in what resembled an auctioneering atmosphere in and around the polling station. Each party also made its ballot distinctive by printing it in a different color and on a different sized sheet from those of the other parties. This assured instant recognition of the ballot by the voters, and, in turn, recognition by the party workers of which party's ballot a person picked up and voted. In addition, the fact that the actual act of voting was usually performed in the open further assured that the people had no right to a secret ballot.[3]

The Australian Ballot system changed all this. It was completely different from the earlier system in concept and orientation. The new ballot was state-prepared and state-administered—hence making it an "official" and uniform ballot which precluded the existence of party-prepared ballots. Secondly, the new ballot was a consolidated or "blanket" ballot, listing the candidates of all parties on it instead of only the candidates of one party. Last, the ballot was secret, an important complement to its being a consolidated ballot. The new system thus offered the voter an impartial, multiple-choice instrument, upon which he was allowed to deliberate and make a decision in the privacy of the polling booth. The intimidating party aura which so permeated the voting situation under the old system had been effectively dispelled.

Most states enacted ballot laws with the basic principles of the Australian Law—officiality, consolidation, and secrecy—intact. This still left them free to determine the internal format of the ballot, a matter on which there was not so much agreement among the states as there had been on the more basic provisions and general orientation of the Australian Law. Some states, following the lead of Massachusetts, looked once again to the original ballot law for cues and basically adopted its nonpartisan practice of aligning candidate names under office blocs. Some modification was made in this format, such as adding party names beside candidate names, but in general the ballot retained its objective, nonpartisan character. Other states followed the lead of Indiana in enacting a party column arrangement of candidate names on the official ballot. This format resembled a consolidation of the old party strips, placed side by side on the same sheet of paper. In essence, these states had overlaid their old party strip system onto the new Australian framework. Today, these two types of official ballot are known as the "Massachusetts office bloc" and "Indiana party column" arrangements.

The popularity of the two types of official ballot varied in this early time period. As Figure 30-1 shows, the office bloc format was the favorite of states in the beginning, but the party column design predominated after 1890, generally increasing in popularity over the years. The inference can be drawn that the early popularity of the office bloc form was due to its association with the original Australian Ballot Law. But this type of ballot, even when modified by the addition of party names, was too objective and non-partisan to be in keeping with the style and heritage of American politics. Americans soon changed the format of the ballot to party column to correspond more with the partisan nature of their political life. They perceived the important contribution of the Australian Law as lying in its basic provisions and not in its specific stipulation of internal format.

States also experimented in this period with adding certain features to the

Figure 30-1 Trends in State Adoption of Partisan Ballot Types and Features

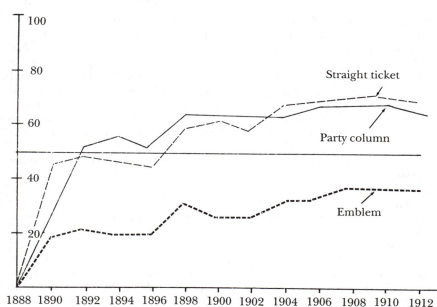

physical format of the ballot, such as straight ticket and party emblem devices. States would try a feature, evaluate its results, and then decide whether or not to keep it on the ballot. Figure 30-1 reveals certain trends in this experimentation and the resulting decisions made. For instance, the straight ticket addition seems to have been well received, since its popularity gained over the years. In part, such a movement is to be understood in the light of the increasing popularity of the party column form, the straight ticket option adding to the partisan flavor of this kind of ballot. This is not to say that such an option could not be or was not offered on office bloc ballots but rather that the general trend was for its incorporation onto the party column format. Party emblem was less used, but it also increased in popularity during this period, primarily, again, as a complement to the party column ballot.

Basic Theory

. . . Two central hypotheses on ballot effects can be formulated. The first is that the Australian Ballot system had a stimulating effect on split ticket voting relative to its predecessor, the unofficial party strip ballot. The second is that the different internal formats of the official ballot themselves had differential effects on split ticket voting; in particular, we may hypothesize that the incidence of such voting was related to the degree of partisan orientation the particular ballot format displayed.

Under the old party strip system, the voter's decision was, for all practical purposes, limited to a single choice—that of which party's ballot to cast. . . . The party strip system did not deny the possibility of a split ticket vote being cast. There were ways to vote a split ticket if the individual had the motivation to find out how and to execute such a decision in an environment emphasizing partisan norms and allowing only an open vote. One method was to "scratch" a name off the ballot and write the name of another party's candidate above it. Another was to take two different party ballots, marking each for certain offices, and then have them attached together before depositing them in the ballot box. Certain variants of these voting schemes existed in other states. But it was rare to find instructions on how to vote "a split ticket" printed on the ballot or for party hawker to mention such a possibility. The electoral environment discouraged deviant voting in most instances—the complete party control of the ballot encouraging and reinforcing a tendency toward straight ticket voting.

The voting situation was different under the Australian Ballot system. The voter no longer had to reduce his several choices to a single dominant choice: he could instead express his multiple preferences as they stood across the new consolidated ballot. If he needed guidance on how to do so, the ballot had voting instructions printed on it, and voting assistance was also obtainable from nonpartisan state officials. The presence of a secret vote gave further notice that the prevailing norms of the partisan world were capable of being broken at the polling station. In fact, the new system encouraged different norms more compatible with the changing milieu. Split ticket voting was on the rise because the opportunity clearly existed to be used. This did not mean that electorates immediately registered large split ticket tendencies overnight; voters had to adjust to the new ballot instrument and the new norms that the changing milieu created. Old habits had to be modified or broken to adjust to the new situation—habits that had been in existence for a long time.

Changes in voting habits (and the rate at which they took place) depended considerably on the internal format of the Australian Ballot. The two different formats of the official ballot could have effects of their own. For instance, the party column format, since it had consolidated the party strips of the earlier period, continued to suggest a more partisan vote than its counterpart, the office bloc ballot. The similarity in style of the Indiana format to its predecessor was compatible with previous voting habits, thereby making it more difficult to recognize and use the ticket-splitting potential of the new ballot. On the other hand, the Massachusetts ballot was conducive to an independent decision being made for each office. The alternatives it defined favored a multi-choice orientation rather than a single-choice one. The difference in orientation between it and the unofficial ballot probably prompted a faster adjustment to its split ticket capabilities than to those of the Indiana format.

The addition of straight ticket and party emblem features to the ballot could also have effects on voting behavior. Such partisan devices suggested some decrease in split ticket voting from the levels normally associated with ballot format alone, but the extent of this decrease depended on the ballot format on which they were displayed. The devices probably had only a small effect on the party column ballot since this format already provided a strong partisan orientation. But because these devices stood in greater contrast to the office bloc format, they were more salient to the voter and thereby considerably decreased the likelihood of split ticket voting on this ballot. . . .

Operational Definitions

. . . In this study, only the dependent variable—split ticket voting—needs to be operationalized. The independent variables of ballot types and forms are usable for analysis purposes directly as they are taken from state laws.

The research literature provides few guidelines for operationalizing the dependent variable. A measure authored by Burnham (1965, p. 9) has gained some currency in the field and is related to one theoretical interpretation of the voting patterns of this period. . . .

The Burnham measure is defined as the difference between the highest and lowest percentages of the two party vote cast for the Democratic party among the array of statewide races in any given state and election year.[4] For example, state A in a certain election year has the following statewide races, with the results expressed as Democratic percentages of the total vote cast for the two major parties: President, 51 percent; Governor, 49 percent; Secretary of State, 48 percent; State Treasurer, 48 percent; and Attorney General, 48 percent. The split ticket value for state A in this election year is 3 percent.

The central focus of the Burnham measure is on the competitive interaction of the two major parties in an electoral situation. This requires the exclusion of uncontested races and the virtual exclusion of races with third party activity from consideration in the split ticket computations.[5] Third party intrusions of a sizable nature would especially create additional variation in the two party vote which could not be considered a true split ticket effect for Burnham's or our purposes.

As an aggregate-based measure, the Burnham index suffers from the same liabilities as other such measures. For example, it assumes that the "gross difference value" it obtains is due solely to ticket-splitting, yet one realizes that some portion of this value is attributable to other causes. Election fraud, accidental miscounting of election returns, etc., can register artificial effects in the index. Also, since the measure is an aggregate difference figure, it would not detect mutual crossovers between the two parties which have the effect of cancelling each other out.[6]. . .

A fault more specific to the Burnham measure is that it does not provide for analysis of "comparable race sets" across states within a given election. The number and kinds of races from which it is computed can vary from state to state. The Burnham measure is rather best suited for analyzing ticket-splitting within states across election years as a means of controlling its "race composition factor".[7] A major part of the analysis in this paper uses the Burnham measure in this context. But an analysis across states is also an important interest. In this situation, use of the Burnham measure needs some intellectual justification since its values could fluctuate from state to state simply because of differences in the races composing it. Whether or not this is a disadvantage depends on how the index behaves as a function of the composition factor and what the relation of this behavior is to the predictions of ballot theory.

Several tests of the Burnham index were conducted, primarily to determine the effect of the race composition factor, but also for the more general purpose of checking to see if the measure was indeed tapping ticket-splitting. With regard to the latter purpose, the measure was found to behave as one might expect, both statistically and theoretically. That is, as one increased the number of races in the index, its value would generally rise as a function of the probability of rare outcomes entering the calculations. As one included the presidential race with two or more state-specific rates, its value also tended to increase in keeping with the theory that the presidential race is a more powerful generator of short-term influences in elections. While these two tests suggested the validity of the measure, they also highlighted the possibility that states contesting larger numbers or given kinds of races could have higher split ticket values simply because of their particular race composition situations. Hence, another test was called for—and this revealed that the race composition factor was not spuriously affecting our own predictions as to ballot effects. That is, it indicated that there were not larger numbers of races or given types of races associated with those ballot conditions predicted by ballot theory to have greater incidences of split ticket voting. A last test also confirmed this lack of spurious correlation and gave further evidence of validity. Three measures devised to have "comparable race sets," and hence to control for the variable factor of race composition, behaved similarly and gave similar results in the ballot analysis as the Burnham measure.[8] The results from all the tests indicated that, assuming some care with the number of races per state, the Burnham index reflected split ticket voting adequately and avoided any noticeable confounding or contaminating effects in its operations.

Introduction of the Australian Ballot

The Burnham split ticket values, when computed for the 1876-1908 time span, are quite revealing. Figure 30-2 displays a trendline of rising values in the years in which the Australian reform took place. However, until ballot has been examined as an analysis variable, such a trend can only be regarded as indirect evidence of ballot's effect on voting. Perhaps there were other ticket-splitting stimuli that were particularly active in the Australian Ballot years. More direct tests of the central hypothesis need to be undertaken in order to determine the role ballot played in this split ticket voting picture.

One test is a within-year analysis of ballot conditions. Such a test also provides us with an election normalization device. Some control on different kinds and intensities of political stimuli can be put into effect by examining the unofficial and official ballot systems with regard to ticket-splitting in the same year. The results of this analysis are presented in Table 30-1.

A few points need to be made about Table 30-1 before it can be analyzed effectively. First, the number of cases in the table is necessarily limited due to

Figure 30-2   Means of Split Ticket Voting Index by Election Year for Nation and Region

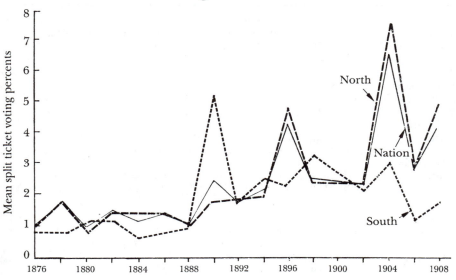

(1) the ballot reform being accomplished in a short period of time, leaving few data points in the unofficial ballot categories, and (2) part of this general period, 1890-1908, being marked by fervid third party activity, making it necessary to drop some of the states (mainly in the Australian Ballot category) from the analysis. Second, the table contains not one but two unofficial ballot categories. Row (1) refers to the general type of unofficial ballot in use during this period—the "pure party strip" which has been described in previous sections. Row (2) includes all unofficial ballot states, combining the ballot cases of row (1) with the very few states (never more than five in the United States at any particular time) that used a deviant form of the unofficial ballot. This deviant form was called the "separate party strip system"—its distinguishing characteristic being that a separate party strip ballot was used for each office contested by the party instead of following the modal pattern of placing all offices contested by the party on a single party strip ballot. Row (3) of the table is, of course, the official ballot category.

The main finding in Table 30-1 follows the predictions of ballot theory. Regardless of whether one compares row (1) or (2) with row (3), the direction of mean values shows that the Australian Ballot states have more ticket-splitting than their unofficial counterparts in every election year in both the North and the nation. The strength and consistency of this pattern of voting values attest to its own importance. The new official ballot allowed and encouraged split ticket voting. As a contrast, the South manifests a ragged, nonconsistent pattern. Partly this can be ascribed to inadequate cases for analysis purposes because of our data

Table 30-1 Split Ticket Voting Means of Unofficial and Australian Ballot States by Election Year for Nation and Region

Ballot Condition	Election Year										Overall Means 1890-1908
	1890	1892	1894	1896	1898	1900	1902	1904	1906	1908	
Nation											
Pure party											
strip	1.5	0.8	—	1.0	0.7	0.4	0.3	2.8	—	3.3	1.5
(1)	(16)	(3)	(0)	(1)	(1)	(2)	(2)	(2)	(0)	(2)	(29)
All party											
strip	2.5	1.0	0.6	4.0	0.7	1.4	0.5	2.6	0.1	4.3	2.2
(2)	(18)	(5)	(2)	(3)	(2)	(4)	(3)	(4)	(1)	(4)	(46)
Australian											
ballot	2.6	2.2	2.4	4.3	2.7	2.6	2.7	7.4	3.1	4.6	3.6
(3)	(7)	(13)	(11)	(34)	(26)	(36)	(20)	(21)	(13)	(21)	(202)
North											
Pure party											
strip	1.7	0.8	—	1.0	0.7	0.4	0.3	2.8	—	3.3	1.5
(1)	(13)	(3)	(0)	(1)	(1)	(2)	(2)	(2)	(0)	(2)	(26)
All party											
strip	1.6	0.8	0.9	1.7	0.7	1.6	0.5	2.7	0.1	4.8	1.7
(2)	(14)	(4)	(1)	(2)	(2)	(3)	(3)	(3)	(1)	(3)	(36)
Australian											
ballot	2.2	2.3	2.1	4.9	2.6	2.6	2.7	9.1	3.2	5.5	3.8
(3)	(6)	(11)	(9)	(28)	(24)	(27)	(19)	(15)	(12)	(16)	(167)
South											
Pure party											
strip	0.4	—	—	—	—	—	—	—	—	—	0.4
(1)	(3)	(0)	(0)	(0)	(0)	(0)	(0)	(0)	(0)	(0)	(3)
All party											
strip	5.4	1.9	0.3	8.5	—	0.9	—	2.2	—	2.6	3.8
(2)	(4)	(1)	(1)	(1)	(0)	(1)	(0)	(1)	(0)	(1)	(10)
Australian											
ballot	4.6	1.7	3.8	1.4	3.4	2.8	2.2	3.2	1.2	1.7	2.5
(3)	(1)	(2)	(2)	(6)	(2)	(9)	(1)	(6)	(1)	(5)	(35)

Note: Category (2) refers to all unofficial ballot states; category (1) refers to those unofficial ballot states which have all major statewide races on a single party strip ballot. Figures in parentheses denote the number of states on which the mean split ticket value was based for any given entry.

screening process. But it also is thought that the deviant form of unofficial ballot, which was used by a few southern states, motivated additional split ticket voting beyond that associated with the modal party strip ballot system. Such a tendency, given the few data cases in the table for the South, would accentuate the importance of this ballot in explaining the idiosyncrasies in this region's ticket-splitting picture.

A comparison of rows (1) and (2) by nation and region comments on the unique split ticket properties of the "separate party strip ballot system," the deviant form of unofficial ballot. For instance, in the nation, in all but one year, the values of row (2) are greater than those of row (1). Since row (2) is an average of row (1) values and those of the deviant unofficial ballot states, one can easily infer that the deviant ballot is associated with the larger split ticket tendencies. The reason for this association lies in the fact that the voter had to choose a separate party ballot for each office for which he wished to vote; in so doing, he was faced with several possible decision-making situations, and unlike the voter in the modal party strip system, he did not have to reduce his several choices to a single dominant choice. The separate party strip system thus encouraged some modicum of ticket-splitting, at least generally greater than that evidenced in pure party strip ballot states. Its effects were more pronounced in the South than in the North, but the general tendency existed in both regions. . . .

A summary of the effects of the unofficial-official ballot conditions across all years can here serve to highlight the effects we have observed within given election years. As shown in Table 30-2, the progression of split ticket values is as predicted and reflects the need to consider the two pre-Australian forms as separate categories with separate effects. This logic fits well with the idea that the two are conceptually different and that this difference is shown to have predictable influences on ticket-splitting behavior. The dominant theme of the two is, of course, registered by the pure party strip system with its low frequency of split ticket voting, since it was the type of unofficial ballot used by about 90 percent of the states. The contrast between the two pre-Australian categories and the Australian Ballot reflects the split ticket potential existing with a secret, consolidated ballot. The opportunity is presented by the ballot and stands in contrast to the party emphasis in the earlier voting system.

Another way to look at the effect of ballot is to take each state separately and compare its split ticket voting before it adopted the official ballot with such voting after adoption. The analysis mode then shifts from comparing mean split ticket scores of the unofficial and official ballot conditions across states within election years to within states across election years. Within this mode, comparisons will usually be made for similar types of elections—keeping presidential and off-year elections distinct because of the differing stimuli associated with each.

Practically speaking, the actual computations involve summing a state's split ticket values for elections of the same type, within each of the two ballot time periods, and then deriving a mean value for each period. Such an aggregation across elections within ballot periods has the advantage of sharpening the accounting of effects attributable to the ballot while dampening out (through mutual canceling) the effects of any unique election year stimuli. The end product of such aggregating and averaging operations should be good estimates of each state's ticket-splitting behavior in the two ballot environments.[9]

The data for presidential elections are presented in Table 30-3 and resemble the other data sets with respect to the effects of the official ballot. All but one state—97 percent of the states in all—have a higher split ticket figure for their official ballot period than for their unofficial ballot period. In almost all of the

Table 30-2   Split Ticket Voting Means of Unofficial and Australian Ballot
States Over All Election Years, 1876-1908

Ballot Condition	*Split Ticket Means*
Pure party strip	1.2 (197)
Separate party strips	3.1 (20)
Australian ballot	3.6 (202)

Note: The first two row categories refer to different types of the unofficial ballot.

states, the split ticket values of the two periods differ quite remarkably. Some
states, such as Iowa, Massachusetts, Michigan, Oregon, and Rhode Island, reveal
very little ticket-splitting in the party strip phase, but mushroom in value when
the reform movement took hold. What is important in this regard is the increment
in split ticket voting from the unofficial ballot condition (as expressed in ratios of
ballot categories) and not a given percentage increase taken to be a standard for
all states to pass or fail. The relative increase is the item of interest, and, in most
cases, such an increase is quite large. A doubling, tripling, or quadrupling of such
voting is commonplace among the various states.

Some excellent summary information can also be gleaned from Table 30-3.
The import of its message is similar to earlier statements, but it can give us some
indication of the average effect of the two ballot time periods. In the table, twenty-
nine states qualify as having both unofficial and official ballot conditions. For
these states, ticket-splitting goes from a mean value of 1.1 to 3.4 for the two ballot
conditions, an increase of approximately three times. This is the average effect of
the official ballot for states having both forms in presidential years. For all states,
the figures deviate even more—1.1 to 4.1.

Several states, of course, were deleted from the first set of figures because of
one or the other of two reasons—they used the unofficial ballot exclusively in this
period, or, the converse, they adopted the official ballot, never having any
previous ballot system. The incidence of ticket-splitting for the first category of
states is very low—0.8 percent. The second category of states, those western states
entering the Union in the early 1890's or later, go in the opposite direction—they
display the highest split ticket average in the study, 7.2 percent. Obviously,
variables other than ballot were contributing to this outcome. The entrance of a
territorial entity into national politics in itself must promote some reactions
similar in kind to those shown for the ballot. The presence of the ballot makes it
easier to implement such reactions. However, even when the large split-ticket
effects of these official ballot states are controlled for, the basic relationship
between ballot and voting behavior still holds, as our example of the twenty-nine
states above indicated.

The same story of ballot effects repeats itself in the off-year election figures
so that little new information is to be gained from this data source. Approximately
85 percent of the states, in the off-year election context, show a rise in ticket-

Table 30-3 Split Ticket Voting Means of Unofficial and Official Ballot
Periods of States in Presidential Election Years, 1876-1908

| | | | | Category Cases | |
State	Unofficial Ballot Period	Official Ballot Period	Difference of Means	Unofficial Ballot	Official Ballot
Alabama	1.10	—	—	1	0
Arkansas	0.65	2.05	1.40	2	2
California	1.12	2.15	1.03	4	2
Colorado	2.62	3.88	1.26	4	5
Connecticut	0.60	—	—	4	0
Delaware	0.28	1.14	0.86	4	5
Florida	0.70	2.70	2.00	3	2
Georgia	—	—	—	0	0
Idaho	—	2.03	—	0	3
Illinois	1.18	1.20	0.02	4	2
Indiana	0.38	1.10	0.72	4	3
Iowa	0.93	3.40	2.47	3	3
Kansas	2.77	0.72	−2.05	4	4
Kentucky	0.45	1.58	1.13	4	4
Louisiana	1.10	—	—	2	0
Maine	—	—	—	0	0
Maryland	0.48	1.54	1.06	4	5
Massachusetts	1.15	6.58	5.43	2	6
Michigan	1.00	6.62	5.62	3	4
Minnesota	2.63	16.58	13.95	3	4
Mississippi	2.00	—	—	2	0
Missouri	1.57	2.00	0.43	6	1
Montana	—	12.90	—	0	3
Nebraska	2.05	3.65	1.60	4	4
Nevada	1.80	4.35	2.55	4	2
New Hampshire	0.72	4.08	3.36	4	5
New Jersey	1.28	—	—	9	0
New York	0.88	2.33	1.45	5	3
North Carolina	0.48	—	—	4	0
North Dakota	—	8.44	—	0	5
Ohio	0.65	1.98	1.33	4	4
Oregon	0.48	3.15	2.67	4	2
Pennsylvania	0.42	0.70	0.28	4	4
Rhode Island	0.55	5.46	4.91	4	5
South Carolina	—	—	—	0	0
South Dakota	—	1.40	—	0	2
Tennessee	1.70	2.30	0.60	4	4

(Table continues)

Table 30-3   *(continued)*

State	Unofficial Ballot Period	Official Ballot Period	Difference of Means	Category Cases	
				Unofficial Ballot	Official Ballot
Texas	0.55	3.40	2.85	2	2
Utah	—	18.65	—	0	2
Vermont	1.92	4.06	2.14	4	5
Virginia	0.30	5.73	5.43	3	3
Washington	—	3.23	—	0	3
West Virginia	0.73	2.40	1.67	3	5
Wisconsin	0.57	1.30	0.73	3	2
Wyoming	—	4.06	—	0	5
Means of state means	1.1	4.1	2.3	128	125

Note: The unofficial ballot category covers the period from 1876 through the last presidential election before change from the unofficial ballot for each state. The official ballot category covers the period from the first presidential election in which the Australian Ballot was used through the 1908 election. The designation "category cases" refers to the number of elections entering the split ticket mean computations for the unofficial and official ballot periods of any given state.

splitting in their Australian Ballot period. When off-year and presidential types of elections are merged, 91 percent of the states revealed the predicted direction.

Demonstration that ballot has an effect on split ticket voting is only one part of an analysis: for ballot theory to be substantiated, split ticket voting patterns must be shown to have changed in the states shortly after the new ballot was introduced. A reasonable prediction would be that, in accord with adjustment patterns, split ticket voting would show a rise in either the first or second election year in which a state used the new ballot. This proposition is first tested across states within these crucial years of ballot change. . . . According to the data, both the first and second years of ballot use seem to be good indicators of the effects of the official ballot. Sizable differences exist between the unofficial and official ballot states. . . . States adopting the new ballot soon changed their voting patterns from those remaining steadfast to the existing system. Voters were seen to be adjusting to the new ballot and its ticket-splitting potential without much difficulty.

A second way to test this proposition of early ballot effects is within states across election years. In Table 30-4, split ticket values are listed for each state in its last election year using the unofficial ballot and the first two elections using the official ballot. Also listed are "difference values" between the last unofficial ballot election and the second election year in which the official ballot was used. . . . The type of election, presidential or off-year, used in these unofficial-official ballot comparisons is decided separately for each state, according to which year its change of ballot occurred.

Table 30-4   Split Ticket Values of States in Last Election Before and First and Second Election Years of Official Ballot Use, for Comparable Election Types

State	Last Election Year Using Unofficial Ballot (1)	First Election Year Using Official Ballot (2)	Second Election Year Using Official Ballot (3)	Difference Values (Column 3 Minus Column 1) (4)
California	0.7	(2.7)	4.0	3.3
Colorado	1.6	1.0	5.6	4.0
Delaware[a]	0.1	0.1	2.1	2.0
Illinois[a]	0.9	(0.5)	1.4	0.5
Indiana[a]	0.4	0.7	(0.5)	(0.1)
Iowa[a]	0.6	(0.8)	6.0	5.4
Kentucky[a]	0.2	—	0.6	0.4
Lousiana[a]	1.9	—	0.6	−1.3
Massachusetts	1.2	3.6	2.2	1.0
Michigan[a]	0.6	(2.2)	0.6	0.0
Minnesota	3.8	(6.3)	(6.4)	(2.6)
Nebraska	2.6	(8.1)	3.2	0.6
Nevada	2.7	(7.2)	4.9	2.2
New Hampshire	1.0	1.4	6.8	5.8
New York[a]	0.5	2.3	1.6	1.1
Ohio[a]	0.0	0.7	0.2	0.2
Oregon	0.7	—	3.9	3.2
Pennsylvania[a]	0.5	0.1	0.3	−0.2
Rhode Island	(0.4)	2.8	3.2	(2.8)
Tennessee	1.1	4.6	1.9	0.8
Vermont[a]	1.6	2.1	4.3	2.7
West Virginia[a]	0.5	0.4	0.2	−0.3
Wisconsin[a]	(1.4)	1.4	(1.1)	(−0.3)
Means	1.1	2.4	2.7	1.6

Note: Most values in the table met the screening requirements of the Burnham index. Those enclosed in parentheses did not but were included as "impure" cases as defined in footnote 5 above. In order for a state to be included in the table, it had to have split ticket values in both the last election before and the second election of official ballot use—thus excluding those states that have no pre-Australian period, those never adopting the official ballot in the 1876-1908 time period, and those screened out of even the "impure data set" in these heavily "third party" election years. For a given state, the "difference value" compares the split ticket scores of similar types of elections (either presidential or off-year), depending on when the ballot change took place. The designation "—" entered for some states in column (2) indicates that these states' split ticket values were not included because of failure to meet the requirements of either the Burnham index or its "impure version."

[a] Denotes states having the party column format in their second election year of official ballot use.

Of first interest in the data is the fact that approximately 80 percent of the states had greater split ticket scores after they adopted the new ballot. The difference values in column (4) show this, and the trend is repeated when one compares columns (1) and (2). Certainly, this finding would be more impressive if higher, yet its consistency with our earlier tables is further evidence of this type of patterning in the data.

The ballot picture is improved if one considers a few additional features of the data. For one thing, the deviations in the difference values are very small for the remaining 20 percent of the states. This is because these states adopted the party column type of official ballot, which in many respects resembled the earlier unofficial ballot situation. Of note here too is the observation that most of the party column states showing the predicted direction also registered but small difference values. (A footnote denotes the party column states in Table 30-4.) The next section will show that the party column form in the first few years revealed similar split ticket figures to the pre-Australian Ballot states. The habits formed by the party strip situation carried over to the party column form, with its arrangement of party strips and straight ticket provision facilitating the continuation of these habits.

Lending further weight to our ballot interpretation is the fact that with continued use of the party column format over time, the split ticket figures do increase. Admittedly, this tendency is not major, yet it does exist, as we shall see in Figure 30-3. The reasons for the increased split ticket use of the party column form over time are probably twofold—a continuing adjustment to the new ballot and a given election producing a desire to use the split ticket property of the ballot.

Thus, an analysis within states across election years substantiates the earlier results found by examining data across states within election years. The new ballot has effects on voting behavior not only, generally speaking, across time, but also fairly immediately after it is introduced in the several states.

Types of Australian Ballots

The general conclusion of the last section was that the introduction and establishment of the official ballot facilitated a rise in split ticket voting. A more detailed question has to do with the relative contributions of the party column and office bloc types of this ballot to such ticket-splitting and also the contrast of their effects with those of the earlier unofficial ballot system.

Figure 30-3 presents the split ticket pictures for party column, office bloc, and unofficial ballot states in the North. The values in the figure are mean scores for each ballot condition within the election years of the 1890-1908 time period. Looking first at just the two types of official ballot states, one notes the wide divergence in their respective split ticket values, suggesting the influence of differing internal ballot formats on voting behavior. Ticket-splitting is significantly higher under the less partisan arrangement of the office bloc form than under the party column type. . . .

Figure 30-3 Split Ticket Means for Three Ballot Conditions of States, North Only

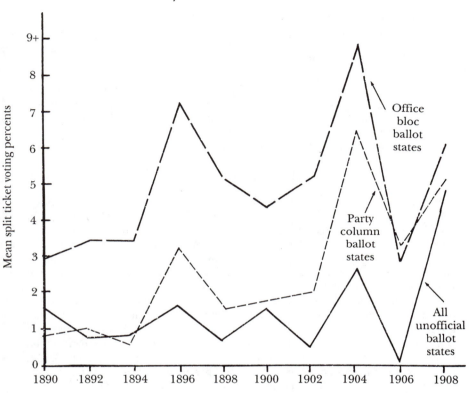

Summary

The findings of this study of the Australian Ballot can be summarized as follows:

1. The introduction and establishment of the Australian Ballot in the states led to an increase in ticket-splitting in comparison to the previous ballot system. . . .
2. The unofficial ballot system in use previous to that time was distinguished by very little split ticket voting. . . .
3. The extent to which ticket-splitting rose from the unofficial to the Australian Ballot depended on the type of internal format used on the Australian Ballot. The party column format displayed a slightly higher split ticket pattern than the unofficial ballot. . . . The office bloc format,

on the other hand, was a complete contrast to the unofficial ballot and therefore revealed much higher split ticket patterns than its predecessor. . . .

4. By implication from the discussion in (3), the party column and office bloc forms themselves had very different split ticket voting patterns. The party column ballot was associated with a low level of ticket-splitting. . . . The office bloc ballot displayed a much stronger split ticket pattern as a result of its multiple-choice orientation.

5. The inclusion of a partisan feature on a ballot format also had consequences on voting patterns [for data, see original article]. . . . Throughout, however, the dominant variable was the ballot format itself. When the partisan devices were included, they decreased ticket-splitting within a narrow range of the levels imposed by ballot format. . . .

Burnham's Theory

To date only one other theory has been advanced to explain the split ticket voting patterns of this period. The theory proposed by Walter Dean Burnham purports to explain the rise in ticket-splitting of this period by a breakdown in party organization and competition and a corresponding alienation of the voter from the political system. Before this breakdown, the electorate was, according to Burnham, quite firmly rooted in the party milieu and "party" served as the main reference group in the system.

Burnham's evidence for his theoretical conclusions is the split ticket records of five states, only four of which will concern us here.[10] But one could contend, given the above ballot analysis, that the increase in ticket-splitting observed by Burnham is, in fact, mainly due to the introduction and establishment of the official ballot in this period. The crucial question is how much variation in voting, if any, is there left to "explain" after ballot has explained all that it can. Any additional variation could be considered "fair game" for other variables, such as Burnham's, to interpret.

In order to answer this question, a series of "expected" split ticket values for the four states were computed—"expected" in the sense that they encompassed the mean effects on split ticket voting of all other states using the same Australian Ballot configuration; then, these figures were compared with the "actual" values of the four states. The results [were calculated] for each state's first election year of official ballot use, its second year of such use, and the remaining time spans for presidential and congressional election years.

"Difference values" . . . sum up for the various years of interest the additional split ticket voting a state had left over after the effects of ballot were removed from the picture. Positive values indicated that some split ticket voting was left over; negative values indicated the reverse—that the states in question did not even achieve a split ticket value as high as the mean figure of other states using the same ballot configuration. A state-by-state analysis reveals that three of the four states had little or no additional split ticket voting for factors other than ballot to explain. The mean difference values for Ohio, New York, and

Pennsylvania across these years are −.1, −.2, and .2, respectively. Only Michigan with a mean of 1.9 provides an exception to the general theme. The mean difference for all states over all years is 0.5, with Michigan providing most of the positive component in the computation. A value of zero would indicate that other explanatory factors were not needed for these states.

The reasons for such small difference values seem clear in the framework of previous ballot analyses. All four states had party column-straight ticket ballots and all save Pennsylvania had an emblem as well. Such states displayed only moderate split ticket increases in their Australian years relative to earlier ballot days. What increases in ticket-splitting there were to explain could easily be done by resort to the ballot variable alone. Only in Michigan did there seem to be other factors entering the picture.

The types of variables Burnham mentioned in his theory were supposed to be making widespread, not minuscule, changes in voting. While this could be the case in Michigan, it definitely is not so in the other three states. It is possible that a study of other states in this context might show additional ticket-splitting beyond what could be explained by ballot—but the crucial point is that the key examples of states used by Burnham do not confirm his theory. Even if other states showed such a tendency, Burnham would still have to account for other plausible features of this period which could cause ticket-splitting.

The ballot variable also seems to contribute to another of Burnham's findings. In his analysis, Burnham was concerned with not only the increased tendency toward ticket-splitting, but also toward "roll-off"—the tendency of the electorate to vote in greater numbers for high than for low prestige offices on the ballot. In the four states examined, Burnham found an increase in roll-off in the exact time period when the official ballot was adopted in these states. The official ballot contributed to roll-off since it was long and consolidated, requiring substantial effort on the part of the voter to mark all offices. But the unofficial ballot required less effort in voting than the official ballot—in many states, merely depositing the ticket in the ballot box, and, in some others, the marking of offices down a single column with no attendant decision-making involved as to partisan choices.[11]. . .

NOTES

1. The history of the American ballot system can be found in various sources such as Albright (1942), Evans (1917), Harris (1934), Ludington (1911), and Wigmore (1889). In general, these references give much better accounts of the Australian Ballot era than the voting systems in use prior to that time. An exception to this is the book by Evans.
2. Although the first Australian Ballots were adopted in 1888 and 1889, they did not become effective in federal elections until 1890.
3. The party strip or unofficial ballot came into use in most states during the first half of the nineteenth century. Before that time, the states (or colonies) had other forms of

paper balloting, voice voting, or such unorthodox procedures as letting corn or beans designate one's vote. At one time, in the early 1800's, several states allowed the voter to make up his own ballot. The parties, noting this, were motivated to print their own ballots in order to thwart the use of handwritten ballots. This practice of party-prepared ballots was upheld in a Massachusetts Supreme Court decision in 1829, setting a precedent which was not challenged until the beginning days of the Australian Ballot reform.

4. The definition of a "statewide race" was expanded in this chapter to include an aggregation of the district congressional vote. As a check on this operation, another measure was constructed excluding the congressional vote, and, when compared, both revealed similar behaviors and interpretations in the subsequent ballot analysis.

5. Burnham did not indicate what screening criteria he used to eliminate third party intrusions in his data. The rule established in this study was that no race would enter the computations if the third party vote contributed six or more percent to the total vote for that race. Admittedly, this figure was somewhat arbitrary and some might consider it too high; however, given the many and large third party movements in this period, the figure seems reasonable. To check this procedure, we also looked at those cases of states having third party vote figures greater than six percent for most of their races and yet where the percentage did not vary greatly across the set of contested races. These data, impure as they were, conformed to the same trendlines in the ballot analysis as the figures generated by the screening criterion selected for use with the Burnham measure. This gave increased confidence in the findings, and on one occasion in the ballot analysis below (Table 30-4), we display the "impure" values of states with the "pure" values of other states carefully distinguishing the two in such instances.

6. Aggregate election analyses usually assume that voters crossover or split their tickets mainly in one direction—the direction of national trends. But even if this were not the case, the phenomenon of mutual crossovers would not contaminate our ballot analysis unless it occurred, for some reason, far more often in unofficial than in official ballot states, a proposition that seems unlikely.

7. By "race composition factor" is meant the types of races entering the Burnham index computations in any given state. Inspection of the data shows that this factor is fairly stable across elections though the index can in no way guarantee a complete control over this.

8. The three measures computed were based on the presidential-gubernatorial, presidential-congressional, and gubernatorial-congressional pairings of races. . . .

9. The voting estimates are "good" except for the fact that there is a rising split ticket curve in this period that makes sense substantively. Better estimates could be obtained by excluding the transition trends in the data.

10. Burnham's fifth state, Oklahoma, is not relevant to this analysis since it entered the Union at the end of the time period covered in this study.

11. . . . Walker (1966) has shown that roll-off also varies according to the type of official ballot in use—the office bloc ballot contributing more to a roll-off effect than the party column ballot. Walker also views his findings as a possible modifying factor on Burnham's theory as the following quotation suggests: "The argument made by both Burnham and Stiefbold that increasing roll-off is an indication of increasing political alienation at least is weakened by our finding that changes in ballot forms directly affect the amount of roll-off" (p. 462).

31. A SOCIALIZATION THEORY OF PARTISAN REALIGNMENT

Paul Allen Beck

Students of politics since the time of Plato have posited the existence of strong linkages between preadult political learning and the operation of political systems. For all their concern, however, there was little systematic research on preadult political learning prior to the late 1950's. Students of socialization outside the field of political science largely ignored socialization into explicitly political roles, while those few students of politics who were interested in political socialization focused narrowly and often impressionistically on civic education in the schools.

In slightly over a decade, all of that has changed. As Herbert Hyman (1959) observed in the preface to a new edition of his inventory of political socialization research:

> Now—by 1969—the study of political socialization has become a large-scale enterprise. It has become the organizing principle for scientific meetings and lengthy conferences. Journals devote special issues to the theme. Texts and theoretical works in political science and monographs on the politics of many countries contain chapters on the topic. Scholarship has developed to the point that collections of articles are ready for the press, and the bibliography already runs to dozens of pages. . . . With this luxuriant scene before our eyes, it is hard to bring back to mind the barren vistas of the previous decade.

The outpouring of socialization research in the past decade has greatly enhanced political scientists' knowledge of the preadult political world. It has provided an increasingly clear picture of what is learned and how it is learned. Yet this research has contributed little to an understanding of adult political behavior or the operations of modern political systems. The reason for this is implicit in almost all political socialization research. Researchers have been content to assume that preadult political learning has important consequences for both individuals and the political system. This assumption has allowed them to avoid coming to grips with the recalcitrant question which motivated students of

Source: Richard G. Niemi and associates, *The Politics of Future Citizens,* Jossey-Bass, 1974. Reprinted with permission of the publisher.

politics to focus on childhood socialization in the first place: what is the relevance of preadult political learning for adult political behavior and, consequently, for political systems?[1]

If political socialization research is to continue to make important contributions to the study of politics, it must deal with these linkage questions. I take some initial steps in that direction here by outlining an explanation of a macropolitical phenomenon which seems critical to the functioning of American politics— partisan realignment. My explanation is grounded in theories of childhood partisan socialization and adult partisan change. Taken together these two theories provide a persuasive new explanation for past realignments as well as for contemporary politics.

Erosion of Childhood Partisanship

Of all the political orientations which develop in the preadult years, none promises to be more durable throughout an individual's life than partisanship. Psychological attachments to the Democratic and Republican parties emerge as early as grade two and become increasingly widespread among elementary school students with each passing year (Greenstein 1965, pp. 64-78; Hess and Torney, 1967, pp. 101-4). Although this partisanship appears to wane after elementary school (presumably as a result of nonpartisan influences in the school), high school seniors have been shown to be only about 10 percent less partisan than their parents (Jennings and Niemi, 1968, p. 453). While childhood partisanship may represent little more than imitation of parental partisan orientations, there is little doubt that it typically provides a strong foundation for adult partisan behavior (Campbell et al., 1960, pp. 146-49).

Partisan orientations normally develop early in the preadult years and persist throughout the life cycle. But during certain phases in American political history, inherited partisan orientations have been noticeably eroded. These periods of sharp change in the distribution of party loyalties in the electorate are termed *partisan realignments*. In the 1820's (before the emergence of the modern two-party system), the 1860's, the 1890's, and the 1830's, partisan changes have been of such force that they destroyed the previous balance of party power and inaugurated new lines of political conflict.

The aggregate characteristics of these realignment phases in American electoral politics are relatively easy to identify. Each has been accompanied by increases in electoral participation, sharp intraparty as well as interparty conflict, extensive geographical shifts in voting patterns, and unusually severe social or economic traumas (Burnham, 1970, pp. 6-9). Each has been preceded by a rise in electoral support for minor parties.

But individual changes during these realignments are difficult to identify. About the only source of data on such changes is the University of Michigan presidential election series, which sheds some light, though indirectly, through recall of past voting behavior, on the realignment of the 1930's. Through analysis of the past and present partisan behavior of the respondents in these voter surveys, Campbell and his colleagues (1960) have been able to piece together a picture of individual change during this political upheaval. In the following pages, I elaborate upon this picture—buttressing it with data drawn from a wider temporal interval and placing it into a broader theoretical context.

The realignment of the 1930's seems in retrospect to have been wrought principally by the new voters during the New Deal realigning phase, not by those who had voted in earlier years. As is demonstrated in Table 31-1, the first votes of these new voters were cast overwhelmingly in support of Franklin Delano Roosevelt. This behavior reflects the tendency for new voters to be swayed more heavily than their elders by the short-run forces in a particular election. It suggests also that the voting dispositions of these young voters were not wholly predetermined by their childhood partisan socialization. Given the likelihood that a majority of these first voters came from Republican homes (Republican identifiers were a majority prior to the 1930's), this first-time voting behavior signifies wholesale defections from inherited partisanship.

Before moving on, Table 31-1 warrants more careful examination. New voters are divided into two separate categories: those who were voting for the first time because they had just attained majority and those who where of age previously but had not voted. The behavior of these two groups of new voters is similar in all but one election—that of 1928. The nomination of a "wet" Catholic, Al Smith, by the Democrats in that year may well have attracted voters to the presidential contest who had been uninterested in presidential politics in previous years.[2] But on the whole, these two groups of new voters are virtually indistinguishable in terms of their voting behavior. The "delayed" voters were undoubtedly young adults moved by the same forces governing the "coming-of-age" voters.

Voting defections of the type portrayed in Table 31-1 are hardly sufficient to spawn a realignment. Realignments occur only when either inherited or active partisan allegiances are changed, producing large-scale shifts in the partisan loyalties of the voting public (Burnham, 1970, p. 6). While the electorate usually contains enough independents to allow some change in the distribution of partisanship, a shift of the magnitude of a realignment seems unlikely without many voters changing their partisan attachments.[3]

Experienced voters in the 1930's seem to have returned to relatively stable partisan loyalties. They support the theory that partisanship progressively hardens over an individual's life cycle, becoming more resistant to change with each passing year (Converse, 1969). Partisan shifts in a realignment are better explained by the recent entry of new age cohorts into the electorate. These young people are probably moving away more from a *nominal* inherited partisanship than from any deep-seated partisan orientations.

This theory of individual change during realignments cannot be tested adequately until a new realignment occurs. It is based on the assumption that adult partisanship is much deeper, and hence less subject to change, than that articulated by a child or even a young adult. Support for this assumption can be found in a panel study comparing young adults and their parents (Jennings and Niemi, 1975). Adult partisan orientations have been reinforced by voting. Childhood partisan identifications, on the other hand, have received little of this

Table 31-1   Reported Presidential Votes, 1924-1940

	Percent Democratic of Two-Party Vote		
Election	All Voters	"Coming-of-Age" Voters	"Delayed" First Voters
1924	35	29	20
1928	41	38	53
1932	59	80	93
1936	62	89	77
1940	55	69	72

Source: Campbell et. al., *The American Voter*, p. 155.

behavioral support and, as socialization research has shown, are rarely buttressed by a well-developed sense of the policy differences between the parties. Although many adults see no difference between parties and although children clearly manifest partisan orientations that are likely to be reinforced in adulthood, nonetheless the weakest link in the transgenerational partisan chain within any family lies in the preadult years.

Circumstantial evidence can be marshaled to support the notion that this weakest link is most likely to be broken during the transition years between childhood and full adulthood—the first time childhood partisanship is tested. Young voter cohorts which supported Roosevelt so overwhelmingly in 1932 and 1936 were overwhelmingly Democratic in their partisanship as well. Their break with tradition to cast a Democratic vote became a permanent rather than temporary defection. This is demonstrated in Figure 31-1: the major discontinuity in the division of party identifiers is found between those who were in their twenties when the Depression of 1929 struck and those who were over thirty at that critical watershed.[4] This change in the distribution of partisanship is both sharp and durable, preordaining the emergence of a new Democratic majority as the process of population replacement worked its inexorable magic.

Given these data, however tentative they might seem, one must doubt that preadult political socialization fully determined the adult partisan orientations of these Depression generations. It seem much more likely that preadult orientations gave way under the impact of strong political forces for those who were in the transition years between childhood and full adulthood. Not yet habituated to a partisanship by actual electoral decision-making, these new voters were mobilized in new partisan directions. In the process, a new Democratic majority was formed.

The newest members of the electorate provide the dynamic element to American electoral politics. They are the ones most likely to break the partisan continuity between past and future and to force comprehensive changes in the policy agenda. Inherited partisan orientations are not always subjected to the intense pressures of a realigning phase, however. The excitement which

Figure 31-1 Party Identification by Four-Year Age Cohort

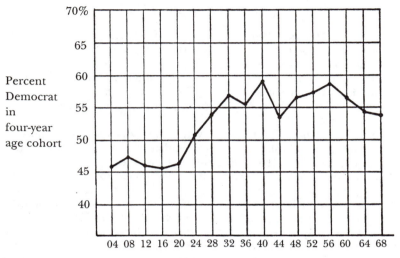

Percent Democrat in four-year age cohort

Presidential election when members of cohort
were first eligible to vote

Note: These are the Democratic identifications of each four-year age grouping–including those who classified themselves as independents on first response but later admitted leaning toward the Democratic party–that were cumulated over every presidential election from 1952 through 1968, using the Survey Research Center election study data. The total N is approximately 9,000 and the N is not less than 100 for any age cohort.

pervades such a period, caused by the critical battle over agenda-setting for the future, cannot be sustained for long. Realignment phases then give way to the long periods of "normal politics," in which the party coalitions and policy agenda remain relatively stable. Normal politics promotes a high degree of intergenerational continuity in partisan orientations. Politics is simply too unexciting and too repetitious to continually subject the inheritances of new voters to severe pressures. Such pressures may be present in individual cases for idiosyncratic reasons, but they are unlikely to cumulate across an entire age cohort.

The study of political socialization has matured and prospered during a normal phase of American electoral politics. Thus it is not surprising that socialization theorists have seen more continuity than change in preadult political orientations and in the political system. It should now be obvious, though, that theories of socialization erected on a normal politics data base—especially those concerning partisanship—are misleading.

Cycles in Partisanship Socialization

If it is true that the politics of realignment are intense enough to cause large numbers of voters to desert their childhood partisanship, it is also likely no other generation has more deeply entrenched partisan orientations and that, as a result, no other generation will transmit partisan orientations as successfully to its offspring as this realignment generation. These two assumptions combine to produce a new and powerful theory of preadult partisan socialization and the dynamics of realignment.

Three different groups of voters are involved in this theory. The members of group one adopt their enduring partisan orientations as emerging adult participants in a realigning phase. The partisanship of these realignment generations should have stronger intellectual underpinnings—a firmer grounding in rational responses to operative political realities—than that of any other age group. Group two includes all individuals who receive their preadult partisan socialization from members of a realignment generation. These "children of realignment," while lacking direct adult exposure to intense partisan conflict, are likely to receive much of the flavor of such conflict "across the dinner table" from their parents. Most group two individuals may be expected to carry into adulthood a partisanship which is supported by visceral if not intellectual underpinnings. Their childhood partisan orientations should be well insulated against change-inducing forces.

The third group of partisan learners is composed of the individuals of the next generation. Their childhood political experience is gained during a period of normal politics; their parents were not direct participants in a realignment. The childhood partisan learning of these "children of normal politics" should provide little insulation from the short-term political forces they encounter as young adults.

A clear similarity exists between groups one and three—the realignment generation and the children of normal politics—even if they are sharply differentiated by age. Both receive relatively weak childhood partisan socialization, but the members of group one experience strong partisan socialization during their years of transition into adulthood, while the members of group three have not passed through this transition period yet. Even though the children of normal politics have become a realignment generation in every previous instance, there also exists the possibility that no such transformation will occur. This distinction is critical: in it lies the difference between political instability (when large numbers of voters reject partisanship) and political change (when large numbers of voters accept new partisanship).

Regular cycles of partisan stability and change have dominated American politics for more than a century. Realignments have occurred at roughly three-decade intervals, and each realignment has been followed by a long period of stable normal politics. This previously puzzling regularity in partisan politics is explicable when change is conceptualized in terms of the movement through the electorate of the realignment generation, the children of realignment, and the children of normal politics. Through the process of population replacement, the relative weight of each of these groups changes continually. Furthermore, the potential for sweeping partisan change depends on which of these groups is just entering the electorate.

This explanation can be grasped more readily if accompanied by a look at the century of American politics postdating the emergence of the modern two-party system. Three realignments have been identified in this time period. The first was associated with the political conflicts over slavery and civil war, the second with the urban-rural conflict of the late 1800's, and the third with the class conflicts of the New Deal. Each of these realignments occurred at a time when the children of normal politics were entering the electorate in full force. These voters seem to have been mobilized during their early adult years and subsequently became a realignment generation.

The fundamental population replacement process which underlies this theory is represented in Figure 31-2. Underlying the visible precision of this figure are several operational assumptions. First, the delimiting of each generation depends upon the location of clear initial and terminal points for every realignment phase. Such precision is difficult because of the very nature of realignments. At times they have emerged nationwide only gradually because of their uneven development in different parts of the nation (such as during the Civil War and the New Deal). The task of specifying the realignment phases is made even more difficult by the fact that each has been preceded by a period of partisan instability which appears, on the surface, to be "of a piece" with the subsequent realigning phase. (Nonetheless, a graphical depiction of my theory of realignment dynamics requires precise delimitation of these rather imprecise phenomena, and thus I have attempted to determine initial and terminal points as carefully as possible by weighing the relevant historical evidence. At the same time, I must reiterate that this is an artificial precision and that these points may be moved within reasonable bounds without disturbing the essential features of the theory.)

The Civil War realignment phase seems to have begun with southern secession from the Union in 1861, not with the long period of partisan instability which preceded it, as is often supposed. The basic structure of this Civil War party system seems to have been set by the peace at Appomattox four years later. A number of scholars (Burnham, 1970; Sellers, 1965; Sundquist, 1973) contend that the Civil War realignment was completed by the beginning of the 1860's. Sundquist (1973, p. 71) for example, concludes: "By 1858 the new alignment was firmly in place thoughout the North." Yet, in retrospect, this assessment seems to overestimate the importance of this time period for the development of long-term partisan orientations. As Sundquist (p. 87) adds: "The heightened polarization of the war years etched the slavery-secession-war-reconstruction-Negro-rights line of cleavage more deeply into the political pattern until old lines dividing the electorate were obliterated. More and more voters made their party choices on the basis of the new line of cleavage rather than the old, especially the new generation of voters just coming to political maturity."

Figure 31-2   Population Replacement and Partisan Change, 1850-1940

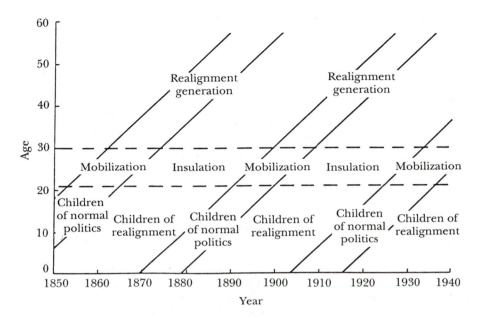

The period prior to the 1860's seems more an era during which the old party system was eroding rather than the new one forming. Pomper (1970, p. 114) argues that the 1864 election, not an earlier election, first registered "the definite break with traditional sources of party support" even in the North; he supports his contention by reporting low correlations between that election and the average of the four preceding presidential elections and high correlations between it and the average of the four subsequent elections. Furthermore, Lipset (1960, chap. 11) shows that the realignment in the South postdated the 1860 election, coming with the referenda over secession several months later.

Scholars agree that the Panic of 1893 initiated the next realignment phase. Sundquist (1973) and Burnham (1970) ascribe to the Panic of 1893 the responsibility for the initial urbanite movement away from the Democrats. This movement was surely crystallized by the Democrats' choice of an agrarian populist as their presidential candidate three years later. Bryan's nomination countered these losses partially by attracting rural, particularly western, voters to the Democratic party. Pomper's (1970, p. 107) correlational analysis shows that the 1896 election was most unlike those that preceded and consistent with those that followed. This realigning phase had clearly run its course by the reelection of McKinley over Bryan in 1900.

While Key (1955) identifies the beginnings of a realignment in New England during the 1928 election, it seems doubtful that the New Deal realignment was fully initiated throughout the nation, and even in that region, prior to the Depression of 1929. The changes in voting patterns in the 1928 election were probably tied to the candidacy of Al Smith and would not have been permanent had the Depression of 1929 not reinforced the short-run lines of cleavage. As Sundquist (1973, pp. 181-82) puts it: "The heavy movement across party lines in presidential voting in the cities in 1928 was obviously caused by the issues that dominated public discussion in that election—religion and Prohibition. These were not the dominant issues of 1932 and 1936. The minor realignment of 1928 in the cities can therefore be considered an episode in American politics distinct from the realignment of the 1930's." The realignment started by the Depression of 1929 and continued in the election of 1932 was probably not consummated until the 1936 election.

The second important assumption underlying Figure 31-2 is that the period during which adults are most likely to change their partisan attitudes comes between the age at which they are first eligible to vote (twenty-one before 1970 and eighteen since) and age thirty. Both are arbitrary bounds for the "adult formative years" and serve only as a first approximation until more is known about the formation of political attitudes in adults.

A third assumption is that the average age differential between parents and children is the conventional twenty-five years. This assumption plays an important role in the spacing of the mobilization phases in Figure 31-2. The generations available for mobilization are, by definition, those whose parents were not adults during the previous realigning phase. Thus, the children of normal politics begin to enter the electorate twenty-five years after the end of that phase. The mobilization phase begins twenty-five years after the termination of the preceding period of realignment and ends with the denouement of the new realignment phase. The children of normal politics may be in the electorate for some years (but no more than nine) before they are realigned.

This theory of realignment suggests that the prior disengagement of young voters from the established party system is a necessary precondition for realignment. The purportedly weak childhood partisan socialization of the children of normal politics only nurtures the "ripeness for realignment," however; a societal trauma, often a depression, seems from past experience necessary to deteriorate the actual realignment. It is clear in retrospect that traumatic events will not have this effect if they are not set in the context of an electorate "ripe for realignment." Other traumas of at least equal magnitude— the economic depressions of 1873 and 1907, two world wars, and the anticommunist hysteria of the early cold war period, for example—had no more than short-lived impacts on partisan behavior.

Manifestations of a decline in the importance of parties are apparent prior to each of the realignments in the past. Third party movements were unusually successful in electoral politics in the 1850's, the early 1890's, and the 1920's. Split-ticket voting also seems to have peaked during the 1920's (Cummings, 1966, p. 37) and may well have risen in the earlier periods if the pre-1900 electoral system had not made ticket splitting virtually impossible (Rusk, 1970). The decline of parties during each of these periods was arrested abruptly by the advent of a traumatic realignment-producing event and the consequent resocialization of young voters to provide a realignment generation.

This theory cannot stand without substantial qualification. First, a certain tentativeness is inevitably involved in any theory which purports to explain a macropolitical phenomenon using micropolitical behavior, without much more than circumstantial evidence linking the two. Second, the operational assumptions incorporated in Figure 31-2 are crude. The time interval between generations, the adult formative years, and the length of each realignment phase all resist precise quantification. Third, individuals in age-defined political generations do not necessarily share experiences during both childhood and the early years of adulthood. Political learning and experience are far too complex to be common for age-related individuals who differ substantially on other fundamental variables. The theory can withstand this qualification, however, because partisan realignments require only partial reshufflings of the electorate.

The most critical qualification to this theory is that it is grounded on assumptions about past individual-level political behavior which cannot be tested empirically. We simply cannot determine whether the partisan orientations of previous realignment generations of voters were more deeply rooted than those of other generations of voters. Furthermore, we know virtually nothing about the relative intensities of partisan socialization when performed by realignment versus normal politics generations. Precise answers to these questions must await another realignment phase in American electoral politics. Partial answers, on the other hand, may be suggested by contemporary political behavior, if they are researched. Even these answers, though, will not be forthcoming unless political socialization researchers recognize the importance of the early adult years for the formation of enduring political orientations and realize that substantial variations may exist in the success with which each successive generation socializes its young.

Contemporary American Electoral Politics

Recent American electoral politics has been marked by unusual instability. After a landslide victory of historic proportions in the 1964 presidential election, the Democratic party descended into bitter internecine strife and electoral defeat, followed by electoral disaster in 1972. During the same time period, pollsters plotted an increase in self-identified independents in the electorate, at the expense of both parties (see Figure 31-3). This change in the distribution of partisan orientations has been parallel by a remarkable increase in split-ticketing voting, particularly in the two most recent presidential elections—1968 and 1972.

Some observers conclude that recent events in American electoral politics signal a new realignment phase. Phillips (1970) trumpets the emergence of a new Republican majority coalition. Burnham (1970, p. 141), on the other hand, is more cautious: "It is particularly doubtful ... that a new majority would be 'Republican' in any well-defined, party-identified sense of the terms; but such a majority, if derived from the 'great middle,' would surely be profoundly conservative." If there has been any realignment, he concludes, its direction has

Figure 31-3   Distribution of Party Identification, 1940-1973

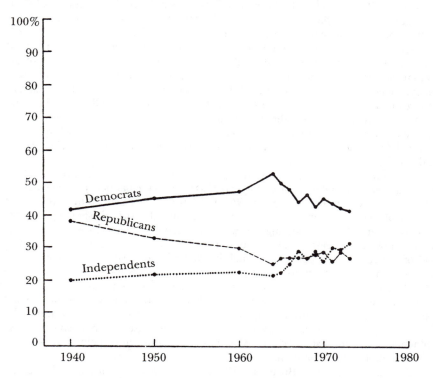

Source: The Gallup Opinion Index, Report No. 95, May 1973 (recent figures represent yearly averages).

been conservative, even though the dynamics of that realignment may well have set in motion a liberal-to-radical realignment to come in the future. A few political commentators have even perceived the birth of a new liberal majority in the politics of the sixties (Dutton, 1971) although they have been virtually silenced by the Nixon landslide in 1972.

Burnham (1969, 1970) also expresses considerable doubt that a realignment is possible any longer in American politics. This important mechanism of electoral change has been rendered inoperable, he maintains, by the "depoliticizing and antipartisan" electoral reforms enacted by the Progressives at the turn of the century. To Burnham, the decline in the importance of party loyalties (and, hence, parties) to the electorate is a long-term trend which was briefly slowed, but not reversed, by the New Deal realignment.

It seems to me that neither the theory of realignment nor that of the decline of parties provide adequate explanations for contemporary electoral politics. Nor does Burnham's combination of the two theories in a single explanation seem satisfactory. The best clues to the state of present politics are found in the political orientations of the youngest generation of voters. Change should be clearest, as well as most prophetic of the future, in this generation. Two logically intertwined characteristics of these maturing voters are conspicuous in recent years. First, this generation is much more heavily independent than older generations were at similar stages in the life cycle,[5] and there is every indication of increased independence among the young. (Data from the University of Michigan congressional election study in 1970 and from the Gallup Poll show that the generations which entered the electorate after 1968 were, if anything, more independent than their immediate predecessors.) Second, the heightened independence of this generation represents an erosion of support for both the Democrats and the Republicans.

Thus not only has there been no aggregate shift in a partisan direction, but there has been no tendency for young voters to flock to the banners of either party. Republican presidential victories in 1968 and 1972 were registered in spite of, not because of, the voting tendencies of this generation. McGovern's showing among these voters in 1972 does not augur well for an emerging Democratic majority. In the absence of changes in the distribution of partisan loyalties in the electorate and of noticeable disproportionate mobilization of young voters into one party, realignment explanations for present policies seem inadequate.

Recent changes in partisan orientations, principally the increase in independents, appear, on their face, to be explained better by the theory of the decline of parties. Upon closer examination, though, this theory too is found wanting. It fails to explain a signal characteristic of the increase in independents: its suddenness. (Sundquist, 1973, p. 353, has made this same point but with a different explanation for it than mine.)

As conceptualized by Burnham (1969, 1970), the decline of parties has been inexorable since the beginning of the twentieth century. Only the onset of the New Deal realignment slowed the spread of this fatal cancer in the party system, but it hardly effected a cure of it. Given this view, it is puzzling why the pace of the decline of parties accelerated so quickly in the sixties.

Beyond the theories of realignment and decline of parties lies an explanation of contemporary electoral politics. The socialization theory of realignment offers an explanation which fits both the present and the past. The 1960's and early 1970's bear striking resemblance to eras in American political history which preceded realignments. The electorate in each case—in the 1850's, the 1890's, the 1920's, and the present—contains a generation of young voters who, as children of normal politics, were (and are) ripe for realignment. The current ripe-for-realignment generation began to enter the electorate in full force in the 1960's (see Figure 31-4), and the decline of parties has been manifest ever since.

What differentiates the present from the earlier mobilization periods is that almost a decade has passed without an event with sufficient force and direction to destroy the old party alignment and mobilize young voters in new partisan directions. A second differentiating feature, making the current decline of parties all the more pronounced, is that a higher proportion of the electorate is in the

Figure 31-4 Population Replacement and Partisan Change, 1920-1980

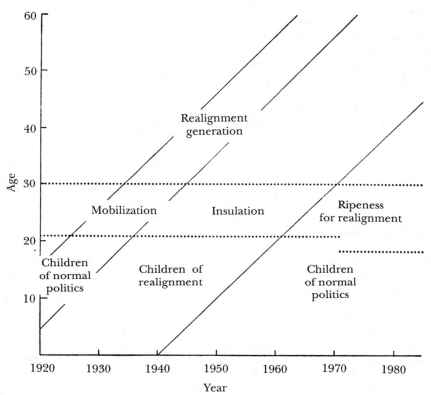

under-thirty age group than has been the case in the recent past. One of the more subtle effects of the post-World War Two "baby boom" and the recent reduction of the voting age to eighteen has been to quicken the pace of partisan decay.

The Future of American Electoral Politics

While my socialization theory of realignments can explain both the periodicity of past realignments and the current drift away from parties, it yields no clear predictions about the future. Several alternative future scenarios may be suggested, each of which seems plausible.

The first scenario assumes that some critical, realigning event is "just around the corner." As in the past, this event may be economic in nature, though the major role government now plays in managing the economy would seem to preclude economic dislocations of the magnitude of past depressions. Current economic problems are sure to make their mark on political dispositions. But it is doubtful that they will catalyze a realignment, particularly since they reflect current partisan cleavages. Another potential realigning event may be the Watergate affair. Past revelations of political wrongdoing have never triggered a realignment, but one cannot be certain whether this is explained by their timing (none occurred when the electorate was ripe for realignment) or by the general nonpartisan "fallout" of such issues over the long run.

The conflict over civil rights for blacks may constitute a realigning issue. But unless there is considerable lag in the impact of events on partisanship, this issue does not seem to have generated the kind of traumatic force necessary to mobilize voters towards a new partisan alignment. Even though it seems premature to write an ending to the importance of this conflict and its realigning potential, there is little evidence that it will produce a realignment, especially since the major questions underlying this conflict are now juridical in nature and outside of the electoral arena.

An alternative scenario portrays a future almost wholly incongruous with the past. In the absence of a catalyzing traumatic event, the current ripeness for realignment may continue, contributing to an increasingly severe decline of party. Some voters in the generation ripe for realignment have already passed their thirtieth birthday and may no longer be available for partisan mobilization. This may lead to the increasing influence of "Madison Avenue politics" and to a perceptible decline in popular influence over public policy because, for all their faults, political parties are valuable instruments for democracy, and no institutions have yet emerged which can supplant them as vehicles for popular control.

A variation of this theme assumes that independence rarely constitutes a meaningful long-run partisan orientation and that independents over thirty will remain available for mobilization. If this assumption is valid, then we may expect a far more sweeping realignment in the future than has ever appeared in the past. Such a realignment could well endanger partisan competition in America by virtually vanquishing the party not favored in the realignment.

Whatever happens in the future, the socialization theory of realignment should considerably enhance our understanding of past and present electoral politics. Ripe for realignment in a system which has failed to generate any mobilizing forces in partisan directions, younger voters are drifting away from both parties to a haven of political neutrality. This drift could fundamentally alter the dynamics of American electoral politics by terminating the century-old cycle of realignments and normal politics. It could culminate in a paralysis in the making of public policy if confidence declines in political parties—the major forces for the policy coordination that occurs in American politics—and if no other institutions arise to take their place.

NOTES

1. One suspects that this linkage question has been ignored because of the ease of collecting data from school children and the difficulty of gathering data which tied adult political behavior directly to preadult political learning.

2. One could infer from these data that Key's evidence of a realignment in 1928 in the industrial Northeast was, in reality, evidence of substantial defections only among older voters. These defections could probably not have forged a realignment by themselves without the subsequent Depression of 1929. See Key (1955).

3. There is a possibility that a realignment could be produced without any partisan changes through the conversion of independents to a partisan disposition. This possibility was unlikely, however, as long as independents were few in number and the least knowledgeable and politically involved of all voters as was the case in the 1950's (Campbell et al., 1960, pp. 142-45). In more recent times, the characteristics of independents seem to be changing, and one can speculate that the absence of realigning forces in an electorate ripe for realignment has created a growing number of knowledgeable, involved independents—particularly among the young. This trend may well differentiate contemporary electoral politics from those of any previous era. Discussion of the implications of such a trend is left until later.

4. This figure parallels one reported in Campbell et al. (1960, p. 154), but it is based on a much wider time interval and is restricted to presidential elections to ensure equivalency. Slightly different conclusions may be drawn from these two distributions of party identification by age cohort. Generational discontinuity in Figure 31-1 is not as sharp as that which appears in the figure from *The American Voter*. One reason is surely that independents have been excluded from the latter figure, but a second reason may be that the passage of time has dulled the apparent effects of the New Deal realignment.

5. In the past twenty years, young voters have continually identified themselves as independents more than have their elders. The common interpretation of this relationship is that it reflects life-cycle differences and that generations would become more partisan as they aged (Campbell et al., 1960, p. 162). While it is too early to determine whether the phenomenon will persist through the life cycle, the life-cycle differences in partisanship which have been common in the past years appear to have been joined recently by pervasive generational differences.

REFERENCES

Abelson, Robert, Donald Kinder, Mark Peters, and Susan Fiske. "Affective and Semantic Components in Political Person Perception." *Journal of Personality and Social Psychology* (1982) 42:619-30.

Abramowitz, Alan I. "A Comparison of Voting for U.S. Senator and Representative in 1978." *American Political Science Review* (1980) 74:633-40.

Abramson, Paul R. *Generational Change in American Politics.* Lexington, Mass.: Lexington Books, 1975.

———. "Developing Party Identification: A Further Examination of Life-Cycle, Generational, and Period Effects." *American Journal of Political Science* (1979) 23:78-96.

Abramson, Paul R., John H. Aldrich, and David W. Rohde. *Change and Continuity in the 1980 Elections,* rev. ed. Washington, D.C.: CQ Press, 1983.

Achen, Christopher H. "Mass Political Attitudes and the Survey Response." *American Political Science Review* (1975) 69:1218-31.

———. "Issue Voting in the 1950's." University of California, Berkeley, 1976.

———. "The Bias in Normal Vote Estimates." *Political Methodology* (1979) 6:343-56.

Agger, Robert. "Independents and Party Identifiers: Characteristics and Behavior in 1952." In *American Voting Behavior,* ed. Eugene Burdick and Arthur G. Brodbeck. Glencoe, Ill.: Free Press, 1959.

Albright, Spencer D. *The American Ballot.* Washington, D.C.: American Council on Public Affairs, 1942.

Aldrich, John H. "Candidate Support Functions in the 1968 Election: An Empirical Application of the Spatial Model." *Public Choice* (1975) 22:1-22.

———. "Turnout and Rational Choice." *American Journal of Political Science* (1992) 36:forthcoming.

Allison, Paul D. "Testing for Interaction in Multiple Regression." *American Journal of Sociology* (1977) 82:144-53.

Almond, Gabriel A. *The American People and Foreign Policy.* New York: Harcourt, 1950.

Almond, Gabriel A., and Sidney Verba. *The Civic Culture.* Princeton, N.J.: Princeton University Press, 1963.

Amemiya, Takeshi. "The Estimation of a Simultaneous Equation Tobit Model." *International Economic Review* (1979) 20:169-81.

Andersen, Kristi. *The Creation of a Democratic Majority, 1928-1936.* Chicago: University of Chicago Press, 1979.

Arcelus, Francisco, and Allan H. Meltzer. "The Effects of Aggregate Economic Variables on Congressional Elections." *American Political Science Review* (1975) 69:1232-39.

Arseneau, Robert B., and Raymond E. Wolfinger. "Voting Behavior in Congressional Elections." Paper presented at the annual meeting of the American Political Science Association, New Orleans, 1973.

Atesoglu, H. Sonmez, and Roger Congleton. "Economic Conditions and National Elections, Post-Sample Forecasts." *American Political Science Review* (1982) 76:873-75.

Baker, Kendall L., Russell J. Dalton, and Kai Hildebrandt. *Germany Transformed.* Cambridge, Mass.: Harvard University Press, 1981.

Barnes, Samuel H. "Left, Right, and the Italian Voter." *Comparative Political Studies* (1971) 4:157-75.

_____. *Representation in Italy.* Chicago: University of Chicago Press, 1977.

Beck, Paul Allen. "Model Choice in Political Science: The Case of Voting Behavior Research, 1946-1975." In *Political Science: The Science of Politics,* ed. Herbert F. Weisberg. New York: Agathon, 1986.

Belknap, George, and Angus Campbell. "Political Party Identification and Attitudes Toward Foreign Policy." *Public Opinion Quarterly* (1952) 15:601-23.

Berelson, Bernard R. "Democratic Practice and Democratic Theory." In *Voting,* Bernard R. Berelson, Paul F. Lazarsfeld, and William N. McPhee. Chicago: University of Chicago Press, 1954.

Berelson, Bernard R., Paul F. Lazarsfeld, and William N. McPhee. *Voting.* Chicago: University of Chicago Press, 1954.

Bishop, George F., and Kathleen A. Frankovic. "Ideological Consensus and Constraint Among Party Leaders and Followers in the 1978 Election." *Micropolitics* (1981) 1:87-111.

Bishop, George F., Alfred J. Tuchfarber, and Robert W. Oldendick. "Change in the Structure of American Political Attitudes: The Nagging Question of Question Wording." *American Journal of Political Science* (1978) 22:250-69.

Blake, Donald E. "The Consistency of Inconsistency: Party Identification in Federal and Provincial Politics." *Canadian Journal of Political Science* (1982) 15:691-710.

Bloom, Harold, and H. Douglas Price. "Voter Response to Short Run Economic Conditions: The Asymmetric Effect of Prosperity and Recession." *American Political Science Review* (1975) 69:1240-54.

Bowman, Lewis, Dennis Ippolito, and William Donaldson. "Incentives for the Maintenance of Grassroots Political Activism." *Midwest Journal of Political Science* (1969) 13:126-39.

Boyd, Richard W. "Popular Control of Public Policy: A Normal Vote Analysis of the 1968 Election." *American Political Science Review* (1972) 66:429-49.

_____. "Decline of U.S. Voter Turnout: Structural Explanations." *American Politics Quarterly* (1981) 9:133-59.

Brody, Richard A. "Change and Stability in Party Identification: A Note of Caution." Stanford University, n.d. Photocopy.

_____. "Communication." *American Political Science Review* (1976) 70:924-26.

_____. "Stability and Change in Party Identification: Presidential to Off-years." Paper presented at the annual meeting of the American Political Science Association, Washington, D.C., 1977.

Brody, Richard A., and Benjamin I. Page. "The Assessment of Policy Voting." *American Political Science Review* (1972) 66:450-58. Reprinted, in part, as Chapter 10 in this volume.

――――. "Indifference, Alienation and Rational Decision: The Effects of Candidate Evaluations on Turnout and the Vote." *Public Choice* (1973) 15:1-17.

Brody, Richard A., Benjamin I. Page, Sidney Verba, and Jerome Laulicht. "Vietnam, the Urban Crisis and the 1968 Election." Paper presented at the annual meeting of the American Sociological Association, San Francisco, 1969.

Brown, Thad, and Arthur A. Stein. "The Political Economy of National Elections." *Comparative Politics* (1982) 14:479-97.

Brunk, Gregory G. "The 1964 Attitude Consistency Leap Reconsidered." *Political Methodology* (1978) 5:347-60.

Budge, Ian, Ivor Crewe, and Dennis Farlie, eds. *Party Identification and Beyond.* London: Wiley, 1976.

Budge, Ian, and Dennis Farlie. "A Comparative Analysis of Factors Correlated with Turnout and Voting Choice." In *Party Identification and Beyond,* ed. Ian Budge, Ivor Crewe, and Dennis Farlie. London: Wiley, 1976.

Burnham, Walter Dean. "The Changing Shape of the American Political Universe." *American Political Science Review* (1965) 59:7-28. Chapter 29 in this volume.

――――. "American Voting Behavior and the 1964 Election." *Midwest Journal of Political Science* (1968) 12:1-40.

――――. "The End of American Party Politics." *Transaction* (1969) 7:12-22.

――――. *Critical Elections and the Mainsprings of American Politics.* New York: Norton, 1970.

――――. "Those High Nineteenth-Century American Voting Turnouts: Fact or Fiction?" *Journal of Interdisciplinary History* (1986) 16:613-44.

Butler, David, and Donald Stokes. *Political Change in Britain.* New York: St. Martin's, 1969, 1970, 1974, 1976.

Cahalan, Don. "The *Digest* Poll Rides Again." *Public Opinion Quarterly* (1989) 53:129-33.

Cain, Bruce, and John Ferejohn. "A Comparison of Party Identification in the United States and Great Britain." *Comparative Political Studies* (1981) 14:31-47.

Cain, Bruce E., John A. Ferejohn, and Morris P. Fiorina. "The Constituency Service Basis of the Personal Vote for U.S. Representatives and British Members of Parliament." *American Political Science Review* (1984) 78:110-25.

――――. *The Personal Vote.* Cambridge, Mass.: Harvard University Press, 1987.

Campbell, Angus. "Surge and Decline: A Study of Electoral Change." *Public Opinion Quarterly* (1960) 24:397-418.

――――. "Voters and Elections: Past and Present." *Journal of Politics* (1964) 26:745-57.

Campbell, Angus, and Howard C. Cooper. *Group Differences in Attitudes and Votes.* Ann Arbor, Mich.: Institute for Social Research, 1956.

Campbell, Angus, and Donald E. Stokes. "Partisan Attitudes and the Presidential Vote." In *American Voting Behavior,* ed. Eugene Burdick and Arthur J. Brodbeck. Glencoe, Ill.: Free Press, 1959.

Campbell, Angus, Philip E. Converse, Warren E. Miller, and Donald E. Stokes. *The American Voter.* New York: Wiley, 1960.

――――. *Elections and the Political Order.* New York: Wiley, 1966.

Campbell, Angus, Gerald Gurin, and Warren E. Miller. *The Voter Decides.* Evanston, Ill.: Row, Peterson, 1954.

Cantril, Hadley. *The Pattern of Human Concerns.* New Brunswick, N.J.: Rutgers University Press, 1965.

Carmines, Edward G., Steven H. Renten, and James A. Stimson. "Events and Alignments: The Party Image Link." In *Controversies in Voting Behavior,* 2d ed., ed. Richard G. Niemi and Herbert F. Weisberg. Washington, D.C.: CQ Press, 1984.

Carmines, Edward G., and James A. Stimson. *Issue Evolution: Race and the Transformation of American Politics.* Princeton, N.J.: Princeton University Press, 1989.

Chambers, William N., and Walter D. Burnham, eds. *The American Party Systems.* New York: Oxford University Press, 1967, 1975.

Christ, Carl F. *Econometric Models and Methods.* New York: Wiley, 1966.

Claggett, William. "Partisan Acquisition Versus Partisan Intensity: Life-Cycle, Generation, and Period Effects, 1952-1976." *American Journal of Political Science* (1981) 25:193-214.

Clarke, Harold D., Lawrence LeDuc, Jane Jenson, and Jon H. Pammett. *Political Choice in Canada.* Toronto: McGraw-Hill Ryerson, 1979.

Conover, Pamela Johnston, and Stanley Feldman. "Belief System Organization in the American Electorate." In *The Electorate Reconsidered,* ed. John Pierce and John L. Sullivan. Beverly Hills, Calif.: Sage, 1980.

Converse, Jean M. *Survey Research in the United States: Roots and Emergence, 1890-1960.* Berkeley: University of California Press, 1987.

Converse, Philip E. "The Nature of Belief Systems in Mass Publics." In *Ideology and Discontent,* ed. David E. Apter. New York: Free Press, 1964. Reprinted, in part, as Chapter 5 in this volume.

———. "On the Possibility of Major Political Realignment in the South." In *Elections and the Political Order,* Angus Campbell, Philip E. Converse, Warren E. Miller, and Donald E. Stokes. New York: Wiley, 1966a.

———. "The Concept of a Normal Vote." In *Elections and the Political Order,* Angus Campbell, Philip E. Converse, Warren E. Miller, and Donald E. Stokes. New York: Wiley, 1966b.

———. "Of Time and Partisan Stability." *Comparative Political Studies* (1969) 2:139-71.

———. "Attitudes and Non-Attitudes: Continuation of a Dialogue." In *The Quantitative Analysis of Social Problems,* ed. Edward R. Tufte. Reading, Mass.: Addison-Wesley, 1970.

———. "Change in the American Electorate." In *The Human Meaning of Social Change,* ed. Angus Campbell and Philip E. Converse. New York: Russell Sage, 1972.

———. "Public Opinion and Voting Behavior." In *Handbook of Political Science,* ed. Fred I. Greenstein and Nelson W. Polsby. Reading, Mass.: Addison-Wesley (1975).

———. *The Dynamics of Party Support.* Beverly Hills, Calif.: Sage, 1976.

———. "Rejoinder to Abramson." *American Journal of Political Science* (1979) 23:97-100.

Converse, Philip E., and Georges Dupeux. "Politicization of the Electorate in France and the United States." *Public Opinion Quarterly* (1962) 26:1-23.

Converse, Philip E., and Gregory B. Markus. " 'Plus ça Change . . . :' The New CPS Election Study Panel." *American Political Science Review* (1979) 73:2-49. Chapter 8 in this volume.

Converse, Philip E., Warren E. Miller, Jerrold G. Rusk, and Arthur C. Wolfe. "Continuity and Change in American Politics: Parties and Issues in the 1968 Election." *American Political Science Review* (1969) 63:1083-1105.

Converse, Philip E., with Richard G. Niemi. "Non-Voting Among Young Adults in the United States." In *Political Parties and Political Behavior,* ed. William J. Crotty, Donald M. Freeman, and Douglas S. Gatlin, 2d ed. Boston: Allyn & Bacon, 1971.

Converse, Philip E., and Roy Pierce. "Basic Cleavages in French Politics and the Disorders of May and June, 1968." Paper presented at the Seventh World Congress of Sociology, Varna, Bulgaria, 1970.

_____. "Measuring Partisanship." *Political Methodology* (1985) 11:143-66.

Coombs, Clyde H. *A Theory of Data.* New York: Wiley, 1964.

Cover, Albert D. "One Good Term Deserves Another: The Advantage of Incumbency in Congressional Elections." *American Journal of Political Science* (1977) 21:523-42.

Cover, Albert D., and David R. Mayhew. "Congressional Dynamics and the Decline of Competitive Congressional Elections." In *Congress Reconsidered,* ed. Lawrence C. Dodd and Bruce I. Oppenheimer. New York: Praeger, 1977.

Crewe, Ivor. "Party Identification Theory and Political Change in Britain." In *Party Identification and Beyond,* ed. Ian Budge, Ivor Crewe, and Dennis Farlie. London: Wiley, 1976.

Cummings, Milton C., Jr. *Congressmen and the Electorate.* New York: Free Press, 1966.

Dahl, Robert A., ed. *Political Oppositions in Western Democracies.* New Haven, Conn.: Yale University Press, 1966.

Dalton, Russell J. *Citizen Politics in Western Democracies.* Chatham, N.J.: Chatham House, 1988.

Davis, Otto A., Melvin J. Hinich, and Peter C. Ordeshook. "An Expository Development of a Mathematical Model of the Electoral Process." *American Political Science Review* (1970) 64:426-48.

Dawes, Robin, and B. Corrigan. "Linear Models in Decision Making." *Psychological Bulletin* (1974) 81:95-106.

de Guchteneire, Paul, Lawrence LeDuc, and Richard G. Niemi. "A Compendium of Survey Studies of Elections around the World, Update 1." *Electoral Studies* (1991) 10:231-43.

Dennis, Jack. "Trends in Support for the American Party System." *British Journal of Political Science* (1975) 5:187-230.

_____. "Some Properties of Partisanship." Paper presented at the annual meeting of the American Political Science Association, New York, 1981.

_____. "Political Independence in America, Part I: On Being an Independent Partisan Supporter." *British Journal of Political Science* (1988) 18:77-109.

Dobson, Douglas, and Duane Meeter. "Alternative Markov Models for Describing Change in Party Identification." *American Journal of Political Science* (1974) 18:487-500.

Dobson, Douglas, and Douglas St. Angelo. "Party Identification and the Floating Vote." *American Political Science Review* (1975) 69:481-90.

Downs, Anthony. *An Economic Theory of Democracy.* New York: Harper and Row, 1957.

Dreyer, Edward. "Change and Stability in Party Identification." *Journal of Politics* (1973) 35:712-22.

Duncan, Otis Dudley. *Introduction to Structural Equation Models.* New York: Academic Press, 1975.

Dutton, Frederick G. *Changing Sources of Power.* New York: McGraw-Hill, 1971.

Duverger, Maurice. *Political Parties,* 2d ed. New York: Wiley, 1959.

Eldersveld, Samuel J. *Political Parties: A Behavioral Analysis.* Chicago: Rand McNally, 1964.

_____. "Party Identification in India in Comparative Perspective." *Comparative Political Studies* (1973) 6:271-95.

Epstein, Laurily L., and Kathleen A. Frankovic. "Casework and Electoral Margins: Insurance is Prudent Policy." *Polity* (1982) 14:691-700.

Erikson, Robert S. "The SRC Panel Data and Mass Political Attitudes." *British Journal of Political Science* (1979) 9:89-114.

Erikson, Robert S., and Kent L. Tedin. "The 1928-1936 Partisan Realignment: The Case for the Conversion Hypothesis." *American Political Science Review* (1981) 75:951-62.

Evans, Eldon C. *A History of the Australian Ballot System in the United States.* Chicago: University of Chicago Press, 1917.

Fair, Ray C. "On Controlling the Economy to Win Elections." Cowles Foundation Discussion Paper No. 397, Yale University, 1975.

_____. "The Effects of Economic Events on Votes for President." *Review of Economics and Statistics* (1978) 60:159-73.

Fenno, Richard F., Jr. "If, as Ralph Nader Says, Congress is 'The Broken Branch,' How Come We Love Our Congressmen So Much?" In *Congress in Change: Evolution and Reform,* ed. Norman J. Ornstein. New York: Praeger, 1975.

_____. *Home Style: House Members in Their Districts.* Boston: Little, Brown, 1978.

Ferejohn, John A. "On the Decline of Competition in Congressional Elections." *American Political Science Review* (1977) 71:166-76.

Ferejohn, John A., and Morris P. Fiorina. "The Paradox of Not Voting: A Decision Theoretic Analysis." *American Political Science Review* (1974) 68:525-36.

_____. "Closeness Counts Only in Horseshoes and Dancing." *American Political Science Review* (1975) 69:920-25.

Field, John Osgood, and Ronald E. Anderson. "Ideology in the Public's Conceptualization of the 1964 Election." *Public Opinion Quarterly* (1969) 33:380-98.

Fiorina, Morris P. "An Outline for a Model of Party Choice." *American Journal of Political Science* (1977a) 21:601-26.

_____. *Congress: Keystone of the Washington Establishment.* New Haven, Conn.: Yale University Press, 1977b, 1989.

_____. "Economic Retrospective Voting in American National Elections: A Microanalysis." *American Journal of Political Science* (1978) 22:426-43.

_____. "Congressmen and Their Constituents: 1958 and 1978." In *The United States Congress,* ed. Dennis Hale. Proceedings of the Thomas P. O'Neill, Jr., Symposium on the U.S. Congress. Boston College, 1981a.

_____. *Retrospective Voting in American National Elections.* New Haven, Conn.: Yale University Press, 1981b.

_____. "Some Problems in Studying the Effects of Resource Allocation in Congressional Elections." *American Journal of Political Science* (1981c) 25:542-67.

Fisher, Franklin. *The Identification Problem in Economics.* New York: McGraw-Hill, 1966.

Formisano, Ronald P. "Federalists and Republicans: Parties, Yes—System, No." In *The Evolution of American Electoral Systems,* ed. Paul Kleppner et al. Westport, Conn.: Greenwood, 1981.

Fowler, Linda L., Jeff Stonecash, and Robert Carrothers. "The Ties That Bind? Casework and Careerism in State Legislatures." Paper presented at the annual meeting of the American Political Science Association, Denver, 1982.

Frey, Bruno S., and Friedrich Schneider. "Economic and Personality Determinants of Presidential Popularity." manuscript, 1977.

Frohlich, Norman, Joe A. Oppenheimer, Jeffrey Smith, and Oran R. Young. "A Test of Downsian Voter Rationality: 1964 Presidential Voting." *American Political Science Review* (1978) 72:178-97.

Gamm, Gerald H. *The Making of New Deal Democrats.* Chicago: University of Chicago Press, 1989.

Gienapp, William E. " 'Politics Seems to Enter into Everything': Political Culture in the

North, 1840-1860." In *Essays on American Antebellum Politics, 1840-1860*, ed. Stephen Maizlish and John Kushma. College Station: Texas A & M University Press, 1982.

———. *The Origins of the Republican Party, 1852-1856*. New York: Oxford University Press, 1987.

Ginsburg, Gerald. "Computing Antebellum Turnout: Methods and Models." *Journal of Interdisciplinary History* (1986) 16:579-611.

Goldberg, Arthur S. "Discerning a Causal Pattern Among Data on Voting Behavior." *American Political Science Review* (1966) 60:913-22.

Goodman, Leo. "Some Alternatives to Ecological Correlation." *American Journal of Sociology* (1959) 44:610-25.

Goodman, Saul, and Gerald H. Kramer. "Commentary on Arcelus and Meltzer: The Effect of Aggregate Economic Conditions on Congressional Elections." *American Political Science Review* (1975) 69:1255-65.

Greenstein, Fred I. *Children and Politics*. New Haven, Conn.: Yale University Press, 1965, rev. ed., 1969.

———. *The American Party System and the American People*, 2d ed. Englewood Cliffs, N.J.: Prentice-Hall, 1970.

Guynes, Randall. "Orientations Toward the Opposition Party." Emory University, n.d. Photocopy.

Guynes, Randall, and Jerry Perkins. "Notes on a Theory of Partisan Identification." Emory University, n.d. Photocopy.

Hadley, Charles D. "Dual Partisan Identification in the Deep South: An Analysis of State Political Party Elite." Paper presented at the annual meeting of the Midwest Political Science Association, Chicago, 1983.

Hagner, Paul R., and John C. Pierce. "Correlative Characteristics of Levels of Conceptualization in the American Public: 1956-1976." *Journal of Politics* (1982) 44:779-807.

Hanushek, Eric A., and John E. Jackson. *Statistical Methods for Social Scientists*. New York: Academic Press, 1977.

Harris, Joseph P. *Election Administration in the United States*. Washington, D.C.: Brookings Institution, 1934.

Hartwig, Frederick, William R. Jenkins, and Earl M. Temchin. "Variability in Electoral Behavior: The 1960, 1968, and 1976 Elections." *American Journal of Political Science* (1980) 24:553-58.

Heckman, James. "Dummy Endogenous Variables in a Simultaneous Equation System." *Econometrica* (1978) 46:931-49.

Heise, David R. "Separating Reliability and Stability in Test-Retest Correlation." *American Sociological Review* (1969) 34:93-101.

Hess, Robert, and Judith Torney. *The Development of Political Attitudes in Children*. Chicago: Aldine, 1967.

Hibbing, John R., and John R. Alford. "Economic Conditions and the Forgotten Side of Congress: A Foray into U.S. Senate Elections." *British Journal of Political Science* (1982) 12:505-16.

Hibbs, Douglas A., Jr. *Mass Political Violence*. New York: Wiley, 1972.

Hinckley, Barbara. "Interpreting House Midterm Elections: Toward a Measurement of the In-Party's 'Expected' Loss of Seats." *American Political Science Review* (1967) 61:694-700.

———. "House Re-Elections and Senate Defeats: The Role of the Challenger." *British Journal of Political Science* (1980a) 10:441-60.

_____. "The American Voter in Congressional Elections." *American Political Science Review* (1980b) 74:641-50.

Holmberg, Sören. *Svenska Väljare.* Stockholm: Lieber, 1981.

Hotelling, Harold. "Stability in Competition." *Economic Journal* (1929) 39:41-57.

Howell, Susan E. "Chasing an Elusive Concept: Ideological Identifications in the 1980 Presidential Campaign." Paper presented at the annual meeting of the Midwest Political Science Association, Chicago, 1983.

Hurley, Patricia A., and Kim Quaile Hill. "The Prospects for Issue Voting in Contemporary Congressional Elections: An Assessment of Citizen Awareness and Representation." *American Politics Quarterly* (1980) 8:425-48.

Hyman, Herbert H. *Political Socialization.* Glencoe: Free Press, 1959.

Inglehart, Ronald, and Hans D. Klingemann. "Party Identification, Ideological Preference, and the Left-Right Dimension Among Western Mass Publics." In *Party Identification and Beyond,* ed. Ian Budge, Ivor Crewe, and Dennis Farlie. London: Wiley, 1976.

Iyengar, Shanto, and Donald R. Kinder. *News That Matters: Television and American Opinion.* Chicago: University of Chicago Press, 1987.

Jackson, John E. "Issues and Party Alignment." In *The Future of Political Parties,* ed. Louis Maisel and Paul M. Sacks. Beverly Hills, Calif.: Sage, 1975a.

_____. "Issues, Party Choices, and Presidential Votes." *American Journal of Political Science* (1975b) 19:161-85.

Jackson, Thomas H., and George Marcus. "Political Competence and Ideological Constraint." *Social Science Research* (1975) 4:93-111.

Jacobson, Gary C. "The Effects of Campaign Spending in Congressional Elections." *American Political Science Review* (1978) 72:469-91.

_____. "Congressional Election, 1978: The Case of the Vanishing Challengers." In *Congressional Elections,* ed. Louis Sandy Maisel and Joseph Cooper. Beverly Hills, Calif.: Sage, 1981.

_____. *The Politics of Congressional Elections.* Boston: Little, Brown, 1983.

Jacobson, Gary C., and Samuel Kernell. *Strategy and Choice in Congressional Elections.* New Haven, Conn.: Yale University Press, 1981, 1983.

Jacoby, William G. "Unfolding the Party Identification Scale: Improving the Measurement of an Important Concept." *Political Methodology* (1982) 8:33-59.

Jennings, M. Kent, and Richard G. Niemi. "Party Identification at Multiple Levels of Government." *American Journal of Sociology* (1966) 72:86-101.

_____. "The Transmission of Political Values from Parent to Child." *American Political Science Review* (1968) 62:169-84.

_____. *The Political Character of Adolescence.* Princeton: Princeton University Press, 1974.

_____. "Continuity and Change in Political Orientations: A Longitudinal Study of Two Generations." *American Political Science Review* (1975) 69:1316-35.

_____. "The Persistence of Political Orientations: An Over-Time Analysis of Two Generations." *British Journal of Political Science* (1977) 8:333-63.

_____. *Generations and Politics.* Princeton: Princeton University Press, 1981.

Jensen, Richard J. "American Election Campaigns: A Theoretical and Historical Typology." Paper presented at the annual meeting of the Midwest Political Science Association, Chicago, 1968.

_____. *The Winning of the Midwest: Social and Political Conflict, 1888-1896.* Chicago: University of Chicago Press, 1971.

_____. "Armies, Admen and Crusaders: Strategies to Win Elections." *Public Opinion* (1980) 3:44-53.

Johannes, John R., and John C. McAdams. "The Congressional Incumbency Effect: Is It Casework, Policy Compatibility, or Something Else?" *American Journal of Political Science* (1981) 25:512-42.

Johnston, J. *Econometric Methods,* 2d ed. New York: McGraw-Hill, 1972.

Judd, Charles M., and Michael A. Milburn. "The Structure of Attitude Systems in the General Public: Comparisons of a Structural Equation Model." *American Sociological Review* (1980) 45:623-43.

Kaase, Max. "Party Identification and Voting Behavior in the West German Election of 1969." In *Party Identification and Beyond,* ed. Ian Budge, Ivor Crewe, and Dennis Farlie. London: Wiley, 1976.

Kabaker, Harvey. "Estimating the Normal Vote in Congressional Elections." *Midwest Journal of Political Science* (1969) 13:58-83.

Kagay, Michael R., and Greg A. Caldeira. "I Like the Looks of His Face: Elements of Electoral Choice, 1952-1972." Paper presented at the annual meeting of the American Political Science Association, San Francisco, 1975.

Katz, Richard S. "The Dimensionality of Party Identification: Cross-National Perspectives." *Comparative Politics* (1979) 11:147-63.

Keith, Bruce E., et al. "The Myth of the Independent Voter." Paper presented at the annual meeting of the American Political Science Association, Washington, D.C., 1977.

Kelley, Stanley, Jr. *Political Campaigning: Problems in Creating an Informed Electorate.* Washington, D.C.: Brookings Institution, 1960.

Kelley, Stanley, Jr., and Thad W. Mirer. "The Simple Act of Voting." *American Political Science Review* (1974) 68:572-91.

Kernell, Samuel. "Presidential Popularity and Negative Voting: An Alternative Explanation of the Midterm Congressional Decline of the President's Party." *American Political Science Review* (1977) 71:44-66.

Kerr, Clark, John R. Dunlop, Frederick S. Harbison, and Charles A. Myers. *Industrialism and Industrial Man.* Cambridge, Mass.: Harvard University Press, 1960.

Kessel, John H. *The Goldwater Coalition: Republican Strategies in 1964.* Indianapolis: Bobbs-Merrill, 1968.

———. "Comment: The Issues in Issue Voting." *American Political Science Review* (1972) 66:459-65.

———. *Presidential Campaign Politics.* Homewood, Ill.: Dorsey Press, 1980.

Key, V.O., Jr., *Southern Politics.* New York: Alfred A. Knopf, 1949.

———. *Politics, Parties, and Pressure Groups,* 5th ed. New York: Crowell, 1964.

———. "A Theory of Critical Elections." *Journal of Politics* (1955) 17:3-18.

———. *American State Politics.* New York: Knopf, 1956.

———. *The Responsible Electorate.* Cambridge, Mass.: Harvard University Press, 1966.

Key, V.O., Jr., and Frank Munger. "Social Determinism and Electoral Decision: The Case of Indiana." In *American Voting Behavior,* ed. Eugene Burdick and Arthur J. Brodbeck. Glencoe, Ill.: Free Press, 1959.

Kiewiet, D. Roderick. "Policy-Oriented Voting in Response to Economic Issues." *American Political Science Review* (1981) 75:448-59.

Kinder, Donald R., and D. Roderick Kiewiet. "Sociotropic Politics: The American Case." *British Journal of Political Science* (1981) 11:129-61.

Kleppner, Paul. *The Cross of Culture.* New York: Free Press, 1970.

———. *The Third Electoral System, 1853-1892.* Chapel Hill: University of North Carolina Press, 1979.

———. "Critical Realignments and Electoral Systems." In *The Evolution of American Electoral Systems,* ed. Paul Kleppner et al. Westport, Conn.: Greenwood, 1981.

———. "Were Women to Blame? Female Suffrage and Voter Turnout." *Journal of Interdisciplinary History* (1982a) 12:621-43.

———. *Continuity and Change in Electoral Politics, 1893-1928.* New York: Greenwood, 1987.

Klingemann, Hans D. "Measuring Ideological Conceptualizations." In *Political Action,* ed. Samuel H. Barnes et al. Beverly Hills, Calif.: Sage, 1979a.

———. "Ideological Conceptualization and Political Action." In *Political Action,* ed. Samuel H. Barnes et al. Beverly Hills, Calif.: Sage, 1979b.

Knight, Kathleen. "Ideology and Public Opinion." *Micropolitics* (1990) 3:59-82.

Knoke, David, and Michael Hout. "Social and Demographic Factors in American Party Affiliation: 1952-1972." *American Sociological Review* (1974) 39:700-13.

———. "Reply to Glenn." *American Sociological Review* (1976) 41:905-08.

Kostroski, Lee. "Party and Incumbency in Post-War Senate Elections." *American Political Science Review* (1973) 67:1213-34.

Kramer, Gerald H. "Short-Term Fluctuations in U.S. Voting Behavior." *American Political Science Review* (1971) 65:131-43.

———. "The Ecological Fallacy Revisited: Aggregate- versus Individual-Level Findings on Economics and Elections and Sociotropic Voting." *American Political Science Review* (1983) 77:92-111.

Kramer, Gerald H., and Susan Lepper. "Congressional Elections." In *Dimensions of Quantitative Research in History,* ed. William O. Aydelotte. Princeton, N.J.: Princeton University Press, 1972.

Kuklinski, James H., and Darrell M. West. "Economic Expectations and Voting Behavior in United States House and Senate Elections." *American Political Science Review* (1981) 75:436-47.

Ladd, Everett C., Jr., and Charles D. Hadley. *Transformation of the American Party System,* 2d ed. New York: Norton, 1978.

Lane, Robert E. *Political Life.* New York: Free Press, 1959.

———. *Political Ideology.* New York: Free Press, 1962.

Lane, Robert E., and David O. Sears. *Public Opinion.* Englewood Cliffs, N.J.: Prentice-Hall, 1964.

Lazarsfeld, Paul, Bernard Berelson, and Helen Gaudet. *The People's Choice.* New York: Columbia University Press, 1944, 1948.

LeDuc, Lawrence. "The Dynamic Properties of Party Identification: A Four-Nation Comparison." *European Journal of Political Research* (1981) 9:257-68.

Lepper, Susan. "Voting Behavior and Aggregate Policy Targets." *Public Choice* (1974) 18:67-81.

Levitin, Teresa E., and Warren E. Miller. "Ideological Interpretations of Presidential Elections." *American Political Science Review* (1979) 73:751-71.

Lewis-Beck, Michael S., and Paolo Bellucci. "Economic Influences on Legislative Elections in Multiparty Systems: France and Italy." *Political Behavior* (1982) 4:93-107.

Lipset, Seymour Martin. *Political Man.* Garden City, N.Y.: Doubleday, 1960.

Lipset, Seymour Martin, and Stein Rokkan. "Cleavage Structure, Party Systems, and Voter Alignments." In *Party Systems and Voter Alignments,* ed. Seymour M. Lipset and Stein Rokkan. New York: Free Press, 1967a.

———. *Party Systems and Voter Alignments.* New York: Free Press, 1967b.

Lodge, Milton, Kathleen McGraw, and Patrick Stroh. "An Impression-Driven Model of

Candidate Evaluation." *American Political Science Review* (1989) 83:399-419.

Ludington, Arthur C. *American Ballot Laws: 1888-1910.* Albany: New York State Library, 1911.

Luttbeg, Norman. "The Structure of Beliefs Among Leaders and the Public." *Public Opinion Quarterly* (1968) 32:398-409.

Macaluso, Theodore. "The Responsiveness of Party Identification to Current Political Evaluations." University of Kentucky, n.d. Photocopy.

McClosky, Herbert. "Consensus and Ideology in American Politics." *American Political Science Review* (1964) 58:361-82.

McClosky, Herbert, Paul J. Hoffmann, and Rosemary O'Hara. "Issue Conflict and Consensus among Party Leaders and Followers." *American Political Science Review* (1960) 54:406-27.

McCormack, Richard P. "Political Development and the Second Party System." In *The American Party Systems,* ed. William Chambers and Walter Dean Burnham. New York: Oxford University Press, 1967, 1975.

McDonald, Michael D., and Susan E. Howell. "Reconsidering the Reconceptualization of Party Identification." *Political Methodology* (1982) 8:73-91.

McGerr, Michael E. *The Decline of Popular Politics: The American North, 1865-1928.* New York: Oxford University Press, 1986.

Maggiotto, Michael A., and James E. Piereson. "Partisan Identification and Electoral Choice: The Hostility Hypothesis." *American Journal of Political Science* (1977) 21:745-67.

Mann, Thomas E. *Unsafe at any Margin: Interpreting Congressional Elections.* Washington, D.C.: American Enterprise Institute, 1978.

———. "Congressional Elections." In *The New Congress,* ed. Thomas E. Mann and Norman J. Ornstein. Washington, D.C.: American Enterprise Institute, 1980.

Mann, Thomas E., and Raymond E. Wolfinger. "Candidates and Parties in Congressional Elections." *American Political Science Review* (1980) 74:617-32. Chapter 20 in this volume.

Marcus, George. "The Structure of Emotional Response: 1984 Presidential Candidates." *American Political Science Review* (1988) 82:737-62.

Margolis, Michael. "From Confusion to Confusion: Issues and the American Voter (1956-1972)." *American Political Science Review* (1977) 71:31-43.

Markus, Gregory B. "Candidates, Parties and Issues: A Feedback Model of the Voting Decision." Center for Political Studies, University of Michigan, 1976.

———. "Political Attitudes during an Election Year: A Report on the 1980 NES Panel Study." *American Political Science Review* (1982) 76:538-60.

Markus, Gregory B., and Philip E. Converse. "A Dynamic Simultaneous Equation Model of Electoral Choice." *American Political Science Review* (1979) 73:1055-70. Chapter 14 in this volume.

Marvick, Dwaine, and Charles R. Nixon. "Recruitment Contrasts in Rival Campaign Groups." In *Political Decision Makers: Recruitment and Performance,* ed. Dwaine Marvick. New York: Free Press, 1961.

Mayhew, David R. *Congress: The Electoral Connection.* New Haven, Conn.: Yale University Press, 1974a.

———. "Congressional Elections: The Case of the Vanishing Marginals." *Polity* (1974b) 6:295-317. Reprinted, in part, as Chapter 18 in this volume.

Meier, Kenneth. "Party Identification and Vote Choice: The Causal Relationship." *Western Political Quarterly* (1975) 28:496-505.

Meltzer, Allan H., and Mark Vellrath. "The Effects of Economic Policies on Votes for the

Presidency: Some Evidence from Recent Elections." *Journal of Law and Economics* (1975) 18:781-98.

Merriam, Charles E., and Harold F. Gosnell. *Non-Voting*. Chicago: University of Chicago Press, 1924.

Miller, Arthur H. "Normal Vote Analysis: Sensitivity to Change Over Time." *American Journal of Political Science* (1979) 23:406-25.

Miller, Arthur H., and Richard Glass. "Economic Dissatisfaction and Electoral Choice." manuscript, 1976.

Miller, Arthur H., and Warren E. Miller. "Ideology in the 1972 Election: Myth or Reality—A Rejoinder." *American Political Science Review* (1976) 70:832-49.

_____. "Partisanship and Performance: 'Rational' Choice in the 1976 Presidential Election." Paper presented at the annual meeting of the American Political Science Association, Washington, D.C., 1977.

Miller, Arthur H., Warren E. Miller, Alden S. Raine, and Thad H. Brown. "A Majority Party in Disarray: Policy Polarization in the 1972 Election." *American Political Science Review* (1976) 70:753-78.

Miller, Arthur H., and Martin P. Wattenberg. "Policy and Performance Voting in the 1980 Election." Paper presented at the annual meeting of the American Political Science Association, New York, 1981.

Miller, Warren E. "The Cross-National Use of Party Identification as a Stimulus to Political Inquiry." In *Party Identification and Beyond,* ed. Ian Budge, Ivor Crewe, and Dennis Farlie. London: Wiley, 1976.

Miller, Warren E., and Teresa E. Levitin. *Leadership and Change: The New Politics and the American Electorate.* Cambridge, Mass.: Winthrop, 1976.

Miller, Warren E., and Donald E. Stokes. "Constituency Influence in Congress." *American Political Science Review* (1963) 57:45-56. Reprinted, in part, as Chapter 17 in this volume.

Mills, C. Wright. *The Power Elite.* New York: Oxford University Press, 1956.

Nelson, Candice J. "The Effect of Incumbency on Voting in Congressional Elections, 1964-1974." *Political Science Quarterly* (1978) 93:665-78.

Nelson, Forrest, and Lawrence Olson. "Specification and Estimation of a Simultaneous-Equation Model with Limited Dependent Variables." *International Economic Review* (1978) 19:695-709.

Nie, Norman H., with Kristi Andersen. "Mass Belief Systems Revisited: Political Change and Attitude Structure." *Journal of Politics* (1974) 36:541-91. Reprinted, in part, as Chapter 6 in this volume.

Nie, Norman H., Sidney Verba, and John R. Petrocik. *The Changing American Voter.* Cambridge, Mass.: Harvard University Press, 1976, 1979.

_____. "Reply to Abramson and to Smith." *American Political Science Review* (1981) 75:149-52.

Niemi, Richard G. *How Family Members Perceive Each Other.* New Haven, Conn.: Yale University Press, 1974.

_____. "Costs of Voting and Nonvoting." *Public Choice* (1976) 27:115-19

Niemi, Richard G., Richard S. Katz, and David Newman. "Reconstructing Past Partisanship: The Failure of the Party Identification Recall Questions." *American Journal of Political Science* (1980) 24:633-51.

Niemi, Richard G., and Herbert F. Weisberg. *Controversies in Voting Behavior,* 3d ed. Washington, D.C.: CQ Press, 1992.

Niemi, Richard G., and Anders Westholm. "Issues, Parties, and Attitudinal Stability: A

Comparative Study of Sweden and the United States." *Electoral Studies* (1984) 3:65-83.

Nisbett, Richard E., and Timothy D. Wilson. "Telling More Than We Know: Verbal Reports on Mental Processes." *Psychological Review* (1977) 84:231-59.

Norpoth, Helmut. "Party Identification in West Germany: Tracing an Elusive Concept." *Comparative Political Studies* (1978) 11:36-61.

————. "The Parties Come to Order! Dimensions of Preferential Choice in the West German Electorate, 1961-1976." *American Political Science Review* (1979) 73:724-36.

Page, Benjamin I. *Choices and Echoes in Presidential Elections: Rational Man and Electoral Democracy.* Chicago: University of Chicago Press, 1978.

Page, Benjamin I., and Richard A. Brody. "Policy Voting and the Electoral Process: The Vietnam War Issue." *American Political Science Review* (1972) 66:979-95.

Page, Benjamin I., and Calvin Jones. "Reciprocal Effects of Policy Preferences, Party Loyalties and the Vote." *American Political Science Review* (1979) 73:1071-89. Chap. 14 in this volume.

Palfrey, Thomas R., and Howard Rosenthal. "A Strategic Calculus of Voting." *Public Choice* (1983) 41:7-53.

————. "Participation and Provision of Discrete Public Goods." *Journal of Public Economics* (1984) 24:171-93.

————. "Voter Participation and Strategic Uncertainty." *American Political Science Review* (1985) 79:62-78.

Percheron, Annick, and M. Kent Jennings. "Political Continuities in French Families." *Comparative Politics* (1981) 13:421-36.

Petrocik, John R. "An Analysis of Intransitivities in the Index of Party Identification." *Political Methodology* (1974) 1:31-47. Reprinted, in part, as Chapter 26 in this volume.

Phillips, Kevin. *The Emerging Republican Majority.* Garden City, N.Y.: Doubleday, 1970.

Pierce, John C. "Party Identification and the Changing Role of Ideology in American Politics." *Midwest Journal of Political Science* (1970) 14:25-42.

Pierce, John C., and Douglas D. Rose. "Non-Attitudes and American Public Opinion." *American Political Science Review* (1974) 68:626-49.

Piereson, James E. "Presidential Popularity and Midterm Voting at Different Electoral Levels." *American Journal of Political Science* (1975) 19:683-94.

Piven, Francis Fox, and Richard A. Cloward. *Why Americans Don't Vote.* New York: Pantheon, 1988.

Pomper, Gerald M. *Elections in America.* New York: Dodd, Mead, 1970.

————. "From Confusion to Clarity: Issues and American Voters, 1956-1968." *American Political Science Review* (1972) 66:415-28.

————. *Voters' Choice.* New York: Dodd, Mead, 1975.

Popkin, Samuel, John W. Gorman, Charles Phillips, and Jeffrey A. Smith. "Comment: What Have You Done for Me Lately? Toward an Investment Theory of Voting." *American Political Science Review* (1976) 70:779-805.

Powell, Lynda W. "Constituency Service and Electoral Margin in the Congress." Paper presented at the annual meeting of the American Political Science Association, Denver, 1982.

Prewitt, Kenneth, and Norman H. Nie. "Election Studies of the Survey Research Center." *British Journal of Political Science* (1971) 1:479-502.

Prothro, James W., and Charles M. Grigg. "Fundamental Principles of Democracy: Bases of Agreement and Disagreement." *Journal of Politics* (1960) 22:276-94.

Ragsdale, Lyn. "The Fiction of Congressional Elections as Presidential Events." *American Politics Quarterly* (1980) 8:375-98.

Rahn, Wendy, John Aldrich, Eugene Borgida, and John Sullivan. "A Social-Cognitive Model of Candidate Appraisal." In *Information and Democratic Processes*, eds. John A. Ferejohn and James H. Kuklinski. Urbana: University of Illinois Press, 1990.

RePass, David E. "Issue Salience and Party Choice." *American Political Science Review* (1971) 65:389-400.

———. "Comment: Political Methodologies in Disarray: Some Alternative Interpretations of the 1972 Election." *American Political Science Review* (1976) 70:814-31.

Riker, William H., and Peter Ordeshook. "A Theory of the Calculus of Voting." *American Political Science Review* (1968) 62:25-42.

———. *An Introduction to Positive Theory.* Englewood Cliffs, N.J.: Prentice-Hall, 1973.

Robinson, Michael. "The Three Faces of Congressional Media." In *The New Congress,* ed. Thomas E. Mann and Norman J. Ornstein. Washington, D.C.: American Enterprise Institute, 1980.

Rosa, J. J., and D. Amson. "Conditions Economiques et Elections." *Révue Française de Science Politique* (1976) 26:1101-24.

Rosenberg, Milton J., Sidney Verba, and Philip Converse. *Vietnam and the Silent Majority.* New York: Harper and Row, 1970.

Rosenstone, Stephen J., and Raymond E. Wolfinger. "The Effect of Registration Laws on Voter Turnout." *American Political Science Review* (1978) 72:22-45.

Rosenstone, Stephen J., Raymond E. Wolfinger, and Richard A. McIntosh. "Voter Turnout in Midterm Elections." Paper presented at the annual meeting of the American Political Science Association, New York, 1978.

Rostow, Walt W. *The Stages of Economic Growth.* Cambridge, Mass.: Harvard University Press, 1960.

Rusk, Jerrold G. "The Effect of the Australian Ballot Reform on Split Ticket Voting: 1876-1908." *American Political Science Review* (1970) 64:1220-38. Chapter 30 in this volume.

———. "Comment: The American Electoral Universe: Speculation and Evidence." *American Political Science Review* (1974) 68:1028-49.

Rusk, Jerrold G., and John J. Stucker. "The Effect of the Southern System of Election Laws on Voting Participation: A Reply to V. O. Key, Jr." In *The History of American Electoral Behavior,* ed. Joel H. Silbey, Allan G. Bogue, and William H. Flanigan. Princeton, N.J.: Princeton University Press, 1978.

Salisbury, Robert. "The Urban Party Organization Member." *Public Opinion Quarterly* (1965-66) 29:550-64.

Sani, Giacomo. "A Test of the Least Distance Model of Voting Choice: Italy, 1972." *Comparative Political Studies* (1974) 7:193-208.

———. "Political Traditions as Contextual Variables: Partisanship in Italy." *American Journal of Political Science* (1976) 20:375-405.

Särlvik, Bo, and Ivor Crewe, *Decade of Dealignment.* Cambridge: Cambridge University Press, 1983.

Schattschneider, E. E. "United States: The Functional Approach to Party Government." In *Modern Political Parties,* ed. Sigmund Neumann. Chicago: University of Chicago Press, 1956.

———. *The Semi-Sovereign People.* New York: Holt, Rinehart, and Winston, 1960.

Schlesinger, Arthur M. "Tides of American Politics." *Yale Review* (1939) 29:217-30.

Schulman, Mark A., and Gerald M. Pomper. "Variability in Electoral Behavior: Longitudinal Perspectives from Causal Modeling." *American Journal of Political Science* (1975) 19:1-18.

Sears, David O., Carl P. Hensler, and Leslie K. Speer. "Whites' Opposition to 'Busing': Self-Interest or Symbolic Politics?" *American Political Science Review* (1979) 73:369-84.

Sellers, Charles. "The Equilibrium Cycle in Two-Party Politics." *Public Opinion Quarterly* (1965) 30:16-38.

Shapiro, Michael J. "Rational Political Man: A Synthesis of Economic and Social-Psychological Perspectives." *American Political Science Review* (1969) 63:1106-19.

Shepsle, Kenneth A. "The Strategy of Ambiguity: Uncertainty and Electoral Competition." *American Political Science Review* (1972) 66:555-69.

Shively, W. Phillips. "Voting Stability and the Nature of Party Attachments in the Weimar Republic." *American Political Science Review* (1972) 66:1203-25.

_____. "Information Costs and the Partisan Life Cycle." Paper presented at the annual meeting of the American Political Science Association, Washington, D.C., 1977.

_____. "The Development of Party Identification among Adults." *American Political Science Review* (1979) 73:1039-54.

Silbey, Joel H. "Beyond Realignment and Realignment Theory: American Political Eras, 1789-1989." In *The End of Realignment? Interpreting American Electoral Eras*, ed. Byron E. Shafer. Madison: University of Wisconsin Press, 1991.

Smidt, Corwin E. "Negative Political Party Identification in the United States: 1964-1972." Paper presented at the annual meeting of the Southern Political Science Association, Nashville, 1975a.

_____. The Changing Patterns of Political Party Identification in the United States: 1964-1972. Ph.D diss., University of Iowa, 1975b.

_____. "The Dynamics of Partisan Change in the United States: An Analysis of the Relationship Between Change in Partisan Affections and Partisan Self-Images." Paper presented at the annual meeting of the Midwest Political Science Association, Cincinnati, 1981.

Smith, Eric R. A. N. "The Levels of Conceptualization: False Measures of Ideological Sophistication." *American Political Science Review* (1980) 74:685-96.

Smith, Tom W. "The First Straw: A Study of the Origins of Election Polls." *Public Opinion Quarterly* (1990) 54:21-36.

Squire, Peverill. "Why the 1936 *Literary Digest* Poll Failed." *Public Opinion Quarterly* (1988) 52:125-33.

Squire, Peverill, Raymond E. Wolfinger, and David P. Glass. "Residential Mobility and Voter Turnout." *American Political Science Review* (1987) 81:45-65.

Steeper, Frederick T., and Robert M. Teeter. "Comment on 'A Majority Party in Disarray.'" *American Political Science Review* (1976) 70:806-13.

Stimson, James A. "Public Support for American Presidents: A Cyclical Model." *Public Opinion Quarterly* (1976) 40:1-21.

Stimson, James A., and Edward G. Carmines. "The Continuing Issue in American Politics." Paper presented at the annual meeting of the Southern Political Science Association, New Orleans, 1977.

Stokes, Donald E. "Some Dynamic Elements in Contests for the Presidency." *American Political Science Review* (1966) 60:19-28.

Stokes, Donald E., Angus Campbell, and Warren E. Miller. "Components of Electoral Decision." *American Political Science Review* (1958) 52:367-87.

Stokes, Donald E., and Warren E. Miller. "Party Government and the Saliency of

Congress." In *Elections and the Political Order,* ed. Angus Campbell, Philip E. Converse, Warren E. Miller, and Donald E. Stokes. New York: Wiley, 1966. Reprinted, in part, as Chapter 16 in this volume.

Sullivan, John L., James E. Piereson, and George E. Marcus. "Ideological Constraint in the Mass Public: A Methodological Critique and Some New Findings." *American Journal of Political Science* (1978) 22:223-49. Chapter 7 in this volume.

Sundquist, James. *Dynamics of the Party System: Alignment and Realignment of Political Parties in the United States.* Washington, D.C.: Brookings, 1973.

Taylor, A. H. "The Proportional Decline Hypothesis in English Elections." *Journal of the Royal Statistical Society* Series A (1972) 135:365-69.

Theil, Henri. *Principles of Econometrics.* New York: Wiley, 1971.

Thomassen, Jacques. "Party Identification as a Cross-National Concept: Its Meaning in the Netherlands." In *Party Identification and Beyond,* ed. Ian Budge, Ivor Crewe, and Dennis Farlie. London: Wiley, 1976. Reprinted, in part, as Chapter 16 in this volume.

Tingsten, Herbert. *Political Behavior.* Totowa, N.J.: Bedminster, 1937.

Tufte, Edward R. "Determinants of the Outcomes of Midterm Congressional Elections." *American Political Science Review* (1975) 69:812-26.

———. "On the Distribution of Published R^2: Consequences of Selection of Models and Evidence," manuscript. 1977.

———. *Political Control of the Economy.* Princeton, N.J.: Princeton University Press, 1978.

Tullock, Gordon. *Toward a Mathematics of Politics.* Ann Arbor: University of Michigan Press, 1967.

Uhlaner, Carole J. "Rational Turnout: The Neglected Role of Groups." *American Journal of Political Science* (1989) 33:390-422.

Valentine, David C., and John R. Van Wingen. "Partisanship, Independence, and the Partisan Identification." *American Politics Quarterly* (1980) 8:165-86.

van der Eijk, C., and B. Niemöller. *Electoral Change in the Netherlands.* Amsterdam: CT Press, 1983.

Van Wingen, John R., and David C. Valentine. "Biases in the Partisan Identification Index as a Measure of Partisanship." Paper presented at the annual meeting of the Midwest Political Science Association, Chicago, 1979.

Verba, Sidney, and Richard A. Brody. "Participation, Policy Preferences, and the War in Vietnam." *Public Opinion Quarterly* (1970) 34:325-32.

Verba, Sidney, Norman H. Nie, and Jae-on Kim. *The Modes of Democratic Participation.* Beverly Hills, Calif.: Sage, 1971.

Wainer, Howard. "Estimating Coefficients in Linear Models: It Don't Make No Nevermind." *Psychological Bulletin* (1976) 83:312-17.

Walker, Jack L. "Ballot Forms and Voter Fatigue: An Analysis of the Office Bloc and Party Column Ballots." *Midwest Journal of Political Science* (1966) 10:448-63.

Wattenberg, Martin P. "Party Identification and Party Images." *Comparative Politics* (1982) 15:23-40.

Weisberg, Herbert F. "A Multidimensional Conceptualization of Party Identification." *Political Behavior* (1980) 2:33-60. Chapter 27 in this volume.

———. "Party Evaluations: A Theory of Separate Effects." Paper presented at the annual meeting of the Midwest Political Science Association, Milwaukee, 1982.

———. "A New Scale of Partisanship." *Political Behavior* (1983) 5:363-76.

Weisberg, Herbert F., and Bernard Grofman. "Candidate Evaluations and Turnout." *American Politics Quarterly* (1981) 9:197-219.

Weisberg, Herbert F., Jon A. Krosnick, and Bruce D. Bowen. *Introduction to Survey Research and Data Analysis,* 2d ed. Glenview, Ill.: Scott, Foresman, 1989.

Wigmore, J. H. *The Australian Ballot System as Embodied in the Legislation of Various Countries.* 2d ed. Boston: Boston Book Co., 1889.

Wiley, David E., and James A. Wiley. "The Estimation of Measurement Error in Panel Data." *American Sociological Review* (1970) 35:112-17.

Yiannakis, Diana E. "The Grateful Electorate: Casework and Congressional Elections." *American Journal of Political Science* (1981) 25:568-80.

Zeckman, Martin. "Dynamic Models of the Voter's Decision Calculus." *Public Choice* (1979) 34:297-315.

Zeidenstein, Harvey. "Measuring Congressional Seat Losses in Mid-Term Elections." *Journal of Politics* (1972) 34:272-76.

NAME INDEX

SUBJECT INDEX

definen m, dealizin p. 285